VICTORY
DENIED

By the same author

THE BOMBER'S EYE
'BOMBER' HARRIS: THE AUTHORISED BIOGRAPHY
BERNARD LOVELL: A BIOGRAPHY

VICTORY DENIED

THE RISE OF AIR POWER AND THE DEFEAT OF GERMANY 1920-45

DUDLEY SAWARD

FRANKLIN WATTS
NEW YORK
1987

Library of Congress Catalog Card Number: 86-50894
ISBN: 0-531-15045-3

Copyright © 1985 by Dudley Saward

First published in 1985 by Buchan & Enright,
Great Britain
First published in the United States in 1987
by Franklin Watts, New York
All rights reserved
5   4   3   2   1

CONTENTS

LIST OF ILLUSTRATIONS

Flight Lieutenant E. J. Dickie*
Dr A. C. B. Lovell*
Dr P. I. Dee*
Saundby and Harris examining bomb-damage photographs (*IWM*)
Arnold, Harris and Eaker in 1943 (*IWM*)
Arnold and Portal at Quebec, 1943 (*US National Archives*)
Churchill, Roosevelt and Stalin at Yalta, 1945 (*US National Archives*)
Churchill, Brooke and Montgomery on the Rhine (*IWM*)
Air Chief Marshal Sir Arthur T. Harris, C-in-C, Bomber Command, 1942-45*

* Illustrations marked with an asterisk are from the author's collection, and in many cases were taken by him.

MAPS

DIAGRAMS

AUTHOR'S PREFACE

My sources of information for Part 1 of this book were primarily from: Air Ministry files covering the years 1918 to 1939; *Keesing's Contemporary Archives – Weekly Diary of World Events*, 1931 to 1940; Martin Gilbert's excellent *Winston S. Churchill*, Vol. V 1922-1939; *Hansard*; Sir Winston Churchill's *The Second World War* Vol. I; *The Memoirs of Sir Anthony Eden* Vols. I and II; John Laffin's *Swifter Than Eagles*, a biography of Marshal of the Royal Air Force Sir John Salmond; Helmut Heiber's biography *Adolf Hitler*, and Hitler's own *Mein Kampf*; Air Marshal Sir Robert Saundby's *Air Bombardment*; Peter Lewis's *The British Bomber Since 1914*; and Hanfried Schliephake's *The Birth of the Luftwaffe*. Information in the Prologue came from *The Times History of the War* (First World War) Vols. VIII, X and XIII. References to the Royal Air Force College, Cranwell, are partly from Professor Rupert de la Bere's *A History of Cranwell*, which was published in 1934 in a limited edition, and from my own experience of Cranwell as a cadet from 1932-1934.

I am greatly indebted to the late Anthony Eden, Earl of Avon, for assistance with Part 1. He permitted me to interview him on several occasions at Manor House, his home at Alvediston, near Salisbury, where he allowed me to see a number of his own documents relating to the period between the two world wars, thus providing me with much valuable information on diplomatic history from 1918-1939.

I must also thank the Public Record Office, in particular Wing Commander Lambert (now retired from his post at the PRO), and the Air Historical Branch of the Ministry of Defence, in particular Group Captain E.B. Haslam (now retired from the post of Head of Branch). Not only did I receive much assistance from these two in my researches for Part 1 of the book, but also for Parts 2 and 3. Others to whom I am indebted for information in connection with Part 1 are Mrs Anne Baker, the daughter of Sir Geoffrey Salmond and the niece of Sir John Salmond, and Mr E.M. Boyle, ALA, of the Salisbury Reference Library, who devoted much time to assisting me with my searches into reference books at the library.

Sources for Parts 2 and 3 were primarily from Air Ministry files covering the period 1940-1945; Bomber Command files from 1940-1945; War Cabinet Minutes, Chiefs of Staff Minutes, and Prime Minister's (Churchill's) files 1939-1945. For access to the War Cabinet Minutes, Chiefs of Staff Minutes and Churchill's files, I am greatly indebted to Mr Clifton Child, the former Head of the Historical Section of the Cabinet Office; and again too the late first Earl of Avon, who kindly ensured that I received full co-operation in my researches into documents of the Cabinet Office.

Considerable assistance with Part 2 was also obtained from *The Royal Air Force, 1939-1945* by Denis Richards and Hilary St George Saunders; *The Narrow Margin* by Derek Wood and Derek Dempster; and from Sir Winston Churchill's *The Second World War*, Vols. II and III.

Details of bomb loads and damage assessments in Part 3 are taken from the Bomber Command Weekly Digest, Nos. 1 to 174, covering the period 18 April 1942 to 19 August 1945. Bombing results are supplemented by bomb-damage assessments made by Büro Ha of the Swiss Intelligence Service. Copies covering the period 2 June 1942 to 31 December 1944 were kindly provided to me by the late Hans Hausemann, formerly Head of Büro Ha. In addition, the late Doctor Albert Speer permitted me to spend many days at his home in Heidelberg studying his private papers and reports on production in connection with the armaments situation in Germany from 1942 to 1945 – these disclosed the disastrous effects of the bombing by the Royal Air Force and the US Eighth Air Force. He also allowed me to tape-record many hours of conversation with him, and I am greatly indebted to him for his co-operation.

I have also drawn on Sir Winston Churchill's *The Second World War*, Vols. IV, V, and VI in part 3.

Whilst engaged upon the writing of the official biography of Marshal of the Royal Air Force Sir Arthur Harris, the Commander-in-Chief of Bomber Command from February 1942 until the end of the war in 1945, I received invaluable assistance from Sir Arthur not only in connection with that biography, but also in connection with this book. In Part 3 I have drawn on these sources to a considerable extent. Having served on his Staff from February 1942 to May 1945, I have also drawn on my own personal knowledge of those years. Prior to joining Harris's Staff I served in No.2 Army Co-operation Squadron from September 1939 until the end of May 1940, when France collapsed. In July 1940 I joined the Blind Approach Technical & Development Unit in England at Boscombe Down, which was charged with investigating and disrupting the German blind-bombing beam system known as *Knickebein* and *X-Gerät*. I have, therefore, drawn on my own knowledge of the collapse of France as well as upon official sources, and upon my knowledge of the defeat of the German blind-bombing tactics. In 1941 I was at the Air Ministry with the responsibility for operational requirements for RDF (later radar)* for Bomber Command, and at the beginning of 1942 I was posted to Bomber Command Headquarters as Wing Commander, RDF on the Staff of the C-in-C (later to become Group Captain, Radar). Consequently, I have again drawn on my own knowledge of radar in Bomber Command as well as on official sources.

Others to whom I am indebted for information connected with Part 3 include Marshal of the Royal Air Force Lord Elworthy, the late Air Chief Marshal the Hon. Sir Ralph Cochrane, Professor Sir Bernard Lovell, Lieutenant-General Ira C. Eaker, USAAF, and Colonel James Parton, formerly of the USAAF and now a member of the US Air Force Historical Foundation. Colonel Parton provided me with much useful information on the US Eighth Air Force, including extracts of comments by prominent German industrialists and senior German officers on the effectiveness of the bombing of Germany. These comments were made during interrogations, and are recorded in Book 7 of *Impact*, a documentary series of eight books sponsored by the US Air Force Historical Foundation, published in New York in 1980.

Finally, I have to thank Gerald Pollinger, my agent, and Toby Buchan, my publisher, both of whom encouraged me in my endeavours from the very start of this project. I am truly grateful to them both for their constant guidance and advice – their help has been inestimable.

---

* RDF = Radio Direction Finding; radar = RAdio Detection And Ranging.

Part 1

AN ARMISTICE
FOR TWENTY YEARS

Dedicated to the memory of
Sir Winston Churchill, who wisely supported
the development of air power in the Twenties and
Thirties in the face of massive opposition, and who used
it effectively from 1940 to 1945 to bring about the total defeat
of Nazi Germany; and to the memory of Marshal of the
RAF Viscount Trenchard, the 'Father of the Royal
Air Force', who defended that service in its
infancy from destruction by the
politicians

PROLOGUE

Late on the night of 2 September 1916, the most formidable German Zeppelin attack up to that date in the First World War was made upon England by thirteen of these airships. They crossed the North Sea into the Eastern Counties, making for the Midlands and London. Most of the raiders were confused by the almost complete blackout conditions on the ground, only recently imposed as a protection against the night bombing, and they wandered over East Anglia dropping their bombs indiscriminately. Three, however, succeeded in reaching the outskirts of London, two of which were driven off by the defences. But the third was shot down – the first Zeppelin to be brought down on British soil.

This epic fight took place within the view of hundreds of thousands of people, and it was a riveting spectacle. London was lying in almost complete darkness, only relieved by faint flickering lamps in the streets and shaded lights through curtained windows. The warning of the impending attack had been spread through the City, and hospitals, ambulances, fire services and police stations had all been alerted. In many homes families had moved to lower rooms for greater safety. But masses of people had gone onto roofs and into the streets to watch what was happening. Searchlights explored the clear star-lit sky and the sound of guns was matched by the sight of shells bursting in great flashes in the darkness above. Suddenly the searchlights concentrated northwards and a thrill passed through the crowds as the shape of a Zeppelin, locked in the swaying beams, became clearly visible. It was moving towards the south and west, and for a short while was unable to escape the unwanted attention of the searchlights. Then, to every observer's amazement, the gunfire ceased and the searchlights were doused. What had happened? was the question on everybody's lips. But as they wondered, the image of a Chinese lantern seemed to appear in the sky, glowing from a soft pink to a fiery red and finally bursting into a great blazing mass such as had never been seen before. Twenty miles away people claimed they could read their newspapers by the flaming ball of fire as the Zeppelin, alight from stem to stern, plunged earthwards. It was 2.30 on the morning of 3 September 1916.

At first it was thought that a shell had scored a direct hit, and a great shout of jubilation went up from the crowds wherever they were. But later it was learnt that it had been shot down from the air by a twenty-one-year-old officer of the Royal Flying Corps by the name of Lieutenant William Leefe Robinson who, with several other pilots, had taken to the air in pursuit of the enemy. He had been at 8,000 feet when he sighted the airship about 2,000 feet above him, caught in the searchlights. It was when it was realised by the searchlight and gun crews that an aircraft was pursuing the Zeppelin that the ground defences ceased firing, and within seconds of getting above his target Leefe Robinson was pumping his fire into the enemy.

The great mass of the wreckage fell on a field at Cuffley, near Enfield, the crew of sixteen being burnt almost beyond recognition. The remains of the Zeppelin, from the Imperial German Naval Air Service, revealed that it was of a new construction, being wooden-framed, a type known as the Schütte-Lanz.

Despite much public opposition to the idea of giving the crew a military funeral, members of the RFC insisted that the commander and his men should be accorded this honour. They took the view that the Germans were brave men who, in attempting to bomb London, had only obeyed orders and, in doing so, had run great risks. They reasoned that this crew had earned the right to the last token of a soldier's respect, a respect which, they knew, they themselves would receive at the hands of the German Army if the situation was reversed. And so, on 3 September 1916, the coffin containing the body of the Zeppelin's commander was borne by six officers of the RFC, and each coffin of the fifteen crew was borne by six other ranks of the RFC as they were taken from a lorry to be interred in the cemetry at Cuffley. The officer was buried separately in one grave and the coffins of the crew were laid together in one large grave. The coffin of the officer was marked with a simple inscription:

AN UNKNOWN
GERMAN OFFICER
WHILE COMMANDING
ZEPPELIN L. 21.
3RD SEPTEMBER, 1916

At the conclusion of the service the Last Post was sounded while officers and men stood to attention. The age of chivalry had not yet quite passed.

A few weeks later the name of the commander was given in the German casualty lists as Kapitän Wilhelm Schramm.

Lieutenant Leefe Robinson, who was awarded the Victoria Cross for his feat, was from a flight of No. 39 Squadron equipped with BE2C two-seat biplanes and based at Sutton's Farm, later to become RAF Hornchurch. His Flight Commander was Captain A.T. Harris who, in the Second World War, became Commander-in-Chief of RAF Bomber Command. This initial success by No. 39 Squadron, which had been charged with the defence of London against the Zeppelins, was quickly followed by further victories. A few days later the L33 was hit simultaneously by gunfire from the ground and by bullets from an aircraft piloted by Lieutenant A. de B. Brandon, and the L32 was destroyed by Lieutenant F. Sowery, both pilots being from Harris's flight. Then, on the night of 1 October, 2nd Lieutenant W.J. Tempest* took off from North Weald, where another flight of No. 39 Squadron was based, and engaged Zeppelin L31 which he shot down in flames over Hertfordshire, where it fell in the grounds of the Tower House in Heath Road, Little Heath, on the outskirts of Potters Bar. This was a major victory, for the L31 was commanded by Kapitänleutnant Heinrich Mathy, the most resolute and successful of all Zeppelin commanders; Tempest was awarded the Distinguished Service Order. These four quick victories by the RFC brought a sigh of relief from the British public; the Zeppelin was not invincible, despite the danger and difficulties of night-flying in those days, and the primitive nature of aircraft and instruments.

By November the Zeppelin raids on England, which had started early in 1915, almost ceased, but in the spring of 1917 the Germans began a more serious strategic air offensive against this country. Having established bomber bases in Belgium they were now capable of attacking the south and south-east coast with aircraft, and on 25 May 1917 a squadron of Gothas, their latest bomber, a large, well armed, twin-engined biplane, attacked Shorncliffe camp and Folkestone, killing 95 people and injuring another 195. Even though seventy-four British aircraft went up to intercept and engage the enemy, only one German bomber was shot down. This raid revealed the inadequacy of the defences. The aircraft used against the Germans were a mixed bag, and there was absolutely no co-ordination of tactics. In fact, many of the pilots were still under training and, for all their gallantry, they failed to find the enemy through lack of experience. And, into the bargain, no

---

* Until the formation of the Royal Air Force on 1 April 1918, there were two British air forces, the Royal Flying Corps and the Royal Naval Air Service, which were amalgamated to form the new service. Until then, ranks were as they would have been in either the Army or Royal Navy.

warnings of the impending attack were given to the towns concerned.

On the morning of Wednesday, 13 June 1917, twenty-one Gothas crossed the south coast of England and bombed several small towns in Kent and Essex. Fourteen of these aircraft, flying in a diamond formation, continued on to London, which they reached at 11.35 am and upon which they dropped their high-explosive bombs with a fair degree of indiscrimination, killing 162 people and injuring 432. The air defences did not succeed in bringing down one single enemy aircraft, although ninety-two British aircraft of varying types went up to intercept and attack the raiders. Nearly a month later, on 7 July, a second daylight raid was made upon London in which 65 people were killed and 245 were injured. Only one of the German Gothas was destroyed by the ninety-five British aircraft that took to the air to intercept the enemy.

After the raid of 13 June, not only did the Americans express horror at the bombing of civilians, but even in Germany the newspaper *Volkswacht*, of Breslau, openly deplored 'this massacre' of civilians. Furthermore, a semi-official telegram from Berlin to Amsterdam in neutral Holland professed that the grief was no less in Germany than in Britain that so many civilians, particularly children, should have fallen victims to 'this attack for military objects'. A few days later, however, the British Government received a telegram of equal authority which stated that if it was wished to spare civilians then they should be evacuated from places such as Dover, Folkestone, Sheerness and London, which were 'storehouses for military requirements'.

These raids of May, June and July demonstrated the intention of the Germans to mount a major strategic offensive against England. They also revealed the inadequacy of Britain's defences, and this forced the War Cabinet to recognise the seriousness of the situation. The life of the capital was threatened, and in consequence the conduct of the war was in danger of being undermined. The defence of what was in effect the political and military base of the war effort was the first charge of the armed forces, but the military were at loggerheads as to the best method of providing proper protection. The Cabinet wanted fighter squadrons brought back from France for the defence of London and those towns within range of the enemy's aircraft, but powerful members of the Imperial General Staff argued that every fighter was required on the Western Front and that the best method of defence was to reconquer Belgium as soon as possible and thereby overrun the enemy's airfields. Unfortunately, the solution to defence and offence, using aircraft, was not helped by the split control of this new weapon of war. Since their inception, the Royal Flying Corps and the Royal Naval Air Service had remained quite separate services, the only link between them being an Air Committee, later named the Air Board. This body had completely failed to control inter-Service rivalries and, therefore, had also failed to produce any co-ordinated use of this new dimension of war. Now, however, in July, 1917 it was quite apparent that urgent action was imperative and David Lloyd George, the Prime Minister, took a firm line. Through the War Cabinet he formed a committee of two, consisting of himself and General Jan Smuts (who had commanded the South African forces against the British in the Boer War), to review the air situation and make recommendations. Shrewdly, Lloyd George left the task to Smuts, and on 17 August 1917 the latter submitted his report.

Smuts's first recommendation was the establishment of a better organised defence, and Major-General E.B. Ashmore was appointed Commander-in-Chief for the defence of London with control of observers, anti-aircraft guns, balloon barrage and fighter squadrons. His command extended over a wide area, and the recommendation provided for some strengthening of the fighter squadrons under him. But Smuts's second and most far reaching recommendation was that the Royal Flying Corps and the Royal Naval Air Service should be amalgamated under one ministry, which would control and administer all matters in connection with aerial warfare of any kind, including lighter-than-air as well as heavier-than-air craft. He it was, in fact, who set out the plans for the formation of the Royal Air Force, the amalgamation of the two flying services which ultimately came into being on 1 April 1918, under the governance of the newly formed Air Ministry. In a concluding part of his report he displayed his remarkable vision in prophetic words:

> Air Power can be used as an independent means of war operations. Nobody that witnessed the attack on London on 7th July, 1917, could have any doubt on that point. Unlike artillery an air fleet can conduct extensive operations far from and independently of both Army and Navy. As far as can at present be foreseen there is absolutely no limit to the scale of its future independent war use. And the day may not be far off when aerial operations with their devastation of enemy lands and destruction of industrial and populous centres on a vast scale may become the principal operations of war, to which older forms of military operations may become secondary and subordinate.

More immediately the defence of London and the Home Counties, under 'Splash' Ashmore, improved considerably and the Germans soon found their daylight losses too great to sustain. Inevitably came the switch to night bombing, using the full-moon periods to aid navigation. On the evening of 2 September 1917 the enemy undertook a trial raid on Dover, and on the night of the 3rd there was a raid by six machines which located the visible shape of the Thames Estuary and bombed Margate, but in both cases little success attended these attacks. Whilst the moon lasted the raids continued over a wide area, and then ceased during the dark period. They began again during each successive full-moon period up until 22 December, but still with very limited effect. For the first four weeks of 1918 England was left in peace, but seven more raids were made upon Kent, Essex, Hertfordshire, Bedfordshire and London before they finally ceased after the last raid on 17 June 1918. None of the raids caused any serious industrial damage and, with the exception of the raid on the night of 28/29 January 1918, casualties were very low; the losses suffered by the enemy, by contrast, were significant enough to be a serious deterrent. The night raid on 28/29 January, when two attacks were made on London, resulted in 65 civilians and 6 servicemen being wounded. Just following this raid, a savage bombing onslaught was made upon Paris on 30 January. The interesting corollary to this attack was the publicised statement by the Germans that the Paris attack was merely a reprisal for French raids on German towns, whereas the object of the raids on London, although partly to cause damage, was chiefly to force Britain to maintain an enormous ground and aerial defence around London and the east coast at the expense of aerial and ground services on the Western Front. In this the Germans certainly achieved some success. Even by the end of 1916, 17,340 officers and men were serving in the home anti-aircraft services and twelve RFC squadrons consisting of 200 officers, 2,000 other ranks and 110 aircraft were stationed in England, despite the urgent need for them on the Somme. After the May, June and July raids of 1917 these numbers were further increased.

As 1918 progressed, the British were bombing German towns from bases in France, not by way of reprisal, but to force the Germans onto the defensive and thus win the war.

In fact, the whole question of bombing from the air had become a matter of great controversy, and one displaying little understanding of the true morality of this new method of warfare. Great Britain had for centuries been protected by the seas around her shores from military action within her own boundaries, and her civilian population had therefore suffered none of the real terrors of war such as the sacking of towns and villages by sword, gun, military and naval artillery, or reduction and starvation by siege. Long forgotten were the invasions of the Romans, the Angles, Saxons, Danes and, finally, the Normans, all of which had involved the civilian population in the attendant horrors of war. Even the Civil War, in which civilians suffered at the hands of both Cromwell's armies and those of the King, had faded into the pages of the history books. There had been fears of a military invasion at the time of the Napoleonic Wars, but the Channel had preserved the British people from the threat and the battles were all fought on the soil of Continental Europe instead. Indeed, Continental Europe had been the scene of many wars for hundreds of years (including many of Britain's wars), and her civilian population had been constantly in the front line, suffering the fearful casualties resulting from artillery bombardment and starvation by siege, as well as the 'ordinary' hardships of being caught up in war. An example was the Siege of Paris of 1870-71 during the Franco-Prussian War, when between 20,000 and 25,000 people were estimated to have been killed or to have died of starvation. 17,000 are definitely known to have been killed because their burial costs, which were paid for by the Municipal Council after the Paris Commune's defeat in May 1871, are recorded in the City annals.

America, too, had mainly been isolated from wars on her own soil by the oceans, apart from the American War of Independence and the Civil War, and had become accustomed to the idea that civilian populations were immune from the direct tragedies of war.

The truth was that in the war of 1914-18 the bombing aeroplane had extended the range of 'artillery', and the population of Great Britain was thereby brought into the front line. Nothing had really changed in regard to the rules of war with reference to civilian populations. It was a case of the Channel no longer being wide enough to offer complete protection to the British public. America, however, was still safe, given the limited range of early aircraft.

CHAPTER I

The Second Little Corporal

On 20 April 1889, the wife of an obscure Austrian customs official gave birth to a boy in their home town of Braunau on the Inn River, which coursed its way along the Bavarian-German border with Austria. The father, a strict and dictatorial patriarch at home, exercised a repressive authoritarian influence upon his son almost from the moment that the child could speak and walk. After his retirement in 1895, the family finally moved to Leonding, near Linz, after an unsuccessful attempt to run a farm in Trauntal, Upper Austria. At this time the father became increasingly short-tempered and even more domineering, so that the boy grew up in an atmosphere lacking in love, except for that small amount which his mother was able to lavish on him, if not in secret, then surreptitiously. The boy's performance in elementary school was excellent, driven on, as he was, by his father. But when his father died in 1903, while he was at the Realschule (college preparatory school) in Linz, he became rebellious, a reaction to his father's authoritarian rule, and began to fall behind in his studies. He was transferred to another school in the hope that he would settle down to his previous studious behaviour, but the move was to no avail and, in 1905, at the age of sixteen, he finally left school for good.

Still resistant to the discipline of authority, he avoided a regular job and began a long period of aimless existence, reading, writing poetry, painting, sketching buildings, wandering in the woods, and dreaming of becoming a famous artist and eminent architect. Then, in 1907, he moved to Vienna and attempted to enrol as a student in the Academy of Fine Arts. He sat the entrance exam and failed miserably. Next he tried to

15

study as an architect, but that profession unfortunately required a qualification which he did not possess – a secondary school certificate.

His failures led him into a deep depression, and this was increased by the death of his mother four days before Christmas of the same year, 1907. He cut himself off from his friends and, in almost total seclusion, lived on in Vienna on his orphan's pension, supplemented by what money his mother had left him, and by what he could earn by painting and selling picture postcards. During this time of disappointment he became fascinated by Karl Luegar, the Mayor of Vienna, and his nationalist Christian-Socialist Party. What impressed him was the efficiency of the party's propaganda machine and the potential of mass political manipulation as demonstrated by Luegar's use of propaganda to whip up anti-Semitic feeling for political gain. Under Luegar's influence, and that of the former Roman Catholic monk and race theorist, Lanz von Liebenfels, the youth first developed his fanatical hatred of the Jews and his vision of the ideology of a master race of pure Aryans.

In 1913, to avoid being called up for Austrian military service – having already failed to register for conscription – he slipped across the German border to Munich, only to be arrested and handed over to the Austrian police. He was not punished for his offence, and voluntarily agreed to present himself to the military authorities for call-up, but fate took a hand and he failed on medical grounds. He returned to Munich. On the outbreak of the First World War in August 1914 he immediately volunteered for service with the German Army, and on this occasion was accepted with no question of rejection on medical grounds. He served in the army for four years with the List Regiment, a Bavarian unit, on the Western Front. Although he fought with distinction, he gained no promotion beyond that of corporal; he was, however, wounded twice, and won several awards for bravery, including the Distinguished Service Cross (Second Class) and the coveted Iron Cross (First Class). Then, in the evening of 13 October 1918, less than a month before the Armistice, he was temporarily blinded by chlorine gas in a British attack near Comines.

During November, while he lay blind and helpless in Pasewalk Hospital in Pomerania, with the piercing pain in the sockets of his eyes only slowly diminishing, he heard from his bed the rumours of revolt in the German Navy, of the rise of the people against the continuation of the war, and of the seeds of a Marxist left-wing revolution that would soon overtake Germany.

In November, [he wrote] the general tension increased. And then one day, suddenly and unexpectedly, the calamity descended. Sailors arrived in trucks and proclaimed the revolution; a few Jewish youths

16

were their leaders in this struggle for the 'freedom, beauty and dignity' of our national existence. None of them had been at the Front. By way of a so-called gonorrhoea hospital, the three Orientals had been sent back from their second-line base. Now they raised the red rag in the homeland ... My first hope was still that this high treason might still be more or less a local affair.

But he was quickly to learn that the revolt was widespread, that Germany had been forced to capitulate, that the House of Hohenzollern would no longer bear the German Imperial Crown, and that the Fatherland was to be degraded to a republic. Shocked and depressed, with his eyes still burning like hot coals, he buried his head in his pillow. His own failure as a young man became merged in his mind with the defeat of Germany, the collapse of law and order, and the triumph of the hated French – bitterly hated since the ravaging of the German States by the armies of Napoleon a century earlier. It was the profound grief he felt at the downfall of his country, as he, an Austrian, now regarded Germany, that set him thinking of the causes of the catastrophe. With his narrow political background derived from Luegar and Lanz von Liebenfels, he began to blame those same undermining activities by another race about which he had been taught in Vienna – the exploiters of the Nordic world – the Jews. As many others were to proclaim at this time, he too was convinced that the war had been lost as a consequence of a 'stab in the back' of the victorious German Army delivered by a civil population aroused to disaffection by the greedy Jews, who saw their wealth evaporating in any further continuation of hostilities. Soon his patriotic anger grew into an overpowering hatred, and the seeds of revenge and of the dream of the restoration of a pure Germanic race were sown in his mind. Adolf Hitler, the son of Alois Hitler – himself the illegitimate son of a peasant girl, Anna Schicklgrüber, by an unidentified father before she married Johann Georg Hitler – had begun to see his mission in life some thirty years after his birth.

Corporal Adolf Hitler was discharged from hospital at the end of November 1918, and posted to Traunstein. Then, in March 1919, he was posted to Munich, the town to which he had fled from Austria before the war to escape national service with the Austrian Army. He spent his thirtieth birthday, 20 April, under the rule of the Soviet Republic of Bavaria, which had been illegally proclaimed on 7 April. A week after his birthday, the supporters of the new regime tried to arrest him. Hitler stood firm and confronted those sent to take him into custody with his rifle, and as it was clear that he meant to use it if needs be, and as they were unarmed, the arresters withdrew. His resolute action on this occasion and, in early May, his leadership as a corporal in assisting loyal troops of the Munich garrisons, supported by volunteers from the civilian population, to overthrow the Soviet regime of Communists and mutinous soldiers, brought his name to the attention of the officers of his regiment, who were already deeply alarmed by the seditious and revolutionary temper of their men. They had found one, at least, of their NCOs who was disciplined and loyal to the kind of society Germany had for generations upheld. With confidence, they appointed him to a commission of enquiry into revolutionary activities in the 2nd Bavarian Infantry Regiment; in effect a witch-hunt aimed at routing out the revolutionaries. Hitler's successes in this purge were to the entire satisfaction of his superiors, and within a few weeks he was put on a course at Reichswehr Command Headquarters, to be trained as a political agent for the purpose of bringing back to reason the unruly elements amongst the Army who had become tainted with Marxism. His task was to indoctrinate these disaffected soldiers with the patriotic spirit of Bismarck's German Empire. During this specialised political schooling Adolf Hitler gained great favour with his officers because of his pronounced anti-Semitism. As a result, he was appointed Education Officer to the 1st Bavarian Rifle Regiment, a position which made him a kind of political commissar.

On the evening of 12 September 1919 he was given the official duty of attending, in a Munich brewery, a meeting of the German Workers' Party, with the object of ascertaining its politics. Here he heard for the first time people stating, in accordance with his own secret convictions, that the profiteering Jews, and the Communists in their international conspiracy of Jewish intellectuals, had been the real 'November Criminals' of 1918 (as he called them), intriguing behind the Western Front to force defeat upon an undefeated German Army in the interests of preserving their own financial gains from the war years – the 'stab in the back'. Shortly after this meeting he joined the German Workers' Party, although still continuing his military work, but he was not enthusiastic about its effectiveness and therefore took upon himself the task of developing its propaganda. His memories of Karl Luegar and Lanz von Liebenfels, and of the efficiency of Luegar's pre-war nationalistic Christian-Socialist Party propaganda machine, were to assist him in his own approach to establishing a nationalist party, which already he had visions of leading himself. He organised the first mass meeting of the party (which from then became known as the National Socialist German Workers' Party – the NSDAP), on 24 February 1920, in the festival hall of the Hofbräuhaus in Munich, and there he presented to his audience, some two thousand people, the party programme, a mixture of Pan-Germanic nationalistic, anti-Semitic, and Socialist concepts. Central to the programme was the philosophy that it was the duty of all patriotic

Germans to save Germany from the Jews and the Bolshevik Communists, to avenge her wrongs, and to lead the Master Race back to its position as an unassailable world power.

On 31 March 1920, he left the army. Adolf Hitler had become a politician – a nationalist, and a dedicated anti-Jew and anti-Communist.

While an unknown Austrian ex-corporal was embarking upon his political career, more famous politicians and military men at the Paris Peace Conference had been rapidly propagating the seeds of a new European conflict in their efforts to resolve the form of peace which should follow the one that, in 1914, had come to an end. Opinions differed, largely in accordance with the sufferings of the individual countries which had comprised the Allied cause. This war had been one of peoples, not just of governments and their armies. Millions had perished, and whole generations had been decimated, leaving a terrible gap in the continuity of life amongst the nations involved. No longer could the peace treaties be negotiated as they had been in the eighteenth and nineteenth centuries, when aristocratic statesmen, victor and vanquished alike, negotiated in polite and courtly fashion, redrawing the frontiers on maps and reshaping national policies on foundations upon which all were agreed. This war had savaged nations, in particular France and Belgium, and also Britain and her Empire. A million and a half Frenchmen had lost their lives defending their country against the German invader. Thirteen French provinces had come under the heel of Prussian military rule; vast regions had been systematically devastated by the German Army; towns and villages and huge agricultural areas had been left in ruins by artillery bombardment; hardly a cottage or house in the length of the country did not mourn its dead or shelter its cripples. 'Five times in a hundred years,' wrote Churchill, 'in 1814, 1815, 1870, 1914 and 1918, had the towers of Notre Dame seen the flash of Prussian guns and heard the thunder of cannonade.' Now France demanded retribution. Her victory was a miracle, and the people who had suffered so much had no intentions of letting their leaders sign away, at the peace conference table, what their soldiers had at last won on the bloody battlefields of their beloved country. For nearly a hundred years from the time of the Napoleonic Wars, France had lived under the terror of German arms, now, with this great victory, the French people were determined that never again should the threat of German aggression disrupt their lives. Germany had fought almost the entire world single-handed, and on several occasions the result had hung in the balance as she came close to conquering all Europe. Certainly France, Belgium and Italy would have succumbed to the onslaught but for the two to three million men of Britain and her Empire who sprang to Europe's defence, followed by the final support, in the last year of the war, of two million Americans.* If defeat had come, then Holland, Spain and Portugal, and probably all of the Scandinavian countries, would have fallen under the domination of the new German Empire. Having been spared this awful prospect, France wanted security, without which all that had now been gained would be valueless.

After the Armistice of November 1918, the German armies were intact, as indeed was the High Seas Fleet. In truth, the armies had not been overwhelmingly defeated on the battlefield, and they had marched home in good order. The war had ceased not by a military defeat and the pleas of the German Army for a surrender, but by the fears of the politicians of an overwhelming defeat demanding unconditional surrender if fighting was not quickly halted. In addition, German politicians were faced with the wrath of a public facing the horrors of starvation brought about by the success of the British naval blockade, which had already caused more than 800,000 deaths. Marshal Ferdinand Foch, the Supreme Commander of the Allied Forces, said of his enemy: 'They fought well, let them keep their weapons', but he demanded that the French frontier should henceforth be the Rhine. Foch took the view that Germany might be disarmed and her defences dismantled; she might be impoverished and loaded with vast reparations; she might even be fragmented by internal strife arising from differing political elements eager to blame each other for the catastrophe, and each seeking to gain control of the remnants of defeat. But he was convinced that the might of Germany would rise again and, therefore, the broad, deep and swift-flowing Rhine must be fortified and held by the French Army, to act as a barrier against aggression behind which France could shelter for generations. The views of Britain and the United States, however, without whose aid France would surely have perished, were very different and, as a result, the territorial provisions of the Treaty of Versailles, signed on 28 June 1919, left Germany practically intact, although some areas had been returned or ceded, and still the largest homogeneous racial block in Europe. When Foch heard of the signing of the Peace Treaty with its generous territorial concessions, he remarked acidly: 'This is not Peace. It is an Armistice for twenty years.'

The economic clauses of the Treaty were, by contrast, so vindictive as to be unenforceable. Germany was condemned to pay reparations on an entirely unrealistic scale, thus giving expression to the vengeance of the victors. While the politicians were, for the most part, aware that a defeated nation could never pay damages on a scale which would meet the cost of a modern war, and that reparations could only be made from

---

* Technically, the United States of America was not one of the Allies, President Wilson having insisted, when he declared war on 6 April 1917, that his country be regarded as a co-belligerent 'associated power'.

indigenous raw materials, industrial production, and services, all of which demanded a recovery in German industrial output and trade, they were not prepared to make these facts known to the multitudes at large. The public wanted retribution, and, steeped as they were in ignorance of economic facts, they howled for Germany to be squeezed 'till the pips squeaked', as one French politician put it. The politicians, seeking the votes of the victorious nations, were, for their part, not prepared to undeceive the people of those nations; no one in authority had the courage or honesty to detach himself from the public folly of unlimited revenge, and to tell the various electorates that no profit would be gained by trying to destroy economically the defeated German nation.

In fact, most of the economic clauses of the Treaty of Versailles were never enforced. £1,000 million of German assets were certainly appropriated by the victors, but almost immediately afterwards £500 million was lent to Germany by the USA and Britain to enable her to repair the ruin caused to her basic industries by the war. Indeed, the extortion of indemnities from Germany was only possible because of profuse loans made to her, principally by the USA. In fact, from 1926 to 1929, the repayment by the Allies to the USA of loans made before America came into the war, loans which enabled the Allies to continue the struggle, represented only *one-fifth* of the money that the USA was lending Germany without chance of repayment. The truth was that, by borrowing successfully in all directions, Germany gained 2,000 millions sterling in loans against the 1,000 millions which reparations demanded from her in one form or another. She borrowed more than she had to pay, and thus was able to re-establish her industries. This assistance to the vanquished reaped no gratitude or good will, however, for the embittered populations of the victorious nations were still vociferously insisting that Germany should be made to pay 'to the uttermost farthing'. No German would be grateful for that.

Perhaps one of the greatest errors of the Peace Treaty was the insistence by the victorious Allies that they would only deal with Germany as a republic, and never as a monarchy. This prejudice against monarchy came mainly from America, supported by France (both republics), and as a result Kaiser Wilhelm II was sent into exile and the Weimar Republic (so named after the town in which the first National Constituent Assembly gathered in February 1919) was established to replace the reign of emperors. Lloyd George, the British Prime Minister, was the only leading politician in favour of the retention of the monarchy,* but he made no visible effort to counteract the views of the Americans and

---

* Wilhelm II, Emperor of Germany and King of Prussia, was one of Queen Victoria's grandsons. Exiled after the First World War, he died in Holland in 1941, with a new generation of German invaders outside his gates.

French. The result was that nonentities were elected to lead Germany, men who commanded scant respect from the mighty, defeated, but largely uninjured nation. As Churchill wrote:

> Wise policy would have crowned and fortified the Weimar Republic with a constitutional sovereign in the person of an infant grandson of the Kaiser, under a Council of Regency. Instead, a gaping void was opened in the national life of the German people. All the strong elements, military and feudal, which might have rallied to a constitutional Monarch, and for its sake respected and sustained the new democratic and Parliamentary processes, were for the time being unhinged. The Weimar Republic, with all its liberal trappings and blessings, was regarded as an imposition of the enemy. It could not hold the loyalties or the imagination of the German people.

It was indeed a nonentity, Friedrich Ebert, who was made the first President of the Weimar Republic in 1919.

In the period from 1919 to 1923, German feelings were aroused to a high pitch of impotent rage. Raymond Poincaré, the French President who, in 1922, succeeded Georges Clemenceau as Prime Minister of France, attempted to create an independent Rhineland under the patronage and control of France, and, in January 1923, to enforce the payment of reparations by a French and Belgian invasion and occupation of the Ruhr. Although the troops encountered only passive resistance, the fury unleashed by this treatment led the Germans to a deliberate, irresponsible, and reckless printing of paper money, with the object of destroying the whole basis of the Deutschmark and thereby reducing war debts to worthless dimensions. In the final stages of this inflation, fostered by the speculators, the mark stood at forty-three million millions to the pound sterling. The consequences of this runaway inflation were far reaching. The savings of the middle classes were wiped out, and thus was created the potential support for any forceful and dynamic leader, however wild, with new political philosophies. The path to Communism or a dictatorship of the right was opened, but as yet the Nazi* Hitler was not far enough along the route to take over. After Ebert, who died at the beginning of 1925, Germany was to have Field-Marshal Paul von Hindenburg as President of the Republic from 1925 to 1934, and with his reign there came some degree of stability.

---

* The word 'Nazi' is the abbreviated form of the German for National Socialist German Workers' Party. The term was originally used derisively.

CHAPTER II

Trenchard's Royal Air Force

In 1919 and 1920, the Royal Air Force, formed as a separate service on 1 April 1918 by the amalgamation of the Army's Royal Flying Corps and the Navy's Royal Naval Air Service, was already suffering from a kind of April Fool's Day hoax attendant upon its creation. As a result of the expansion for war and of this amalgamation, the RAF had become the largest air force in the world. Consistent, however, with the hasty demobilisation of all the services immediately after the Armistice was signed, it was rapidly whittled down to a negligible force. Of the three services, the Royal Air Force was subjected to the most vicious cuts because the British Admiralty and the War Office regarded it as nothing more than a wartime expedient, and were determined that the newly formed Air Ministry should be disbanded. Their desire was to kill General Smuts's creation and have the flying forces revert to the organisation that existed up to April 1918, that is to say, a Naval Air Service under the thumb of the Admiralty, and a Flying Corps under the War Office. Air Marshal Sir Hugh Trenchard, who had commanded the RFC for most of the war and who was the first Chief of the Air Staff of the newly formed Royal Air Force, had other ideas, for he was convinced of the necessity for a powerful, centrally controlled air arm in the interests of national security. Moreover, he was persuaded that much of the Empire, including the Middle East territories for which Britain had accepted administrative responsibility from the League of Nations after the war, could be more economically policed and controlled by the Royal Air Force than by the Army. He therefore fought diligently and intelligently for the survival of his force, with the able support of two brothers, Air Vice-Marshals Sir John and Sir Geoffrey Salmond, both heroes and senior officers from the war, and the pair of them Trenchard's most trusted colleagues. Apart from demonstrating that savings in costs could be made if the Royal Air Force was used for control and administration in the Middle East, Trenchard decided to use a public relations ploy to capture the imagination of the people of Britain. In fact, he planned a master stroke. Britain would see for itself its air force, watch its skill in the skies and on the ground, and be thrilled by the hair-raising performances of the men in their flying machines.

On Saturday, 3 July 1920, just two weeks before his marriage to Katharine Boyle, Trenchard staged the first Royal Air Force Pageant at Hendon Aerodrome, close to London.

The Pageant was not his only success in 1920. From the moment of the inception of the Royal Air Force as a separate service, many steps were taken to ensure its continued existence. One of the most important was the decision, in 1919, to establish at Cranwell a Cadet College, on the lines of the Royal Military College at Sandhurst and the Royal Military Academy at Woolwich, for the purposes of training officers for permanent service and to create an air force spirit and a sense of career in the new service. This college, to be known as the Royal Air Force College, Cranwell, was inaugurated on Thursday, 5 February 1920, with Air Commodore C.A.H. Longcroft, a notable pioneer of flight, as its first Commandant, and Wing Commander L.W.R. Rees, VC, OBE, DFC, AFC, as its first Wing Commander, Flying.

At the inauguration, Trenchard said:

> This College will have the making or marring of the future of a Service which was built up during the war by gallant pilots, observers, and other ranks who fought through it, and won a name in the air second to none in the world.
>
> If it is to continue its great work, which I am convinced that it will do, we realise that it has to live up to its reputation, and we must ensure by every means in our power that it does.
>
> Therefore you will have to work your hardest, both as cadets at the College and subsequently as officers, in order to be capable of guiding this Service through its early days, and maintaining its traditions and efficiency in the years to come.

But Trenchard's masterstroke at this time was the support he won for the employment of the Royal Air Force in the Middle East and, later, India, at great saving to the British taxpayer.

After the Armistice, the President of the USA, Woodrow Wilson, conceived the idea of a League of Nations, as a consortium of the victorious nations, later to include the vanquished, which would stand together against any country that made aggressive advances against any one or more members of the League. The idea was that the war just finished should remain as 'the war to end wars', and that international differences should in future be settled by negotiation, with all members of the League participating in the attempts to resolve differences – a form of collective security. The basic covenant of the League of Nations was contained in the Treaty of Versailles, and since it was initially Woodrow Wilson's brain-child, it was expected that initial membership would include the USA. But no sooner had the League been created than the United States abandoned Wilson's offspring, despite his determined campaign to win American support. An election demolished his party and his policies. In 1920 the United States elected a Republican President, Warren Harding, and returned to its old principles of isolationism, and to its view that Europe should be left to stew in its own juice.

The European nations did not, however, abandon the League. Until 1934 the power vested in the European allies in the name of the League, and under its moral and international reputation, was enough to limit the armed strength of Germany, and to exert restraint upon Mussolini's ambitions to extend Italy's empire in North Africa. But its more immediate task in 1919 and 1920 was to find ways of administering the territories formerly ruled by the Ottoman sultans and now removed from Turkish rule by the defeat of this former ally of Germany. The idea was to form these areas into the new states of Palestine, Transjordan, Mesopotamia, Syria, the Lebanon, the Hejaz, and the Yemen. Of these, Mesopotamia, Palestine, Transjordan, the Hejaz, and the Yemen were mandated to Britain. Rule by mandate was a new concept, giving a Great Power responsibility for defence, internal security, and political and economic development of the new state until it was fit to fend for itself, when it would become a member of the League of Nations itself and the Mandatory Power would withdraw.

The British public were not in favour of these commitments, for they recognised that considerable British forces would be needed to defend hundreds of miles of disputed frontiers, and to maintain law and order amongst wild people, costing the taxpayer a great deal of money for no return. The rebellion in Mesopotamia in 1920 proved them right; it cost 2,000 casualties and about £100,000,000 to subdue, a very considerable sum in those days. As a result the public pressed the Government to withdraw from all the mandated territories. The Government knew, however, that withdrawal would be an irresponsible act, leading to the whole area erupting in inter-state feuding or open warfare, an attempt by Turkey to reimpose its rule throughout the Middle East, and the probable annihilation by the Arabs of the growing Jewish settlement in Palestine. The British Government therefore looked desperately for more economic and effective ways of undertaking its obligations to the League. Trenchard had already seen a way out of the dilemma by using the Royal Air Force for the tasks normally assigned to the Army. He first of all requested Air Vice-Marshal Sir Geoffrey Salmond, then Air Officer Commanding, Middle East, to study the possibilities of exercising an air control of Mesopotamia, which he was convinced would result in substantial savings in troops, equipment and costs. Salmond completed his report and made recommendations which showed that immense savings could be made in lives and money by employing aircraft to police and control these large tracts of difficult territory; he submitted it under cover of a letter dated 25 May 1920, from RAF Headquarters, Baghdad, addressed to the General Officer Commanding, Mesopotamia, and to Trenchard. In the meantime, Trenchard, with Air Vice-Marshal Sir John Salmond's aid, had drawn up a preliminary scheme for the military control of Mesopotamia by use of air forces, and this he discussed with Churchill prior to submitting it to the Cabinet on the 12 March 1920. This scheme, later supported by Sir Geoffrey's report and recommendations, impressed both Churchill and the Cabinet, the former, in particular, seeing in it very significant savings when compared with traditional methods. There followed, in March 1921, a conference in Cairo – Egypt was then a protectorate of the British Empire – to investigate possible ways of exercising control in the mandated territories both effectively and at a much lower cost. Churchill was chairman of this conference, and it was there that he took the bold step of giving the responsibility for the protection of Mesopotamia and Transjordan from external incursions, and for the maintenance of law and order internally, to the Royal Air Force. This experiment in the use of the air force proved so successful, and made such great savings in men, materials and money, that RAF responsibility was extended, yet again, to cover the Aden Protectorate.

The RAF's massive striking force, which had numbered ninety-six squadrons in France alone by the time of the Armistice, had, within six months, shrunk to twenty-three, as a result of demobilisation. By the end of 1920 the number of squadrons had risen to twenty-five and a half; of these, Trenchard based nineteen overseas to meet his commitments in the Empire and to carry out the newly won responsibilities in the mandated territories. Three were established in Mesopotamia, seven in Egypt (of which one was transferred, in 1922, to Mesopotamia), eight in India, and one was allotted for division between various naval bases. This left only two fighter squadrons for the defence of Britain, two for army co-operation, and two and a half for work with the Home Fleet.

Despite the meagre size of his air force, Trenchard had gone a long way towards securing its future, for he had wisely foreseen that if he could save the taxpayer's purse, he could rely on the latter's support. At Hendon he was showing the public what it owned, small as it was, and in the Middle East he was demonstrating how what the public owned could save it money. But he was not satisfied with the success he was having in the Middle East alone, for by 1922 he reckoned that what was being achieved there could also be accomplished on the North-West Frontier of India. Here, however, he had a different problem. Although the RAF had been a separate autonomous service since 1918, with its own budget introduced to Parliament by its own Secretary of State, in India it had remained under the thumb of the Army, its budget being one of the cost centres of Army expenditure in the Military Services Budget, which was controlled by the Commander-in-Chief, India, as Army member on the Viceroy's Council. The result was that the RAF's requirements were sadly neglected, even to the extent that the eight squadrons were so ill supplied with spares and maintenance facilities that at one stage, early in 1922, only four aircraft out of ninety-six were in flying condition. Indeed, the treatment of the RAF in India seemed to amount almost to sabotage. These appalling conditions were fortunately revealed to the public in a letter to *The Times* from Lord Montagu of Beaulieu, who, as Adviser on Mechanical Transport to the Government of India, had recently returned from a visit to that country. The letter created such a scandal that it gave Trenchard the opportunity he had been seeking to have the control of the RAF removed from the Army in India. To this end he sent Sir John Salmond to the sub-continent to make a detailed, on-the-spot enquiry into the situation.

Sir John left England at the end of May 1922, arrived in India at the end of June, and completed his tour of inspection on 27 July. His report was shattering. 'The Royal Air Force in India', he stated, 'is to all intents and purposes non-existent as a fighting force at this date.' The total number of aircraft shown as serviceable, he said, was only seven, or 15 per cent of expectation, and he added that a number of the serviceable aircraft were 'so old and decrepit that they should have been already struck off charge.' Others, he reported, were 'flying without the incorporation of technical equipment essential to safety.' His recommendations included a complete reorganisation of the RAF in India, independent of the Army and under the direct control of the Air Ministry, with a proper system of budgeting kept separate from the Army's budget. He also recommended specific increases in establishments, the provision of adequate barracks and technical buildings, and increased status for the Air Officer Commanding in India to that befitting the commander of an autonomous service. These proposals were submitted to the British Government, and were approved. Trenchard had again won the day. The RAF in India, under proper Air Force control, was quickly to perform with the same effectiveness as it had in the Middle East, and was to be accepted by the Army as a much-needed ally in policing the North-West Frontier.

The future of the Royal Air Force, despite its pathetically small size in Britain, had now been assured by Trenchard, and he was at last able to concentrate on fighting for its increase in the United Kingdom to a size essential for national security. This was just as well, for the future of another phenomenon of the twenties was, by 1924, also largely assured – that of Adolf Hitler.

CHAPTER III

Hitler Emerges

In 1920 and 1921, Hitler was still only the recruiting officer for the National Socialist German Workers' Party. In fact, in January, 1921, at a regular meeting of the members, he was elected to no significant office, although he had hoped for the appointment of Deputy Chairman, if not Chairman, of the Party. His disappointment turned to intense annoyance. He had not become a politician solely to spend his life making publicity for other people. Certainly it was, in the main, his organisation, his writing activities, and his speech-making, which were winning NSDAP members from the ranks of ex-soldiers who had failed to come to terms with civilian life; from those Germans who had been cut off from their country by war and its aftermath of boundaries redefined by peace treaties, and who were living with seething resentment abroad or on the borders of their homeland; and later from the middle classes who were already suffering a severe diminution of their standard of living. Indeed, by 1922 and 1923 Hitler was even receiving, on the Party's behalf, both social and financial assistance from such major industrialists as Borsig and Thyssen.

The time had come, he decided in 1921, to assume command of the Party, and he chose as his battleground the split in Party opinion over the question of amalgamation with another nationalist group, the German Socialist Party, based in North Germany with a strong supporting element in Nürnberg, and led by a man named Julius Streicher. The proposed union was to come under a joint, and more-or-less democratic, action committee with equal representation from both sides. The action committee would in effect be above the two parties, and would reach

29

agreement on Party issues and policies and instruct the parties accordingly. Hitler viewed this as the path of procrastination and weakness in pushing forward any programme which his party had already ratified. If the German Socialist Party, or any other party for that matter, wished to join forces with the National Socialist Workers' Party, then, he avowed, they should abandon their parties as such and transfer their membership and allegiance to the NSDAP. He was opposed in this view, and, since it looked as though he would be defeated, he resigned from the Party on 11 July 1921. This was, however, a planned move – having resigned, he promptly wrote a letter to the Party Committee, couched in the most arrogant terms, and setting out the conditions under which he was prepared to return to the fold. These conditions included the retention of the Munich headquarters, of the Party programme as previously approved, and of the Party name, but the *pièce de résistance* was his demand that he should be given 'the position of Chairman with dictatorial powers'. The Party Committee, well aware of Hitler's success in rallying increasing numbers of people and, more importantly, money, to the Party's standard, gave in, and he duly emerged as the unchallenged leader. By December 1921, the Bavarian press was hailing him as 'Leader of the National Socialist Party', and on 30 November 1922, when he spoke at five mass meetings, the posters announced him as: 'Our Führer, Adolf Hitler.' And in October 1922 he had gained a valuable adherent to his cause when Hermann Göring, a wartime pilot of considerable renown, had joined the Party.

In the following year, 1923, Hitler was aided in his recruitment of more supporters, particularly from the middle classes, by the French occupation of the Ruhr and the inflation that followed. In Germany, the Weimar government was accused of impotence in the face of French 'aggression', the Communists were accused of plotting to bring about a state of anarchy in the once proud German nation, and the Jews were blamed for creating inflation in order to fill their pockets with gold at the expense of the rest of the population. This disaffection proved to be a good recruiting ground. By November, the Party boasted 56,000 members, four times as many as at the beginning of the year, and ten times the membership at the beginning of 1922. Now, it seemed was the time to stage something dramatic to maintain the momentum of growth.

On 8 November Hitler marched on Munich with his supporters, and with the prestigious support of General Ludendorff, with the vague idea of usurping the power of the Bavarian State Government, before marching on Berlin and establishing a right-wing government. He reached the inner city with much backing from the populace, but the march collapsed at the Feldeherrnhalle under a few salvoes from the numerically far inferior Bavarian State Police. Sixteen of the marchers were killed. Hitler's National Socialists had little confidence in themselves at this time, and preferred flight to a premature end to their lives and careers. Hitler himself was arrested and sent for trial on 24 February 1924, at the Munich People's Court, where he conducted his own defence and made an impassioned attack on all who had dragged Germany down into the dust, accusing the Reich President of high treason and denigrating all who opposed his own high ideals of the restoration of his country to its proper place amongst nations. By the time he had finished he had won most of those present to his side, including the Court President. But he was found guilty of treason and was sentenced to five years' detention at the fortress of Landsberg – in fact, the minimum sentence, and backed by a strong recommendation for early parole. In addition, the Nazi Party was banned throughout Germany, even in its home state of Bavaria.

As the gates of the fortress closed upon him, so began his literary career – designed to further his political career in the future. Behaving as a model prisoner, in contrast to many of his rowdy followers who had also been jailed, he began work on a book to be called *Four and a Half Years' Struggle Against Lies, Stupidity, and Cowardice'*, which he later renamed *Mein Kampf* – 'My Struggle'. Hitler dictated his work to a young follower, also imprisoned for his part in the 'Munich Putsch', who was devoted to him and who acted as his secretary – Rudolf Hess. For the time being Adolf Hitler was out of circulation, but not for long. His sentence was reviewed and, as a result, reduced to six months' imprisonment followed by four years' probation, although he was forbidden to take an active part in politics, or to speak in public. He was released in 1924, and in the two following years the two volumes of *Mein Kampf* appeared.

Hitler may have made his impact on Bavaria at this time, but to the world at large he was unknown, and even in Germany he was regarded as being of little importance, other than as a nuisance factor to the Weimar Republic. In fact, a long interval was to pass before his National Socialist Party, or Nazi Party, as it increasingly came to be known, was to gain a significant hold on the masses of the German people, the armed forces, and the majority of those industrialists who were already fearful of Communism.

In 1922, there appeared a new leader in British politics. A Member of Parliament since 1908, he had from 1916 been Financial Secretary to the Treasury, and had passed unknown and unnoticed in a world at war, playing his modest part in domestic affairs. Unlike Hitler, however, he was already a politician of some experience, practising in a legitimate and recognised party of considerable standing. It was from his subsequent

31

position as President of the Board of Trade that he became the ruling force in British politics when, in October 1922, he assisted Andrew Bonar Law in challenging the National Coalition Government which, under the premiership of Lloyd George, had governed for most of the war. The result of the challenge was a General Election in which the Conservatives, quitting the Coalition, gained a majority of 120 seats and Bonar Law became Prime Minister. The name of the man who had assisted him to power was Stanley Baldwin.

Early in 1923, Bonar Law resigned the leadership because of ill-health, and on 22 May Stanley Baldwin succeeded him as Prime Minister, although his term of office was to be short-lived by his own design. Baldwin was suspicious that Lloyd George, a Liberal and 'free-trader', would gather to his side enough dissenting ex-Conservative ministers who had lost office when the National Coalition Government had been challenged and defeated, to cause a split in his government's majority. The issue, he recognised, would be 'Protection versus Free Trade', and he forestalled the Liberals by raising the matter first in a speech at Plymouth on 25 October. Its effect was, as he had calculated, to force a dissolution of Parliament before October ended. A General Election was then held on Thursday 6 December, the second in 1923. The Conservatives won 258 seats, the Liberals 159, Labour 191, and others 7, a result so evenly spread between Conservatives, Liberals and Labour, that a combination of any two of the three major parties could command a majority in the House of Commons. Baldwin declined to form an administration in these circumstances, and H.H. Asquith for the Liberals also declined. Thus it came about that, on 22 January 1924, Ramsay MacDonald, at the head of little more than two-fifths of the House, became Britain's first Socialist Prime Minister. He stayed in power for a year, largely thanks to quarrels between the two Opposition parties, who divided in the House more for the purpose of defeating each other than to oppose the Government, even when they disagreed with government policy.

Before the end of 1924, however, the Liberals and the Conservatives had come to see eye-to-eye over a major issue, and the two Opposition parties combined to bring down the Labour Government. So yet another General Election was held on Wednesday, 29 October 1924, the third within two years. Baldwin's Conservative Party was returned with a majority of 223 over all the parties, the distribution of seats being Conservatives 419, Liberals 40, Labour 151, Communists 1, and others 4. Stanley Baldwin once more became Prime Minister, but this time with a healthy majority. He was to lead his country with great skill for the next five years through a difficult period in both internal and international affairs. In this he was ably supported: Churchill was Chancellor of the Exchequer, Austen Chamberlain Foreign Secretary, and an as-yet unknown MP, Anthony Eden, was soon to become Parliamentary Private Secretary to the Foreign Secretary.

A few days before the election, on 25 October, several British newspapers published a letter allegedly written in Russian by Grigori Zinoviev, Chairman of the Comintern (the Communist Third International), to the Communist Party of Great Britain. The letter urged British Communists to promote a revolution in their own country, and advised them on methods of undertaking the task. Because the minority Labour Government, led by Ramsay MacDonald, had formally recognised the Communist regime in Russia earlier in the year, and had then tried to negotiate a trade treaty with the USSR, many voters believed that the Labour Party must contain 'fellow-travellers',* secret sympathisers with Communist Russia and its plans for a revolution in Britain, and treacherously ready to sell their country to the enemy. It is estimated that the Labour Party lost some 42 seats at the election as a result of the publication of the Zinoviev Letter, although its genuineness is still disputed. But even if this episode had never occurred, the Conservatives would still have won the General Election of October 1924 with a handsome majority.

---

* A term coined by Trotsky, implying a person in sympathy with a political party, but not a member of it. It is most commonly used of Communist sympathisers.

CHAPTER IV

The Secret Rebirth of Germany's Armed Forces

With the death, in February 1925, of Friedrich Ebert, the leader of the pre-war German Social Democratic Party and the first President of the new Weimar Republic, Field-Marshal Paul von Hindenburg was elected to the Presidency by a very narrow majority. The distribution of votes cast on Sunday 26 April, was: Hindenburg, 14,655,766; Marx of the Catholic Party, 13,751,615; and the Communist, Thaelman, 1,931,151. Hindenburg, the military idol of Germany during the First World War, had remained faithful to the exiled Kaiser and had favoured a restoration of the Imperial monarchy. He was now seventy-seven, and had been in retirement for several years, but his return to public life, which he had been urged to undertake by nationalist politicians, was welcomed in Germany because the population had for many decades been brought up under a kind of paternal autocracy, albeit one which had always made room, by years of custom, for free speech and Parliamentary opposition. Field-Marshal Hindenburg was an illustrious commander from an old famous military family, and a great patriot, and as such he was looked upon by the people as a man who would provide the nation once again with a sense of pride and dignity. His election was also welcomed by Britain, whose rulers believed that Hindenburg would give Germany stability, help her to recover her honour and self-respect, and to put aside the bitterness of defeat.

Early in 1925 there occurred an event which, nurtured by Hindenburg, came to assume great importance. The Weimar Republic declared a willingness to accept a pact with those Allied powers – Britain, France and Italy – which, as a result of the Peace Treaty, were providing the military occupation of the Rhineland, not to wage war against each other, the trustees for such a solemn agreement to be the United States of America. Implicit in this pact was to be a guarantee of the existing territorial status of the Rhineland; in effect, the Germans wished to ensure that the Rhineland, nominally an independent republic under the Treaty, would remain a part of Germany after the Allies withdrew from occupation. Austen Chamberlain, the British Foreign Secretary, was in favour of the German proposal and made the news public in the House of Commons on 5 March, but added a proviso – there could be no agreement outside the League of Nations and, therefore, a condition must be the entry of Germany into the League. He also insisted that Belgium be included amongst the contracting powers. In this he was backed by Churchill, the Chancellor of the Exchequer, who, like Chamberlain himself, passionately believed that the principal interest of the British people in Europe lay in the abatement of the long-standing Franco-German feud, and in the unification of Western Europe into an assembly of independent states supporting each other's national security. Austen Chamberlain's outlook also commanded the respect of all parties in Parliament.

In July, the Germans accepted the condition of entry into the League of Nations prior to the ratification of the Western Pact of Non-Aggression which they had proposed, but they wanted concessions themselves. These included agreement upon general disarmament, deletion from the Peace Treaty of the 'war guilt' clause, and the immediate evacuation of Cologne by the occupying Allied troops, although these concessions had not, in fact, been pressed by the German Government when Gustav Stresemann, the German Foreign Minister, had been made aware that Britain and France were adamant that Germany must join the League of Nations without reservations. A conference was held at Locarno in Switzerland, starting on 4 October 1925, attended by delegates from France, Britain, Belgium, Italy and Germany, to discuss the terms of the proposed Western Pact. Out of this conference were born the Treaty of Mutual Guarantee between the five powers; Arbitration Treaties between Germany and France, Germany and Belgium, Germany and Poland, and Germany and Czechoslovakia,, effectively guaranteeing the existing boundaries of those countries; special agreements between France and Poland and between France and Czechoslovakia, by which France undertook to go to the aid of these countries in the event of a breakdown of the Western Pact being followed by unprovoked aggression by any signatory – which meant, in effect, by Germany. Then, by what came to be known as the Treaty of Locarno, the Western European democracies agreed to keep the peace amongst themselves, and to unite against any one of their number who broke the contract and used aggression against another. As between France and Germany, Britain became pledged to go to the aid of whichever of those two nations was the object of unprovoked aggression by the other. Whilst France remained armed and Germany disarmed, Germany could not attack France, and it was almost a certainty that France would never attack Germany if that meant Britain allying herself with Germany. Thus there seemed little likelihood of Britain being involved in a Continental war as a result of this commitment, and the condition was therefore accepted by Parliament and warmly endorsed by the nation as a whole.

The Treaty of Locarno, completed at the end of 1925, was first signed by Stanley Baldwin; Austen Chamberlain, the main instigator of the Treaty and the man who steered it to a successful conclusion, was made a Knight of the Garter and awarded the Nobel Peace Prize. All now seemed set for the future peace of Europe. No agreement on general disarmament followed the Locarno Treaty, however, and neither was there any discussion on the subject of withdrawal of the occupation forces from the Rhineland. These matters, with German resentment still smouldering over the French and Belgian invasion of the Ruhr in 1923 in order to extract reparations, were the cause of much dissatisfaction among the German General Staff. Helping to fire this discontent even more were the military terms imposed by the victorious Allies at the end of the war. By the Treaty of Versailles, at the suggestion of Lloyd George, the German Army was limited to 100,000 men, and conscription was forbidden. Additionally, the Treaty prohibited a German air force (that which had existed at the Armistice being officially dissolved in May 1920), and only a small naval force was permitted, with a maximum strength of 15,000 men. All of these restrictions were a bitter blow to the pride of the German Army – the Reichswehr – and Navy, and it was not long before secret efforts were being made to build up a nucleus from which military forces could ultimately expand.

Without conscription it was inconceivable that a force of 100,000 men could be expanded into an army of millions, even over a comparatively long period. On the other hand, the German General Staff recognised at the outset that if those hundred thousand men were of the highest quality, and capable of leadership as officers and senior NCOs, then the essential nucleus of a skilled and disciplined army could be formed which could be rapidly expanded when the time came. As early as 1921 the creator of this nucleus, General Hans von Seeckt, Chief of the Army General Staff, was planning in secret a full-sized German Army whilst arguing deferentially with the Allied Military Control Commission about his limited military forces. Although, for example, the Peace Treaty demanded a decrease in the officer corps from 34,000 to 4,000, von Seeckt was successfully increasing the number by every subterfuge; under the pseudonymous Departments of Reconstruction, Research, and Culture, thousands of plain-clothes staff officers and their assistants were being assembled in Berlin to examine the warfare of the past and to plan for the army of the future. New principles of training and instructional courses were prepared, all existing manuals were rewritten and brought up to date, the use of mobile warfare was studied, including the major use of armoured divisions and the employment of air support, and this, not for an army of 100,000, but for the ultimate armed might of the German nation. The main principle was to develop an integrated military force with all the services, ground, sea and air, tactically interwoven and strategically supported. In the summer of 1926, von Seeckt held his first major military exercise for commanders. He had no troops, the exercise being for generals, commanding officers and general staff officers. It was designed to introduce these officers to the art of future warfare, when the army would be of the size commensurate with that befitting a nation as great as Germany.

During this time also, von Seeckt prepared the resuscitation of the German Air Force with skill and immense cunning. Reading the opening and closing paragraphs of his Order of the Day, for 6 May 1920, one wonders whether he had already formulated his plans at that early date. This order, drafted by Hauptmann Wilberg, von Seeckt's air defence adviser, was on the subject of the disbandment of what had been known as the flying corps. 'As from May 8, 1920', it read, 'a young branch of the armed forces, which has served with bravery in action and earned fame in the course of its relatively short history, will lay down arms in silence and with pride. On this day, the German Flying Corps fulfils the demand laid down in the Peace Treaty for the complete disbanding of all its formations and establishments.' After an account of the history of the German Military Air Service, von Seeckt ended his order by saying: 'We shall not abandon the hope of one day seeing the Flying Corps come to life again. The fame of the Flying Corps engraved in the history of the German armed forces will never fade. It is not dead, its spirit lives on!'

Von Seeckt's first move to preserve a foundation for military aviation was to hide a reserve of trained pilots, aircrew and ground staff within his permitted army of 100,000 and under the cover of his phoney civilian departments in Berlin. But without flying practice, and without training facilities for a new generation of pilots, aircrew, and maintenance staff, the benefit of such artifice was minimal. Moreover, the Treaty of Versailles had not only removed aircraft from the German Army, but had laid down such stringent performance limitations for the aircraft that Germany was to be allowed to design and build in the future, that production of military types was effectively precluded. The importation of military aircraft was also forbidden. But von Seeckt found a way around these problems with the aid of a most unexpected ally. On 6 May 1921, Germany and the Soviet Union concluded a Trade Agreement which led to discussions between the two countries not only on economic matters, but also on military matters. As a result, von Seeckt came into contact with the Russian negotiator, Radek, and the two debated the possibilities of military collaboration. Arising from these talks the Soviet Union and Germany concluded, on 16 April 1922, the Treaty of Rapallo, which re-established diplomatic relations between the two countries, each renouncing existing financial claims upon the other. More importantly, the treaty opened the way to a period of co-operation between the Reichswehr and the Soviet Army. For this purpose a commission of members of the unofficial German military, naval and air staffs was sent to Moscow, led by Colonel von der Lieth-Thomsen, who had been Chief of Air Staff to the C-in-C of the German Flying Corps during the war. On the completion of the work of this mission, von der Lieth-Thomsen, having shortened his name to Herr von der Lieth to conceal his identity, remained in Moscow with a small staff, the reduced mission now operating as a liaison unit.

By the end of 1925, a German military flying training school had been established at Lipezk in north-west Russia, fifty Fokker DXIII fighters fitted with British 450-hp Napier Lion engines, illegally purchased from the Dutch manufacturer, had been shipped from Stettin to Lipezk via the port of Leningrad, and the first training course for German pilots had begun. From then onwards, until Hitler put a stop to them in 1933, the courses became a regular feature. The deception of the Allies was complete, due to the unholy pact between Germany and Russia. Even the Napier Lion engines used in the Fokker DXIII were shipped back to the makers in England for repair, and re-shipped again to Leningrad, without anyone in Britain realising that they were assisting the rebirth of German military aviation, in contravention of the terms of the Peace Treaty which British politicians had helped to draft. Lipezk continued to be used for training right up to 1933, and was unquestionably the birthplace of the Luftwaffe, as the German Air Force was to become known.

None of this, however, solved the problem of Germany's aircraft industry. Von Seeckt was determined to keep that industry alive, and so gave encouragement to Ernst Heinkel, an aircraft designer and constructor, to begin designing and building in absolute secrecy, military-type aeroplanes at his small factory at Warnemünde, just to the north of Rostock. It was not difficult to conceal the company's operations, hidden away in this corner of the Baltic coast, and even as early as 1923 and 1924 Heinkel were building limited numbers of military types. In some cases they designed and built the aircraft parts and shipped them to Sweden for assembly, where they were also fitted with British engines acquired by Sweden on Germany's behalf, since engines of German manufacture were not then available. The aircraft were then packed and warehoused in bond at Stockholm harbour, as a reserve for their future use. Finally, some were shipped to Lipezk for testing and for purposes of flying instruction and operational training.

The irony was that while Britain was reducing her armed services, in particular the Royal Air Force, to a level that was totally inadequate for her security, Germany was successfully preparing for a return to armed might under the very noses of the Allies. Hitler's military power of the thirties and forties was, in the twenties, being underwritten for him, although at this stage he was still a comparative nonentity from the State of Bavaria.

After his release from Landsberg at the end of 1924, Hitler was quick to persuade Franz Gürtner, the gullible Bavarian Minister of Justice, to lift the ban imposed upon his former Party, on the understanding that his future methods of conducting politics would be above reproach, and would be controlled in a democratic fashion. He also managed to have the proscription of the Party's newspaper, the *Völkischer Beobachter** reversed. Equally quickly, he re-established himself as leader of the National Socialist Party. At a mass meeting in the Bürgerbräukeller in Munich on 27 February, he electrified his audience of 4,000 people with his speech, and had them acclaiming him in hypnotic delirium as they clambered over tables, embraced each other, and gave vent to thunderous applause. Adolf Hitler was once more in the saddle of what was now to become the Nazi Party. Step by step, from 1925 onwards, he was to found this authoritarian movement, a movement in which only one man would give the orders, and would be answerable to no one but himself. Slowly his following would expand to encompass the blindly trusting masses of the entire German people, but in 1925, Hitler and his Party, with its membership of barely 100,000, were looked upon by their opponents as a joke. Under Hindenburg the Germans were for the moment happy with their lot, particularly now that substantial foreign loans had arrived from the USA and Britain, now that the currency had stabilised, and now that a period of more settled economic conditions had begun, bringing increased industrial activity and fuller employment. It was, in fact, to take Hitler a little more than five years from 1925 to build his following to a size capable of making a significant challenge to the major political parties of all Germany, and, in the event, he was fortuitously helped by the international economic collapse which occurred at the outset of the thirties. For the time being, however, he

* *'The People's Observer'*.

39

retired to Berchtesgaden in the Obersalzberg to write the second volume of *Mein Kampf*, which was published in December 1926.

Whilst von Seeckt was thinking about future wars and secretly preparing a German army against such eventualities, and whilst Hitler was rebuilding his National Socialist Party, Britain was putting her efforts behind finding a formula for the future peace of Europe, as witness the Treaty of Locarno in 1925, which was followed by Germany's election to the Council of the League of Nations in March 1926. At this time there was one Briton who was deeply concerned about the prospect of another war, and who was so convinced that a second world war would truly reach the proportions of an Armageddon, that he sought every means to preserve the peace. Winston Churchill was ready to support force in order to defy tyranny or ward off ruin, but he believed that another war could be avoided by the enforcement of international law through international collective security. It was his incredible foresight that made him detest war more than many so-called pacifists, and which made him seek at all times *rapprochement* in Europe, particularly between France and Germany. In 1925 he made a prophecy which was the basis of his fears about the unprecedented horrors of a future war, writing:

> May there not be methods of using explosive energy incomparably more intense than anything heretofore discovered? Might not a bomb no bigger than an orange be found to possess a secret power to destroy a whole block of buildings – nay, to concentrate the force of a thousand tons of cordite and blast a township at a stroke? Could not explosives even of the existing type be guided automatically in flying machines by wireless or other rays, without a human pilot, in ceaseless procession upon a hostile city, arsenal, camp or dockyard?

Then, in 1928, he wrote:

> Mankind has never been in this position before. Without having improved appreciably in virtue or enjoying wiser guidance, it has got into its hands for the first time the tools by which it can unfailingly accomplish its own extermination. That is the point in human destinies to which all the glories and toils of men have at last led them. They would do well to pause and ponder upon their new responsibilities. Death stands at attention, obedient, expectant, ready to serve, ready to shear away the peoples en masse; ready, if called on, to pulverise, without hope of repair, what is left of civilisation. He awaits only the word of command. He awaits it from a frail, bewildered being, long his victim, now – for one occasion only – his Master.

In 1926 Britain was hit by a General Strike, which began on 4 May. It arose out of a dispute over pay and working hours between the mine owners and the miners, and as a result of support for the miners by the Trades Union Congress, all rail and other transport workers, the men working in the docks, power station employees, and those in many other industries came out on strike. Baldwin, the Prime Minister, had foreseen the possibility of a lightning strike and had quickly made plans to operate essential services with troops and volunteers. By the second day skeleton services of buses, trams and trains were being run reasonably satisfactorily by volunteers, while troops and more volunteers were unloading ships in the docks to maintain food supplies, and the executive staffs of the electricity and gas supply companies, also with the aid of volunteers, were keeping power supplies going effectively. In the same way, water supplies were maintained. Since the printing trades had joined the strike, there were no newspapers, but the Government issued its own official newspaper, which it called the *British Gazette*. In addition, the Government had the use of the BBC with which to make its views known. The rights and wrongs of the cause of the strike were beyond the understanding of most people, including a good few politicians of the day, but the then new idea of bringing the nation to a standstill by the action of those working in industries not involved in the dispute, infuriated the vast majority of ordinary people who had no union affiliations and wanted to get on with their jobs. Consequently, many volunteers came forward to run essential services, men and women and university students who were determined to preserve the established order of everyday life. The buses, trams, and trains were frequently attacked and stoned by the more militant strikers in an effort to intimidate the volunteers, but the volunteers proved to be tough. One bus with broken windows announced in large letters on the advertisement panels: 'The driver's a Guy's Hospital Doctor, the conductor's a Guy's Hospital Student, and if you attack this bus you'll be a Guy's Hospital Patient!' The bus unquestionably carried reinforcements.

The strike lasted for only nine days up to 12 May, primarily because of those who so successfully kept the essential services going. When it ceased, Stanley Baldwin carried out his promise: 'Call off the General Strike first and then I will negotiate.' As Lord Avon, formerly Anthony Eden, wrote of this time: 'In the aftermath of the General Strike, he [Stanley Baldwin] rejected vengeful acts. No British statesman in this century has done so much to kill class hatred. He was able to do this because he neither believed in class distinctions nor felt them.' But while Britain was disunited, Germany was secretly re-arming.

CHAPTER V

Hitler's Power Grows

One of the German Army officers who had initiated Hitler into political life in 1919 was Major Ernst Röhm who, with General von Epp, both of the Reichswehr Command Headquarters in Munich, had been mainly responsible for the training of a corps of political agents charged with the task of bringing to reason unruly elements amongst the troops who had become tainted with Marxism after the war. The aim was to reinculcate a patriotic attitude after the old style of Imperial Germany.

Röhm, nearly two years Hitler's senior, had been in the German Army since 1906, and in the First World War had distinguished himself as a courageous soldier, attaining his rank of major. From 1919 to 1923, during Hitler's early political days, he had helped the latter to win the support of the army in Bavaria. Initially Röhm had commanded a body of military men whose purpose was to maintain law and order in Bavaria in the chaotic conditions that had immediately followed the ending of hostilities. Then, in October, 1921, with the aid of Army funds, he had formed his own private strong-armed force, the *Sturmabteilung* ('storm troopers'), known as the SA. As Hitler progressed politically at the beginning of the twenties, Röhm became more and more his supporter, for he saw the National Socialist leader as an effective instrument against Communism and an upholder of German nationalism. Although, as a soldier, Röhm wished for no personal involvement in politics, he put himself and his SA at Hitler's disposal in order to support his meetings and protect them from the efforts of Communists and other left-wing factions, who attempted to break them up by force. Röhm met force with force. By 1923, the financing of the SA, apart from Army funds, was greatly eased by contributions from the growing number of Hitler's Party members, and by support from industrialists who were becoming increasingly discontented with the weakness of the Weimar Republic in international affairs, and disturbed by the advances of Communism in Germany. Then, after the November 1923 Munich Putsch, when Hitler, Röhm and others were imprisoned, the SA was banned, and remained inactive until late in 1924.

The famous meeting in the Bürgerbräukeller in Munich on 27 February 1925, which marked Hitler's active return to politics after his imprisonment and which was followed by a number of rowdy branch meetings, caused the Bavarian State Government to impose a public-speaking ban upon Hitler, a ban that was soon to be extended to other provinces, including Prussia, which was a growing centre of support for the Party in North Germany. Hitler was, however, left with the freedom to speak in public in Thuringia, Brunswick, and Mecklenburg-Schwerin, but it was not until 5 March 1927 that he was again permitted to mount the rostrum in Bavaria, and it was as late as 28 September of the following year before the ban upon him in Prussia was lifted. Almost coincident with the Bavarian ban, in April 1925, Röhm gave up his position with the SA and went to live in Bolivia for several years. His decision was influenced by a desire to maintain the independence of this paramilitary force in order to support any political party that opposed Communism and that sought to re-establish German military might. Indeed, he had wanted the SA to absorb, or even supplant, the regular army, and to become entirely independent of any one political party. Hitler, to the contrary, wished the SA to be subordinate to the National Socialist Party, and to act as the Party's own army to assist it to achieve ultimate power. Hitler's will prevailed, since by this time he had greater control of the SA and its funds. Röhm's successor was Hauptmann Pfeffer von Salomon, relatively a nonentity. Thus it was that the man who had done more than most for the early rise of Hitler, and who had been his constant and close friend, left the stage. He was to return, however, at Hitler's request, early in 1931.

With the ban on public speaking, the requirements for SA assistance were diminished. Moreover, Hitler's efforts to increase support for his Party were seriously handicapped by the ban, for there could be no doubt among those who had seen and heard him speak that he was an orator *par excellence*, capable of exerting an hypnotic effect upon his audience, enslaving minds in an uncanny fashion. His faith in and enthusiasm for what he said – and in those days much of it was appealing to any German who wished to raise his head above the shame of national defeat and to see the way to a new self-respect – transferred themselves, with a mighty impact, to those who listened.

But if Hitler was to be silenced for a while in public, he was free in the meantime to establish his position more firmly in his Party, and to strive for a closer unification with another nationalist group in North Germany with whom he had already secured an affiliation which recognised him as the overall leader. This group, originally that same German Socialist Party over which he had resigned from the NSDAP in 1921 and which had such strong support from the element headed by Julius Streicher and based on Nürnberg, was led by two brothers, Otto and Gregor Strasser. Just after his release from prison in 1924, Hitler had temporarily delegated the expansion of his National Socialist Party in North Germany to the Strasser brothers, and by the end of 1925 they had built up a surprisingly strong organisation with a substantial following. The Strasser's group, however, which only just recognised Hitler as its leader, was rapidly becoming independent under the name of the National Socialist Freedom Movement, and was basing its politics much too far to the left for Hitler's liking. It had developed a strong anti-capitalist and federalist programme, including a move to unite with left-wing Socialists over the dispossession of the Princes and the Imperial Royal Family, and a massive nationalisation of industry. This programme was totally at variance with Hitler's views, for he was resolutely against Marxist doctrines, and preferred to make use of the Reichswehr, the nobility, and the industrialists, as well as the middle- and working-classes, to achieve his ultimate goal – undisputed power that would enable him to re-create Germany as an unassailable nation and master race. The breakaway group, which had gained adherents largely on Hitler's reputation, must therefore be brought to heel.

The final clash over who ruled the rebellious party came as a result of a congress of North German Gauleiters (district leaders) in Hanover on 24 January 1926, to which Hitler was not invited and about which he was not advised. But one of his adherents, Feder, was present, and faithfully reported back to his master. Also at the meeting was Gregor Strasser's private secretary, a partly crippled Doctor of Philosophy who had gained his doctorate, in literature, at Heidelberg University in 1922. Born on 29 October 1897 at Rheydt, the son of a pious Catholic family, he was then only twenty-eight years of age; his name was Josef Goebbels. Apart from the Congress making common cause with left-wingers, and replacing Hitler's programme for the National Socialist Party with a heretical 'pink' one drawn up by Otto Strasser, this man Goebbels delivered an inflammatory oration demanding the expulsion from the Party of 'the petty bourgeois Adolf Hitler'!

Hitler took swift action. He ordered all the Party Gauleiters to attend a conference at Bamberg on 14 February, where he delivered a rousing speech which not only routed the mutineers, but swung the overwhelming majority behind him as undisputed leader. In the first volume of his *Mein Kampf*, sub-titled *Eine Abrechnung* ('A Reckoning'), published on 19 July 1925, he wrote: ' ... the greatest revolutions have never been directed by a goose-quill! ... But the power which has always started the great religious and political avalanches in history rolling has, from time immemorial, been the magic power of the spoken word, and that alone.' On this occasion he exercised his belief successfully, not for the first time; only Gregor Strasser rose to criticise. The eloquent Josef Goebbels, who the mutineers had expected to speak for them, remained silent. He had witnessed the solidarity of the Party's South German supporters and the way in which Hitler had swayed the North German delegates back behind him. Goebbels, as an ambitious young man, with no sincere convictions, leaped on to the Hitler bandwagon. He had recognised where the future power lay.

Hitler proceeded to consolidate his victory. Shrewdly, instead of revenging himself upon Goebbels for what he had said previously, he appointed him Gauleiter of Berlin in November. He had used the whip, and now he felt sure the little cripple would jump at the carrot; he had judged him to be an opportunist who would be loyal to any tide which swept him to greater authority. Moreover, the man understood the force of the word, both written and spoken. Hitler proved correct in his choice. In no time, Goebbels set about eliminating the influence of his former patrons and purging Berlin, by force when necessary, not only of left-wingers, but also of heretics in his own camp. Later, he founded *Der Angriff* ('The Attack'), the Party's weekly newspaper, and in 1928 he took charge of the Party propaganda machine.

In August 1927 the ban on Hitler's speaking in Bavaria was lifted, and he was once more able to hold the Party Congress in his own state. In the autumn of that year he selected Nürnberg as the most eminently suitable site, and marked the day by declaring the place the 'city of the Reich Party Days', where all future congresses and major rallies of the Nazi Party would be held. More than 50,000 SA marched from all parts of Germany to attend the rally, many to admire their Führer for the first time, and dressed — again for the first time — in the storm-troopers' uniform, from which they earned the nickname 'Brownshirts'. The rally was a staggering success, even though the Party and its leader were still very small fry in politics, judged by the size of its following compared to the size of the German population. Neither party nor leader would be small fry for long, however.

Hitler's was a complex personality. Although born an Austrian, he had come into the world only just beyond the German border, and he had grown up with a love of Germany and an increasing disillusionment with the decaying Hapsburg dynasty, a decline which he blamed on the conglomeration of races of which it was composed – Czechs, Slavs, Hungarians and Jews. He grew up under influences which ultimately convinced him that a nation could never be proud and great unless its entire people had but one loyalty – an undivided patriotism to the nation of their forefathers and their birth. He believed that nations of mixed ethnic races must inevitably be divided in their loyalties, and therefore must carry the seeds of decay. Above all, he distrusted the Jews and the Marxists, whom he regarded as being of the same origins. They were international by the very nature of their creeds, and neither owed, nor gave, any allegiance to the country of their adoption. In his opinion, they were prepared to destroy the patriotic nationalism of a country in order to gain world-wide domination by the imposition of their dogmas on an international scale. He accepted that religion went beyond nationalism, but he was convinced that the very ideals of the Christian Catholic and Protestant faiths encouraged a loyalty to the nation of the individual's birth and upbringing. These religions were not in fact racial. Indeed he did not attack the Jews for their religious faith, but for their race, to which he believed they were at all times patriotic at the expense of loyalty to the nation of their birth or adoption. After the First World War he had found a home in the country for which he had fought so gallantly and which he loved dearly and fanatically – Germany. To see his 'hero' defeated in war, degraded by what he considered to be the injustice of the Peace Treaty, and then cringing in front of the victors because its politicians had abandoned their national pride and courage, was too much for him. Possessed of high ideals, albeit tainted with his hatred of Jews, Hitler decided that he must devote his life to the re-establishment of the honour and greatness of his beloved country. He identified the greatest obstacles to that return to honour and greatness as the Jews and the Marxists, because their loyalty was not to the Germany of the Germans. His habit of relating Jewishness to Marxism sprang from the fact that Karl Marx, although born in Prussia and brought up as a Lutheran, was a Jew, both his father and mother having descended from a long line of rabbis. Hitler always referred to Marx as 'the Jew, Karl Marx', but in a peculiar way he admired the Socialist for his success in spreading his doctrine so swiftly and widely during the nineteenth century. In a similarly perverse manner he also admired the Jews for their uncompromising racialism, which kept their race intact and internationally interwoven, bound by strict religious laws against intermarriage with peoples of other ethnic races, and which provided them with a herd instinct so powerful that wherever they existed in the world their first loyalty was to the Jewish race. In the philosophy of Karl Marx Hitler saw an attempt by the Jews to impose an international control over states and their peoples by introducing an international political creed – Marxist-Communism.

In 1924 Hitler wrote, on the subject of Marx:

Actually Karl Marx was only the 'one' among millions who, with the sure eye of the prophet, recognised in the morass of a slowly decomposing world the most essential poisons, extracted them, and, like a wizard, prepared them into a concentrated solution for the swifter annihilation of the independent existence of free nations on this earth. All this in the service of his race. His Marxist doctrine is a brief spiritual extract of the philosophy of life that is generally current today. And for this reason alone any struggle of our so-called bourgeois world against it is impossible, absurd in fact, since this bourgeois world is also essentially infected by these poisons, and worships a view of life which in general is distinguished from the Marxists only by degrees and personalities. The bourgeois world is Marxist, but believes in the possibility of the rule of certain groups of men (bourgeoisie), while Marxism itself systematically plans to hand the world over to the Jews.

Adolf Hitler's mistake was to believe that the Communism of the Russian Bolsheviks would remain forever a tool of the Jews, even if, as seems unlikely, it had ever truly been one. Had he concentrated on the defeat of expansionist Russian Communism with the same objectivity as that with which he tried to destroy the Jewish race, he might have found more support in the world when he was rising to the peak of his power.

Referring to nationality, he bemoaned the fact that as a result of the Thirty Years' War, with its constant invasions of the German states, including Austria, Germany was no longer based on a unified racial nucleus. Those years of war had, he believed, led to a decomposition not only of the blood, but also of the soul. The great 'herd of Attila the Hun' had been infected by 'un-German foreign bodies' because of the 'open borders of our Fatherland'. Hitler looked lovingly back at the ancient Nordic history.

The German people [he wrote] lack that sure herd instinct which is based on unity of the blood and, especially in moments of threatening danger, preserves nations from destruction in so far as all petty inner differences in such people vanish at once on such occasions and the solid front of a unified herd confronts the common enemy ... If the German people in its historic development had possessed that herd unity which other peoples enjoyed, the German Reich today would doubtless be mistress of the globe. World history would have taken a different course, and no one can distinguish whether in this way we would not have obtained what so many blinded pacifists today hope to gain by begging, whining and whimpering: a peace, supported not by the palm branches of tearful, pacifist female mourners, but based on the victorious sword of a master people, putting the world into the service of a higher culture. The fact of the non-existence of a nationality of unified blood has brought us untold misery. It has given capital cities to many small German potentates, but deprived the German people of the master's right.

Hitler determined to set Germany on a course that would make her once more a unified nation, cleansed of foreign blood. In *Mein Kampf* he clearly set out his beliefs and his programme for the future of Germany, should he ever attain his cherished ambition of becoming undisputed leader of the country. Those aims were basically to make Germany a master race of absolute purity, purged of Jews and Marxists, free from the control of other nations, militarily all powerful, and capable of regaining all her lost provinces by force if necessary, and of increasing her territory in Europe for her own expansion. For European expansion, he regarded Russia, in particular the Baltic states, as most suited to his plans for territorial gain. He indicated that there were only two possible allies for Germany in the future, England, which had in the past been a traditional ally and whom he admired above all other nations, and Italy. Within his programme he hinted at an ultimate domination of Continental Europe, including Russia, and a position of unassailable power in the world. The struggle and gradual emergence of Adolf Hitler still passed unnoticed in the rest of Europe, however, and few politicians inside or outside that continent bothered to read *Mein Kampf*. That book was initially only possessed and devoured by Hitler's followers, and then, in Germany, by those who began to see in him and his Party a bulwark against Communism. But in 1929 a corner of the veil of obscurity was lifted.

Since 1927 the US Commissioner for the Peace Treaty, an American banker by the name of Young, had administered and controlled the German budgets and collected the heavy payments demanded by the Allies as reparations. Because he thought the demands were far too onerous and could not therefore continue to be paid for much longer, Young framed, proposed, and negotiated, with the aid of a 'committee of experts', a scheme of mitigation which put a final limit to the period of reparation payments. The plan recommended a further fifty-nine annual payments on a sliding scale, each to be an average five hundred million marks lower than the previous payment. In addition, his scheme, which came to be known as the 'Young Plan' and which was finally proposed on 7 June 1929, included the freeing of the Reichsbank and the German railways from Allied control, and the replacement of the Reparations

Commission by a 'Bank for International Settlements'. Two months later, Gustav Stresemann, the German Chancellor and Foreign Minister, succeeded in persuading Aristide Briand, the French Foreign Minister, to concede the complete evacuation of the Rhineland by the Allied Armies by the end of June 1930, a date long before that which the Peace Treaty demanded – the British and Americans had already indicated their agreement to the evacuation, and the only stumbling-block had been the French. These concessions did not completely fulfil German wishes, but they were a good step forward. However, industrial and commercial interests in Germany, in conjunction with the right-wing parties, launched a savage campaign against the acceptance of the proposals, hailing the plan as 'Young's Slavery' – fifty-nine years of slavery. The fact that the Government of the Weimar Republic had approved the Young Plan in the Reichstag by only 224 votes to 206 lent encouragement to those who wished for far greater concessions towards freedom from Allied interference to increase their attack upon the hated Weimar system. This they did by pressing for the early liquidation of the war debt and the right to build up the country's military defences to a strength which was right and proper for a nation of Germany's size. The loudest and most vigorous voice in this campaign against the Government and its acceptance of the Young Plan, was that of Alfred Hugenberg, a powerful industrial and commercial magnate who also controlled a vast network of newspapers and news agencies, as well as the Ufa film combine. And it was Hugenberg, controlling as he did the media, if not the votes, of the electorate, who in 1929 decided to back Hitler and his National Socialist Party. Hugenberg recognised that if his support could bring wide recognition and political power to this man who seemed to put Germany's future greatness in the forefront of all his ambitions, then the weak-kneed Weimar Republic, along with the Communists and other left-wing organisations, could be routed for all time.

This alliance between the magnate and the rising politician made Hitler a well-known, even acceptable figure. The entire Hugenberg-controlled media, films and all, poured out *ad nauseam* Hitler's commentaries on the Young Plan and the real need to restore Germany once more to her position as a powerful nation. Hitler's opinions were relentlessly drummed into millions of German brains. His face-to-face talks with the people, enabling him to exert his hypnotic oratory, backed by impassioned physical presentation, on all and sundry, were made possible by the Ufa-produced news films. Hitler was now in the political arena arm-in-arm with one of Germany's most renowned industrialists. A corner of the veil of obscurity had indeed been lifted.

On 23 January 1930, in the Landtag elections, Hitler's Party gained its first major victory when its candidate, Wilhelm Frick, became the first Nazi Minister of State, for Thuringia. In March the Young Plan was rescinded by the Reichstag. On 14 September the Germans cast their votes for elections to the Reichstag, and in the early hours of the 15th the world learnt that in a massive poll there had been a landslide in favour of the Party led by an unknown man called Hitler. Out of the blue he had won 107 seats in the new parliament. At last Hitler had arrived. He did not have a majority in the Reichstag, but it was a substantial body of members under his single control.

Heinrich Brüning, who had succeeded Stresemann as Chancellor on 28 March 1930, held the majority in the Reichstag with his Catholic Centre Party, and it was Brüning who foresaw the danger to Germany of the growing following of Hitler's National Socialist Party. He recognised the nation's natural desire to turn to a man who was vociferously demanding action which would throw off the shackles the victorious Allies had placed upon Germany, and who boldly stated his determination to rebuild Germany's military strength. Brüning himself agreed with these patriotic sentiments, and he was equally a foe of the Marxists and Communists. But he regarded Hitler and his Party as an opportunist rabble that, in the end, would bring disaster to the nation. Brüning had a solution which he believed would preserve the peace and safety of Germany and re-establish her former glory – the restoration of the monarchy, but this time a constitutional monarchy based upon English lines. Such a step, if taken, would fill the void at the summit of the German nation towards which Hitler was now inexorably advancing, and would draw back the middle-class and industrial elements which were fast drifting to the ranks of Hitler. What was needed was the reinstatement of Kaiser Wilhelm, but Brüning knew that neither the Social Democrats nor the trade unions would tolerate the return of the old Kaiser, or even of his son, the Crown Prince. The alternative was to appoint one of the sons of the Crown Prince as the new Kaiser, with von Hindenburg acting as Regent during his last term of office, albeit on the assumption that he would again be elected President in the forthcoming Presidential election due in 1932. But the aged and senile field-marshal regarded the suggestion as an insult to his military honour. He was the trustee for the Kaiser, and legitimacy must not be violated by picking and choosing amongst the royal princes. If the monarchy was to be restored, then the Kaiser must return to the throne and, in due course, be followed by the Crown Prince. In the face of such opposition the monarchical solution had to be abandoned, thus leaving the way wide open for Hitler, who was already being helped forward by the world economic collapse, which had originated in America in October 1929 with the onset of the 'Great Depression'. In February 1930 total unemployment in Germany was three and a half millions; a little later it had risen to five millions; and in 1931 it reached over six millions. The unpopular Weimar Republic was castigated for what was, in fact, a world-wide catastrophe, and Hitler and his National Socialists, now backed by the German industrial and commercial powers, used the situation to capture the support of the massive army of unemployed of all classes.

In the same year – 1929 – that Hitler was becoming, with Alfred Hugenberg's help, 'respectable', and thus at last reaching out towards political power in Germany, the second Baldwin administration came to an end. Since the end of 1924, the Conservative Government had achieved what appeared to be some significant success in its foreign policy and had contributed notably to a return to prosperity in Britain itself. Indeed, at the end of the twenties Europe was tranquil, a state which had been unknown since before the Napoleonic Wars. Once again, the traditional British friendship with Germany was renewed, born of past alliances in the eighteenth and nineteenth centuries, and of the succession to the British throne by George I of Hanover in 1714, which had established the line of British royalty from the Hanoverian house. The Treaty of Locarno had been negotiated, the evacuation of the Rhineland by the French Army and other Allied contingents had been completed, the new Germany, now a republic*, had joined the League of Nations, and the alliances in Europe which France had negotiated at the time of the Locarno Conference seemed secure. The war was rapidly fading into mists of forgetfulness, and under the benevolent influence of vast American and British loans, Germany's industry was recovering rapidly, while her international trade was advancing at a pace that was increasing internal prosperity faster than anyone had believed possible. The disarmament clauses of the Treaty of Versailles were apparently being observed; the German Navy was non-existent, the German Air Force had been disbanded and its rebirth prohibited, and the German Army was so strictly limited that it could only be regarded as a kind of armed police force. At home, Britain's industrial transformation from war to peace production had been achieved with reasonable success, bringing with it substantial reductions in unemployment, greatly increased international trading, and consequent prosperity. In fact, by the time of the 1929 General Election, the Conservatives could claim to have given the country five years of competent administration. Their only fault was to have been blind to the secret forces in Germany that were successfully laying the foundations of that country's future armed might.

---

* The constitution of the German Federal ('Weimar') Republic dated from 1919, and was to survive until 1933.

The General Election, which took place on Thursday, 30 May 1929, was greeted by an over-confident Conservative Party convinced of its own return to power for a second term of office. The electorate had other ideas, however, and the normal desire for change, not always born of wisdom, produced a quite dramatic swing of the pendulum. The result was 288 seats for Labour, 260 for Conservatives, 59 for the Liberals, and 8 'others'. Effectively, this meant that whichever of the two major parties took office, the Liberals would hold the balance of power, and with the Liberal Party still under the leadership of Lloyd George it was expected that they would be hostile to the Conservatives. In these circumstances Baldwin, supported by Churchill, his Chancellor of the Exchequer, declined to form a Government, and so, on 7 June, Ramsay MacDonald became Prime Minister and, for the second time, led a majority Labour Government which was dependent for survival in the House of Commons upon the Liberal vote. There was, however, one new Conservative member elected to the House, representing North Paddington, whose adoption by the Conservative Party for this constituency had received Churchill's support. His name was Brendan Bracken.

The new Labour Government was quick to react in the areas of the Empire and of foreign policy. At the outset it proposed far-reaching constitutional changes in India, the intention being to press forward with plans to give India self-government. At the same time, it made major concessions to Egypt and other of Britain's overseas territories as evidence of its intention to liquidate the Empire. In line with these idealistic policies, the Labour Government made a renewed effort to achieve world disarmament, but so pacifist and short-sighted was its outlook that it became hell-bent on disarming Britain alone, supposedly to show a lead to the rest of the major powers; MacDonald's government seemed ready to strip the country of its ability to defend itself against aggression in the erroneous belief that other nations would instantly follow suit. In these aims it was fully supported by the Liberals and, therefore, could be confident of commanding a Parliamentary majority. Strangely, however, Baldwin, given his not insignificant Conservative Opposition, declined to confront the Government on these issues, his view being that Britain was no longer in a position to assert British Imperial greatness and, in the case of disarmament, that pressure for retaining too much in the way of defence spending would incur the displeasure of the electorate and rebound against the Conservatives at a future General Election. Churchill was resolutely opposed to this attitude, believing that the Conservative Opposition 'should strongly confront the Labour Government on all great Imperial and national issues and should identify itself with the majesty of Britain as under Lord Beaconsfield [Disraeli] and Lord

Salisbury, and should not hesitate to face controversy, even though that might not immediately evoke a response from the nation.' But Churchill found little or no support from the rest of his party, except from the new member for North Paddington, Brendan Bracken, a staunch Imperialist.

It was this divergence of views upon Indian policy and Imperial issues as a whole which caused the breakdown of the close relationship that had existed between Baldwin and Churchill, and which led to Churchill being out of favour and out of office in the thirties when, from the end of 1931 to the beginning of the Second World War in 1939, the Conservatives held power. But during his years in the political wilderness he had one constant supporter in the House of Commons who spoke for his views on every possible occasion – Brendan Bracken, whom Baldwin called 'the faithful Chela of Winston Churchill'.

The Labour Party's term of office was to be brief. Up until the autumn of 1929 the prosperity of the Western world seemed to be on the increase, particularly in the United States of America. But in October of that year came the crash on Wall Street. A sudden loss of confidence in the economy, fired by runaway inflation, caused an unprecedented wave of selling of stocks and shares, which in turn brought on an unheard-of collapse in trading and production. The easy credit facilities and loans which had encouraged people to buy most things on the instalment system, from houses to every conceivable gadget of modern living, even stocks and shares, suddenly dried up. Twenty thousand local banks suspended payments. Those who had spent their earnings before they had earned them were left destitute in the wave of unemployment that followed the dislocation of economic life in the country, caused in turn by the contraction of trade and production. The savings of rich and poor alike were wiped out. Unemployment rose at an alarming pace. The 'Great Depression' had begun, spread rapidly to the rest of the world and, with America's imposition of tariffs to protect its own collapsing industries, quickly began to bite deeply into the economies of the countries of the rest of the world. In Britain, the years of 1930 and 1931 saw a rise in unemployment to more than two million seven hundred thousand; in the USA it reached nearly ten millions; in Germany, as has been said, it rose to over six millions.

Ramsay MacDonald's Labour Party proved to be utterly unable to cope with the problems that confronted it. Founded upon attacking capitalism and riddled with strong left-wing doctrines, the Labour Government found it difficult to preserve the confidence and credit so essential to the highly artificial economy of Britain, which was dependent upon importing raw materials and manufacturing and exporting finished goods profitably even in normal times of international prosperity, let alone in a period of deep world recession. It quickly became evident that the Government, unable to command party discipline or to reject ingrained doctrinaire socialist policies, incapable of exercising the vigour necessary to balance the budget, and deprived of all financial confidence, could no longer govern. The collapse of the country's financial credit internationally led to the formation, in the late summer of 1931, of a government of all parties, which Stanley Baldwin supported, expressing his willingness to serve under Ramsay MacDonald. The Liberals, under Sir John Simon, also rallied to this coalition. There quickly followed a General Election, on 27 October, from which a substantial Conservative majority emerged. The voting produced 473 seats in the House for the Conservatives, 13 for National Labour, 35 for National Liberals, 33 for Liberals, 4 for Independent Labour, 52 for Labour, and 5 others. Despite the overwhelming Conservative majority, Stanley Baldwin believed that only a government of all parties could undertake an administration with success in the extreme crisis prevailing, and it was on this principle that he had appealed to the country at the election. MacDonald and his Chancellor of the Exchequer, Philip Snowden, attempted, with patriotic zeal, to carry the majority of the Labour Party into this combination, but, with the party split by an uncompromising left wing, they failed to take more than the National Labour members with them. The Liberal Party, which had fared none too well in the election, was again led by Sir John Simon into an all-party coalition. Stanley Baldwin magnanimously agreed to continue to serve under MacDonald in a continuation of the former National Government. His generous attitude was, however, probably stimulated by his knowledge that, in fact, he now held the power in the House.

The new National Government appeared to many to be an immensely strong administration because it had brought together the best in all parties to rule the country at a time of economic crisis. It proved, however, to be the weakest on record in respect of foreign and imperial policy, and, as a corollary, of defence and the security of the nation.

CHAPTER VI

The Folly of Disarmament

The 'Great Depression' struck Germany as forcibly as any other European country. There, however, with the after-effects of the war only partially overcome despite foreign aid, in particular from the USA, the world-wide economic catastrophe was even more pronounced. The German economy had, in a way, been duped into assuming an air of prosperity due to the short-term loans from abroad, and it was therefore even more vulnerable than the rest of Europe to the collapse of international trade. To sharpen its problems, foreign capital dried up, loans were recalled, export trade collapsed, factories closed, service industries were bankrupted, and many banks failed – the failure of the Danat Bank in the summer of 1931, and the closing of the stock exchanges, emphasised the scale of the disaster. The level of wages dropped swiftly and drastically where it was possible to maintain employment, and unemployment in 1931 rose to over six millions – six million people on the streets who, with their families, were both declassed and destitute. These millions came from all income groups and all professions and skills, and their very existence was in peril. Whilst all were disenchanted and discontented with what they believed to be the failure of the Weimar Republic to govern them effectively, and so to provide them with national security, it was the youth of the country that was most bitter. The young were growing up in an age of wretchedness with little prospect of employment, and with a feeling that the old politicians, of whatever political colour or creed, had let them down. So where to look for leadership?

It was Adolf Hitler who was ready to point a finger at a scapegoat –

55

the Weimar Republic – and to offer himself as the man who could lead Germany out of the dilemma. He told the nation that the Germans were of a race of such purity that it was superior to all others and deserved a place among, and equal to, the great world powers – even above these powers. The tactics he offered by which to achieve the greatness that was Germany's due were shrewdly calculated to encourage the dispirited masses to follow him. He demanded land reform and 'dispossession without compensation' to the 'Jewish land speculation societies'. He accused the Jews and their Communist allies of exploiting all classes, and of attempting to turn Germany into a slave state of Bolshevik Russia; the Germans, he said, in their totally dejected circumstances, were ready to believe anything. He hinted at the elimination of Communism as a political force in Germany, and at the removal of the Jews from the country. He offered an agrarian programme that fulfilled all the wishes of the farming community. His plans for industrial revival he made dependent upon support for the industrialists. 'Do you think,' he said to the Marxists and Socialists, 'I am so crazy as to want to destroy German heavy industry? The entrepreneurs have worked their way to the top by their efficiency. And on the basis of their superiority, which only the higher race evinces, they have a right to lead.'

Hitler's proposed policies for making Germany a leading nation once more rapidly became popular. They included the use of the industrial giants, the intent to re-arm and re-create Germany's Navy and Air Force, plans to rebuild German cities and communications, and his often stated resolve to extend the borders of Germany to embrace those territories, such as Austria and parts of Poland and Czechoslovakia, which were populated by people he regarded as belonging to Germany. Here, thought the masses, was a man who could make Germany, like the Phoenix, rise from the ashes. Here, thought the industrialists, was a man who was resolutely against Communism and who would firmly dispose of any left-wing efforts to impose a Marxist state like that which existed in Russia. Hitler was still far from being a leading political figure, however, even with Alfred Hugenberg's support, but he was beginning to make his impact in a hitherto untouched area. In 1929, he had begun to woo the military – the officer corps and the generals of the Reichswehr, who already held the Weimar Republic in ill-concealed contempt. By 1931, he was making considerable headway.

The most powerful personality in the Ministry of Defence was General Kurt von Schleicher, who had inherited the sound foundations of a new army, navy and air force from General Hans von Seeckt. Von Schleicher was one of those military men who had political ambitions, and was convinced that an officer from the High Command could be a great and welcome leader for the German people, if not as President initially, then at least as Chancellor prior to succeeding Hindenburg as President. In Hitler he saw a rallying point for popular support, a banner to which all sections of the population would flock – military of all ranks and civilian of all classes. If he played his cards correctly, and pulled strings cunningly, he could ride to power on Hitler's back. But, like so many others, he underestimated Hitler's unscrupulous character and political skill, and failed to recognise his ruthless determination to rule the nation as a despot.

It was von Schleicher who persuaded von Hindenburg to give Hitler an audience, which took place on 10 October 1931, just seventeen days before Britain's General Election which returned a National Government under the pacifist Ramsay MacDonald, supported by an overwhelming Conservative majority under Stanley Baldwin. Von Hindenburg was unimpressed by Hitler, and is reputed to have remarked after the interview that at most he might become the Postmaster-General one day and 'lick stamps with my head on them'. Nevertheless, the meeting was a success for Hitler, since the very fact that it had taken place indicated to the population that he was now a man who had to be recognised at the highest level in the land.

Now Hitler's advance to ultimate power was swift. Earlier in 1931 he had persuaded Ernst Röhm to return from Bolivia to take over the command of the SA, as Chief of Staff, from Hauptmann Pfeffer von Salomon. At the end of that year Hitler was persuaded by his followers to contest the forthcoming Presidential Election, and on 22 February 1932 he agreed to have his candidature announced by Goebbels at a Nazi rally in the Berlin Sportpalast, an announcement that was greeted with tumultuous applause and fanatical enthusiasm. The problem of his statelessness, arising from his release in 1925 from Austrian citizenship at his own request, was quickly resolved; the Nazis now held control in the State Government of Brunswick, and Hitler's naturalisation was obtained without opposition on the grounds that he was required to fill the post of Regierungsrat,* representing Brunswick in Berlin. The election was held in March 1932, and in the first poll Hitler managed to win just short of 11,500,000 votes. Von Hindenburg finished ahead of his rivals, Hitler, the Communist Thaelmann, and the German Nationalist Duesterberg, but he was 0.4 per cent short of the votes required to give him an overall majority. On the second ballot, Duesterberg having withdrawn from the election, von Hindenburg succeeded in holding the Presidency for another term of office, but Hitler increased his vote by another 2 million, giving him over 37 per cent of the poll.

In the following month, on 24 April, the Landtag elections produced

---

* An administrative adviser, not unlike a kind of Privy Councillor.

more gains for Hitler, making the Nazis the strongest party in Prussia and giving them an overwhelming majority in Oldenburg. Then, in May 1932, von Schleicher, whose influence with Hindenburg had been growing, successfully contrived to bring about the fall of Chancellor Brüning, and to have him replaced by Franz von Papen, who he believed would be his willing tool. With his eye on the Presidency, von Schleicher also made a bargain with Hitler and his Party. In April, Brüning had placed a ban on the SA and a relatively new Party formation, the SS (*Schutzstaffeln*, literally, 'protection detachments', but also known as 'Black Shirts', from the uniform), which had been formed under Heinrich Himmler, another of Hitler's adherents. Von Schleicher offered, in return for Hitler's support of von Papen, to arrange for the removal of this ban; he also promised fresh elections to the Reichstag. With the SA back on the streets, supported by the Army through von Schleicher's influence and his co-operation with Röhm, the 'bully-boy' tactics began again, and months of bloody fighting ensued as the Nazis sought to scare off would-be Communist voters, and to intimidate others into voting for the Party. The new Reichstag was elected with Hitler gaining 13,800,000 votes, nearly 40 per cent of the electorate. In the new Reichstag the National Socialists – or Nazis – held, with the Communists, an absolute majority, but a coalition of the Nazis with the Centre Party, now led by von Papen, could give Hitler the chance of controlling the Reichstag. He therefore made a bid for the Chancellorship in August 1932, but was unsuccessful because both von Papen and von Schleicher persuaded Hindenburg to reject the Nazi leader's demand.

In a further election on 6 November – 1932 came to be known as the 'year of elections' – Hitler lost 2 million votes and thirty-four seats. The moderates in Germany heaved a sigh of relief; National Socialism was on the wane. Ironically, however, the most striking gains in this election were made by the Communists who, with eleven further seats, increased their representation in the Reichstag to one hundred, only ninety-six seats fewer than the Nazis. Within the nation, the Army and the moderates were shocked. Believing that the Nazis were a more acceptable alternative to a growing Communist Party, and believing, quite mistakenly, that it was possible to negotiate with the Nazis and therefore bring them to heel, von Schleicher brought about the fall of von Papen and, with the backing of the Reichswehr and of von Hindenburg, seized the Chancellorship for himself. His bid failed, however, for he underestimated Hitler's ruthless determination to gain ultimate power. The Centre Party combined with Hitler's Nazis to oppose von Schleicher. With the aid of the President's son, Oskar von Hindenburg, and the prominent Cologne banker, von Schroeder, Hitler and von

Papen, the latter thirsting for revenge, were brought harmoniously together, and together intrigued to oust von Schleicher. Finally Hitler, suddenly and cunningly adopting the tactic of supporting the idea of a return of the monarchy, a move which he had absolutely no intentions of implementing if he won ultimate power, at last endeared himself to the aged and decrepit President.

On Monday, 30 January 1933, Adolf Hitler was sworn in as Chancellor of Germany by Field-Marshal Paul von Hindenburg.

That night, Goebbels wrote in his diary: 'The whole German Nation is on the march.' At his Reich Chancellery window, as he watched an endless torchlight procession wend its way through the Brandenburg Gate and up to the Wilhelmstrasse in celebration of his victory, Hitler swore: 'No power on earth shall ever bring me out of here alive.' A truly prophetic vow.

In February 1932, just two weeks before Goebbels announced that Hitler was entering the contest for the Presidency (a bid which, though unsuccessful, was the first significant move in his meteoric rise to the Chancellorship), the Disarmament Conference assembled under the aegis of the League of Nations at Geneva. Disarmament had long been a policy close to the heart of Ramsay MacDonald and the many pacifist supporters of the Labour and Liberal Parties. It was certainly their desire to encourage all the nations of the world to bury their arms for good, and it was the Labour Party's avowed intent to strip Britain naked, if necessary, to give a lead to the rest of the world. The Conference, to which sixty nations sent delegations, was probably doomed to failure from the very start. Although an international preparatory commission had worked for years to formulate a work schedule for the Conference, the fundamental weakness of any disarmament plan to be discussed was the reluctance of every nation, except Britain, to propose specific limitations on their own armed forces. All, however, were prepared to suggest drastic limitations for Germany. The result was an open conflict between the Germans and the other delegates, in particular the French. Germany firmly demanded equality of armaments; the war had ended fourteen years ago and impositions against parity in arms were unacceptable when the nations around her could maintain greater forces and thereby threaten her security. In fact, Germany had already exceeded the armament limits imposed upon her by the Versailles Peace Treaty, a situation about which the French were well aware, and to which they had drawn the attention of Sir John Simon, the British Foreign Secretary. Indeed, the leadership of the German Reichswehr had in every respect laid the foundations for the revival of the armed forces, including the Navy and the forbidden Air Force. In the case of the Air Force the Germans had even put in hand the development and production of advanced types of bombers, fighters, and reconnaissance aircraft, using the leading firms of the aircraft industry – Dornier, Heinkel, Rohrbach, and Junkers, including the Junkers branch factory in Sweden. The Army was fast mechanising, developing the principles of armoured mobile warfare, and producing the tanks for future Panzer divisions.

France's disenchantment with disarmament, given her fear of yet another war, was understandable. But Britain blundered blindly onward with her ideological dreams, in spite of the disturbing changes that were taking place in Germany. There were also, of course, economic reasons behind Britain's desire to pursue the ideological path. The Government felt impelled to enforce severe reductions in British armaments because of the financial crisis from which the country was barely beginning to recover. MacDonald and his Conservative and Liberal colleagues therefore pressed ardently for international disarmament equal to that which had been forced upon Germany by the Treaty of Versailles, or at least to a level approximating to those limitations. Tragically, Britain turned a blind eye to what was happening in Germany, despite the warnings of the French; at this stage only Churchill and Brendan Bracken began to cast doubts upon the wisdom of disarmament on a massive scale. The general public itself seemed disinclined to worry about Germany, and consequently there was no outcry of public opinion against the process of reducing Britain's armaments below a safe level. Remarkably, even when, in July 1932, the German delegation to Geneva categorically demanded the right to re-arm – the Chancellor, then still von Papen, had stated: 'The conditions of affairs in which we are definitely forbidden the use of arms, which other states are allowed to possess as indispensable weapons of defence, cannot continue' – Germany found considerable support for its military aspirations in the British press. *The Times* spoke of 'the unqualified recognition of the principle of the equality of States'. So here was Britain, on the one hand condoning the principle of Germany being allowed to re-arm, whilst on the other hand deliberately disarming herself, in the face of the clearly stated intentions of this man called Hitler, who was now well within reach of a position of absolute power in Germany.

In the absence of an agreement to recognise its claim for equality of armaments, the German delegation walked out of the Conference in July. It was not until December of 1932 that Germany agreed to rejoin the Conference after Edouard Herriot, the French Prime Minister, supported by the British, agreed to offer Germany: 'Equality of rights in a system which would provide security for all nations.' It was a meaningless proposal. In November, the British delegation to Geneva was falling over backwards in attempts to break the deadlock, and was ready to sacrifice the Royal Air Force as a hostage to fortune. Marshal of the RAF Sir John Salmond, who had succeeded Trenchard as Chief of the Air Staff, was bitterly opposed to further cuts in the strength of the Royal Air Force, and to any prohibition of bombers and other aircraft capable of bombing. He knew that the stern test of war would break down conventions, and he saw disarmament as a game for fools – while Britain disarmed, other countries would not necessarily keep their promises, and might well use the situation to arm secretly and gain a dominant position of international power. He was backed up energetically in his views by his brother, Air Chief Marshal Sir Geoffrey Salmond, who was to succeed him as Chief of the Air Staff in April 1933.* In fact, it was Sir Geoffrey who attended the Disarmament Conference as an observer for air matters when, late in November 1932, the British delegation was graced by the presence of Ramsay MacDonald, Sir John Simon, and Anthony Eden, the latter having been in Geneva as a substitute delegate since 2 November. At a breakfast meeting with the three politicians, Salmond had his worst fears confirmed. MacDonald and Simon were definitely prepared to sacrifice all bombers and aircraft capable of bombing in order to show the way to disarmament, thus leaving Britain with a so-called Metropolitan Air Force consisting only of fighters of strictly limited range. This was totally at variance with the advice given by the Air Staff, and Sir Geoffrey Salmond was furious. He told MacDonald: 'The fighters in your proposed Metropolitan Air Force could not even fly as far as Paris and back. We will be restricted to a close defence of Britain, and the aircraft will be so handicapped that retaliation will be impossible.' British morale would be hard hit, he added. In the event, the plan to emasculate the air forces of the Allies, which meant the British, French and Italian air forces, was finally defeated by the French, who voted against it.

Sir Geoffrey Salmond, however, incensed by the lack of concern for Britain's security and, like his brother Sir John, convinced that Germany was already rebuilding her air force, felt impelled to criticise those who were ready to abandon the air arm as a gesture to encourage others to disarm. On 26 November 1932, at the annual reunion of the Comrades of the Royal Air Forces' Association held in Harrods's Georgian Restaurant, he gave vent to his feelings. After outlining the highly successful activities of the Royal Air Force in the Empire, and in policing the territories mandated to Britain by the League of Nations, all at a considerable saving to the taxpayer when compared to the previous military methods of policing, Salmond turned to the subjects of the home-based air force

* Sir Geoffrey Salmond only held the post of Chief of the Air Staff for a few weeks. He died unexpectedly on 27 April 1933.

and of disarmament. 'Whenever disarmament is spoken of,' he said, 'one heard the Air Forces of the world very clearly mentioned. It is a tribute to Air Power that people should be so fearful of the might of this tremendous force – a somewhat different state of affairs from the days before the war of 1914-1918, when a high military authority referred to aeroplanes as very pretty toys.' He asked whence came the present eagerness for the abolition of air forces, adding that to his mind it came from 'the misconception on the part of many people that you can make war humane.' That was impossible, he said. 'War is a business of legalised killing. Air Forces are the greatest deterrent against war. Statesmen and others who contemplate war in the future,' he continued, 'know very well that thereby they would lay open their country to terrible attacks by an enemy who would take no notice of frontiers and would disregard the old boundaries observed by the armies and navies in the past, and would transfer the attack to the home front.' If such a possibility existed, he questioned whether politicians or demagogues would be so likely to assume the responsibility of starting a war. He added as a corollary that the danger to civilisation arose from prolonging wars; anything that would shorten them if they were forced upon a nation should be retained – and air forces were the most potent weapon to do just that. Salmond finished by stating that he did not believe the outcome of the Geneva Conference would, as the sentimentalists believed, abolish air forces as a nation's legitimate form of military defence and retaliatory offence.

Sir Geoffrey's speech caused an uproar when it was debated in the House of Commons on 6 December. Much of the fury came from Labour and Liberal members who were blindly pacifist, and who considered that all military men should be muzzled and forbidden to warn the country of dangers to its security which, given their professional experience and skill, they genuinely believed to exist. Salmond was well defended in the House, however, by Sir Philip Sassoon, the Under-Secretary of State for Air, who drew attention to the fact that Stanley Baldwin, the leader of the Conservatives, had recently made the cautionary statement in the House that 'any form of disarmament which would leave Great Britain relatively weak in the air in proportion to other nations, as we are at present, does not commend itself to the Government.' Since Baldwin, with an overwhelming Conservative majority in the National Government and the House, could sway events, the disarmers inside and outside the Government were held at bay. Then, with Hitler's advent to power on the 30 January 1933, Britain finally began to question the desirability of leading the way to disarmament.

After the burning down of the Reichstag in Berlin on 27 February, for which the Communists were blamed, less than a month after he had been proclaimed Chancellor of Germany, Hitler persuaded von Hindenburg to sign an emergency decree 'For the Protection of People and State'. Armed with the almost dictatorial powers provided by this decree during the so-called emergency, Hitler proceeded to strengthen his position. Prior to the new elections to the Reichstag, set for 5 March, Göring, now Minister of the Interior, clamped down on the Communists, arresting some 4,000 leading members and detaining many others in improvised concentration camps; in addition the Marxist press was banned. For the Nazis, Goebbels manipulated the propaganda media of the State to good purpose. The results, however, were not exactly proportional to the violence of the campaign, Hitler obtaining 288 seats in the Reichstag for the Nazis, with 52 going to his allies, giving him a bare majority in a parliament of 647 seats. He was not deterred. After the first sitting of the new Reichstag in the Garrison Church in Potsdam, conducted with great pomp and ceremony in the presence of the aged President von Hindenburg and everybody of rank, including the Diplomatic Corps, Hitler staged a further meeting in the Kroll Opera House that same afternoon. There he pushed through a Bill, called the Enabling Bill, which gave him a free and despotic hand for the next four years to enact laws – including laws which could alter the Constitution – without consulting the Reichstag. By process of arrests, coupled with intimidation of non-Nazi members of the Reichstag by the presence of SA and SS troops threateningly filling the corridors of the Opera House, he won a vote of 444 out of 538 Deputies present, giving him the powers of a dictator. Some years earlier, Hitler had written in *Mein Kampf*:

> From the smallest community cell to the highest leadership of the entire Reich, the State must have the personality principle anchored in its organisation. There must be no majority decisions, but only responsible persons, and the word 'council' must be restored to its original meaning. Surely every man will have advisers by his side, but the decisions will be made by one man.

Adolf Hitler was now that man.

In April of 1933, Nazi nominees were appointed as *Reichsstatthaltern* (Reich governors) in every state. Then, on May Day, that traditional workers' holiday was renamed 'The Day of National Labour', and the trade unions were liquidated, their funds sequestered, and their members absorbed into a newly founded 'Labour Front'. The former trade union leaders were arrested and placed in concentration camps, since they were by now all regarded as Marxists and Jews. At the same time, Hitler restored what he called the 'Professional Civil Service' by sacking all Jews and Marxists holding civil service posts, including the judiciary, and banned Jews and Marxists from practising in other professions such as the law and medicine. In June and July, he brought about the dissolution of the other political parties in the Reich, the Centre Party finally disbanding on 5 July. Nine days later, a Government law, put into force by Hitler's 'Enabling Bill', ruled that the Nazi Party was to be 'the only political party' and that the formation of new parties was henceforth a punishable offence. Without delay, the posts in government were systematically passed over to Hitler's faithful supporters; democracy in Germany, now so threatened, was soon to vanish completely. Ironically, Hitler had cleverly emulated the tactics of the Marxists in the earliest stages of his march to power, and from them he had learned the art of breaking up meetings by bully-boy tactics. The Marxist principle was to prevent any political party conveying views to the public other than those of the Marxist-Communist philosophy, and to achieve this end they had consistently employed hundreds of thugs, using the greatest brutality, against all those attending such meetings, as well as against the organisers. Hitler built up an army of tough men to counter these tactics, Ernst Röhm's SA. Initially, the SA was used to defend the early National Socialist meetings against the Marxists, but it became so immensely effective that it was later used as an instrument to intimidate the masses into joining the Nazi Party. Indeed, out of Marxist tactics designed to impose a Marxist state upon Germany, grew the Nazi counterblast which gave the country a ruthless Nazi dictatorship instead of a Communist oligarchy. The moderates in the middle were squeezed out of existence, and from Marxism sprang Nazism.

During this year of 1933, Hitler did not neglect the question of the armed forces. By May, Hermann Göring had become the Air Minister, with Erhard Milch reporting to him as Secretary of State for Air. Milch's task was to form the German Air Force, to be known as the Luftwaffe, as an independent force of the armed services. The Army and Navy were given the go-ahead to re-arm. In the autumn, Hitler ordered the evacuation of the secret Lipezk training base in Russia for ideological reasons – there must no longer be any flirting with the Russian Communists. On 14 October 1933, he ordered the withdrawal of Germany from the Disarmament Conference and from the League of Nations. Germany was now openly re-arming.

Elsewhere in Europe, men like the Salmond brothers were proved to have been justified in their scepticism of disarmament.

CHAPTER VII

Advances in British Aircraft Design

In the early 1930s the fate of the Royal Air Force hung very much in the balance. It had survived earlier attacks by the Navy and the Army upon its independent existence, but now its future lay under a poised Damoclean sword in the form of Ramsay MacDonald and his pacifist Labour disarmers, ably supported by the Liberals. There can be no doubt that these were sincere in their desire for a Utopian world, but all were totally gullible about the intentions of Germany and of Bolshevik Russia, and were therefore blind to the basics needed for the security of their own nation. Neither was the Conservative Party immune from blame, for its members fought only half-heartedly for the necessary military forces required for the preservation of Britain's independence and freedom, the notable exceptions being Winston Churchill and his 'faithful Chela', Brendan Bracken, later to be joined by the up-and-coming Anthony Eden. Churchill recognised that the only successful means of defence depended upon the ability to strike back at an aggressor, and he was therefore in favour of the development of the bomber aircraft as an indispensable weapon of defence. Eden, at first ready to side with Ramsay MacDonald and Sir John Simon in every effort to achieve international disarmament, soon turned his back upon the disarmers when he saw that they were prepared to ignore what was happening in Germany, and thus put Britain at risk, for the sake of personal ideals.

In 1932 and 1933 a bitter battle was being waged by the Chief of the Air Staff, Sir John Salmond, for both the preservation of the Royal Air

Force, and for its expansion to a size that had been planned under his predecessor, Sir Hugh Trenchard, as early as 1925. In this, he was supported by his brother Geoffrey, whose speech at the end of November 1932 had so scathingly admonished the politicians for their disarmament proposals as they affected the Royal Air Force. As the Salmond brothers well knew, Britain's air force was yet again at the cross-roads. In 1919 a dictum termed 'The Ten-Year Rule' had been enunciated by the War Cabinet as part of an economy campaign for the Service Departments in the aftermath of the 1914-1918 war. This stated that Service Estimates should be based on the assumption that 'the British Empire will not be engaged in any great war during the next ten years, and that no Expeditionary Force will be required.' Even Churchill had fully supported this dictum, and when he became Chancellor of the Exchequer in Baldwin's administration in 1924, he had further backed it after asking the Committee of Imperial Defence to review the ruling, whose members made no recommendations for its alteration. In 1927, however, the War Office proposed that the 1919 ruling should be extended, for the Army only, to cover ten years 'from the present date'. Then on 5 July 1928, the matter was again discussed and Churchill proposed 'that the basis of Estimates for the Service Department should rest upon the statement that there would be no major war for a period of ten years, and that this basis should advance from day to day, but that the assumption should be reviewed every year by the Committee of Imperial Defence.' Effectively, this meant that as each year passed 'The Ten-Year Rule' applied for yet another ten years, instead of decreasing yearly. With no enemy in sight during the twenties there was little chance of Britain's military services improving their budgets. And of the three Services it was the Royal Air Force which had felt the economy most harshly.

In 1925, the constitution of the Air Force at home was determined by certain guide-lines, the principal one being that the ratio of bombers to fighters should be two to one, and that the force should build up to thirty-five bomber squadrons and seventeen fighter squadrons; of the bomber squadrons twenty should be of day-bombers and fifteen of night-bombers. The target date for this new force was 1928, but by 1931 the Royal Air Force had reached a total home-based strength of only twenty-six regular squadrons and eleven Auxiliary and Reserve squadrons, these latter squadrons being manned by volunteer personnel and reservists, somewhat on the lines of the Territorial Army. During the Geneva Disarmament Conference in the same year, the British Government imposed a ban on any increase in armaments in order to show its sincerity in trying to reach an agreement on the international reduction of arms. This embargo was particularly disastrous for the Royal Air Force, which was in any case far below its originally approved strength. Moreover, this lack of size was not compensated for by any great advance in modernisation of aircraft types, for the Royal Air Force was still largely equipped with obsolete aeroplanes dating back to the last war. The quality of flying training and technical training were, however, of the highest standard, and the educational levels demanded of officers were exceptional; indeed, of the three Services it was the most difficult to enter.

In 1933 the initial flying training aicraft for the Royal Air Force College, Cranwell, was the Avro 504N, a wooden-framed biplane which had first been passed over from service use to training duties in 1927. It was a modified version of the old Avro 504K, which had seen war service before being turned over to flying training at Cranwell in 1920. Virtually the only difference between the two types was the engine, the 504N being fitted with the radial Armstrong-Siddeley Lynx engine in replacement for the 504K's Gnôme rotary. The two service training aircraft then in use were also wooden biplanes; the Armstrong-Whitworth Siskin IIIA for fighter training, and the Armstrong-Whitworth Atlas I for bomber training, aircraft which had been in service up to 1927 and 1930 respectively, and which were only just being replaced by yet more wooden biplanes. The new aircraft for the fighter squadrons were the Bristol Bulldog and the Hawker Fury, with the Hawker Hart and Hind for day-bomber squadrons, the Hawker Audax for Army co-operation squadrons, and Vickers Wellesleys and Handley-Page Harrows and Heyfords, also wooden biplanes and hopelessly obsolete, for the night-bomber squadrons. In fact, the Royal Air Force was a force of obsolete wooden biplanes, and was to remain as such for a number of years to come. Britain had ceased to have the most powerful and up-to-date air force in the world, having by 1933 slipped way down the ladder. On 14 March of that year, just after the British Air Estimates had been revealed in the House of Commons, Winston Churchill, now in the political wilderness, was so appalled that he was constrained to say:

> I regretted to hear the Under-Secretary say that we were only the fifth air power, and that the ten-year programme was suspended for another year. I was sorry to hear him boast that the Air Ministry had not laid down a single new unit this year. All these ideas are being increasingly stultified by the march of events, and we should be well advised to concentrate upon our air defences with greater vigour.

Churchill not only supported the Salmond brothers in their view that the bomber was as much a weapon of defence as offence, but he also pressed his views on the matter of weapons for the Army. As early as May 1932, when he had already been out of office for three years, he had challenged those who extolled the virtues of disarmament – members of all parties – when Sir John Simon, the Foreign Secretary, had presented to the House of Commons the new classification of weapons which should be allowed or discouraged as a result of discussions at the Disarmament Conference. These classifications sought to permit defensive weapons only, and to debar all offensive weapons. Churchill, alone in the House, was mindful of the changed circumstances in Europe; he alone was awake to the changing scene in Germany. Although an ardent supporter of controlling Britain's arms in the past, he was quick to change his opinions when the threat of a resurgent Germany began to appear on the horizon. He was utterly opposed to foolish disarmament by Britain and her former Allies, and forcefully stated:

> The Foreign Secretary told us that it was difficult to divide weapons into offensive and defensive categories. It certainly is, because almost every conceivable weapon may be used in defence or offence; either by an aggressor or by the innocent victim of his assault. To make it more difficult for the invader, heavy guns, tanks and poison gas are to be relegated to the evil category of offensive weapons. The invasion of France by Germany in 1914 reached its climax without the employment of any of these weapons. The heavy gun is to be described as 'an offensive weapon'. It is all right in a fortress; there it is virtuous and pacific in its character; but bring it out into the field – and, of course, if it were needed, it would be brought out into the field – and it immediately becomes naughty, peccant, militaristic, and has to be placed under the ban of civilisation. Take the tank. The Germans, having invaded France, entrenched themselves; and in a couple of years they shot down 1,500,000 French and British soldiers who were trying to free the soil of France. The tank was invented to overcome the fire of the machine-guns with which the Germans were maintaining themselves in France, and it saved a lot of life in clearing the soil of the invader. Now, apparently, the machine-gun, which was the German weapon for holding on to thirteen provinces of France, is to be the virtuous, defensive machine-gun, and the tank, which was the means by which these Allied lives were saved, is to be placed under the censure and obloquy of all just and righteous men ...

Churchill's strictures did not end here. In 1933 he continued his attack upon the disarmers. After the German delegation to the Disarmament Conference had withdrawn in July 1932, unable to get agreement for Germany's demands to be allowed to re-arm to at least equality with France, it became the prime political objective of the British Government to coax Germany back into the fold at almost any cost. Even Britain's former ally, France, was subjected to constant pressure to agree to near-equality of arms with Germany. The 'MacDonald Plan' of 16 March 1933, which accepted as its basis the adoption of the French system of short-service armies under conscription, the period of service being eight months at that time, then proceeded to lay down exact figures for the soldiers of each country. By this injudicious plan the French Army was to be reduced from its peacetime establishment of 500,000 men to 200,000, and the German Army was to be permitted to double its strength from the 100,000 men authorised by the Versailles Peace Treaty to 200,000, and, therefore, to parity with the French. Initially the German military forces could not benefit from the large pool of trained reservists which would accumulate from a succession of annual conscripted quotas. But at this time the Germans, with their SA and SS forces and other paramilitary organisations, all armed with weapons coming from their own arms production, had certainly amassed at least a million ardent volunteers who had received some form of military training. Other aspects of the MacDonald Plan sought to impose upon Britain, France, and other former Allied European countries limitations on the calibre of guns, the banning of certain weapons regarded as offensive, and the reduction of the air forces of France, Britain and Italy to 500 aircraft each, of which none were to be bombers. Where the air forces were concerned, the disarmers argued that the German Air Force had been disbanded under the Peace Treaty and that Germany had been prohibited from forming another military air service. But it was already apparent, to those who were not too blind to see it, that Germany had long since begun to revive its air force clandestinely.

On 23 March 1933, Churchill again attacked the Government over its disarmament policy and, in particular, the pressure being put upon France to agree to equality of arms with Germany. In the House he said:

I doubt the wisdom of pressing this plan [the MacDonald Plan] upon France at the present time. I do not think the French will agree. They must be greatly concerned at what is taking place in Germany, as well as at the attitude of some others of their neighbours. I dare say that during this anxious month there are a good many people who have said to themselves, as I have been saying for several years: 'Thank God for the French Army.' When we read about Germany, when we watch with surprise and distress the tumultuous insurgence of ferocity and war spirit, the pitiless ill-treatment of minorities, the denial of the normal protections of civilised society, the persecution of large numbers of individuals solely on the grounds of race – when we see all that occurring in one of the most gifted, learned and scientific and formidable nations in the world, one cannot help feeling glad that the fierce passions that are raging in Germany have not yet found any other outlet but upon themselves. It seems to me that at a moment like this to ask France to halve her Army while Germany doubles hers, to ask France to halve her Air Force while the German Air Force remains whatever it is — is a proposal likely to be considered by the French Government, at present at any rate, as somewhat unreasonable. The figures that are given in the plan of the strength of the armies and airplanes, secure to France only as many as would be possessed by Italy, leaving any air power possessed by Germany entirely out of consideration.

In April of the same year he returned to the attack.

The Germans demand equality in weapons and equality in the organisation of armies and fleets, and we have been told 'you cannot keep so great a nation in an inferior position. What others have, they must have.' I have never agreed. It is a most dangerous demand to make. Nothing in life is eternal, but as surely as Germany acquires full military equality with her neighbours while her own grievances are still unredressed and while she is in the temper which we have unhappily seen, so surely should we see ourselves within a measurable distance of the renewal of general European war ... One of the things which we were told after the Great War would be a security for us was that Germany would be a democracy with Parliamentary institutions. All this has been swept away. You have most grim dictatorship. You have militarism and appeals to every form of fighting spirit, from the re-introduction of duelling in the Colleges to the Minister of Education advising the plentiful use of the cane in Elementary Schools. You have these martial or pugnacious manifestations, and also this persecution of the Jews of which so many members have spoken ...

Turning to France and pointing out that she was not only the sole great surviving democracy in Europe, but also the strongest military power and the guarantor and protector of the small European states such as Belgium, Poland, Czechoslovakia, Yugoslavia, Rumania, Austria and Hungary, he added:

They all look to France. When any step is taken, by England or any other Power, to weaken the diplomatic or military security of France, all these small nations tremble with fear and anger. They fear that the central protective force will be weakened, and that then they will be at the mercy of the great Teutonic Power.

Finally, it was Hitler who was to put a stop to any question of European disarmament when, in November 1933, Germany withdrew from the Disarmament Conference for the second time, and when Hitler also ordered withdrawal from the League of Nations. No longer was Germany to re-arm in secret. Instead, she openly and boastfully proceeded to build up her military forces.

The Royal Air Force in 1933 was not, in the longer-term view, in quite such a desperate condition as it appeared to be at first sight. Its strength was certainly well below that which had been planned, and even the planned strength was far below what was necessary for the security of Britain in a politically unstable Europe. In addition, the obsolescence of its aircraft was daunting. But if the immediate future only offered a continuation of outmoded wooden biplanes of indifferent performance and armament, there were signs of better things to come, thanks to the enterprise of the privately owned aircraft and engine companies, and to a remarkably patriotic and far-sighted woman, Lady Houston.* For a number of years there had been an international air race held biennially, in which the fastest aircraft from a number of nations competed for a cup known as the Schneider Trophy. The trophy was presented to the entry which covered a set course at the highest speed, the site of the course invariably being in the country of the winner of the last contest. The major winners of the Schneider races in the twenties had been the Americans, the British and the Italians. Britain won again in 1927, after a period of losing the races, when the Vickers Supermarine-Napier Seaplane, flown by Flight Lieutenant S. N. Webster, won at Venice against strong Italian opposition. This seaplane was the product of close co-operation between the High-Speed Flight of the Royal Air Force, the aircraft and engine designers, and the Air Ministry, all backed by Sir Hugh Trenchard, the then Chief of the Air Staff. In 1929 the trophy was again won by Britain, this time with an experimental all-metal monoplane, the Vickers-Supermarine S6, designed by R.J. Mitchell and powered by an experimental engine designed by F.R. Royce of Rolls-Royce. It was an aircraft incorporating many innovations far ahead of the times, and its specially built Rolls-Royce engine was truly advanced. Piloted by Flying Officer H.R.D. Waghorn, the S6 seaplane covered the seven laps of the circuit off the south coast of England at the phenomenal average speed of 328 miles per hour. But entry for the Schneider races absorbed a great deal of money. The Treasury tended to

---

* Dame Fanny Lucy Houston (1857-1936), philanthropist and eccentric, was the widow of an enormously rich baronet. The causes she espoused included women's rights, a rest home for nurses during the First World War (for which she was appointed DBE), coal-miners, tramwaymen and persecuted Russian Christians. She became best known for her 'combative patriotism'; her gift to the Schneider Trophy team was an act of the greatest service to her country. In 1932 she offered £200,000 towards the air defence of London, but Parliament turned down her gift.

condemn enterprises of this kind since they were supported by public money, and with the disarmament-conscious Labour Government in power after 1929, the Under-Secretary of State for Air, Frederick Montague, announced on 18 March 1930, and again on 25 March, that as the Schneider Trophy race was 'in the nature of a sporting event', it was not desirable that it should be supported by public money. The Government, in short, would not support Britain's Schneider entry. The fact that this contest was providing a stimulus for the aircraft industry and the Royal Air Force to develop modern aircraft and engines was ignored. The Labour Party had little interest in the protection of Britain if the means ran counter to dogmatic ideas on disarmament and hallucinations about international socialism. It was in the face of this bitter blow, that Lady Houston stepped in with an offer of £100,000 out of her own pocket – a prodigious sum in those days. This was gratefully accepted by the Air Council, and Britain was thereby enabled to defend her title in 1931, winning the Schneider Trophy yet again with the Supermarine S6B seaplane. Perhaps the most important outcome of the 1931 contest* was its influence on the design of high-speed aircraft. In particular, the work of R.J. Mitchell of Vickers Supermarine, which led to the development of the Spitfire only just in time for the Battle of Britain in 1940, was directly connected with the Schneider Trophy attempts. Equally important was the spin-off from the Rolls-Royce 'R' series of engines which had powered the seaplanes, for from these emerged the Rolls-Royce Merlins and Griffons upon which Britain's wartime fighters and bombers were largely to depend, powering (among many aircraft) Hurricanes, Spitfires, Mustangs, Mosquitoes, and the highly successful four-engined Lancaster bombers.

The privately owned aircraft industry, in co-operation with the Royal Air Force, was also laying the foundations of the future strategic bomber. In the latter half of the twenties, the Fairey Aviation Company produced a single-engined high-wing monoplane designed for long-range flying. It was of composite construction, wood and metal, and was powered by a Napier Lion engine. At the beginning of 1933 this aircraft arrived at Cranwell with its crew, Squadron Leader O.R. Gayford and Flight Lieutenant G.E. Nickoletts, for its take-off on a non-stop flight to South Africa in an endeavour to establish the world long-distance record. Fully loaded with fuel for this venture, the Fairey Monoplane needed the length of aerodrome for take-off that only Cranwell could provide. On 6 February 1933, watched by all the cadets and other Service personnel, this magnificent monoplane (in an age when the majority of aircraft were

---

* This was the last time the Schneider air races were held, and Britain retains the trophy to this day.

biplanes) rumbled and roared across the grass airfield, only just becoming airborne before reaching the boundary. It was an inspiring sight, marking the beginning of a magnificent achievement, for the aircraft flew without a stop to Walvis Bay on the west coast of South Africa, a distance of 5,431 miles, in 57 hours and 25 minutes. A short while later, in the early spring, it returned to Cranwell to an excited welcome – truly a case of 'See the conquering heroes come'. What was impressive about the Fairey Long-Range Monoplane was its immense size, particularly its enormous wing-span. Cranwell's aircraft – Atlases, Siskins, and Avro 504Ns – were positively dwarfed on the tarmac by this vast and beautiful aeroplane.

In the summer of that same year, Cranwell was to be even more impressed by another and yet larger product of the Fairey Aviation Company. This was the Fairey Night-Bomber (designed, like the Long-Range Monoplane, by D.L. Hollis-Williams), a huge twin-engined, low-wing cantilever monoplane of all-metal construction, apart from fabric covering for the fuselage, and powered by two 525-hp Jupiter XF cowled radial engines. The Night-Bomber was the first all-metal framework aircraft to be developed as a bomber, and that development had been done as a private venture by the Fairey Company. The prototype, K1695, which visited Cranwell for part of its trials, had a maximum flying speed of 155 mph, was capable of carrying a bomb load of 1,160 lbs, and had an out-and-home range in excess of 1,000 miles – truly remarkable performance from such a machine in those days. The Fairey Night-Bomber was to become one of the most important milestones in the history of the Royal Air Force, for its development brought about a radical change in the concept and design of the bombers of the future. The final version, as ordered by the Air Ministry, was named the Hendon Mk II and was fitted with two 600-hp Kestrel VI engines. It went into service with No. 38 Squadron at the end of 1936.

If there were gleams of hope for the RAF in the development of new aircraft, this was true also of its personnel. For officer cadets, the course at the Royal Air Force College lasted two years, and was divided into four terms, the terms commencing in September and January of each year. At the end of the first two terms every cadet had to sit and pass what were known as 'first-year examinations' before he could move into his second year of training. At the end of two years there were final exams which, if passed, qualified the cadet to pass out of Cranwell with a commission and enter the Royal Air Force as an officer. It would, however, be wrong to assume that Cranwell only trained the future officer to fly, for the curriculum of training went considerably beyond that. By far the largest proportion of a cadet's time was taken up by academic studies, with the emphasis placed on scientific and engineering disciplines. Subjects included very advanced mathematics, aeronautical engineering, physics, electrical engineering, navigation, military history, English, Air Force Law, Civil Law and accountancy. The engineering subjects were supported by extensive workshop practice, and in the second year every cadet had to complete and submit a thesis on some aspect of aeronautical engineering, choosing his subject from a list provided. Teaching at Cranwell was of the highest order, and the very fact that the entry for each term was some thirty cadets, bringing total cadet strength in any one year to about 120 only, resulted in classes being small, which in turn allowed much individual attention to be given to each student. The academic course was, in truth, equal to a degree course in science at any university, with the advantage that it was backed by some humanistic subjects, including law. That such a course could be covered in two years, as compared to three years at university, was due to the fact that apart from a few days' break at Christmas and the Easter Bank Holiday weekend, leave was confined to one month, August, during the summer.

Navigational training in 1933 was, by today's standards, rather elementary, and consisted of dead reckoning (DR). The cadet was taught how to calculate a compass course to be steered, using a given track between point of departure and destination, and with wind speed and direction supplied by the local meterological office. He was then instructed in the methods of adjusting the compass course in flight when check points on the ground over which he was flying showed that he was drifting from track, indicating changes in wind speed and direction from those supplied for pre-flight planning. At Cranwell, aircraft carried no radio equipment, and therefore no wireless aids to navigation. Squadrons in service, however, operated a number of aids such as radio beacons and direction-finding stations (D/F stations), all of which were crude by modern standards. But the principles of wireless aids and their use were taught in navigation classes on the ground, and the technical function of the equipment in service formed part of the theoretical and practical instruction in the physics and electrical engineering classes. In addition, every cadet had to learn Morse code – essential to the use of wireless aids – the pass level being twenty-five words a minute, sending and receiving. The practical application of DR navigation, and of map-reading, was achieved by cadets being sent on cross-country flights. These consisted of flying to another RAF station, landing there, reporting to the Duty Pilot and obtaining the latest meteorological information for the return flight, obtaining permission to take off, and returning to base. The length of these flights increased as experience was gained, but if unexpected bad weather conditions caught out the unfortunate cadet in the middle of a relatively long flight, the prospect, without wireless or radio, could be disturbing.

The length of flying time put in by a cadet in his two years was relatively short, amounting on average to some sixty hours of dual instruction and eighty hours of solo flying. The dual flying included instrument flying under the hood – literally a canvas cover pulled over the cockpit in which the cadet learned to fly compass courses, perform turns, climb and dive, get out of left- and right-hand spins, make approaches to land and other manoeuvres, entirely blind, using only instruments.

It was via Cranwell that the Royal Air Force obtained the majority of its permanent officers. But in 1919 Trenchard had conceived a plan for increasing the number of officers who flew by creating permanent commissions and short-service commissions. With the support of Churchill, then Secretary of State for War and Air, he obtained approval for the plan, which provided for one-third of the RAF's officers to have permanent commissions, and two-thirds to be recruited as short-service commissioned officers. In time, a third category was added – medium-service commissions to allow for short-service officers to sign for a further five years after their initial period of five years had been completed. The result of this far-sighted plan was the ultimate establishment of a large pool of pilots, all of whom became part of the Royal Air Force Reserve when they had completed their tours of duty, and who undertook refresher training each year to keep their hands in at flying. The training of short-service officers was undertaken at a number of Service Flying Training Schools (SFTSs). These courses were of lesser duration than those at Cranwell, lasting for one year as opposed to two, and the chief emphasis was on flying training.

The Royal Air Force also trained all its technical personnel for servicing aircraft and aicraft equipment, thus providing its own supply of fitters, riggers,* wireless-operators and mechanics, and armourers. The supply of these trades came mainly from the Boy Apprentice Schools – engineering staff from the Engineering School at Halton, wireless mechanics from the Electrical and Wireless School at Cranwell, and armourers from the Armament School at Eastchurch. This recruitment was backed up by direct-entry airmen for the different trades who received specialist training to supplement their civilian training and experience. Even clerical trades were trained at apprentice schools, and so too were canteen staff. In fact, the Royal Air Force was self-supporting by the middle twenties as regards recruiting and staffing. In addition, thanks to the short-service schemes, the RAF possessed a growing number of trained reservists, a reserve capable of supporting any moderate expansion which it might suddenly be called upon to undertake.

By 1934, the home-based force was a small one of 30,000 Regulars

---

* Fitters looked after engines, riggers airframes.

officers and men, and 11,000 Reservists. Its first-line strength numbered a mere 564 aircraft. By September 1939, within the successive restrictions imposed by government, its personnel strength had risen to 118,000 Regulars and 68,000 Reservists, and its aircraft strength had reached 1,476. Given the go-ahead to expand freely, it could undoubtedly have done very much better; as it was the expansion looked dismal beside that achieved by the German Air Force. During the same period, Germany expanded from 400 aircraft in 1935 to a first-line strength of 3,609 military aeroplanes, mostly of modern all-metal monoplane construction, supported by 552 transport aircraft, and from 20,000 officers and men to marginally over 500,000. Hitler, equipped with a savage dictatorship, enabled the German Air Force to expand at an unprecedented rate; British democracy procrastinated almost to the point of disaster.

CHAPTER VIII

Hitler's Third Reich
Takes Shape

Hitler's accession to the Chancellorship of Germany in January 1933 soon sparked off a serious division in the Nazi Party. In April, when at his direction the Jews and so-called Marxists were being ousted from civil service, government, and other professional appointments, as was anyone else who opposed his regime, he said, 'If we make Germany great we have a right to think of ourselves.' At the moment of Hitler's acquisition of power, the SA under Ernst Röhm was nearly three million strong, while Nazi Party membership numbered only one and a half million. Three months later the Party membership figure had risen to two and a half millions, the increase being stimulated by the hope of non-Jews and non-Marxists that they would be permitted to retain their old posts or to obtain new ones if they joined the Party. There was, as a result, a scramble for better jobs, the spoils of Hitler's victory, and those who came off badly called vociferously for the elimination not only of the Jews and Marxists, but also of the old ruling caste, from the most senior posts down to the lowest. Indeed, there were highly placed members of the Party, including the SA, who became ardent for more social revolution and who were fearful that Hitler, whom they had carried forward to power, would as Chancellor now be taken over by the existing hierarchy of the Reichswehr, the bankers and industrialists, thus denying them the chance of high positions in these fields. Under Röhm's leadership, the SA began to support these new revolutionary elements, and Röhm himself unquestionably had his eye on greater things than just his position as Chief of Staff of the SA. His aim was first to have the SA incorporated into the Reichswehr and then, using his huge numbers of supporters and the Party's backing, to absorb the German armed forces and take over supreme command. Almost certainly he saw himself becoming, by this means, the future powerful figure in Germany. Hitler, however, having gained the Chancellorship, wanted to consolidate his position; he had no intention of embarking upon courses of action which might provoke an insurrection from within, and which would almost surely result in chaos. In fact, he recognised that he needed the assistance of the industrial and commercial interests and of the bankers, both to stabilise the economy of the country and to produce prosperity. Above all he needed them to assist in the re-armament of the nation, a condition which was essential if he was to realise his dream of a greater Germany embracing Austria, Czechoslovakian Sudetenland, and all other areas containing German minorities. Equally important to this dream of a 'master race' of Germans dominating Europe was the support of the Reichswehr. He could not afford to alienate them, and Röhm's ambitions in the direction of taking over the German Army by the very power of his growing SA movement was now seen as a threat to the Reichswehr, and one which could bring that body into active conflict with the Nazi Party.

By early 1934 the SA had risen to a force of more than three million men. With warnings from loyal supporters such as Göring, now chief of the reconstituted German Air Force, Goebbels, and Heinrich Himmler, head of the SS, all urged on by Field-Marshal Walther von Reichenau, Field-Marshal Werner von Bomberg, head of the War Ministry, and other senior officers of the Reichswehr who were suspicious of Röhm's intentions, Hitler began to grow uneasy at the mammoth size of the SA, and to fear that perhaps its control really was slipping from his grasp. It was becoming clear that the time was fast approaching when he would have to deal with his 'dear Ernst Röhm', despite protestations from Röhm and his SA of their fervent loyalty to the Führer. Whilst Hitler had supporters in the Reichswehr and the War Ministry, Röhm also had his well wishers, in particular Generals Kurt von Schleicher and Ferdinand von Bredow. Von Schleicher had harboured a grudge, almost amounting to hatred, against Hitler since the latter had ousted him from the Chancellorship in January 1933; in addition he had never forgiven the Army chiefs of the Reichswehr for failing to choose him as the potential successor to von Hindenburg in the event of the President's death. The warnings to Hitler of Röhm's disloyalty, and of his plans in conjunction with von Schleicher to overthrow him, were accompanied by recommendations to deal swiftly and harshly with the situation, but it is somewhat to Hitler's credit that he remembered Röhm's friendship and support from the earliest days of his struggle. Instead of acting instantly in the brutal and ruthless fashion which has always been attributed to him, he attempted reconciliation with Röhm, offering him a post in the Cabinet and public thanks for his 'imperishable services'.

As early as February 1934, however, Hitler was clearly becoming more and more concerned about the growth of the SA, and about its control, as is demonstrated by his conversations with Anthony Eden* in Berlin on the afternoon of the 18th, when Eden, in company with the British Ambassador and Baron Konstantin von Neurath, the German Foreign Minister, met the Führer for the first time. The purpose of Eden's visit was essentially to discover whether he could persuade Hitler to limit his re-armament relative to the proposed disarmament plans of the Allied Powers contained in the 'MacDonald Plan'. The objective was to induce Germany to limit the increase of its army from 100,000 to 200,000 men only, as opposed to its demand for an army of 300,000. Another objective was to prevail upon Hitler to return Germany to the table of the Disarmament Conference in Geneva – in this Eden failed. In discussing military strengths it was inevitable that Eden should raise the question of the paramilitary organisations, the SA and SS, and seek assurances that they should only act as a form of police force, have no arms, receive no instruction in the use of military arms, undergo no training by German Army personnel, take no part in army manoeuvres. Hitler gave these assurances, but in doing so made the unexpected observation, regarding the activities of the SA and SS, that his own common-sense and political instinct would never allow him to sanction the creation of a second army in the state. History, he averred, had proved that second armies were totally undesirable. He added that he was doubtful whether Mussolini had been wise in creating the Fascist Militia in Italy.

On numerous occasions in April and May, von Blomberg, no friend to von Schleicher or Röhm, complained bitterly to Hitler about the activities of the SA and about the insolence of its leaders when confronted by senior officers of the Reichswehr. The pressure from the Regular Army for a final settlement with Röhm increased, and was in fact irresistible if Hitler was to retain the support of the Reichswehr; indeed, by the latter half of May he had to choose between the generals on the one hand, and Röhm and his officers on the other, for it was clear that the SA leader was virtually ready with a plot to seize control of the Army. Finally, the imprudence of von Schleicher in hinting to the French Ambassador in Rome that Hitler would soon be ousted from power, an indiscretion which quickly reached the Führer's ears, made Hitler realise that he had to take swift action. Yet, again, he hesitated, and in a long

* On 31 December 1933, Anthony Eden was appointed Lord Privy Seal to the National Government and Britain's senior representative at the League of Nations.

conversation with Röhm made a last effort to come to terms with him. But Röhm had moved more to the left than had been suspected and was eager for a Proletarian Republic backed by a People's Army. Such a regime was far from the 'mystic hierarchic Greater Germany of Hitler's dreams', as Churchill once described the Nazi leader's ambition.

Events now moved apace, and Hitler came to terms with the Reichswehr. In exchange for the generals' support for his succession as Head of State on the death of von Hindenburg, he agreed to the permanent removal of Röhm and his associates from the SA, and to a clear understanding that the SA and SS should in no circumstances seek to encompass and take over the Regular Army. The stage was now set for the final reckoning with Röhm, described by Eden as a flamboyant figure, 'scarred and scented, with a jewelled dagger at his waist ... he was not just a perverted swashbuckler, he had intelligence of a kind and, a rarity in the modern world, he was a man who boasted of his bravery, yet was brave. But he was hardly of the modern world; a condottiere [sic] of the Middle Ages might have looked and behaved like him.'

Röhm, with Hitler's consent, had called a conference of all the senior leaders of the SA. This meeting was to be held on 30 June (1934) at the Bavarian spa of Bad Wiessee, where Röhm was taking a cure for rheumatism, and Hitler had announced his intention of attending himself. A few days before the meeting, the Reichswehr, with the generals' agreement, were confined to barracks in those main cities of Germany where the SA were prominent. At the same time, Heinrich Himmler's élite SS troops were issued with arms, Himmler having thrown in his lot with Hitler. The plan was to arrest Röhm and the SA leaders and to throw them into prison. Then, on 29 June, Goebbels, who was to join Hitler in Munich in order to present the press releases on the action taken, with due propaganda for the Führer, brought news of an impending revolt in Berlin against the Hitler regime. According to Goebbels, Röhm's adjutant, Karl Ernst, had been given orders to attempt a rising. Hitler acted at once. He ordered Göring to take control in Berlin and, with the aid of the SS, to deal ruthlessly with the dissenters.

Hitler now decided to deal with Röhm himself. In the early hours of the morning of 30 June, having landed in his personal aeroplane at an aerodrome just outside Munich, he went by car to Bad Wiessee, accompanied by Goebbels and an SS bodyguard. Röhm was taken completely by surprise when Hitler, in person, walked into his bedroom to arrest him. It was rumoured that he was caught with two boys in his room, although this story is probably without foundation, more than likely emanating from Röhm's known homosexual activities rather than from the actual incident. Be that as it may, he and those other SA leaders who had already arrived and were staying at Bad Wiessee were arrested without a struggle, and taken by road to Munich where they were thrown into the Landsberg Prison, the self-same prison in which both Hitler and Röhm had been held in 1924 for their attempt to march on Munich and seize control of the State Legislature. The remaining SA leaders who were to attend the conference were arrested by the SS on the streets or as they alighted from their trains. 'Dear Ernst Röhm' was given the opportunity to shoot himself, but declined the invitation; that same afternoon he was riddled with bullets in his own cell.

The executions continued throughout the day and into the week. In Berlin, Göring organised a similar massacre of members in the SA, including Karl Ernst, and of those others whose names had been found on a list of important supporters of the rebellion against Hitler. The most prominent victims outside the SA were von Schleicher and his wife (who threw herself in front of her husband to protect him from the gunmen), General Ferdinand von Bredow, Gregor Strasser, Otto von Kahr (who, as head of the Bavarian Government in 1923/24, had broken the Munich Putsch and imprisoned Hitler), and most of Franz von Papen's staff. Von Papen, the Vice-Chancellor, was listed for extermination but was saved from a firing squad by von Hindenburg's personal intervention. He took the hint, however, and resigned his post a few days after 'the night of the long knives', as the killings in Munich, Berlin, and other major centres, came to be known. In all, between 5,000 and 7,000 people were murdered during these massacres.

On 13 July, Hitler explained his action to the public in an address to the Reichstag, an address which revealed both his remarkable knowledge of the German mind, and his persuasive powers of argument. The climax was:

The necessity for acting with lightning speed meant that in this decisive hour I had very few men with me ... Although only a few days before I had been prepared to exercise clemency, at this hour there was no place for any such consideration. Mutinies are suppressed in accordance with laws of iron which are eternally the same. If anyone reproaches me and asks me why I did not resort to the regular Courts of Justice for conviction of the offenders, then all that I can say to him is this: in this hour I was responsible for the fate of the German People, and thereby I became the supreme Chief Justice of the German People. I did not wish to deliver up the Young Reich to the fate of the Old Reich [a reference to the left-wing revolution of November 1918, which replaced the monarchy with the Weimar Republic]. I therefore gave the order to shoot those who were ringleaders in this high treason ... And I gave the further order to cauterise to the raw flesh the ulcers of this poisoning of the wells in our domestic life, and of the poisoning of the outside world.

Field-Marshal Werner von Blomberg publicly offered profound thanks to Hitler for his resolute steps to secure the nation from civil war, and von Hindenburg also offered his congratulations for, as he saw it, an action which had saved Germany from internal strife. Göring, in a classic statement on the matter to the assembled Prosecutors-General, stated that, 'The law and the will of the Führer are one and the same thing'.

Hitler had now firmly established the 'Third Reich' – the 'Reich of a Thousand Years', as he boasted – and from July 1934 there was nothing to stop him imposing his will upon the people. To the true German, this will appeared to be for his benefit. By the winter of 1933/34 unemployment had dropped from 6,000,000 to 4,000,000, and the downward trend continued until, in April 1935, the figure was below 1,000,000; it was not long, in fact, before the problem had become a shortage of labour. This was by no means all. Hitler's powerful attack on unemployment consisted of a vast programme of motorway construction, designed primarily for strategic military purposes, enormous armaments production, and the reconstruction of dwelling houses. The associated inflation of these activities was minimised by the wave of public confidence in the new regime, which made it possible to risk extension of credit without the hazard of inflationary panic. And the Germans were prepared to work – and work hard – for minimal wages; anything was better than the miserable past, and working for the proud rise of their nation from ignominy was well worth a tightened belt. Furthermore, Hitler knew how to popularise himself in these early days of power by introducing further measures aimed at the ordinary folk. He introduced marriage loans on a very wide and generous basis to facilitate the purchase of homes, encouraging thereby the growth of families. To protect expectant mothers, bountiful schemes of post-natal care were introduced, and as a further easement of family life and as an encouragement to procreate more and more little Germans, holidays for children in the country were organised on a national basis, and crèches and day-nurseries were set up on a vast scale. A re-housing plan, known as the 'Homestead Project', was designed to remove people from the dreary and monotonous conditions of life in tenement housing, and this, coupled with the 'Winter Help Work' – no one shall go hungry and cold – did an enormous amount to relieve the fearful effects of the poverty of the early post-Great War years. These various assistance schemes were financed mainly by voluntary subscriptions. Nor were these the only benefits to the people. There was the introduction of the Volkswagen – literally the 'People's Car' – a car that was in the price range of the majority, and a project which was essentially inspired by Hitler and in which he actively participated. Finally, there were the 'Strength-Through-Joy' holidays, whereby workers could spend eight days on the

Baltic coast for as little as thirty-two marks (a price which included entertainment), or at the less expensive resorts for ten to fifteen marks a week. Senior employees received similar consideration, but in view of their higher wages they had to pay a supplement. A total of nine ships were even bought or chartered, and two other liners were specially built, for cruises to the Mediterranean, Madeira and Norway. From 1934 to 1937, twenty-two million people enjoyed these holidays.

The motives behind these innovations were not entirely philanthropic. To the ordinary family, however, their phenomenal new hero had won his way to the top not, apparently, just to satisfy his own ego and to become a god amongst politicians, but to improve the lot of the people he ruled; on the face of it, Hitler *had* improved their lot immeasurably from the inflationary periods and depressions of the late twenties and the beginning of the thirties. In fact, the ordinary German family was being duped. The people's gratitude, which bordered on worship, was being bought for the purpose of achieving Hitler's grandiose schemes for the future greatness of Germany and for world domination. He needed an unquestioning nation behind him. When he was ready to risk wars to undertake his expansionist policies he would require a people who would instantly, and with blind faith, leap to arms for the honour of Germany and of its Führer.

There was now every sign of Germany's re-armament, yet on 20 July 1934, when the British Government belatedly proposed a totally inadequate increase in the strength of the Royal Air Force by forty squadrons, at a cost of £20,000,000, to be completed within five years, the Labour Party, with the support of the Liberals, greeted the expansion with a Vote of Censure. The Motion regretted that:

His Majesty's Government should enter upon a policy of rearmament neither necessitated by any new commitment nor calculated to add to the security of the nation, but certain to jeopardise the prospects of international disarmament and to encourage a revival of dangerous and wasteful competition in preparation for war.

Clement Attlee, speaking for the Labour Party (of which he was then Deputy Leader) on this Motion made the extraordinary comment: 'We deny the need for increased air armaments ... We deny the proposition that an increased British Air Force will make for the peace of the world, and we reject altogether the claim to parity.' He was no doubt sincere about the peace of the world, but in the face of obvious German increases in her military strength he appeared to care little about the security of Britain, and of those countries of whose safety Britain was a guarantor.

The Liberal Party Motion stated that:

> This House views with grave concern the tendency among the nations of the world to resume the competitive race of armaments which has always proved a precursor of war; it will not approve any expansion of our own armaments unless it is clear that the Disarmament Conference has failed and unless a definite case is established; and these conditions not being present as regards the proposed additional expenditure of £20,000,000 upon air armaments, the House declines its assent.

The Liberal leader, Sir Herbert Samuel, who presented the Motion, said: 'What is the case in regard to Germany? Nothing we have so far seen or heard would suggest that our present Air Force is not adequate to meet any peril at the present time from this quarter.' Here then was yet another ostrich with its head stuck in the sand.

Churchill, now supported by Anthony Eden as well as Brendan Bracken, not only vehemently attacked the Labour and Liberal Motions, but in prophetic vein went as far as to suggest that the planned increases to the Royal Air Force were insufficient. After drawing attention to the fact that the Government which was proposing these increases was led by an extreme pacifist (Ramsay MacDonald), supported by other principal ministers who were also dedicated pacifists or fervent advocates of disarmament, including the Lord President of the Council, Stanley Baldwin, he said that he would have expected the Opposition to consider such a proposal as a proof of the reality of the danger from which even the pacifists sought to protect the country. He added that the Government, in recommending the increase, had done so apologetically and in inoffensive terms – almost meekly – and had emphasised how small was the intended increase in aircraft. Moreover, he said, the House had been assured that if the Geneva Conference on disarmament could succeed, the increase could quickly be suspended. Despite all this, the Opposition's answer was a Vote of Censure. Then, referring to Germany, he said:

> We are in the presence of an attempt to establish a kind of tyranny of opinion, and if its reign could be perpetuated the effect might be profoundly injurious to the stability and security of this country. We are a rich and easy prey. No country is so vulnerable, and no country would better repay pillage than our own ... With our enormous metropolis here, the greatest target in the world, a kind of tremendous, fat, valuable cow tied up to attract the beast of prey, we are in a position in which we have never been before, and in which no other country is at the present time. Let us remember this: our weakness does not only involve ourselves: our weakness involves also the stability of Europe.

Finally, Churchill asserted that Germany was already in violation of the Versailles Peace Treaty, having created an air force which was at this stage two-thirds as strong as Britain's home-defence air force, and which was being expanded so rapidly that by the end of 1935 it would be equal in numbers and efficiency to the home-defence RAF, even if the Government's present proposals were speedily implemented. If Germany continued her present rate of expansion, then, he insisted, she would definitely be substantially stronger in the air than Great Britain, and once that lead had been established, Britain might never be able to re-establish superiority.

> If these assertions cannot be contradicted [Churchill said] then there is cause for the anxiety which exists in all parts of the House, not only because of the physical strength of the German Air Force, but I am bound to say also because of the character of the present German dictatorship. If the Government have to admit at any time in the next few years that the German Air Forces are stronger than our own, then they will be held, and I think rightly held, to have failed in their prime duty to the country.

Since the National Government held a substantial majority in the House of Commons the Vote of Censure was defeated, and the increases in the strength of the Royal Air Force were approved. The Liberals, having withdrawn their own proposed Vote of Censure in favour of Labour's voted with the Labour Party, but to no avail.

Whatever the Government's proposals for an increase in the Royal Air Force, the fact was that it had been laid down in 1925 that the home-based strength should be fifty-two squadrons by 1928, this force consisting of thirty-five bomber and seventeen fighter squadrons. By 1932, as Stanley Baldwin told the House, the target figure of fifty-two squadrons was short by ten, and since the opening of the Disarmament Conference in 1932 no further squadrons had been added, in order to 'set an example to other countries'. The proposal for forty additional squadrons, backed by reserves, as an absolute minimum, had come from the Chief of the Air Staff, Marshal of the Royal Air Force Sir Edward Ellington, who had succeeded Sir Geoffrey Salmond in May 1933. Sir Edward, who foresaw the growth of the German Air Force and the attendant danger to Britain, told his colleagues that Germany could build up a force of 800 aircraft with the necessary reserves within six months, and that she 'could, if she wished, build up rapidly in peace time to a force of 2,000 aircraft, and that preparations which she is now beginning to make may within, say, five years enable her to maintain such a force at practically its full strength in war.' Despite Sir Edward's warnings, the Cabinet decision was, as has been stated, to increase the Royal Air Force by only forty squadrons within five years, at a cost of £20,000,000, and the request for a further £10,000,000 for reserves, for which Sir Edward had pressed, was rejected. This rejection was in the face of Ellington's further caution that 'at present' only five squadrons had war reserves, and that without proper reserves the Air Force 'would not be capable of operating on a war footing for more than a week or two.'

What was finally adopted was a plan known as Scheme A, dated July 1934, by which the Royal Air force first-line strength was, by March 1939, to reach eighty-four squadrons consisting of 960 aircraft for home defence, twenty-seven squadrons with 292 aircraft for the Empire and Protectorates overseas, and sixteen and a half squadrons with 213 aircraft for the Fleet Air Arm, giving a total of 1,465 aircraft, compared to the 1934 strength at home and overseas of only 844 aircraft. The figure of eighty-four home defence squadrons was reached by adding thirty-two squadrons to the fifty-two which should have been in service by 1928. As the squadron strength in 1934 was, however, only forty-two squadrons the real increase planned for 1939 was, in fact, forty-two additional squadrons. Of the home defence squadrons, the division between bombers and fighters was such as to bring the Bomber Force up to a strength of forty-one squadrons and the Fighter Force to twenty-eight squadrons, the remaining fifteen being for army co-operation and coastal duties. This division was not welcomed by the Air Ministry, which would have preferred an even greater increase in the number of bombers, but the Disarmament Conference's opposition to offensive weapons still weighed heavily with the politicians. Another weakness from the point of view of the Bomber Force was that under Scheme A, twenty-two of its forty-one bomber squadrons were to be of light bombers, which were of no use for attacks on Germany. These were, however, cheaper to make, and so the extra squadrons could be formed at lower cost, a point which weighed heavily with politicians; in their ignorance, those same politicians believed that the deterrent of increased numbers, albeit of useless aircraft, would still be effective. It was a fact, however, that no satisfactory medium or heavy bomber had been put onto the drawing board, let alone into production, except for the Fairey Night-Bomber – the Hendon Mk II – which was in the process of being accepted and which was to go into service late in 1936. But events during the rest of 1934 and throughout 1935 were to change Scheme A through a series of revisions – scheme after scheme – as the German threat to European peace increased with Hitler's ascending power. It was little more than a matter of months before Clement Attlee's comment in the House about Hitler – 'I think we can generally say today that his dictatorship is gradually falling down' – would prove to be one of the most stupid remarks to have been uttered by a responsible Member of Parliament in this century.

The air strengths of other countries were estimated at this time as 1,650 first-line aircraft for France, 1,500 for the USSR, 1,385 for Japan, 1,100 for the USA, and 1,000 for Italy. Britain, with a total strength of 884 first-line aircraft for home and overseas, had dropped to a position as sixth air power in the world. Given Germany's undoubtedly quickened re-armament since her withdrawal from the Disarmament Conference and the League of Nations in October 1933, followed by Hitler's denouncement of the Versailles Peace Treaty in March 1935 and his reintroduction of conscription at the same time, it looked as if Britain might well be slipping back to seventh place. Whether the figures estimated were absolutely accurate is open to question, but in relative terms they were of the right order.

In June 1934 the Standing Committee of the Disarmament Conference was adjourned indefinitely. In Europe France, Italy and Russia were now re-arming in fear of Germany, so also were Poland and Czechoslovakia. Germany, which had been flouting the Peace Treaty in secret, now blamed Europe for the necessity of protecting her frontiers against these provocative actions by neighbouring countries.

In the summer of 1934, Hitler made his first move against Austria. He had always regarded the land of his birth as a natural part of Greater Germany. Indeed, at the very beginning of *Mein Kampf* he had written:

German-Austria must return to the great German mother country, and not because of any economic considerations. No, and again no: even if such a union were unimportant from an economic point of view; yes, even if it were harmful, it must nevertheless take place. One blood demands one Reich. Never will the German nation possess the moral right to engage in colonial politics until, at least, it embraces its own sons within a single state. Only when the Reich borders include the very last German, but can no longer guarantee his daily bread, will the moral right to acquire foreign soil arise from the distress of our own people. Their sword will become our plough, and from the tears of war the daily bread of future generations will grow.

In July, a plot to overthrow the Austrian Government and replace it with a pro-Nazi one was hatched in collaboration with the German Embassy in Vienna. The intention was to replace by force the existing Chancellor of Austria, Dr Engelbert Dollfuss, with Anton von Rintelen, a member of the Austrian Diplomatic Corps and a strong Nazi adherent. The coup was uncovered by the Austrian frontier police when a German courier was found to be carrying documents – and, unwisely, the deciphering codes – which revealed the plan of revolt. For some unknown reason Dollfuss and his ministers took little notice of this apparently imminent threat to the independence of their country. Then, in the early hours of 25 July, the Nazis in Vienna mobilised, and shortly after midday an armed rebel party broke into the Chancellory and assassinated Dollfuss, whilst another detachment seized the broadcasting station and announced the resignation of the Dollfuss government and the formation of a new one under von Rintelen. The tactics were typically Hitlerian, but on this occasion they backfired. The President, Dr Miklas, ordered the restoration of order at all costs, appointing Dr Kurt von Schuschnigg to take over as Chancellor. With the Austrian army and police rallying to the new government, the rebellion was for the moment quelled.

Little deterred, Hitler proceeded to encourage armed Nazi supporters from the Austrian Legion* in Bavaria to cross the frontier to continue the rebellion. Mussolini, however, at this time distrustful of Hitler and his ultimate intentions, despatched three Italian divisions to the Brenner Pass and promised full military aid to his neighbour – he had no desire to see Hitler strutting up and down Italy's own northern frontier. With the almost-certain support of France for Italy's protective action, possibly with the moral support of Britain, Hitler hastily withdrew. As yet, he was in no position to risk war. He did not, however, give up hope of the unification of Germany and Austria; he accepted that he had to await a more propitious time and, to this end, he recalled the German officials who were implicated in the rising, including the German Ambassador, whom he replaced with Franz von Papen. The choice of von Papen was cunning. He was known to have escaped 'the night of the long knives' only by von Hindenburg's personal intervention, and might therefore reasonably be thought to be less in favour of the underhand Nazi tactics, and so more to be trusted by the Austrian administration. But his instructions were to prepare, with subtlety, the way for the eventual take-over of Austria, a task which he accepted willingly, for he was ambitious to rise again in the hierarchy of the German Reich, even if it had to be under Hitler.

On 1 August 1934, von Hindenburg died. On the 2nd, Hitler combined the offices of Chancellor and President under his personal leadership, and on that same day the German armed forces swore an oath of 'unconditional obedience' to him as their new Commander-in-Chief.

If the attempt to swallow Austria had failed this time, it was only a temporary failure. Moreover, this reverse to Hitler's fortunes was quickly to be offset by a success in the Saar. After the First World War, Germany had ceded the Saar coal mines to France under the terms of the Treaty of Versailles, with the Saar district being governed by an international commission of five members. After fifteen years, the inhabitants were to

---

* A group of Austrian Nazis who formed, in Bavaria, a rebel military organisation opposed to the Austrian government.

be given the opportunity to choose between continuation of the commission, union with France, or a return to union with Germany, the decision to be decided by a plebiscite or referendum, due to take place in January 1935 under arrangements conducted by the League of Nations. On 13 January, over 90 per cent of the population voted for reunion with the Fatherland, a vote which gave a tremendous boost to Hitler's popularity in Germany. The way ahead was now opening up greater opportunities for his ambitions, encouraging him to take even bolder steps towards creating his mighty Germany.

In March 1935, following the Saar plebiscite, Sir John Simon, the British Foreign Secretary, and Eden visited Germany for meetings with Hitler. Their purpose was to discuss with him control of armaments and possible pacts of mutual assistance, and to attempt to persuade him to return Germany to membership of the League of Nations. The talks took place at the Chancellor's Palace on 25 and 26 March, against the background of Göring's public announcement, on the 9th, of the official existence of the German Air Force, and Hitler's decree on the 16th introducing compulsory military service and proclaiming the organisation of the German Army on a peacetime basis of thirty-six divisions. Now Eden met a Hitler very different from the man he had visited just a year earlier, in February 1934 – this time the Führer was confident, cavalier and uncompromising. He made it abundantly clear that he would build the navy he needed, and would adhere to his programme of thirty-six divisions for Germany's regular army with a strength of 500,000 men; indeed, he intimated that such a force was more or less already in existence. Moreover, he insisted that he would continue with his paramilitary organisations, the SA and SS, but this time he was not prepared to discuss the question of whether they would be armed or not; instead he made a counter-accusation that there were paramilitary organisations in other countries receiving arms training – even in British public schools such as Eton, a reference to Officers' Training Corps (OTCs). In refusing to discuss any modifications to Germany's re-armament plans, he produced a diagram showing the strengths of his neighbours: France had forty-four divisions, Poland thirty-four, Russia a hundred and one. Then came the bombshell, a matter that was of the most serious consequence to Britain. Simon asked about the present strength of the German Air Force. Hitler replied that Germany had already reached parity with Great Britain, and that the Luftwaffe was continuing to expand.

The British, as an island race, had always regarded the separation from the continent of Europe provided by the English Channel as their first line of defence. With a powerful navy, that separation would protect Britain from the would-be aggressor and give her plenty of time to mobilise an army, should that become necessary. The First World War, in which the Germans used Zeppelins and aeroplanes to bomb London and other English towns, had radically changed this thinking. In 1935, the knowledge that Germany had a regular army of 500,000 men, against Britain's total military land forces of approximately 333,000 men (of which only 110,000 were home-based Regulars supported by a part-time Territorial Army of about 133,000, the remaining 90,000-odd being scattered around the Empire and Protectorates), was not what shocked the British. What did, however, was the realisation that Germany now had a powerful and growing air force which could bridge the Channel and bring the war home to the civilian population as never before. Indeed, Germany was better placed to bring air power to bear upon Britain than was Britain to retaliate. London and other towns were, as Churchill had emphasised in the past, far closer to possible German air bases than were Britain's airfields to Berlin and many important German cities. Moreover, if Germany swiftly moved a conquering army through Holland and Belgium, the operating bases for her air force would be on Britain's doorstep. Herein lay the grave concern at any parity of the Luftwaffe with the Royal Air Force, and thus it was air defences, and the ability to retaliate with an air offensive, that was now to become the obsession of those concerned with Britain's defence, very nearly to the exclusion of all other military requirements for the nation's security, with the possible exception of those for the Royal Navy.

While Hitler was adamant about re-armament, he insisted in his conversations with Simon and Eden that there was no threat to Britain. He went as far as to say that had he been Chancellor of Germany in 1914 there would certainly have been no war with England. His obsession was clear enough. It was with Russia. The illusion of a Jewish-Marxist alliance to control the world was the threat to Germany that dominated his mind and his thinking; but the threat, real or unreal, also masked his ultimate intention to expand eastwards, an eventuality which he had plainly stated in *Mein Kampf*. Eden was deeply concerned about the idea of letting Germany expand eastwards, for he feared that it would lead in turn to the annexation of the West, including Britain. He was, in fact, utterly opposed to letting Germany become too strong, in marked contrast to Lloyd George's comment in the House of Commons on 28 November 1934, during a debate on defence, when he warned against treating Germany 'as a pariah'. She had, the former Prime Minister asserted, been driven to her present attitude – 'driven into revolution' were his words – by the formidable re-armament of her neighbours. He went on to say that in a few years' time Britain could be looking towards Germany as a bulwark against Communism; 'If Germany broke down,' he stated, 'and was seized by the Communists, Europe would follow.' In

1935 Eden's fears could well have been realised; equally, Lloyd George's prophecy might yet come true.

Whatever the ultimate outcome would prove to be, the Simon-Eden meetings with Hitler created consternation in Britain, and it was not long before all the metaphorical alarm bells were ringing furiously in Whitehall, and disarmament was being relegated to the wastepaper basket.

CHAPTER IX

The Danger of War

The decision in 1934 to increase the strength of the Royal Air Force was certainly welcomed, but the manner in which the force was to be increased was open to question. For example, twenty-two of the forty-one bomber squadrons which it was planned should be in service by March 1939 were to be light bombers, and it was well known that these would be utterly useless for retaliatory attacks against an enemy, and certainly against Germany, now recognised as a potential belligerent. As has been said, the decision about the number of light bomber squadrons was not, however, that of the Air Ministry. Even so, the Chief of the Air Staff (CAS) was in a quandary, because existing bomber aircraft – light, medium or heavy – were in truth all 'light', hopelessly out of date, and quite inferior in range and bomb-load to those known to be coming into service with the German Air Force. The Heyford, Hart, Hind, Harrow and Wellesley bombers, all biplanes except for the last, were effectively obsolete, and by 1939 would be even more so. The modern twin-engined monoplanes, such as the Whitley, Hampden and Wellington, had been specified in 1932/1933, but they were far from being ready for production. Indeed, the first prototype of the Hampden, K4240, made its maiden flight on 22 June 1936, the first prototype of the Wellington, K4049, on 15 June, and that of the Whitley, K4586, on 17 March of the same year. A medium bomber known as the Blenheim, derived from a Bristol Aircraft Company transport design which first flew early in 1935, was ordered in September 1935 (although the prototype of the bomber version, K7033, did not perform its maiden flight until 25 June 1936), and in consequence the Blenheim was rather more advanced for production than the Armstrong-Whitworth Whitley, the Handley-Page Hampden, and the Vickers Wellington, all twin-engined monoplanes. Despite the timing laid down for the expansion of the Royal Air Force, the CAS, Ellington, was reluctant to permit that expansion to proceed at a pace which, while it would admittedly provide the numbers of aircraft set down by the politicians, would produce types, fighter and bomber, which would be unfit for modern warfare against an enemy equipped with advanced designs. Ellington's views prevailed. More than this, however, he was to be responsible for the initiation of plans for the development and construction of the four-engined bombers which were to become available in 1942, specifications of which were set down in 1936 by Group Captain A.T. Harris as Director of Plans, and Wing Commander R.H.M.S. Saundby of the Directorate of Operational Requirements.

As regards new designs of fighter aircraft, Sir Edward Ellington was more fortunate. The offspring of the Schneider Trophy success, the Hawker Hurricanes and Supermarine Spitfires, all-metal low-wing monoplanes equipped with 1,030-hp Rolls-Royce Merlin II engines and eight ·303-inch calibre guns mounted in the wing, were within sight. Sydney Camm's prototype Hurricane, K5083, undertook its first test flight at Brooklands on 6 November 1935, with P.W.S. Bulman at the controls. On 3 June 1936, an order was placed to cover production of 600 machines, and initial deliveries began on 15 December 1937, to No. 111 Fighter Squadron based at Northolt. R.J. Mitchell's prototype Spitfire, K5054, was first flight-tested on 5 March 1936 by Captain J. Summers. On 3 June 1936, at the same time as the order for the Hurricanes, a further order was placed for 300 Spitfires, the first deliveries being made to the RAF in June 1938, and to No. 19 Squadron at Duxford in August. Interestingly, No. 19 Squadron had been the recipient of the first deliveries, three years earlier, of the then latest fighter, a wooden, open cockpit, two-gun biplane called the Gloster Gauntlet. The speed with which the Hurricane and Spitfire were to proceed through the gestation period from drawing board to first prototype to initial production was remarkable, and the short cuts that were taken were largely thanks to Ellington, who foresaw the necessity, in the first instance, of simply surviving any possible enemy attack, in order to gain time for the provision of an adequate bomber force to undertake the retaliatory action essential to ultimate victory.

At the time of Britain's decision to abandon disarmament and to increase her arms, in particular her air force, Germany was already well ahead with plans for a colossal expansion of her air power. Even before the Eden and Simon meetings with Hitler at the end of March 1935, Germany had achieved a considerable strength in her air force, and many figures for numbers of German military aircraft were quoted by British politicians, members of the Diplomatic Corps, civil servants, and prominent civilians. These figures differed widely, from Churchill's estimate of between 800 and 900 aircraft to Lord Rothermere's alarmist 20,000, numbers which Churchill angrily deprecated in a letter to Rothermere as being: ' ... so fantastic that they simply deprive you of the enormous credit which otherwise would have been due to your foresight and vigilance.' 'Foresight and vigilance' was a reference to the repeated efforts of Rothermere's newspaper, the *Daily Mail*, to alert the British Government and public to the danger of Hitler's growing prestige in Germany, of his territorial ambitions, and of the increasing threat of German air power. Churchill, however, was always critical of overstatement, believing it to be the quickest method of destroying a good case.

Apart from Churchill's and Rothermere's estimates, there were others in 1934 and early 1935 which put German air strength at well below 800 first-line aircraft. The truth is that early in 1934 the Germans planned to have built, by 30 September 1935, 4,021 military aircraft for its reconstituted air force, of which 2,000 were at that time scheduled in detail. This 2,000 included 843 bombers, 51 dive-bombers, 271 fighters (of which 26 were to be naval fighters), 622 long- and short-range reconnaissance aircraft, and a number of other aircraft for naval duties. 1,000 of these had been delivered by the end of 1934, so that on the basis of Britain's official strength of 880 first-line aircraft for home, overseas, and Fleet Air Arm, Hitler's claim at his meetings with Eden and Simon that the Luftwaffe had reached parity with Britain was certainly correct. It is unlikely, however, that Germany's aim of building 4,021 aircraft by September 1935 was realised. According to military records at the Bundesarchiv at Freiburg, German air strength at the beginning of the Second World War in September 1939 was 4,093 first-line aircraft of all types, of which 3,646 were ready for immediate action. Even so, the German build-up in 1934 and 1935 began to leave Britain far behind in aircraft numbers. The timing of this build-up, however, meant that German types entering war at any date from 1939 to 1942 were often less up-to-date than those aircraft becoming available to Britain at the same time as a result of the delayed start in re-arming. By 1935, Britain's ability to defend herself against aggression was certainly balanced on a razor's edge, and Sir Edward Ellington's decision to re-equip the Royal Air Force at a pace which would give it the advantage of a highly modernised force by 1939–42, rather than large numbers of obsolete aircraft, was to be the vital factor in Britain's initial survival in the Second World War, and thus in the final victory of the Western Allies in Europe.

But much was to happen before war came again to Europe. Hitler's abortive attempt to annex Austria had resulted in a closer association between three old allies. Mussolini's action in offering immediate assistance to the Austrian Government had brought Italy back into the welcoming arms of France and Britain. The Italian leader, however, was not only anxious to safeguard Italy's frontiers against any future German threat; he was also hoping to be allowed a free hand with his ambitious plans for expansion in Africa. Well knowing that France and Britain required Italy as an ally in dealing with Germany by the application of 'collective security', Mussolini therefore believed that he might be left alone to resolve his North African problems, in particular his country's uneasy relations with Abyssinia, neighbour to Italy's two colonies of Eritrea and Somalia, where the frontiers were ill-defined and armed clashes were not infrequent. Abyssinia was a member of the League of Nations, her admission having been sponsored by Italy and France in 1923, despite, ironically, reservations on the part of Britain about the wisdom of such a move. The tyranny of the Abyssinian government, its acceptance of slavery as a part of the nation's mode of life, the constant tribal warfare that went on within its borders, and the general backwardness of the country, had caused Britain to feel that Abyssinia was not yet suitable for membership of the League. In fairness to Mussolini, it must be said that he did much to encourage friendly relations between Abyssinia and Italy, including the signing of a 'Treaty of Friendship and Arbitration' in 1928, which undertook to develop and promote trade between the two countries. But by 1934 incidents on the frontiers between Abyssinia and Eritrea and Somalia had become frequent, principally due to the historical lack of adequate demarcation between the territories involved. These incidents provided Mussolini with an excuse to establish his own ideas about frontiers. By 1935, Italy was extending into territory which Abyssinia claimed as her own, following a small confused battle between the Italians and the Abyssinians in December 1934, in a border oasis known as Walwal.

Mussolini's designs upon Abyssinia were not solely prompted by desire for territorial gain in order to expand his North African possessions. To a large extent his retention of power as the Fascist dictator of Italy depended upon prestige. The Italians had for a long time harboured a fury against Abyssinia for their humiliating defeat at Adowa nearly forty years earlier. At the end of the nineteenth century, Italy was attempting to build an empire in Africa comparable to those of the French and British. The death of the Abyssinian Emperor Yohannes IV in 1889 was followed by violent disorder and internal tribal warfare between factions contending for the succession. The Italians, who had already colonised Eritrea, supported Menelek of Shoa to win the throne from his rival and thus become King Menelek II of Abyssinia; in view of their assistance they tried to assume a protectorate over the whole country and, in effect, to incorporate Abyssinia within their African empire. Menelek was not prepared to accept this state of affairs, whereby the Italians were attempting to impose their control by military means, and by 1893 he was making ready for war. The early campaigns resulted in victories for the Italians but, on March 1896, they suffered a fearful rout at the Battle of Adowa, when their army of 20,000 men under General Oreste Baratieri was cut to pieces and driven into disorganised retreat by Menelek's forces of uncivilised warriors, who outnumbered the Italians by four to one. The Italians lost some 4,600 Europeans and 3,000 natives killed and wounded, and more than 2,500 prisoners; many of the latter were mercilessly and disgustingly mutilated. The result of this campaign was Italy's withdrawal of her claim to a protectorate over all Abyssinia, and the delimitation of her colony of Eritrea to a territory of about 80,000 square miles. The desire for revenge, however, lay strong in the heart of every Italian. As Churchill put it: 'They had seen how Britain had, after the passage of years, avenged both Khartoum and Majuba. To proclaim their manhood by avenging Adowa meant almost as much in Italy as the recovery of Alsace-Lorraine in France.'

To Mussolini, the act of subjugating Abyssinia and adding her to the Italian empire seemed to be an ideal way of consolidating his own power by redeeming Italy's honour after the mortification suffered in 1896. He calculated also that this could be done without risk of upsetting his relations with his former European allies; in that, however, he was wrong. After the Walwal incident, Abyssinia, as a member of the League of Nations, appealed for intervention against aggression by another member, supported, albeit half-heartedly, by France and by other members, pressed for the matter to be adjudicated by the League. Mussolini, however, conjectured that force would not be used to restrain him, and at first he doubted whether trade sanctions would be applied against Italy by League members. He was correct about force, but misjudged the matter of sanctions; in the event, however, sanctions proved ineffective. Despite all efforts of the League of Nations, in which Eden played a prominent part, Mussolini made it abundantly clear that Italy regarded the Abyssinian affair as an Italian matter which was hers and hers alone, and had nothing to do with the League of Nations. On the subject of sanctions, he said, 'Italy will meet them with discipline, with frugality, and with sacrifice,' but he was adamant that he would tolerate neither the imposition of any sanctions which interfered with a proposed invasion of Abyssinia, nor any attempt to debar him passage through the Mediterranean and the Suez Canal, threatening that if such actions were taken, then Italy would go to war with whoever stood in the way. Neither Britain nor France really wanted to risk war. Indeed, with the guidance of Britain, and under pressure exerted by Pierre Laval, the French Foreign Minister (and for seven months until January 1936, Prime Minister), the committee set up by the League of Nations to devise sanctions against Italy avoided any proposal to apply ones which might provoke war. The League's efforts to rescue Abyssinia were applied on the precept that nothing must be done to impede the progress of the aggressor.

The heaviest blow to Britain and France was, of course, the fact that the Abyssinian affair was throwing Italy into the arms of Hitler. Moreover, given the threat of Germany's increasing military power as opposed to the sadly depleted strength of British forces, Britain could not afford to go to war with anyone at this stage. Indeed, she was proving that a country without the teeth to support collective security could never influence or restrain a would-be aggressor.

On 28 September 1935, Churchill had a long talk with Count Grandi, the Italian Ambassador to Britain, in a private and desperate last effort to persuade him to try and prevent Mussolini from invading Abyssinia, although he had little faith in the effect that his conversation might have. In truth, Churchill was by no means happy about the Government's handling of the Abyssinian problem, and was secretly critical of its denunciations of Italian policy. He believed that the crisis was diverting attention away from the real danger facing Britain, and that it was against Germany that all of Britain's energies should be directed. On 1 October, in a reply to a letter from Sir Austen Chamberlain,* he wrote:

> I am glad that you agree with the line I took about Abyssinia, but I am very unhappy. It would be a terrible deed to smash up Italy, and it will cost us dear. How strange it is that after all these years of begging France to make it up with Italy, we are now forcing her to choose between Italy and ourselves.

This was a reference to the French attitude that the League should not interfere in the dispute between Italy and Abyssinia, believing it to be a kind of domestic matter for Italy alone. This view had been vigorously contested by Britain. Churchill went on to say:

> I do not think we ought to have taken the lead in such a vehement way. If we had felt so strongly on the subject we should have warned Mussolini two months before. The sensible course would have been gradually to strengthen the Fleet in the Mediterranean, during the early summer, and so let him see how grave the matter was.

* The half-brother of Neville Chamberlain, and a former Foreign Secretary from 1924-9.

The Conservative Party Conference of 1935 opened at Bournemouth on 4 October, the same day that Mussolini launched his campaign against Abyssinia with a heavy aerial bombing attack upon Adowa. This attack probably had no effect on the vitally important Resolution that was passed at the Conference, but if there had been any Conservatives who still wavered on the subject of re-armament, it certainly removed their doubts about the wisdom of strengthening Britain's military forces, for the Resolution received unanimous support. It read:

1. To repair the serious deficiencies in the Defence Forces of the Crown and, in particular, first to organise our industry for speedy conversion to defence purposes, if need be.
2. To make a renewed effort to establish equality in the air with the strongest foreign force within striking distance of our shores.
3. To rebuild the British Fleet and strengthen the Royal Navy, so as to safeguard our food and livelihood and preserve the coherence of the British Empire.

On 14 November there was a General Election at which Stanley Baldwin (who had replaced Ramsay MacDonald as head of the coalition government on 7 June) presented to the country, in strong terms, the need for re-armament. He also drew attention to the firm stand the Government had taken over the Italian invasion of Abyssinia by supporting sanctions through the League of Nations. At the same time, however, he was careful to hold out a hand of conciliation to those who feared aggressive re-armament, assuring them that it was only the defence of the country, and the ability to support collective security through the League, with which he was concerned. Indeed, just two weeks before polling day he made a speech at the Guildhall to what was known as the Peace Society, in which he made this significant statement: 'I give you my word there will be no great armaments.' It was a comment which he must have known he could not stand by in the light of the now-evident German preparations for aggression in Europe. On the other hand, he was almost certainly aware that the return of a Labour Government would result in the swift and nearly total disarmament of Britain, a state in which she would lie helplessly vulnerable to oppression. Baldwin therefore played the political game as best he could in order to win the substantial Conservative majority needed to support a better preparedness of Britain's defences. In the event, his ploy worked well, getting the best of both sides; the result of the General Election was a triumph for Baldwin, his party winning 432 seats against 154 for Labour, 21 for the Liberals, 4 for Independent Labour, 1 for the Communists, and 4 others, thus giving the Conservatives a clear majority over all other parties of 248.

Having won the election with a handsome majority, Baldwin set about re-armament cautiously, at the same time adopting the principle that peace must be preserved at any price, at any rate until Britain could face a foe with confidence. The first situation which needed to be defused was the Italian-Abyssinian conflict. It was Britain who had been mainly responsible for leading the League of Nations against Mussolini's invasion of Abyssinia, an action which had proved totally ineffective and which had led Italy to look towards Germany as a possible friend rather than a potential foe. This could obviously lead to the disruption of the Franco-Italian agreement, signed at the beginning of 1935, and of the military terms which were a part of this agreement. The military convention with Italy meant that eighteen French divisions could be spared from the French-Italian frontier and transferred to the German frontier. In the circumstances, the French had always remained lukewarm about confronting Italy over Abyssinia, particularly when the only military aid Britain could offer if Germany moved against France was two paltry divisions at the outset of hostilities. Moreover, when it had come to the crunch, Britain had failed to exercise her naval power in the Mediterranean by closing the Suez Canal and preparing to battle with the Italian fleet if the need had arisen. Consequently, France was anxious to mend the breach in Franco-Italian relations. Britain, for her part, was now also concerned to halt the deterioration in her relations with Italy, but at the same time to lose as little face as possible. There resulted, in December 1935, a proposal known as the Hoare-Laval Pact, by which Abyssinia should cede approximately one-fifth of her empire to the Italians in exchange for peace. When these proposals were made known to the House of Commons, the Cabinet having approved them on 9 December, the same day that they were put to the League of Nations, there was considerable disgust that such a dishonourable compromise should ever have been suggested. Sir Samuel Hoare, who in June had succeeded Sir John Simon as Foreign Secretary when Baldwin had taken over as Prime Minister from MacDonald, was bitterly attacked for allowing such a morally unacceptable solution to be adopted, and the Cabinet was forced to abandon the proposals on 18 December. Baldwin then apologised to the House for allowing the Hoare-Laval Pact to be approved by the Cabinet in the first place. Hoare, as the scapegoat, resigned, and on 22 December Anthony Eden was appointed Foreign Secretary.

Relations with Italy now deteriorated even further. Britain had committed herself to opposing Italy over Abyssinia, dragging a reluctant France along with her, but had not been prepared to confront Italy firmly and with force. Then, too late, she had tried, with France, to be conciliatory. In fact, from the point of view of European politics, Italy should either have been left alone to continue her plans for Abyssinia, or military force should have been used to restrain her. Instead, nothing was done, and Britain and France lost an important ally, while the Italians went ahead unchecked in Abyssinia. By May of 1936, after a campaign in which the bombing of civilian populations and the use of poison gas against the armies of the Emperor Haile Selassie had played their parts, Abyssinia finally collapsed. On 1 May, the Emperor abdicated and received a safe escort under British protection from the besieged capital, Addis Ababa, which was now largely ruins. On 9 May, Victor Emmanuel III, by the Grace of God and Benito Mussolini King of Italy, became Emperor of Ethiopia.

Hitler, having helped Mussolini all he could by ignoring sanctions, now established a relationship of friendship with Italy which was soon to grow into a powerful alliance. Britain and France, by indecisive measures against Italy through the League of Nations, lost their partner of the First World War, and the Franco-Italian agreement of January 1935 became a worthless piece of paper. On 7 March 1936, even before the collapse of Abyssinia, Hitler had taken advantage of the preoccupation of France and Britain with Mussolini's African adventure. Claiming that France was attempting to encircle Germany, and that his country therefore required a fortified Rhineland for security, he marched into the demilitarised zone, making as much noise as possible for home publicity purposes; orders to retreat if necessary were, however, in the pockets of the German military commanders involved. By this action, Hitler delivered a last hefty blow to the 'shameful dictate' of Versailles, as he described the Peace Treaty, and in addition he had broken Germany's word, given voluntarily under the Treaty of Locarno, that the Rhineland, although relieved of the presence of the Allied Armies of Occupation, should remain free of any German military presence. Somewhat to his surprise (although he had been encouraged by Mussolini's successful African exploits, which had proceeded without real interference), his military re-occupation of the zone was completed without any practical reaction on the part of Britain and France. There was, admittedly, a great outcry among the French, who wanted to mobilise and drive Hitler out of the Rhineland, but Britain persuaded her ally to stay her hand and to put the case to the already discredited League of Nations. The exhortations of Flandin, the French Foreign Minister who had replaced Laval when Albert Sarraut had become Prime Minister in January 1936, that Britain and France should simultaneously mobilise all land, sea, and air forces, and order Hitler out of the zone, fell on deaf ears. Pacifist Britain wanted to take any course short of confrontation, and so nothing was done – much discussion, endless protests, but no marching. '*Herrgott*', Hitler declared, 'am I glad it went off so smoothly. Yes, the world belongs to the man with courage!' To the Germans, it was clear that the Führer knew how to deal with the weak, vacillating nations of Britain and France. To the Italians, Mussolini had proved himself the leader who would make their nation and empire the pride of the world.

The danger of a European war had come even closer, because Britain, in particular, had attempted to control the militaristic aspirations of Germany and Italy without the physical power to support her high moral purpose and her desire for peace.

From all of these international problems Churchill had been excluded. He had held no ministerial post since 1929, and, although expecting an appointment after the November 1935 General Election (indeed, he was hoping for the Admiralty), he was yet again left in the wilderness – to the consternation of many and the delight of a few. But his exclusion was probably to Britain's benefit in the long run, for increasingly he became the man whom all trusted for the very reason that he had been forced to remain aloof from the inept handling of Britain's defences and foreign relations, except as a backbencher throwing out warnings, time and time again, of the growing threat of Germany to peace. It was his single-mindedness about German intentions, and therefore about the necessity for Britain to prepare herself for what might prove to be an inevitable war, that made him a number of powerful enemies both in and behind the political scene.

In ironical contrast, Stanley Baldwin wrote of his own decision to exclude Churchill from the Government in these words: 'I feel we should not give him a post at this stage. Anything he undertakes he puts his heart and soul into. If there is going to be war – and no one can say that there is not – we must keep him fresh to be our war Prime Minister.'

CHAPTER X

Britain Prepares

Late in July 1935, there occurred a number of events which were to have an important bearing upon the survival of Britain in the coming war. Robert Watson-Watt was a scientist, who, as early as the beginning of the 1920s, had conducted some successful research into methods of locating thunderstorms by the transmission and reflection of radio waves, and who had then perfected his system in order to measure movements of the ionised layer around the earth, the object being to determine related weather patterns and the effect of the movements of the layer on wireless reception. He had put forward the opinion that aircraft could be detected in a similar manner. His theory was both simple and infallible. It depended upon the principle of transmitted radio waves being reflected back by objects, such as aircraft and ships, struck by the radio waves, the echoes being received at the source of the transmission. Since the speed of travel of radio waves is the same as that of light, 186,000 miles per second, and therefore known, the distance of an aircraft could, he postulated, be measured by timing the period between the moment of despatch of the outgoing transmission and its return to source after striking the aeroplane or other object and being 'bounced' back. In addition, since radio waves, again like light, travel in straight lines, the direction of a target object from the source of transmission could be calculated and, therefore, its position, direction of movement and speed could be constantly monitored. This, clearly, was an important discovery if the theory could be proved in practice, since it meant that a hostile air attack could be detected ahead of its arrival and defending fighters could be despatched directly from their bases to a point of interception before the enemy aircraft reached the shores of Britain.

The Air Ministry gave instant backing for expenditure to enable Watson-Watt to conduct experiments to prove his theories, and Lord Londonderry, the Secretary of State for Air, approved the formation of a steering committee under Sir Henry Tizard, Rector of the Imperial College of Science and Technology, and with H.E. Wimperis, Director of Scientific Research at the Air Ministry, Professor A.V. Hill and Professor P.M.S. Blackett as members, with A.P. Rowe as secretary. This committee held its first meeting on 28 January 1935, but in July was re-formed under the Committee of Imperial Defence as the Air Defence Research Sub-Committee, its composition remaining the same. However, Sir Philip Cunliffe-Lister (created Viscount Swinton in that year), who had been appointed Secretary of State for Air when Baldwin took over as Prime Minister from Ramsay MacDonald at the beginning of June, induced Baldwin to persuade Churchill to become a member of the Sub-Committee. The latter agreed to the proposal, subject to Professor Frederick Lindemann, later Lord Cherwell, being invited to join as well; Churchill had for many years depended upon the Professor's aid in matters of science and technology. Lindemann, affectionately known as 'the Prof', was Professor of Experimental Philosophy at Oxford University and during the First World War had distinguished himself in the field of aerodynamics, in particular by conducting a number of experiments in the air to discover the cause of the 'spin' – a major hazard in the early days of flying – and to find ways and means of reducing the problem. Churchill attended his first meeting of the Air Defence Research Sub-Committee on 25 July, when Tizard reported that Watson-Watt's experiments for detecting aircraft had reached a successful stage and were producing results that warranted the construction of a chain of stations. The Sub-Committee recommended such a course of action, and RDF – radio reflection-direction-finding, later known as radar – had thus come of age. In addition, the Sub-Committee advocated the acquisition of Bawdsey Manor in Suffolk, where Watson-Watt conducted many of his experiments, as the centre for research work on RDF, and in December the Treasury granted authority for the building of four RDF stations for the defence of Britain, and for the purchase of Bawdsey Manor. By March 1936 the first chain of stations was being erected along the south coast, and in July 1937 there was a complete review by the Air Defence Research Sub-Committee of the new RDF defence system, which resulted in approval for the expenditure necessary to construct and install, by 1939, a chain of twenty stations providing coverage from west of the Isle of Wight to north of the Tees. The money involved was estimated as being somewhat in excess of £1,000,000.

It was Churchill's presence on the Air Defence Research Sub-Committee which supplied the impatient push to get things done quickly, and ensured that the attention of ministers was drawn to any delays which he considered unwarrantable, while Lindemann's fertile brain put forward many ideas for consideration, stimulating the thinking of the Sub-Committee. A number of Lindemann's proposals were not entirely practicable, however, and sometimes Churchill's pressure for faster progress was unreasonable, endangering sound research into, and the development of, those projects which held high promise of success and which fitted in with the defence tactic being developed by the Air Staff. It was Tizard who, in very difficult circumstances, kept the balance effectively, and thus ensured that this remarkable team of scientists worked together in reasonable harmony, despite the inborn individualism, laced with intolerance of other people's opinions and ideas, which is so often the major characteristic of this breed – a characteristic from which, incongruously, stems scientific genius. Nevertheless, friction between Tizard and Lindemann became acute when the Sub-Committee failed to give sufficient priority to many of the ideas put forward by 'the Prof', ideas which Tizard and the other members regarded as being of no real value. Among Lindemann's suggestions was a scheme to encircle London and other major cities with a curtain of aerial mines suspended by balloons, into which the enemy would fly to their destruction; another plan was to drop the mines from aeroplanes by parachute, into the path of the attacking hordes. In the Committee's view such tactics were unlikely to be effective. The operating heights of German bombers could well be above the heights at which the balloons could suspend the mines, and the parachuted mines could more than probably be by-passed. Low-flying attacks might be deterred, but there was no evidence that these would constitute Germany's bombing strategy; certainly low flying had not been the method employed in 1917. Tizard and his supporters preferred to give priority to the RDF chain, to the problems of identification of friend or foe on the RDF screens and, in conjunction with the Air Staff, to the tactics of interception by fighters of bomber formations 'sighted' by RDF. The solution to this last problem involved a comprehensive system of communications to a central operations room, linking that room to the RDF stations, the fighter bases, and the intercepting squadrons in the air. Furthermore, in the event of night attacks which, it was thought, would almost certainly form a part of the enemy bombing campaign, it was essential not only to develop techniques of directing the fighters by RDF on to the hostile bombers, but also to investigate the possibilities of airborne forms of RDF which would enable the fighter to 'see' his target in the dark.

In the end, the friction between Tizard and Lindemann became so intense that, on 5 July 1936, Tizard told Lord Swinton that he would resign from the Sub-Committee unless Lindemann was removed, and a few days later duly did resign. Lindemann, however, was dropped on 2 November, and Tizard returned to the Chairmanship. In fact, Tizard and his supporters, and the Air Staff, were to be proved correct in what they saw as the priorities for air defence methods, and Churchill later magnanimously recognised their achievements. The weakness of the Sub-Committee, however, was that it was not charged at this stage with the task of examining ideas and scientific methods that would enable bombers to navigate to, locate, and accurately bomb their targets at night. It had been accepted that the retaliatory offensive required to support the defence of Britain would have to be undertaken mostly under cover of darkness, and although night-bombers were being designed for the purpose, insufficient attention was being given to the navigational aids they would need if they were to succeed. RDF was not yet being considered for offensive action.

For the British, 1936 was unquestionably a year of mixed national experience. On 20 January, King George V died at Sandringham, and his body was brought to London to lie in state at Westminster Abbey, before being taken by train to Windsor Castle for burial on the 28th. The spectacle at Paddington Station when the coffin left for Windsor was a most impressive one. Lining the platform, in front of the Royal Coach and the special coach into which the coffin was placed for its last journey, were guards of honour from the three Services. Marching in the funeral procession were the Kings of Norway, Denmark, Rumania, Bulgaria and Belgium; there too were Lebrun, the President of France; the Crown Princes of Sweden, Norway, Italy, Egypt, and Greece; Prince Paul, Regent of Yugoslavia; Baron von Neurath, the German Foreign Minister; Litvinov, the Russian Foreign Minister; Norman Davis, the American Ambassador-at-Large, as well as military representatives from those countries who were soon to be Britain's allies or enemies. Queen Mary and the other ladies of the Royal Family followed in horse-drawn carriages. By the time the funeral procession had reached Paddington, some of the more elderly marchers had been reduced to a shuffle, and had looked distinctly the worse for wear. The Prince of Wales, now King Edward VIII, had marched immediately behind the gun-carriage upon which the coffin was borne, and which was drawn by Bluejackets of the Royal Navy; with him were his brothers, the Dukes of York, Gloucester and Kent.

Sadly, the reign of Edward VIII was to be short-lived, due to his determination to marry an American divorcee, Mrs Wallis Simpson. Having succeeded his father on 20 January 1936, he signed a Deed of

Abdication on Thursday, 10 December of the same year, having reigned for under a year. His brother, Albert Frederick Arthur, Duke of York, succeeded him, becoming King George VI. It was an extraordinary event in world history, and a sombre moment in the history of Britain, but the idea of a King of the United Kingdom marrying a divorcee had proved totally unacceptable not only to the British government and people, but also to those of the Dominions.

On 3 March 1936, the first signs of official plans to increase Britain's military power were made visible when the Government issued a new Defence White Paper, which declared that the country's defences were to be reviewed in the light of 'the present state of the world'. The White Paper also stated that provisions were to be made both for adequate home defence, and for joint international action abroad within the framework of the League of Nations. Two new battleships and a new aircraft-carrier were to be laid down, the Army was to be increased by four battalions, and the Air Force was to be increased by 250 aircraft to a first-line strength of 1,750 for home defence. Munitions factories were to be extended, and industry was to be organised for rapid conversion to war production as and when required. It was on 7 March, just four days later, that Hitler ordered German troops into the Rhineland, and it was only two days after that shaking event that the House of Commons debated the Defence White Paper. Clement Attlee, for the Labour Party, moved the rejection of the Government's proposals because they were 'bellicose'. Churchill, in contrast, praised the White Paper as a step in the right direction, even if it was somewhat late in the day, and he also praised a decision by Neville Chamberlain, the Chancellor of the Exchequer, to set up a financial committee charged with ensuring that the money to be granted for increases to the armed services was spent effectively. In voicing his support, however, he added:

> When things are left so late as this, no high economy is possible. That is part of the price nations pay for being caught short. All the more must every effort be made to prevent actual waste ... it will not be possible for us to overtake Germany and achieve air parity, as was so solemnly promised, unless Germany herself decides to slow down or arrest her air expansion. Clearly a saturation point would be reached when Germany will have created as great an air power as she thinks wise, having regard to other demands upon her warlike energies. If then we continue our development, we shall ultimately achieve air parity. But this day will be fixed by Germany and not by us, whatever we do. Let us, however, see what we are doing. There is a general impression that we are overhauling Germany now. We started late but we are making up for lost time, and every month our relative position

will improve. That is a delusion. The contrary is true. All this year and probably for many months next year Germany will be outstripping us more and more. Even if our new programmes are punctually executed, we shall be relatively much worse off at the end of this year than we are now, in spite of our utmost exertions. The explanation of this grievous fact lies in the past.

Churchill's strictures over the past few years against the Government's slow and inadequate measures to provide the country with a military preparedness effective enough to discourage any power from making war against Britain, and his repeated warnings about the growing belligerence of Germany under Hitler, had been loyally supported by men such as Sir Austen Chamberlain, Lord Winterton, Sir Robert Vansittart of the Foreign Office, Brendan Bracken, Robert Boothby, and more recently by Anthony Eden, the Foreign Secretary since the Hoare-Loval Pact débâcle of 1935. During 1936, however, a number of Churchill's closest friends tried to dissuade him from pointing the finger at Germany and declaring that country to be the inevitable enemy in a future war. Amongst these were Lord Rothermere of the *Daily Mail*, who previously had backed Churchill ardently from outside the House; the Duke of Westminster; the retired General Sir Ian Hamilton, who had commanded the Expeditionary Forces at Gallipoli in 1915; and the Marquess of Londonderry, one of Churchill's cousins. All had become impressed by Hitler and his regime. Lord Londonderry, who had been Secretary of State for Air from 1931-5 and who was now Lord Privy Seal and Leader of the House of Lords, had visited Germany early in the year, and had been granted a two-hour interview with Hitler in Berlin. He tried hard to persuade Churchill 'to consider the German situation from a different angle'. He believed that Germany could not risk a war for at least four years, and urged that it was Britain's duty to do everything in her power to create a situation in which war could be eliminated, or at least postponed for a number of years. While agreeing that Churchill had been largely responsible for changing the Government's attitude towards Britain's defences, resulting rightly in re-armament, Lord Londonderry said in a letter to Churchill, dated 4 May:

I am bound to say, however, that I regret what I may call the 'defeatist' attitude of this country in assuming that nothing can be done to avert hostilities between this country and Germany. When I saw Hitler in the course of a two hours' interview he spoke chiefly of the Communistic menace and I found myself in agreement with a great deal of what he said ... We in this country, owing to the fact that Communism is non-existent, take the view that Germany is exaggerating the Communistic danger, but I am quite sure that they are doing nothing of the kind ...

Churchill replied that he did not take the view that war between Britain and Germany was inevitable. What he feared was that unless something happened to the Nazi regime there would be a devastating war in Europe, which could well come earlier than people thought.

> The only chance of stopping it [he wrote] is to have a union of nations, all well armed and bound to defend each other, and thus confront the Nazi aggression with overwhelming force. In this way there is the best chance that an internal revolution rather than an external explosion may avert an ever growing danger.

A Cabinet Meeting on 11 March, following the German military occupation of the Rhineland on the 7th, discussed a French request to Britain to act in concert with her, and through the League of Nations, to force the German armed forces to withdraw from the demilitarised zone. Baldwin was firmly against taking any action which involved confrontation with Hitler. Indeed, Cabinet papers show that he believed that at some stage it would be necessary to warn the French that their proposals – that Britain and France should mobilise and order Germany out of the Rhineland – would not only bring about another major European war, but the crushing of Germany could result in that country 'going Bolshevik'. Anthony Eden was of a different opinion, however, and at the meeting expressed his view, similar to that of the French and Belgians, that 'if Germany is allowed to remain unmolested in military occupation of the Rhineland, war in two years' time is a certainty and will be fought under very unfavourable conditions ...' In fact, as has already been mentioned, nothing was done, and Eden was proved more or less accurate in his forecast. But at least the Government was shocked into a more aggressive approach to re-armament, and the public at large began to suspect the worst from Hitler, all of which helped the Services to plan ahead more effectively.

By the middle of 1936, Spitfires and Hurricanes, the latest high-speed fighters, had been ordered, and the modern bombers – Whitleys, Wellingtons, Hampdens and Blenheims – were well advanced in their prototype trials, and had also been ordered for production. Then, on 15 July, Air Ministry Specification B12/36 was promulgated, calling for a high-performance heavy bomber, equipped with four engines. Such an aircraft was to be capable of a speed of not less than 230 mph at 15,000 feet on two-thirds power, a minimum range of 1,500 miles and a maximum of not less than 3,000 miles, a minimum ceiling of 28,000 feet with a 2,000-pound bomb load, and a maximum bomb load of 14,000 pounds ($6\frac{1}{4}$ tons). There was to be a crew of six, comprising two pilots, one observer, two air-gunners, and a wireless operator.

On 18 September, Specification P13/36 was issued, seeking to provide a twin-engined medium bomber with a minimum crew of four, consisting of two pilots, a wireless operator, and a gunner; since however, it was later stipulated that the aircraft should be armed with two gun-turrets, one mounted in the nose with two guns and one in the tail with four guns, it was expected that it would in fact have a crew of five. The minimum bomb load was to be 8,000 lbs. The Short Stirling eventually resulted from B12/36 but, oddly enough, it was Specification P13/36 – aimed at producing a *twin*-engined bomber – which ultimately produced the four-engined Avro Lancaster,* the greatest bomber of the war, having an exceptionally high performance that in most respects exceeded the maximum called for in B12/36. It was closely seconded by the four-engined Handley-Page Halifax. Of these four-engined types, only the Stirling was to be available for service before the beginning of 1942, but what was satisfactory about the issue of the Specifications was that, after years of shameful neglect, the strength of Britain's future bomber force was being given greater attention and some priority.

On 26 October 1936, the Joint Planning Sub-Committee of the Chiefs of Staff Committee of the Committee of Imperial Defence produced its 'Appreciation of the Situation in the Event of War Against Germany in 1939', a remarkable document which might well be described as both a warning and a proposal for more effective planning. Two years earlier, on 9 October 1934, the Chiefs of Staff had decided that it was necessary, in considering defence preparations, to contemplate the possibility of war with Germany, and on 2 November of that same year a paper was prepared on this principle, entitled 'Defence Plans for the Event of War Against Germany: Provisional Report'. This paper was subsequently revised several times, the fourth and last version being submitted to the Chiefs of Staff on 31 October 1935. The new 'Appreciation' of 1936 was to have been an up-dating of the previous papers, but in fact it became a very different document, based as it was on the radically changed military situation in Europe.

The authors of this far-sighted Appreciation, which proved to be a very accurate forecast of the course of the Second World War and the means by which victory could be attained, were Captain T.S.V. Phillips, RN,†

---

* The Lancaster derived from the twin-engined Avro Manchester, designed to meet Specification P13/36 but never in fact put into production. Similarly, the Halifax was a re-engined version of Handley-Page's twin-engine design for the same Specification.

† Later Vice-Admiral Sir Tom Phillips, KCB, who went down with HMS *Prince of Wales* when she was sunk, with HMS *Repulse*, by Japanese bombers off the Malayan coast on 10 December 1941.

representing the Naval Staff, Colonel R. Forbes Adam* for the Army, and Group Captain A.T. Harris†, representing the Air Staff. The assumptions that the Chiefs of Staff had laid down were that Allied forces might have to be employed towards the end of 1939 against a Germany which was in an advanced state of war preparedness, and that war would arise from German aggression. It was also assumed that the machinery which then existed for the peaceful settlement of international disputes would not, in 1939, be able to restrict Germany's military action in any way. In their examination of the probable line-up of powers, the three authors took the pragmatic view that self-interest would determine the attitudes of the chief world powers towards war between Britain and Germany. They forecast that in the first stage of war arising from a German attack on France and Belgium, the most probable belligerents would be France, Belgium and Britain against Germany, and in the less likely event of a German attack against Britain alone, the line-up would be the same, although this would depend upon France and Belgium having effective governments with sufficient determination to oppose German aggression. It was assumed that Holland would remain neutral, as she had in the First World War, unless German troops attempted to move into and through her territory. Notwithstanding the Franco-Russian Pact of May 1935, which guaranteed mutual assistance in the face of aggression against either signatory over a period of five years, it was considered that no reliance could be placed upon Russian intervention. Nevertheless, it was felt that Germany would feel it necessary to be prepared for active Russian hostility at short notice. Italy was expected to be sympathetic to Germany, but it was hoped that she would remain neutral on the premise that the preoccupation of Britain and France with Germany would leave her free to pursue her policy in Africa. As long as neither Russia nor Italy intervened, it seemed possible that the remaining European countries would remain neutral, but it was believed that Russia would inevitably become involved, and that therefore the whole of Europe would most probably be caught up in the war. The authors also counted upon the assistance of most of Britain's Dominions, and of India, and stated their belief that Japan would pursue her ambitions in the Far East, and that the USA would remain neutral. In these assessments they were, in the event, largely correct. It was only Japan's unprecedented attack upon Pearl Harbor on 7 December 1941, without a declaration of war, that upset the apple cart and brought

* Later General Sir Ronald Forbes Adam, Bt, GCB, OBE.
† Later Air Chief Marshal Sir Arthur Harris, KCB, OBE, AFC, Commander-in-Chief Royal Air Force, Bomber Command, from February 1942 to the end of the war in 1945. Awarded the GCB and promoted Marshal of the Royal Air Force, 1 January 1946. Created a Baronet for his war services on 1 January 1953, on the recommendation of Winston Churchill.

America into the war on the side of the Western Allies, and Japan into the war on the side of Germany. Italy, too, did not meet the authors' expectations, joining the war on Germany's side on 10 June 1940.

In their preface to the comparison of military forces available, the authors of the Appreciation made some significant remarks about the problems that would beset a democracy mobilising for war. They emphasised that the forces a nation employed in war were no longer limited to the fighting services, but now included the whole industrial resources, manpower and morale of the people, and the capacity to wage war now depended upon the efficiency of a nation's preparations in regard to those matters. In the past, it had been after the outbreak of war that industry had been adapted and expanded to meet war requirements, and manpower organised for the conflict. But, they wrote:

> In Germany as in other totalitarian States, these processes are now being perfected in time of peace. The dragooning of the populace and their submission to economic hardship to a degree previously only associated with war time, or acceptable under war conditions, is being enforced during the peace period preceding the actual campaign. Relief from this discipline and these hardships is only sought or expected as the reward of a successful outcome of war. The German people can be made to submit to this system under the stern discipline of their totalitarian regime, but in no way does democracy lend itself to the experiment. The specialised mass production of the mechanised weapons essential to success in modern warfare, as much for defence as for aggression itself, can only be attained, and the personnel trained to man them, by a vast national effort over a period of years. The problem which this country has to face is how to prepare an equivalent war potential under the democratic conditions which prevail within the British Empire.

In forecasting naval strength as it would be at the end of 1939, the Appreciation took into account the Anglo-German Agreement of June 1935, under which it was agreed that the strength of the German Navy should not exceed 35 per cent of that of the British Fleet in each category of ships, except for submarines, which by transference of tonnage from other categories could be increased to 45 per cent of the submarine tonnage maintained by the British Empire. The Appreciation also noted Germany's declared intention to achieve that ratio of 35 per cent by the end of 1942, and her intention to complete by the end of 1939 one new 35,000-ton capital ship, three 8-inch cruisers, one aircraft-carrier, sixteen destroyers and forty submarines, in addition to the two battle-cruisers of 26,000 tons, *Scharnhorst* and *Gneisenau*, and one 6-inch cruiser already under construction. From this starting point, and with the detailed knowledge of existing British and French strengths and planned increases, the authors produced their forecast. Even neglecting France's contribution, the comparison of naval forces was in Britain's favour, and in order to give a more comprehensive picture of the general situation the estimated naval forces of Japan and Italy were included. The table read as follows:

FORECAST OF FLEET STRENGTHS AT END OF 1939

	British Empire	France	Franco-British Total	Germany	Japan	Italy
Battleships	12	7	19	1	9	5
Battle-cruisers	3	2	5	2	–	–
Armoured ships	–	–	–	3	–	–
Aircraft-carriers	8	1	9	1	6	–
8-in. cruisers	15	7	22	3	12	17
6-in. cruisers	50	12	62	8	23	12
Contre torpilleurs	–	36	36	–	–	–
Large destroyers	142	39	181	28	90	51
Small destroyers	–	19	19	12	30	49
Submarines	60	86	146	66	64	80
Motor Torpedo Boats	24	9	33	17	3	200

The comparison of army forces, assuming that the chief alliance against Germany would comprise Britain, France and Belgium, showed a reasonable balance, the main Allied strength deriving from the French Army. It was reckoned that during the first three or four days Germany would have about thirty-six infantry and three mobile divisions, while the mobilised Allied troops would consist of frontier and fortress (Maginot Line) troops equivalent to only four divisions, although, owing to the strength of the fortifications, these troops were of higher defensive value. It was estimated, however, that under favourable circumstances the Allies could reach equality with the German armed forces by the end of the first week of war. Then, after the third week, the authors believed the Allies might have a slight superiority which, after four to six months, might increase to as much as a proportion of three to two, based mainly on the estimated French mobilisation rate of reserves and the addition of colonial divisions brought in from abroad, to bring the French Army strength up to three fortress divisions, five mobile divisions and forty-eight infantry divisions. After six months these infantry divisions were expected to number fifty-six, and with the addition of twelve infantry divisions and one mobile from Britain by that time, with twelve infantry and three mobile divisions from Belgium, the German estimated figure of fifty-six infantry and five mobile divisions mobilised thirty days after the outbreak of hostilities would be outmatched. But the authors had some doubts about France's industrial capability to sustain her rate of mobilisation and, at the same time, they felt that Germany could conceivably exceed the estimates outlined in the Appreciation:

> Although even in the worst case, the German superiority appears but slight and would, to some extent, be offset by the fact that to gain success the Germans must assume the offensive, yet this superiority would be enhanced by their unity in opposition to three separate Allies and by their possession of the most modern equipment and of war reserves far exceeding those of their opponents. Their superiority might therefore be sufficient to expose the Allied cause on land to considerable danger.

With Allied naval forces definitely outmatching those of Germany, and the land forces apparently reasonably well balanced, the question mark hung over the air forces. France had already announced her intention of building up to a metropolitan air force of 2,000 first-line aircraft by 1938/9, but Group Captain Harris (who was principally responsible for the 'air' part of the Appreciation) was of the opinion that the French aircraft industry was in a state of chaos, an opinion well supported by evidence. The Appreciation therefore took the line that France would have great difficulty in achieving her aim of 2,000 first-line aircraft even by the end of 1939; moreover, it was agreed that, at best, she would not achieve more than 50 per cent reserves, which was utterly inadequate to support such a first-line strength in war. In Germany, Hitler had already stated that he would maintain air parity with France, so the assumption was made that Germany would build up to a first-line strength of 2,000 aircraft. The members of the committee believed that fear of Russia would in fact cause Germany to exceed this figure substantially, but even so they felt that the best Germany could achieve by 1939 was 2,500 first-line aircraft, backed by 100 per cent reserves. Since all reports and information current at that time indicated that the German aircraft industry was exceptionally well organised, was already changing over to war production, and was being dispersed to reduce its vulnerability to attack, Germany's ability to reach such figures was not held in doubt.

When the Appreciation was being prepared, the strength of the Royal Air Force was barely 1,000 first-line aircraft. The authors therefore planned for an absolutely essential build-up to 2,204 first-line aircraft by 1939, of which 1,736 would be metropolitan aircraft, the remainder being for service in Britain's overseas territories, the total figure being backed by 200 per cent reserves. Of the Metropolitan Force, 420 aircraft were to be fighters and 990 were to be bombers, this being in line with the bomber strength put forward earlier in 1936 by Harris, as Deputy Director of Plans at the Air Ministry, and which had been approved by the Air Staff.

It was considered that, of Germany's 2,500 aircraft, 1,700 would be first-line bombers and 270 would be fighters, the rest being for other duties. France's air force of 2,000 aircraft was planned to include 755 bombers and 500 fighters, so that her bombers combined with Britain's would constitute a force of 1,745 aircraft. The general opinion of the authors of the Appreciation, however, was that France would fail in her air re-armament programme, and that her bomber force would not mature. In fact Phillips, Forbes Adam and Harris displayed a grave lack of confidence in France's ability to wage war against Germany, and in the event they were more than justified. This lack of confidence is very much evidenced in their consideration of Germany's likely strategy at the outset of war. Under the heading 'Germany's Choice of Initial Objective' the authors became positively prophetic:

> By concentrating her main offensive against France, Germany would be able to employ her army and her air force, in co-operation, with a single object. Germany might well consider that her best prospect of breaking through the French fortifications might occur during the first few weeks, when her attacks would have the advantage of initiative and surprise. A rapid success against France might give Germany control of Holland, Belgium and Northern France and so place her in a strategical position from which she might hope to dominate the United Kingdom. An offensive against France would be popular in Germany, where France is regarded as the hereditary enemy rather than Great Britain.

Nonetheless, the Appreciation also considered Germany's alternative, that of directing her initial strategy against Britain. This, it was pointed out, would mean that Germany could employ only her naval and air forces in offensive action, and would have to use her army mainly in a defensive role to protect her frontiers with France and Belgium, a situation which would be very unpopular in Germany. The vulnerability of Britain to air attack was, however, so apparent that it was felt that the possibility of the Germans concentrating on this form of attack at the outset could not be lightly dismissed. Germany, the authors averred:

> realises the extent to which the power of the British effort can develop as the war progresses, and, by attacking us at the outset with the advantage of the initiative, she might hope for decisive success before

our country could be organised for war. If such an offensive were postponed, Germany could hardly hope to obtain such great results.

Given that Britain could achieve a strength of 1,736 first-line metropolitan aircraft, of which 420 would be fighters, it was assumed that the air attacks would be contained, and that German losses would prove to be a powerful deterrent as well as having a cumulative effect upon the morale of pilots.

The question of a counter-offensive in the air was also considered, although it was only a whisper compared to the space given to the defence necessary for Britain's survival. It did emphasise, however, the necessity for the Allied air forces to destroy the enemy's war potential by bombing, prior to the ultimate defeat of Germany by a land offensive.

Ironically, while Britain was preparing for a war with Germany, Hitler had become, after his success in the Rhineland, scornful of France, the 'inexorable and mortal enemy of the German people'. He began to believe that he could neutralise France bloodlessly by the systematic disruption of her position in Central and South-Eastern Europe. The Abyssinian war and the intervention of Germany and Italy in the Spanish Civil War, which broke out in July 1936, brought the relationship between Germany and Italy much closer, a closeness which, by Hitler's reckoning, posed the first major threat to France. The supreme irony, however, lay in Hitler's long-held belief in the possibility of an alliance with Britain. Compared with the re-armament of the German Army and the Luftwaffe, he had deliberately neglected the German Navy in the hopes of securing from Britain a favourable attitude towards Germany. He seemed confident, moreover, that Britain would grant him a free hand in Central and Eastern Europe because, he reasoned, she feared Communism more than she feared Germany. In the latter half of 1936 he sent Joachim von Ribbentrop to London as German Ambassador, charging him with the express instruction: 'Bring me the British alliance!'

CHAPTER XI

After Spain What Next?

Since 14 April 1931, when, following Municipal Elections, King Alfonso XIII of Spain had been deposed and a Socialist Republic proclaimed in place of the monarchy, there had been an increasing degeneration of parliamentary rule in that country. The growing strength of the Communists, backed surreptitiously by Soviet Russia, led to a series of insurrections aimed at the ultimate conversion of Spain to Communist-domination. The Communists had consistently followed Marxist-Leninist doctrine, aiding all movements which leaned towards the Left, and helping into office weak constitutional socialist governments which they would be able to undermine, and so seize power for themselves. There was still a strong Monarchist faction in Spain, however, and while the Communists were plotting the overthrow of the country's existing democracy, a secret military counter-plot was being developed, its aim being to set up a Government of the Right. In January 1932 there was a widespread Communist uprising in Catalonia, which the Government army quickly suppressed. Then, in August of the same year, there was a Monarchist rebellion in Madrid, which was also promptly put down by the army. In January 1933, there was renewed left-wing rioting all over the country, in which attacks on churches featured heavily. This was immediately followed by the discovery of a left-wing plot aimed at overthrowing the Republican Government. Many Communists were arrested when the plot came to light, but the episode was counterbalanced by the arrests, in July 1933, of large numbers of Monarchists, Fascists, and church clerics throughout Spain. These had also been plotting against the Republican Government with the intention of overthrowing it, and putting into power a regime which, once and for all, would crush Communist attempts to take over the country and bring it under the domination of Soviet Russia. The last of this 'ding-dong' series of uprisings occurred in October 1934 (by which time the Socialist Government had been replaced by that of the Centre-Right), when there was a major left-wing revolt in Catalonia, at its most serious in Asturias, which resulted in Communist extremists gaining control of a large part of the north of Spain. It was a number of days before the army was able to suppress this revolt.

In February 1936, the 'Government of the Popular Front', essentially left-wing, succeeded that of the Centre-Right Party. Matters swiftly came to a head, however, when the Communists* came into open confrontation with the Monarchists and the military, the Republican Government having become the target for both of these factions, neither of which, in truth, had any legal or moral right to govern the country. Unfortunately, civilised behaviour had already been despoiled by the perverted excesses of the Communists, who now indulged in the practice of seizing their political opponents in the streets or dragging them from their beds, and of murdering them indiscriminately and bestially. Retaliation inevitably took place, these assassinations by both sides being most numerous in and around Madrid. The climax was reached with the murder of Señor Calvo Sotelo, a staunch Monarchist and the leading figure amongst the opponents of the Government. On 16 June 1936, after details of the most recent outrages perpetrated by the Communists had been reported in the Cortes (the Spanish parliament), Sotelo spoke out boldly against the behaviour of these left-wing extremists, demanding stern action by the Government to restore proper democratic conduct to the politics of Spain. He was immediately screamed at by a wild woman Communist member of the Cortes, known as 'La Pasionaria', who shouted: 'That is your last speech!' A month later, on the night of 13/14 July, Sotelo was assassinated by Communist gunmen.

Within five days, on 18 July, the Republican Government was fighting the beginnings of a revolt led by General Francisco Franco, the commander of the Spanish garrison in the Canary Islands, a revolt which was to grow into the Spanish Civil War. The military had finally become tired of the provocative tactics of the Communists, and of their increasing influence over the Government, and had decided to act by attempting a military coup. Franco quickly gained control in the Canaries and then flew at once to Spanish Morocco, where he also drew the army to his support. By the end of July, with the bulk of the Spanish

* The Republican 'Popular Front' was virtually a coalition, being made up of a group of parties and trade unions: Republican Left, Republican Union, Socialists, Communists, Trotskyites, Anarchists and Syndicalists.

Army behind him, including the rank and file, and with the blessing of the Church and nearly all the elements of the Right and Centre in Spain, Franco was on the mainland fighting the Government, which had by now come under the complete control of the Communists. The Spanish Civil War had begun. Within weeks it was to become the testing ground for the weapons and military prowess of Germany and Italy championing Franco, and of Soviet Russia shoring up the Communists.

Hitler and Stalin were greatly concerned with the outcome of this war, and in that concern there was much self-interest; indeed the outcome affected the future strategy that would follow from their aspirations. The primary object of Hitler's designs was increased territory in Eastern Europe for the expansion of the great German race's *Lebensraum* – 'living space'. This territory included not only Czechoslovakia, which he regarded as being essentially a natural part of Germany, but also a deep penetration into Russia, 'the giant country in the east ripe for collapse', as he described the Soviet Union. His aggressive intentions in this direction were not only inspired by the desire for land expansion, but also by his belief that Communism would be an eternal enemy unless crushed once and for all. Russia was the cradle of Communism and the breeding ground for international Communism, and as such she was a menace to German national security – and, Hitler frequently avowed, to European freedom. Therefore she had to be eliminated. Besides Russia, France, the traditional enemy, must be crushed as well, in revenge for the humiliation she had brought upon Germany as a result of the First World War. Hitler's plans for the ultimate annexation of Austria into the Third Reich would obviously be assisted by his new friendship with Mussolini, but more than this, with Italy in alliance with Germany (a situation which Hitler was now confident of achieving), France would be forced to man her frontier with Italy with army divisions which could otherwise be spared for the Franco-German frontier. If only General Franco could gain control of Spain, if necessary with the help of Germany and Italy, and install a strong right-wing government, or even a military dictatorship, then France would also have to protect her southern frontier with Spain, thus pinning down more divisions. On the other hand, and in the light of the Franco-Soviet Pact of May 1935, a success for the Communists in Spain would be enormously to the advantage of Soviet Russia and France, a fact which Stalin well knew. Such a victory would free France from worries about her frontiers with Spain, and the more France could threaten Germany, the weaker Germany must become on her eastern frontier with Russia. In fact, Stalin felt no concern for the Spanish people or, for that matter, for the Spanish Communists, any more than Hitler had any love for Franco and his supporters. It was the advantage that would be gained indirectly by Germany if Franco won, or by Russia if the Communists were victorious, that stimulated the two countries' active interest in the outcome of the battle for power in Spain.

Germany and Italy overtly rushed aid to Franco, admittedly at the latter's request. The Soviet Union had for a long time been providing surreptitious succour to the Spanish Communists by way of funds, and now provided even more money and materials, to which were added troops and pilots, all of them described as 'only a small number of technicians'. By December 1936 both Germany and Russia were accusing each other of intervention in another country's affairs. Von Ribbentrop, the German Ambassador to Britain, accused Russia of already having 50,000 men in Spain. Ivan Maisky, the Soviet Ambassador in London, denied that the number of his countrymen approached anything near this figure, and counter-accused Germany of planning to send 60,000 fully trained troops to help Franco, quite apart from contingents that were to be sent by Italy.

In *Mein Kampf*, Hitler had published his intentions with regard to Soviet Russia, and unquestionably the book had been read as avidly in the Soviet Union as it had in other countries of Europe. No doubt Stalin had taken due note of the threat to Eastern Europe posed by the Führer, just as many politicians in England, including Baldwin, had heeded Hitler's aggressive plans for German expansion. It is unlikely, however, that Stalin's sentiments on the subject were the same as Baldwin's. At the end of July 1936, speaking of Hitler, Baldwin made this statement: 'None of us know what goes on in that strange man's mind ... We all know the German desire, and he has come out with it in his book, to move east, and if he should move east I should not break my heart ... I do not believe he wants to move west ...' He concluded by saying:

I am not going to get this country into war with anybody for the League of Nations or anybody else or for anything else. There is one danger, of course, which has probably been in all your minds – supposing the Russians and Germans got fighting and the French went in as the allies of Russia owing to that appalling pact they made [a reference to the Franco-Soviet Pact of mutual assistance in the event of either country being attacked, signed in May 1935] you would not feel you were obliged to go and help France, would you? If there is any fighting in Europe to be done, I should like to see the Bolshies and the Nazis doing it.

These feelings were echoed by a large section of the country, both amongst officialdom and the general population. There were, however, those who perhaps shared the wish that Germany and Soviet Russia should knock each other out, but who felt that in reality it would be Germany which would overwhelm Russia, and thus become so powerful that the rest of Europe would have to bow to Nazi dominance. Churchill was one such. In the matter of the Spanish quarrel he was neutral; 'How could I be otherwise,' he stated, 'when if I had been a Spaniard they would have murdered me and my family and my friends?' – a reference to the Communists. He was, however, utterly opposed to British intervention in the Spanish Civil War for another reason besides his inborn hatred of dictators, be they from the Left or Right. The British Government, he considered, had enough on its hands preparing the country's defences in readiness for what he believed would be the real threat to Western democracy – the unbridled aggression of Nazism. Churchill was also opposed to Britain's support for the French proposal that there should be a Non-Intervention Agreement between France, Britain, Soviet Russia, Germany, Italy and Portugal, whereby the signatories should deny both sides in the Spanish Civil War all military aid, whether in the form of military equipment or troops, and should leave the opponents to fight it out without any external assistance. Churchill felt that it would be more equitable to recognise the belligerence of both sides, as had been the case with the American Civil War of 1861-65. He was convinced that, whatever agreements were signed, Franco would get all the military aid he needed from Germany and Italy, whereas the Spanish Government, even though it was in the hands of Communists and would therefore receive whatever aid Russia could supply from such a considerable distance, would have a fairer chance if it was not deprived of the right to purchase arms for which it had the money to pay. Nevertheless, the policy of non-intervention was adopted in the end, and a Non-Intervention Committee was formed, holding its first meeting, in London, on 9 September, attended by twenty-six European countries, including Russia, Germany, Italy, France and Great Britain. The Agreement was strictly observed by the British Government, but Germany and Italy on the one side, and Russia on the other, broke their pledges from the very beginning, throwing their weight into the Spanish Civil War, and thus effectively against each other. The French Government under Léon Blum, which had succeeded the Flandin administration in May, came under pressure from the Communists in the Chamber of Deputies to support the Spanish Republican forces, weakening in the process the strength of the already decaying French Air Force.

The French action drew from Churchill a purely personal note to Charles Corbin, the French Ambassador to Britain:

One of the greatest difficulties I meet with in trying to hold on to the old position is the German talk that the anti-Communist countries should stand together. I am sure if France sent aeroplanes, etc., to the present Madrid Government, and the Germans and Italians pushed in from the other angle, the dominant forces here would be pleased with Germany and Italy, and estranged from France. I hope you will not mind my writing this, which I do of course entirely on my own account. I do not like to hear people talking of England, Germany and Italy forming up against European Communism. It is too easy to be good. I am sure that an absolutely rigid neutrality with the strongest protest against any breach of it is the only correct and safe course at the present time. A day may come, if there is a stalemate, when the League of Nations may intervene to wind up the horrors. But even that is very doubtful.

Germany did not, in fact, send as many troops to Spain as has been suggested by different sources; the truth is that the Spanish Civil War was principally a testing-ground for the Luftwaffe. There it gained combat experience which could never have been acquired by theoretical instruction or tactical exercises. Its first task, when General Franco appealed for military assistance from Germany, was to ferry Moroccan soldiers and Spanish Legionnaires from Spanish Morocco, troops which would provide the initial military forces for action on the mainland. Hitler had immediately consented to the operation and had placed the necessary air transport capacity at Franco's disposal, and by 28 July 1936 the first flight by a Junkers Ju52 aircraft of the Luftwaffe had ferried twenty-two Moroccan soldiers from Tetuan to Jerez de la Frontera, near Seville, the first air transport operation in the history of German military aviation. All in all, the initial twenty Ju52s made available to Franco, complete with ground- and air-crews, ferried 13,523 troops and 570,000 pounds of war material, including 36 field guns and 127 machine-guns, from Morocco to Spain. On 1 August, eighty-six personnel, together with six Heinkel He51 fighters and twenty anti-aircraft guns for the protection and support of this airlift, left Germany on the SS *Usaramo*, posing as tourists booked by a fictitious travel company named the Union Travel Agency. The *Usaramo* successfully breached the blockade around Spanish waters and disembarked its 'passengers' and cargo at Cadiz on the night of 5/6 August. A special staff was established for the Luftwaffe in Spain under the code letter 'W', and this Spanish Mission was placed, interestingly, under the control of Generalleutnant Wilberg, who as a Hauptmann at the end of the First World War had been on the Air Staff under General Hans von Seeckt, and who had later been primarily responsible for the secret training of the illicit German air force based at Lipezk in Russia. On 14 August, the Luftwaffe contingent in Spain, soon to be known as the Legion Kondor, undertook its first bombing mission, when a Ju52 attacked the Republican battleship *Jaime I*, which was put out of action by two direct hits from 1,500 feet. Then, on the 21st, a consignment of food supplies was dropped on the beleaguered city of Alcazar in Toledo, where the cadets of the Military Academy of Alcazar were holding out against Republican forces with the utmost tenacity. They were soon to be relieved by Franco's troops, fighting their way up from the south and leaving a trail of vengeance behind them in every Communist village, town or other centre.

In November, a further contingent of 4,500 Luftwaffe 'volunteers' sailed for Spain from Swinemunde and Stettin, this time with twenty Junkers Ju52 bombers, fourteen Heinkel He51 fighters, six Heinkel He45 reconnaissance aircraft, one Heinkel He59 and one Heinkel He60 coastal aircraft, to form the Legion Kondor. Later, ten more Ju52 bombers were added to the force, with twelve He70 and a few more He45 reconnaissance aircraft, and nine He59 and a few He60 coastal aircraft. In addition, the He51 fighter strength was brought up to three squadrons. Generalmajor Sperrle was appointed Commander-in-Chief, with Oberstleutnant Wolfram, Freiherr von Richthofen, a cousin of the famous First War fighter ace,* as his Chief of Staff. By 1937, the Germans had found that the He70s did not come up to expectations either as reconnaissance aircraft or light bombers, and they were replaced by He111s and Dornier Do17s. Furthermore, the He51s had proved to be no match for the Russian fighters used by the Republicans, many of which were flown by Russian pilots. The Heinkels had therefore been replaced with the new Messerschmitt Bf109B-2, a superb low-wing monoplane fighter designed by Willi Messerschmitt, which quickly won, and held, complete mastery of the air for Franco's Nationalist forces for the duration of the Civil War. The Me109s were later to become a scourge for the British and French air forces of 1939 and 1940.

In November 1936, von Richthofen was promoted Generalmajor and took command of the Legion Kondor, serving as its last Commander-in-Chief until the Spanish Civil War came to an end with the victory of Franco's forces over the Communists and Republicans on 1 April 1939. When von Richthofen took command, the Legion Kondor had at its disposal forty He111s, forty-five Me109s, five Do17s, five He45s, eight He59s, and three Ju87B-1s; these last, known as Stukas, were the latest German dive-bombers and had been sent to Spain expressly for bombing trials under operational conditions. And in addition to the Luftwaffe strength, the Italians had 134 aircraft operating in support of

* Rittmeister Manfred, Freiherr von Richthofen, who was the highest-scoring pilot, from any side, in the First World War, with 81 Allied aircraft shot down and confirmed. He was killed in action on 21 April 1918, although argument still rages today over whether he was brought down by aircraft or ground fire. Among members of his Jasta (squadron) during the 1914-18 war were Hermann Göring and Ernst Udet.

Franco by the last months of the war. The total Luftwaffe losses in Spain amounted to ninety-six aircraft, of which only about forty were due to enemy action. From August 1936 until April 1939, Spain had indeed been the proving ground for Hitler's new German Air Force, a conflict in which such aircraft as the He111s, Do17s, Me109s and Ju87 dive-bombers were tested, with their crews, under rigorous operational conditions. All were now ready for war on the direct behalf of Germany as soon as Hitler should name the date and point the finger at each victim blatantly listed in *Mein Kampf*, warnings ignored so pathetically by Britain for so long.

Once the Spanish Civil War had ended, a team of experts led by Generalmajor von Richthofen, assisted by a young Luftwaffe officer, Adolf Galland,* set up a special headquarters staff for the task of working out guide-lines for the organisation, training, and operation of ground-attack formations, based on the experience gained in Spain. What had happened in Spain was to form the blueprint for the Blitzkriegs to come.

In that extraordinary year of 1936, it seemed that many British politicians, of all persuasions, were anxious to find excuses for Hitler's every move. Their reasons were mixed, but were in part based upon fear of Communism, recognition of the weakness of Britain's defences, and apprehension at the reaction of the British electorate to the massive expenditure on re-armament necessary to face any foreign confrontation. Britain was fast rising from the despondency of the days of the 'Great Depression', and was moving into a period of prosperity. No one wanted that prosperity to be placed in jeopardy by going to war, for whatever reason, and the face of Britain was, therefore, for the most part set against military expansion at a level which would make serious inroads into the economy, increasing taxation and, possibly, encouraging aggression against Britain because such re-armament might be construed as bellicose. Even Lloyd George could find it in his heart to pay homage to Hitler, having visited the Führer at Berchtesgaden on 4 and 5 September. At these meetings he had agreed with Hitler that a Communist victory in Spain would constitute a serious danger to the peace and freedom of Europe; indeed, after the meeting on the 5th, Lloyd George had described his host as 'the greatest German of the age', who had restored Germany's honour and made the entire world recognise her 'equality of rights'. It was little wonder, therefore, that Hitler felt confident of Britain's ultimate alliance with Germany, the alliance which he had

* Galland became a high-scoring fighter pilot of the Second World War, and a Luftwaffe general.

instructed von Ribbentrop to negotiate when the latter had been sent as German Ambassador to Britain in August 1936. During 1937, von Ribbentrop made a number of soundings on the possibilities of such an alliance, and approached Churchill, inviting him to the German Embassy for a discussion on Anglo-German relations. Churchill held no Ministerial position at this time, but von Ribbentrop well understood the influence that he still wielded in Parliament and in the country, and he therefore recognised that the British politician could be an important factor in procuring Anglo-German rapprochement, if his support could be won.

Churchill later described his visit to von Ribbentrop: 'He received me in the large upstairs room at the German Embassy. We had a conversation lasting for more than two hours.' The gist of von Ribbentrop's discussion was to the effect that Germany sought the friendship of England with all sincerity. He told Churchill that he could have been Foreign Minister of Germany, but that he had asked Hitler to let him come over to London in order to make the full case for an Anglo-German entente, or even alliance. Whilst Germany might ask for the return of her colonies, ceded after the First World War, this would not be central to any agreement; what was required, however, was that Britain should give Germany a free hand in Eastern Europe. Germany must have her *Lebensraum* for her increasing population, and to this end Poland and the Danzig Corridor must be absorbed, while White Russia and the Ukraine must also be enshrined within the confines of the new and growing Nazi state. In return for Britain's non-interference in Hitler's affairs in Eastern Europe, Germany would be prepared to 'stand guard for the British Empire in all its greatness and extent', whenever that should be necessary. It was an astonishing proposition. In describing the interview, Churchill wrote:

> After hearing all this I said at once that I was sure the British Government would not agree to give Germany a free hand in Eastern Europe. It was true we were on bad terms with Soviet Russia and that we hated Communism as much as Hitler did, but he might be sure that even if France were safeguarded, Britain would never disinterest herself in the fortunes of the Continent to an extent which would enable Germany to gain domination of Central and Eastern Europe. We were actually standing before the map when I said this. Ribbentrop turned abruptly away. He then said: 'In that case, war is inevitable. There is no way out. The Führer is resolved. Nothing will stop him and nothing will stop us.' We then returned to our chairs.

In October 1937, von Ribbentrop tried hard to persuade Anthony Eden of the dangers of Europe presented by Soviet Russia and the spread of

International Communism, and of the need for Britain and Germany to stand together to combat this threat to Europe's liberty. Again he urged that Germany should be left alone to deal with Eastern Europe, but his advocacy was to no avail. Eden, like Churchill, disliked the prospect of a Nazi domination of Europe as much as he disliked the idea of a tyrannical Communist rule.

On 28 May 1937, Neville Chamberlain had become Prime Minister in place of Baldwin, who had retired because of ill-health. Chamberlain, formerly Chancellor of the Exchequer, was convinced that it was his personal duty to re-establish friendly relations with Italy, and to effect an amicable rapport with Germany. Europe's peace must be maintained at almost any cost, and he was determined from the very beginning of his administration to come to terms with Mussolini and Hitler. In July he invited Count Grandi, the Italian Ambassador, to Downing Street to discuss Abyssinia and Italy's intervention in Spain, but while he advised Eden, his Foreign Secretary, of his intention to discuss the matter, he did not ask him to be present. It is almost certain that Chamberlain did not agree with Eden's past foreign policy, under Baldwin's leadership, of opposing the dictators, any more than Eden approved of Chamberlain's readiness to recognise the Italian conquest of Abyssinia as a prelude to improving Anglo-Italian relations, or of his willingness to offer colonial concessions to Hitler in order to establish some form of friendship with Germany. Furthermore, Chamberlain was anxious to play down re-armament and to avoid any conspicuous collaboration with France in military and political affairs. He was desperately concerned to reduce tension, because he was a true pacifist at heart and, like so many pacifists in an imperfect world, blind to the dangers of weakness in a nation, and incapable of realising that strength is an essential buttress to great moral purpose and that, together, strength and purpose have the best chance of maintaining peace. In fairness to Neville Chamberlain, however, it must be said that he was probably aware of the continuing weakness of Britain's defences in 1937, in comparison with the growing power of Germany, and may well have been prepared to continue with his policy of appeasement in order to gain time for a build-up of Britain's strength.

By contrast, Anthony Eden was convinced that any arrangement with Italy must be part of a general settlement in the Mediterranean, including withdrawal from intervention in Spain, and he also felt strongly that such an agreement must be reached in close accord with France. To throw away a bargaining counter such as Abyssinia as a prelude to settling Anglo-Italian differences was, in Eden's view, unwise, and he was quite opposed to Chamberlain's wish to come to terms with Hitler. Eden was convinced that nothing short of a free hand to interfere in Central and Eastern Europe would satisfy Hitler and, even then, any Anglo-German agreement would not be worth the paper it was written on, unless Britain was strong enough to enforce the terms of such an agreement and to ensure that Germany did not interfere in the rest of Europe. And Britain had not that strength. In fact, Eden was utterly against doing any deals with the dictators, as was Churchill and his small but growing band of supporters. He was, however, in favour of greatly increased priorities for Britain's re-armament in order to be strong enough to dissuade, or at least discourage, the dictators from risking war by their greed. His attitude led Chamberlain to believe that the Foreign Office was obstructing his attempts to discuss with Germany and Italy proposals to bring about harmony between the three countries. On the other hand, Chamberlain's known desire to negotiate and appease encouraged Hitler to be confident that an Anglo-German alliance could be achieved, an alliance which he could ultimately dominate. At worst, he felt that Britain would not cross swords with him if he moved against Central and Eastern Europe. Adolf Hitler came to believe that Central and Eastern Europe could be swallowed into the German Reich with very little opposition, to be followed by the rest of Europe.

No doubt it was just this situation which encouraged von Ribbentrop to take his soundings from Churchill and Eden in the second half of 1937. Although thoroughly discouraged by the reactions of these two powerful influences in Britain, and finding it difficult to understand why Chamberlain, as Prime Minister, could not, like the Führer, say 'it shall be done' and thereby have it done, von Ribbentrop did not give up hope. His next move was to invite Lord Halifax who, as Lord President of the Council in Chamberlain's Government, was known to have the Prime Minister's ear, to visit the International Sporting Exhibition in Berlin in November. This invitation came from Göring, as sponsor for the German Hunting Association, and was addressed to Halifax as a Master of Foxhounds in England. Chamberlain agreed that he should accept, particularly as the British Ambassador to Germany had advised that it was the intention that Lord Halifax should meet Hitler whilst in Berlin. In fact, Hitler stayed in Berchtesgaden during the Exhibition, and Halifax had to proceed there for his meeting with the Führer. Danzig, Austria and Czechoslovakia were the main subjects for discussion. Hitler had always regarded Austria as a legitimate target for incorporation into Germany; the neighbouring country was, in his view, German. The other two areas, Danzig and Czechoslovakia, were the subjects of Hitler's strong and emotional reaction to the Versailles Peace Treaty, a reaction that was not entirely without reason. After the First World War, a 'corridor' dividing East Prussia from the rest of Germany had been created to provide Poland with an outlet to the Baltic Sea, the city of Danzig, at the north end of the corridor, being declared a Free City and

Port under the administration of a League of Nations Commissioner. Hitler viewed such a solution as an indefensible injustice which had to be remedied. In 1933 the city senate of Danzig had come under control of the local Nazi party, but the Versailles Treaty and League of Nations provisions remained, and the Danzig Corridor was still, in 1937, a reality. The arrangement was, to say the least, clumsy and to all Germans, particularly those separated by the Corridor, totally abhorrent. In Hitler's eyes, however, the provisions made by the Versailles Treaty for the Sudetenland were even less tenable than those made for Danzig. This highly industrialised strip of former Austrian territory (Northern Bohemia), containing three and a quarter million Germans, had been annexed in 1919, under the Versailles Treaty, to the new State of Czechoslovakia, a state which had been carved out of the old Austro-Hungarian Empire by the Treaties of St Germain (1919) and Trianon (1920).* The Allied intention, enshrined in the Versailles Treaty, was that the Sudetenland strip should form a topographically defensive frontier between Germany and Czechoslovakia, since it lay to the east of mountains forming a natural strategic barrier between the two countries. Hitler had clearly announced in *Mein Kampf* his ultimate intention of re-incorporating the Sudeten Germans, and the land in which they lived, into the German Reich, although that population had never been a part of Germany. In his conversations with Halifax, however, he had made assurances that a German settlement with Austria and Czechoslovakia could be reached peaceably. The agreement between Austria and Germany, signed on 11 July 1936, by which Germany agreed to refrain from giving active support to the banned Austrian National-Socialist (Nazi) movement, and from attempting to influence in any way the internal affairs of Austria, had, Hitler said, led to the removal of all differences between the two countries. As regards Czechoslovakia, it was only required that she should treat the Germans living in the Sudetenland fairly and well, in which case friendly relations could be maintained. Halifax, in turn, expressed the hope that his talks with the Führer might be followed up by direct Anglo-German negotiations, to which Hitler replied with the hope that Britain and Germany might at least be able to retreat from the atmosphere of 'imminent catastrophe' arising from the activities of an excitable and malevolent press. According to Halifax, Hitler remarked: 'Of course, if you believed the newspapers, you would expect to wake up one day to see German armed forces in Vienna or Prague.'

* The Treaty of Versailles (28 June 1919) provided for the Allied settlement with Germany after the First World War. Separate treaties, of St Germain (10 September 1919) and of Trianon (4 June 1920) dealt with the settlements with Austria and Hungary respectively.

To some extent impressed by Hitler's assurances, and having learned a little of German intentions, Lord Halifax returned to London on 22 November to report on his talks.

There was considerable irony in Hitler's witticism about newspapers and waking up to find troops in Vienna or Prague. On 5 November 1937, before his meeting with Halifax, Hitler had called together his Foreign and War Ministers, the Commanders-in-Chief of the three Services, and a number of other high officials, to lecture them on Germany's future plans. He had emphasised the German lack of 'living space', and had outlined the actions necessary to ease the position. The problem could only be resolved by force, and timing was crucial. In order to take advantage of the maximum state of German re-armament as then planned, it was essential, he had said, to strike eastwards against Russia between 1943 and 1945, perhaps earlier. But, in any event, the first move necessary to improve Germany's strategic position would be the invasion and 'crushing' of Austria and Czechoslovakia, which must be done in 1938, the first stage, in the case of Czechoslovakia, being the occupation of Sudetenland.

Although everything which Hitler had outlined in this exposé of his plans had already been enunciated in *Mein Kampf*, and should have been known and expected by his followers, there were a few of his audience on that afternoon who had been so appalled at his proposals that they had voiced strong objections. Amongst them were Field-Marshal Werner von Blomberg, War Minister and Commander-in-Chief of the Armed Forces, General Werner von Fritsch, Commander-in-Chief of the Army, and the Foreign Minister, Baron Konstantin von Neurath. Three months later to a day, these three had been dismissed from their posts. Von Neurath was partially spared by being appointed to the nebulous post of President of the 'Cabinet Privy Council', which never met. Von Fritsch was accused of being homosexual and therefore no longer fit to command the Army. Von Blomberg was found to be unfit to remain as War Minister and C-in-C of the Armed Forces because it had been discovered that his newly wedded wife was an ex-prostitute. Hitler himself took command of the Armed Forces and the Ministry of Defence, and appointed Field-Marshal Walther von Brauchitsch as C-in-C of the Army, while von Neurath was replaced with von Ribbentrop, who was recalled from London to take up his new post.

Now Hitler prepared for the moment when the world would wake up and discover that the newspapers were, after all, to be believed.

CHAPTER XII

Peace With Honour?

During 1937, Churchill and his followers kept up their pressure to speed the increase in the RAF's strength, and this pressure continued into and throughout 1938. Schemes of expansion followed one another at frequent intervals, each scheme being replaced by a fresh one before it could be implemented. New squadrons were formed, although these were mostly numbers on paper; moreover, squadrons that were up to strength were for the most part equipped with obsolete aircraft. By the end of 1937, however, the new Hurricane fighters were beginning to trickle through, followed by the Spitfires, the first of which were delivered in August 1938. The numbers were still pitifully small, but it was a start. The modern bombers, too, began to flow; the Blenheims and Whitleys coming into service in March 1937, the Hampdens in September 1938, and the Wellingtons in October 1938. Set against this, however, was the knowledge that the Luftwaffe was outstripping the Royal Air Force, and was variously estimated to be as much as two to three times larger in terms of first-line aircraft. In addition, the intervention in the Spanish Civil War was revealing the quality of Germany's modern bombers and fighters.

On the face of it, a German offensive in 1938 could well have resulted in the invasion and defeat of Britain. There was an urgent need therefore to give first priority to Britain's Fighter Command, to include proper gun-power for the new fighters and the completion of Watson-Watt's chain of Radar Stations which, with the Hurricanes and Spitfires, could provide powerful opposition to the enemy bomber formations that were expected to be used against British towns – against London and the South

Coast towns in particular. Indeed, it was estimated that the new fighters could, with radar guidance and their eight machine-guns,* successfully take on odds of more than two to one. In fact, numbers were not the only consideration; as the Air Staff well knew, quality of performance of both aircraft and pilots, linked with radar, could minimise the importance of an enemy's superior strength. Which was not to say that equality in numbers with the Germans was not desirable – it was, so long as the other considerations were not forgotten. The same arguments applied to bombers. The measurements that critics of the bomber force's size should have been examining were bomb-load capacity and the armament required for protection against enemy fighter defence. The Air Staff had recognised these factors, as well as the need for navigational aids, since German targets would be at such a great distance that, because of the absence of suitable escort fighters for daylight operations, night-bombing would be the only viable way of conducting a bomber offensive. The bomb-carrying capacity had been taken care of in the case of the new Whitleys, Hampdens and Wellingtons, which outclassed the three principal German bombers in this respect (although the Hampden's 4,000-pound capacity was slightly less than that of the He111), and even greater bomb capacity was to become available with the four-engined Stirlings, Halifaxes and Lancasters. Admittedly, these four-engined bombers were not expected to be in service until 1941/1942, but each type, when to hand, would have the equivalent in lift of three to four German bombers. Their defence had also been well planned, with power-operated gun-turrets included in nose and tail – a deficiency, as regards tail defence, in the German bombers which proved to be their undoing in the Battle of Britain. But despite the development of the RAF's new heavy bombers, not all was success. The Air Staff had failed to push for adequate research and development effort into the provision of effective navigational, target-finding and bombing aids for offensive operations under cover of darkness, since what scientific and development effort was available inevitably had to be concentrated, in the first instance, on the country's survival against air attack.

So, while considerable urgency needed to be applied to Britain's overall re-armament, the greatest danger to the country, now, was attack from the air, and thus the Royal Air Force had to be the first priority. Germany's moves in 1938, following on the military occupation of the Rhineland and the continuing intervention in Spain, soon made the politicians and the British public realise that, however distasteful, heavy re-armament could no longer be avoided. Germany's aggressive policy

---

* The first marks of Hurricane and Spitfire were armed with eight rifle-calibre machine-guns, four in each wing.

could have been halted over the Rhineland, but the chance had been missed because Britain had dallied. Italy could have been stopped in her tracks over Abyssinia, but the League of Nations had only false teeth. Now, wholesale destruction delivered from the skies seemed inevitable, and Britain's air defences were, for the moment, utterly powerless to prevent such a catastrophe.

1938 started ominously. In Britain, Anthony Eden finally clashed with Neville Chamberlain over the latter's determination to seek rapprochement with Mussolini by recognition of Italy's conquest of Abyssinia, and his further intention to improve Anglo-German relations by granting almost any concessions demanded by Hitler. Eden found his position as Foreign Secretary undermined, and on 20 February he resigned. As if to support Eden's views on the hopelessness of contemplating any deals with Hitler, moves against Austria began in February with Hitler's demands to Kurt von Schuschnigg (the Austrian Chancellor who had replaced Dr Dollfuss after his assassination by Nazis in July 1934), to eliminate all fortifications on the frontiers with Germany, to appoint the Austrian Nazi von Seyss-Inquart as Minister of Security in the Cabinet, to recognise the banned Austrian Nazi Party as a legal political force, and to grant an amnesty for all Austrian Nazis under detention. Von Schuschnigg was given three days in which to execute these terms, otherwise Germany would invade Austria. The terms were accepted and acted upon immediately, and von Schuschnigg told the Austrian Parliament on 24 February that, while he welcomed a settlement with Germany which would preserve Austria's independence, Austria would never make any further concessions beyond those specific terms contained in this last agreement with Hitler. At the same time he appealed to Mussolini, who had come to Austria's aid in 1934, to lend his support again. Then, on 9 March, von Schuschnigg officially announced that a plebiscite would be held on the 13th, to determine whether the Austrian people wished to remain independent of Germany. His reasons were based on the fond hope that a resounding 'yes' would strengthen the political position in Austria, and thus make it difficult for Hitler to embark on any predatory moves with the eyes of the world upon him. On 11 March, von Seyss-Inquart called on the Austrian Chancellor, and announced that Göring had telephoned to say that the plebiscite must be called off within an hour. Having, a few hours earlier, been advised by his Consul-General in Munich that a German army corps had been mobilised, with Austria as its destination, von Schuschnigg had no option but to postpone the plebiscite. Von Seyss-Inquart informed Göring of the cancellation, and within a quarter of an hour he was back again with the following message for von Schuschnigg: 'The situation can only be saved if the Chancellor resigns immediately and if within two hours Dr

Seyss-Inquart is nominated Chancellor. If nothing is done within this period the German invasion of Austria will follow.'

Von Schuschnigg tendered his resignation at once to Dr Miklas, the President, who refused to accept it; he was determined to force Hitler's hand, believing that Mussolini would come to Austria's assistance, and that so too would other European countries. All failed Austria, but in any case, Hitler's moves were too swift. He had planned for the military occupation of Austria well before putting his initial demands to Schuschnigg – in fact, it is probable that Hitler was annoyed that the Austrian Chancellor should have accepted those demands, so denying him the chance to move at once.

On 11 March 1938 the Luftwaffe was given its third opportunity to shine. The first opportunity had been when Germany's new air force had flown into the demilitarised zone of the Rhineland, an exercise in efficiency with no shots fired; the second had been the success of the Legion Kondor in Spain, where plenty of shots were still being fired. Now, under the code-name 'Operation Otto' (the plan for the military occupation of Austria), fighter and reconnaissance aircraft accompanied the massed troop movements over the frontier, providing air cover against any – admittedly unlikely – resistance. On the 12th, while German troops were marching on the capital and other major cities, bomber squadrons landed at Aspern aerodrome on the outskirts of Vienna after dropping leaflets on the city, and they were quickly followed by a large number of transport aircraft carrying more troops. There was no resistance and the take-over was completed by the 13th, despite numerous heavy tanks and motorised artillery breaking down, which caused a monumental traffic jam on the road from Linz to Vienna, an incident which earned the Führer's profound displeasure. The poor serviceability of vehicles during this relatively simple campaign indicated that Hitler's military might was not at that stage of efficiency where it could risk a campaign in which it was likely to be confronted with angry resistance. Nevertheless, the object of this particular exercise was achieved satisfactorily, and within days Hitler declared the dissolution of the Austrian Republic and the incorporation of its territory into the German Reich. The land of his birth was at last German, thus fulfilling one of his most cherished wishes. The inefficiency of the German Army would be put right without delay – a remark that was as much a threat as it was a statement of fact.

For Mussolini's lack of intervention, Hitler promised: 'I will never forget it, whatever may happen. If he should ever need any help or be in danger, he can be convinced that I shall stick to him whatever might happen, even if the whole world were against him.'

On the 16th, the merging of the Austrian Air Force with the Luftwaffe got under way with the setting up of Luftwaffe Command, Austria, under Generalmajor Löhr. The *Anschluss* – the union of Austria with Germany – was now a fact, and Nazi strength in Europe was greatly increased.

On 14 March, Churchill had said in the House of Commons:

The gravity of the event of March 12th cannot be exaggerated. Europe is confronted with a programme of aggression, nicely calculated and timed, unfolding stage by stage, and there is only one choice open, not only to us but to other countries, either to submit like Austria, or else take effective measures while time remains to ward off the danger, and if it cannot be warded off, to cope with it ... If we go on waiting upon events, how much shall we throw away of resources now available for our security and the maintenance of peace? How many friends will be alienated, how many potential allies shall we see go one by one down the grisly gulf? How many times will bluff succeed until behind bluff ever gathering forces have accumulated reality? ... Where are we going to be two years hence, for instance, when the German Army will certainly be much larger than the French Army, and when all the small nations have fled from Geneva [a reference to the League of Nations, which had its headquarters there] to pay homage to the ever waxing power of the Nazi System, and to make the best terms for themselves?

Chamberlain took little notice of Churchill's or Eden's warnings. As a result of his resolve to restore friendly relations with Mussolini, negotiations took place between Lord Halifax, who had replaced Eden as Foreign Secretary, and Count Ciano, the Italian Foreign Secretary. On 16 April, an Anglo-Italian Agreement was signed, by which Britain recognised Italy's conquest of Abyssinia, and effectively left her a free hand in Spain, all for a rather nebulous acknowledgement of Britain's position in the Mediterranean, which included the withdrawal from Libya of Italian troops then threatening Egypt. The British object was to wean Italy away from her growing friendship with Germany, an aim which proved to be singularly naive. All it achieved was to allow Mussolini to have his own way in Abyssinia, and to encourage Hitler into believing that Britain, when it came to the test, would never oppose Germany's territorial aspirations with armed force.

Following the *Anschluss* in Austria, the next stage of Hitler's plans was put into operation. Lord Halifax had already woken up one day to discover that German troops were in Vienna, and that, after all, the newspapers could be believed. Soon he was to wake up to see German armed forces in Prague.

The disruption of good relations between the Czechs and the Sudeten

Germans was entrusted to the Sudeten leader, Konrad Henlein, who had been instructed by Hitler, in a secret interview in March 1938, how to conduct a campaign of agitation against the Czech Government. The Germans in the Sudetenland were to be encouraged to step up their complaints about unfair treatment and, at the same time, Henlein was to press the Czechs for more political and economic freedom for the inhabitants of the Sudetenland, making it clear that he was seeking Germany's support for greater independence. The campaign soon produced bloody riots as the Germans clashed with the Czech authorities, enabling Hitler to claim that he must protect his fellow Germans and secure for them 'general freedom, personal, political and ideological'. In the meantime, a carefully prepared plan for the take-over of the Sudetenland, under the code-name 'Operation Green', was ready to be put into action the moment the Führer gave the order. In May 1938 Henlein, on Hitler's instructions, visited London to seek support for his proposals for greater autonomy for the Sudetenland. In brief, these proposals were:

> That the central Parliament in Prague should have control of foreign policy, defence, finance and communications. All Parties should be entitled to express their views there, and the Government would act on majority decisions. The frontier forces could be manned by Czech troops, who would have unhindered access thereto. The Sudeten German regions should enjoy local autonomy; that is to say, they should have their own Town and County Councils, and a Diet in which matters of common regional concern could be debated. All Parties would be free to organise and offer themselves for election, and impartial Courts of Justice would function in autonomous districts. Postal, railway and police officials in the German-speaking region should be German speaking. A reasonable proportion of the total taxes collected should be returned to these autonomous regions for their administration.

On the face of it, they seemed fairly innocuous requests, and Jan Masaryk, the Czech Minister in London, could see no reason to oppose them. But they were, in fact, a part of the plan to build up to a situation when Germany could invade, with some semblance of justification, first the Sudetenland, and then the rest of Czechoslovakia, once Hitler had convinced himself that his army was in a fit state to undertake such a risk. He was by now convinced that Soviet Russia would not intervene, any more than would Britain, and even France, he reckoned, would fail to honour her Locarno Treaty obligations to Czechoslovakia. Mussolini was now safely in his pocket, so the Führer had no fears from that corner. Finally, he was prepared when the time came, to encourage Poland and

Hungary to expand their territories at the expense of Czechoslovakia – after all, he would deal with those two countries in due course. First, however, he would deal with the Sudetenland.

In the months from May to September, the Sudetenland's demands to the Czech Government multiplied. Henlein, instructed by Hitler, pressed for increasingly impossible concessions, until the stage was reached when the Czechs were no longer prepared to negotiate further. On 12 September 1938, at a Party rally in Nürnberg, Hitler made a violent attack on the intransigence of the Czechs, in a speech in which he hinted at the use of force to support the Germans in the Sudetenland. To this the Czechs responded by imposing martial law in the region, quickly putting down what was now fermenting into a revolt. On 15 September Henlein had to flee to Germany for safety. Hitler had now brought about the situation that he had desired in order to satisfy his conscience.

The French and British Governments were, by this time, in urgent consultation, the French being anxious to know what practical support they could expect from Britain if France went to war with Germany over Czechoslovakia. They were told that the most they could expect was two divisions and 150 aeroplanes during the first six months, a statement that was enough to encourage France to leave the Czechs to their fate. On the night of 13/14 September, the French Prime Minister, Edouard Daladier, had contacted Chamberlain in order to propose a joint approach to Hitler in an attempt to reach a peaceful solution to the Sudetenland crisis, only to discover that Chamberlain had already telegraphed Hitler offering to go to Germany to meet him immediately, and that an invitation had been the prompt response. Chamberlain left Heston airport for Munich on the 15th. Before departing he had this message for the people of Britain:

> I am going to meet the German Chancellor because the present situation seems to me to be one in which discussions between him and myself may have useful consequences. My policy has always been to try to ensure peace, and the Führer's ready acceptance of my suggestion encourages me to hope that my visit to him will not be without results.

Chamberlain arrived at Munich airport in the afternoon, and travelled to Berchtesgaden by train. Even before he had arrived at Hitler's mountain retreat German radio stations were broadcasting a proclamation by Henlein, demanding the annexation of the Sudeten areas to the German Reich, news which Hitler had planned should reach Chamberlain's ears before their meeting. During the discussions, Hitler convinced the British Prime Minister that nothing short of the cession of the Sudetenland to Germany would dissuade him from ordering the invasion of Czechoslovakia. The Sudeten Germans were entitled, he insisted, to the rights of self-determination; a national minority had a claim to just treatment which it was not receiving. He emphasised that he was only 'championing the small man against the Czech bully', and he therefore recommended 'a policy for immediate and drastic action ... the transfer of predominantly German districts to Germany.' In that event, he was prepared to give his word that there would be no more territorial demands. Chamberlain was convinced that agreement to Hitler's demands, and acceptance of his guarantees, would resolve the crisis and ensure peace in Europe. He therefore undertook to fly back to London to obtain the agreement of the British and French Governments to such an arrangement, by which the Sudetenland would be ceded to Germany.

When Chamberlain arrived back in England on the 16th he greeted the British public with this message:

I have come back again rather quicker than I expected, after a journey which, had I not been so preoccupied, I should have found thoroughly enjoyable. Yesterday afternoon I had a long talk with Herr Hitler. It was a frank talk, but it was a friendly one, and I feel satisfied now that each of us fully understands what is in the mind of the other. You will not, of course, expect me to discuss now what may be the results of these talks. What I have got to do is to discuss them with my colleagues, and I would advise you not to accept prematurely any unauthorised account of what took place in the conversation.

There now followed meetings of the Cabinet on the 17th, and consultations with Daladier and Georges Bonnet, the French Foreign Secretary, on the 18th, resulting in the issue of a joint communiqué, which read:

After full discussion of the present international situation, the representatives of the British and French Governments are in complete agreement as to the policy to be adopted with a view to promoting a peaceful solution of the Czechoslovak question. The two Governments hope that thereafter it will be possible to consider a more general settlement in the interests of European peace.

On 29 September, Chamberlain left for Munich once more, this time to complete the sell-out of a friendly European state – what the Czechs called the 'Betrayal of Czechoslovakia' by the British and French. Leaving Heston, his parting words were: 'When I was a little boy I used to repeat: "If at first you don't succeed, try, try, try, again." That is what I am doing. When I come back I hope I may be able to say, as Hotspur said in *Henry IV*, "Out of this nettle, danger, we pluck this flower, safety."' In Munich a Four-Power Agreement was signed, on the same day, by Germany, France, Italy and Great Britain, whereby the German

Reich was to occupy the Sudetenland by progressive stages, and the Czechs were to withdraw from the Sudeten German districts peacefully and without destruction of any installations, industrial or otherwise; the same four powers guaranteed what remained of Czechoslovakia against further unprovoked aggression. The signatories were Hitler, Daladier, Mussolini and Chamberlain – there was no Czech representative present. Before Chamberlain left for England on the 30th he had another meeting with Hitler to discuss Anglo-German relations, and on his arrival back he announced that he had had, that very morning,

> a talk with the Führer, and we both signed the following declaration: 'We, the German Führer and Chancellor and the British Prime Minister, have had a further meeting to-day and are agreed in recognising that the question of Anglo-German relations is of the first importance for our two countries and for Europe. We regard the agreement signed last night and the Anglo-German Naval Agreement as symbolic of the desire of our two peoples never to go to war one with another again ...'

A tumultuous welcome was given to Chamberlain when he landed at Heston, where he was greeted by the entire Cabinet, the Lord Mayor of London, the High Commissioners of the Dominions and the Diplomatic Corps, and by crowds of thousands of cheering men and women. In an emotional outburst the British people expressed to the Premier their appreciation for saving them from the menace of war. Arriving at Downing Street, he said in a short speech to the crowd which waited to greet him:

> My very good friends, this is the second time in our history that there has come back from Germany to Downing Street 'peace with honour'.* I believe it is peace for our time. We thank you from the bottom of our hearts. And now I recommend you to go home and sleep quietly in your beds.

On that same day, Hitler rejoiced that his opponents were such 'little worms'.

Between 1 and 10 October, Hitler's 'Operation Green' was launched, ensuring a thoroughly provocative occupation of the Sudetenland, very far from the gentlemanly moves envisaged by Chamberlain. Nearly 500 aircraft of the Luftwaffe took part during the movement of German troops into the Sudetenland, and the Luftwaffe High Command also took precautions against any last-minute military resistance that might be put

---

* The first occasion had been in 1878, when Lord Beaconsfield (Benjamin Disraeli) returned from the Congress of Berlin: 'Lord Salisbury and myself have brought you back peace – but a peace I hope with honour ...'

up by the Czechs. These precautions included a standby air force comprising 400 fighters, 600 bombers, 200 dive-bomber and ground-attack aircraft, and 30 reconnaissance aircraft. In addition, plans were made to use, for the first time, parachute units should it prove necessary, the intention being to employ one battalion to overpower Czech frontier posts, whilst other parachute units captured specified airfields. In the event, these forces did not have to be used, although some parachute and airborne troops were employed to give them operational experience, in an operation code-named 'Exercise Freudenthal'.

Hitler intended not merely to content himself with the annexation of the Sudetenland alone, but also to invade the rest of Czechoslovakia and incorporate it into the Reich, contrary to the pledges given to France and Britain in Munich. This intention caused the Luftwaffe to take precautions against the possibility of Britain going to war with Germany, in spite of Hitler's conviction (correct, as it proved) that Britain would never intervene on behalf of Czechoslovakia. General Felmy, who was entrusted by Göring with the task of making the necessary plans against the eventuality of British and French intervention, submitted a memorandum to Göring in September entitled 'The Conducting of Air Operations against England', in which he concluded that 'a war of destruction against England with the means at present available appears to be out of the question'. In fact, Luftwaffe records reveal that Germany had a strength of 3,307 aircraft, which included 308 transport aircraft, at the end of September 1938. Against this force Britain had 1,982 aircraft at home and overseas, with reserves of 4 or 5 aircraft per squadron, or somewhere between 600 and 700 immediate reserves. A very large proportion of this force was still equipped with obsolete aircraft; indeed, all in all, Felmy seriously overestimated the strength and effectiveness of the Royal Air Force at that time. This report, however, resulted in orders from Hitler to the Luftwaffe General Staff for the immediate development of an air armament programme for the period from autumn 1938 to autumn 1942, allowing for an enormous increase in the strength of the German Air Force in order to provide for war against France and Britain, and probably against Russia. Despite such preparations, it seems almost certain that Hitler still cherished the hope that Britain would not go to war with Germany over the latter's East European intentions, or even in the event of war between France and Germany, although he had probably given up his hopes of an alliance between Germany and Britain. The Führer was determined, however, to be ready for all eventualities.

In contrast, the British Air Staff had put forward a scheme for expansion of the Royal Air Force that went further than all previous schemes. Known as Scheme K, it was submitted to the Cabinet on 14 March 1938 by Lord Swinton, the Secretary of State for Air, with the comment that it was 'below what the Air Staff regarded as the minimum insurance'. Under the Scheme there were to be 1,320 first-line bombers and 544 fighters by March 1939, with full reserves by March 1940, and included in the strength would be the other aircraft types required. Proposals were also made in connection with the industrial capacity that would be necessary to support this new RAF expansion. However, the maximum expenditure that the Chancellor of the Exchequer, Sir John Simon, a Liberal in the National Government, wished to authorise for all three Services was that already agreed, namely, £1,570 million, while Swinton's Scheme K would increase the total defence expenditure to £1,735 million. Simon therefore opposed the proposal on two scores, 'to avoid any public impression of the increase being a panic decision', and because 'the danger was we might knock our finances to pieces prematurely'. So the Scheme was dropped, and the previous plan for 1,736 first-line home-based aircraft (990 bombers and 420 fighters, with other types), and 468 first-line aircraft for Empire commitments was, for the time, to remain.

At the end of October 1938, after the rape of Austria and the annexation of the Sudetenland, the new Secretary of State for Air, Sir Kingsley Wood, tried hard to win increases for the Royal Air Force. He pointed out that the first-line strength was at that date 1,606 aircraft with another 412 in reserve, whereas German first-line strength was estimated at 3,200 aircraft with 2,400 in reserve. Given Britain's existing rate of production, the RAF could have, at best, a total of 1,890 first-line aircraft and 1,502 reserves by 1 August 1939, as compared to an assumed German figure of 4,030 first-line and 3,000 reserves – a comparative strength of 3,392 British to 7,030 German. (This estimate for the German first-line strength was very close to the mark; in fact, as has already been mentioned, the strength of the Luftwaffe at the outbreak of war in September 1939 was 4,093 first-line aircraft, of which 3,646 were ready for immediate action. The figures for reserves, however, were questionable – and still are.) Kingsley Wood asked for immediate authority to build half the aeroplanes he believed would be needed by 1942, and to this end he sought to place orders for 1,850 fighters and 1,750 bombers 'at a very early date'. He, too, like Lord Swinton, was to get the cold shoulder. On 1 November Sir Horace Wilson, the Chief Industrial Adviser to the Government who, at Chamberlain's request, had been seconded to the Treasury for special service, explained to Kingsley Wood that the Air Ministry's proposed increase in the production capacity 'to a level equal to the estimated German capacity' could not be accepted because it would be interpreted by Germany 'as a signal that we have decided at once to sabotage the Munich agreement.' Ironically, it was not to be long before Hitler himself did just that for the British Government.

On 1 November 1938, the same day on which Wilson told Kingsley Wood that no action would be taken which might imply to Hitler that Britain was not to be trusted, Dr Emil Hacha was elected President of the remnants of Czechoslovakia and a new Government took office in Prague. Before long, with Hitler's connivance, the 'Versailles' Czechoslovakia was being eaten away by Poland and Hungary, as well as by Germany. Soon Hacha, an old and sick man 'kept alive' by the Führer's personal physician, appealed to Hitler for German protection for the Czechs, and 'confidently placed the fate of the Czech people in the hands of the Führer.' At 06.00 hours on 15 March 1939, German troops, supported by the Luftwaffe, began their entry into Czechoslovakia, occupying the areas known as Bohemia and Moravia. Before the day was out they had reached Prague, and on the 17th hundreds of aircraft of the Luftwaffe staged a victory fly-past over that city. Thus Lord Halifax was to discover for the second time that the newspapers were to be believed, as he awoke one day to see the German armed forces in Prague.

CHAPTER XIII

War With Germany

At the time of Germany's occupation of the Sudetenland early in October 1938, the Poles had taken advantage of the situation to demand from the Czechs that they hand over the district of Teschen, which lay on the Czechoslovakian frontier with Poland. There were no means of resisting this demand, and Hitler made no move, at that stage, to protest against Poland's action. Indeed, it suited his purpose, for it was to provide him with the pseudo-moral reason for his entry into Bohemia and Moravia in March 1939, when he proclaimed from Prague a 'German Protectorate over Czechoslovakia'. At the same time as Germany took over Czechoslovakia, Hungarian troops crossed into that country's Eastern Province, seeking to satisfy Hungary's long-held demand for the Carpatho-Ukraine area to be incorporated into Hungarian territory. This also suited Hitler, for, after the annexation of Austria, Hungary had indicated her wish to be allied to Germany. A week after the occupation of Prague, Lithuania offered, under pressure, to return to the German Reich the district and predominantly German port of Memel, which she had occupied since 1923, and on 23 March 1939 aircraft of the Luftwaffe's East Prussia Command crossed the Lithuanian frontier and circled for an hour over Memel. On the same day, after this vital Baltic port and district had been occupied by German troops, a victory fly-past was staged over the town and surrounding area.

This latest success extended the German control of the Baltic, leaving Danzig, the Free Port at the end of the Polish Corridor, vulnerable to yet another take-over. With Bohemia and Moravia in his pocket, and with Hungary, as an act of self-preservation, declaring herself to be in the German camp, Hitler now had Poland surrounded. The last remaining stumbling-block in the way of his plans for expansion into Soviet Russia – Poland – could now be eliminated easily. Initially, his aim was to incorporate Danzig into the Reich and to acquire an extra rail and road link with East Prussia through the Corridor. These demands he put to the Polish Government, imagining that, due to their isolation, the Poles would find themselves compelled to accede to his requests. Indeed, encouraged by the ease with which Austria and Czechoslovakia had fallen into his hands with no effective protest from the rest of Europe, Hitler was even confident that Poland would feel obliged to range herself on the side of Germany as an ally. In fact, he told von Brauchitsch on 25 March that he did not intend to solve the Danzig question by force, in order to avoid the possible risk of driving the Poles into the arms of Britain and France.

On 26 March, the Polish Government rejected the German demands, and on the 31st, after Poland had appealed to Britain and France for support, a Franco-British guarantee of Poland was declared. Chamberlain and his Government had at last woken up to the fact that Hitler was not to be trusted, and on that same day Chamberlain made this statement to the House of Commons:

> I now have to inform the House that ... in the event of any action which clearly threatened Polish independence and which the Polish Government accordingly considered it vital to resist with their national forces, His Majesty's Government would feel themselves bound at once to lend the Polish Government all support in their power. They have given the Polish Government an assurance to this effect. I may add that the French Government have authorised me to make it plain that they stand in the same position in this matter as do His Majesty's Government ...

Hitler was furious. The 'little worms' had at last, if unexpectedly, turned. Obviously the Anglo-German Naval Agreement of 1935 did not, as he had fondly believed, confer upon him the right to exercise a free hand in Eastern Europe in exchange for his voluntary restriction of German naval armaments. Clearly, Britain would now oppose the far-reaching ambitions of Nazi territorial policy, and the Poles would draw comfort from this promise of support, which in turn would make them sufficiently confident of military backing from Britain and France, in the event of a German attempted invasion to oppose any such threat with force. Or, wondered Hitler, as he began to calm down, would the British and French still prove to be 'little worms' when the time came? On 3 April 1939, he ordered plans to be prepared for an all-out attack upon Poland, under the code-name 'Operation White', to be launched in the autumn with the aim of the swift elimination of that country. He had finally decided – and his views were supported by von Ribbentrop – that Britain and France would not, in the end, honour their obligations to Poland; therefore, if he could dispose of Poland without intervention from the West, he could then complete a redeployment of his forces for a sudden and surprise attack on France, the Lowlands, and Britain in the autumn of 1940 or, at the latest, in 1941. Lastly, with threats from Western and Central Europe sterilised, he could turn on Russia and indulge his wish, so clearly enunciated in *Mein Kampf*, of expanding eastwards and subjugating the hated Communists. In the meantime, however, and in order to keep Soviet Russia quiescent, he now began extremely secret and ardent negotiations with the leaders of the Soviet Union for a pact of mutual non-aggression. Hitler's flirtation with the 'blood-stained sub-humans', Stalin, and his new Foreign Commissar, Molotov, began in earnest in the late spring of 1939. At least, as he put it, the Jew Litvinov, Molotov's predecessor as Foreign Commissar, had been dismissed in May and was thus out of the way, which made Hitler's to him unpalatable association with these Marxists marginally less unpalatable. On 23 August, the Devil's pact was signed in Mosow by Molotov and von Ribbentrop. At the same time, a secret protocol was made defining German and Russian spheres of influence and, particularly, partitioning Poland against the day of its conquest.

While the talks with Soviet Russia were going on, 'Operation White' was being prepared, the plan of attack allowing for major participation by the Luftwaffe. The date for launching the campaign against Poland was to be at any time from 1 August 1939 onwards. A map exercise was drawn up under the code-name '*Generalstabreise 1939*' – literally, 'General Staff Journey 1939' – which detailed the Luftwaffe deployment and battle directives for 'Operation White'. The air plan called for a blitzkrieg, aimed at destroying the Polish Air Force on the ground by means of a series of lightning raids. Once this objective had been achieved, the Luftwaffe was to be used in full support of military operations on the ground, taking its target orders from the Army. Its role would encompass full-scale attacks on towns with the intention of disrupting and destroying industrial services, communications and government administration, of killing and intimidating civil populations, and of making and spreading general chaos. The whole plan was designed to bring about the speediest possible eradication of all Polish resistance.

At 05.30 hours on the morning of Friday, 1 September 1939, Germany attacked Poland from East Prussia, Slovakia, and the main body of the German Reich. No declaration of war was delivered to the Polish Government, but at 05.40 hours, just ten minutes after the order to invade was given, Hitler issued a proclamation to the Army stating that Poland had refused 'the peaceful settlement' desired by him and 'had appealed to arms'. At 11.40 hours, the German Supreme Command issued the following order: 'Soldiers of the German Army. After all other means have failed, weapons must decide. As successors of the proud traditions of the old army, the young National Socialist Army will now take over the defence of Germany. We will fight under the supreme command of the Führer.' A little time later, Hitler addressed the Reichstag:

For months [he said] we have been suffering under the torture of a problem which the Versailles 'Diktat' created – a problem which has deteriorated until it becomes intolerable for us. Danzig was and is a German city. The Corridor was and is German. Danzig was separated from us, the Corridor was annexed by Poland. As in other German territories of the East, German minorities have been ill-treated in the most distressing manner ... I attempted to bring about, by making proposals for revision, an alteration of this intolerable position. It is a lie when the outside world says that we only tried to carry through our revisions by pressure. I have, not once but several times, made proposals for the revision of intolerable conditions. All these proposals have been rejected ... In the same way, I have also tried to solve the problems of Danzig and the Corridor, by proposing a peaceful discussion ... These proposals have been refused and met, not only at first with mobilisation, but with increased terror against our German compatriots, and with a slow strangling of the Free City of Danzig – economically, politically, and in recent weeks by military and transport means. I made one more final effort to accept a proposal for mediation on the part of the British Government. They suggested, not that they themselves should carry on the negotiations, but rather that Poland and Germany should come into direct contact once more to pursue negotiations.

Hitler then went on to describe what he regarded as the intransigence of the Polish Government who, he said, showed no willingness 'to conduct serious negotiations with us.' Now he was determined to solve the question of Danzig and the Corridor, but he emphasised that he had no quarrel with France or Britain – 'I have declared that the frontier between France and Germany is a final one. I have repeatedly offered friendship and, if necessary, the closest co-operation to Britain, but this cannot be offered from one side only.'

Turning to Russia, the Führer went on to say that he was particularly happy to be able to tell the German people of one great event. 'Russia and Germany are governed by two different doctrines. There was only one question that had to be cleared up' – a reference to the negotiation of the Nazi-Soviet Non-Aggression Pact, signed in Moscow on 23 August.

Germany has no intention of exporting its doctrine. Given the fact that Soviet Russia has no intention of exporting its doctrine to Germany, I no longer see any reason why we should oppose one another. This political decision means a tremendous departure for the future, and it is a final one. Russia and Germany fought against one another in the World War. That shall and will not happen a second time.

He completed his speech with this assurance:

I will not war against women and children. I have ordered my Air Force to restrict itself to attacks on military objectives ... If, however, the enemy thinks he can from that draw 'carte blanche' on his side to fight by other methods he will receive an answer that will deprive him of hearing and sight.

His last words were about his successors.

I ask no better than to be the Nation's first soldier. If anything should happen to me, my first successor will be Field-Marshal Göring, and, if anything should happen to him, my next will be Herr Hess. Should anything happen to Herr Hess, a successor will be chosen from among the bravest and most capable in Germany.

On that same day, the reunion of Danzig with the German Reich was proclaimed by Gauleiter Albert Forster, the Free City's Nazi leader, who informed Hitler that the Danzig Senate had passed the following resolutions and wished the Führer to ratify them:

1. The Constitution of the Free City of Danzig is cancelled with immediate effect.
2. All legislative and executive power is in the hands of the Head of State.
3. The Free City of Danzig with its territory and population shall immediately form part of the territory of the German Reich.
4. Until the Führer makes a definite decision about the introduction of German Reich law, all legal provisions of the Constitution remain in force as they are at the moment of the issue of this constitutional law.

Hitler replied at once, ratifying the resolutions and introducing German Reich law, although the official annexation of Danzig was not ratified until 1 November. He also appointed Forster head of the civil administration of Danzig, while Dr Burkhardt, the League of Nations Commissioner, was ordered to leave the territory within two hours. As with the Sudetenland, Hitler had done his homework both in advance and in secret.

Perhaps unexpectedly, the Polish armed forces immediately went into action on land and in the air, putting up a spirited, if hopeless, resistance and thus disappointing Hitler's hopes of an unopposed invasion similar to that of Czechoslovakia. Moreover, and also on 1 September, the Polish Government invoked the Anglo-Polish and Franco-Polish Mutual Guarantee Treaties, with the result that Britain and France demanded the withdrawal of all German troops from Poland. Unless this was done at once, Germany was advised that both countries would without hesitation fulfil their obligations to Poland. On the same day, Neville Chamberlain informed the House of Commons of the situation and of the joint warning by Britain and France to Germany. 'If a reply to this last warning is unfavourable,' he stated, 'and I do not suggest that it is likely to be otherwise, H.M. Ambassador is instructed to ask for his passports. In that case we are ready.' He concluded his long speech with these words:

> We have no quarrel with the German people except that they allow themselves to be governed by a Nazi Government. So long as that Government exists and pursues the methods it has so persistently followed during the last two years there will be no peace in Europe. We shall merely pass from one crisis to another and see one country after another attacked by methods which have now become familiar to us in their sickening technique. We are resolved that these methods must come to an end. If out of the struggle we can re-establish in the world the rules of good faith and the renunciation of force, then even the sacrifices that will be entailed upon us will find their fullest justification.

With the invasion of Poland on 1 September, full mobilisation was publicly proclaimed in Britain, although the three Services, including all Reservists, Territorials, Auxiliary Air Force personnel, and Volunteer Reservists of the Royal Navy, and the Royal Air Force, had in fact received their call-up orders by 24 August. Moreover, advance parties for the British Expeditionary Force (BEF) were already proceeding to France by 4 September to prepare, in conjunction with the French, for the reception of the BEF units. By 1 September the air defence system of Great Britain, including the new radar chain of detection stations around the South and East Coasts, was fully manned, and Fighter Command was at the ready with all Regular and Auxiliary Air Force squadrons fully armed. Bomber Command was bombed-up and on immediate standby, and Coastal Command's North Sea patrols were watching for German raiders seeking to prey on commercial shipping.

On the 2nd, eight squadrons of Fairey Battles and two of Bristol Blenheims from Bomber Command, which, backed by two squadrons of Hurricanes, were to form the Advanced Air Striking Force (AASF) of the British Air Forces in France, flew across the Channel to their new bases in the Champagne country of Northern France. The Battles were single-engined bombers, and, having a relatively short range, were totally incapable of attacking targets in Germany from bases in England. Their departure left Bomber Command reduced to a force of only twenty-three squadrons which, although pathetically small, was at least equipped with the more modern and faster medium-range Blenheims and the long-range heavy Whitleys, Hampdens and Wellingtons. The squadrons of the Air Component to the BEF, the air force sent to work in co-operation with the Army, were scheduled to move to France during September and early October in the event of a declaration of war. The Air Component consisted of five squadrons of Westland Lysanders* for tactical reconnaissance and photographic survey of the BEF front, four Blenheim squadrons for strategic reconnaissance beyond the French and Belgian frontiers as far as the Rhine, and four Hurricane fighter squadrons for the protection of reconnaissance aircraft, British bases and troops against enemy air attack. Later these Hurricane squadrons were to be increased to six.

The original purpose of the AASF was to bring the short-range Battles within effective striking distance of German industry, but this intention had to be abandoned in favour of much wider responsibilities. As the French could muster less than one hundred bombers, of which only twenty-five could be classed as nearly modern, the AASF would have to serve the needs of the entire Allied front. This meant that its ten squadrons of Battle and Blenheim bombers would now be required to attack advancing columns at such natural bottle-necks as bridges and road-junctions, while its two Hurricane squadrons were to support the bombers and help defend the area around Rheims, where the AASF was based, against attacks by German aircraft. These two Hurricane squadrons, which were additional to those allocated to the Air Component, were to be reinforced by two more squadrons at an early date.

The mobilisation of the Army was also proceeding apace, aimed at providing an initial four divisions, formed into two army corps, for the BEF, to be ready to move to take up positions in France on the frontier with Belgium by mid-October.

On the morning of 3 September, Neville Chamberlain, the Prime

---

* The Lysander was a two-seater high-wing monoplane with fixed undercarriage, each wheel-spat housing a single ·303 Browning machine-gun, both of which were fired by the pilot. In addition, a Vickers K-gun armed the rear cockpit. They were hopelessly obsolete aircraft, although they were later to prove themselves in roles more suited to their short take-off and landing capabilities, notably in the dropping of agents into Occupied Europe.

Minister, informed the House of Commons of the presentation of a final Note to Germany. The Note had stated that unless a reply was received by 11 o'clock that morning to the effect that Germany would withdraw her invading troops at once, Britain would go to war in support of Poland. France, he told the assembled MPs, had sent a similar Note. No reply had been received, and he had therefore to advise the House that Britain and Germany were at war with each other. At the same time the announcement of the British declaration of war on Germany was made in the House of Lords by Lord Halifax.

At 11.15 hours Chamberlain broadcast to the nation, while virtually every man, woman and child listened in sombre silence.

This morning [he said] the British Ambassador in Berlin handed the German Government a final Note stating that, unless we heard from them by 11 o'clock that they were prepared to withdraw their troops from Poland, a state of war would exist between us. I have to tell you now that no such undertaking has been received, and that consequently this country is at war with Germany ... Up to the very last it would have been quite possible to have arranged a peaceful and honourable settlement between Germany and Poland, but Hitler would not have it. He had evidently made up his mind to attack Poland whatever happened, and although he now says he put forward reasonable proposals which were rejected by the Poles, that is not a true statement. The proposals were never shown to the Poles, nor to us, and, although they were announced in a German broadcast on Thursday night, Hitler did not wait to hear comments on them, but ordered his troops to cross the Polish frontier. His action shows convincingly that there is no chance of expecting that this man will ever give up his practice of using force to gain his will. He can only be stopped by force. We and France are today, in fulfilment of our obligations, going to the aid of Poland, who is bravely resisting this wicked and unprovoked attack on her people. We have a clear conscience ... At such a moment as this the assurances of support that we have received from the Empire are a source of profound encouragement to us. The Government have made plans under which it will be possible to carry on the work of the nation in the days of stress and strain that may be ahead. But these plans need your help. You may be taking your part in the fighting Services or as a volunteer in one of the branches of Civil Defence ... You may be engaged in work essential to the prosecution of war for the maintenance of the life of the people – in factories, in transport, in public utility concerns, or in the supply of other necessaries of life ... Now may God bless you all. May he defend the right. It is the evil things that we shall be fighting against – brute force, bad faith, injustice, oppression and persecution – and against them I am certain that the right will prevail.

France declared war at the same time. On the day before, in a statement to the Chamber of Deputies, the French Prime Minister, Daladier, had made this comment:

... France and Britain will not stand by at the destruction of a friendly people. The aggression against Poland is a new enterprise of violence against Britain and France. It is not a question of conflict between Germany and Poland, it is a question of a new attempt by the Hitlerian dictatorship to dominate Europe and the world ...

Within a few minutes of the end of Chamberlain's broadcast to the nation the air-raid sirens began their wailing sound – a new noise in Britain's life, but one that was to become ever more familiar. This time it was, in fact, a false alarm caused by a British aircraft flying along the South Coast on its way back to base. Everybody laughed about the incident, but somehow it seemed to bring home forcibly that war, with all its modern attendant horrors, was at Britain's threshold.

Just after the 'All Clear' had sounded, Churchill made his way to the House of Commons, where Chamberlain told him that he wanted him to take up the appointment of First Lord of the Admiralty, with a seat in the War Cabinet. Churchill accepted, and later that day the Admiralty signalled the Fleet: 'Winston is back'.

On 1 September Hitler, having decided that the British and French warnings about Poland were a cunning bluff, and having therefore launched his attack on that country to the applause of an elated nation, changed into his Party uniform of field-grey on his way to his field headquarters, declaring: 'Now, once more, I have put on that uniform which was to me in the past the holiest and most dear. I shall not take it off until after victory – or I shall not survive the end.' When, two days later, Britain and France declared war on Germany, the Führer was initially stunned; 'What now?' he questioned, almost hopelessly. But he was quick to regain his nerve. 'Of course we are in a state of war with England and France, but if we on our side avoid all acts of war, the whole business will evaporate,' he said to his entourage.

Hitler completed his Polish invasion in eighteen days, without Britain or France being able to exert even a disturbing interference upon his campaign. The abysmal lack of readiness on the part of the two Western Allies forced them to remain passive while Poland was destroyed; indeed, they needed as much time as possible to mobilise to a military strength equivalent to that of Germany's 108 divisions, which was being rapidly increased to 117 divisions. In the first stages such military strength had to come from France, Britain's contribution being, at best, a mere four divisions by mid-October. The maximum that France could mobilise by late October was seventy-two divisions, which were additional to her Maginot Line fortress troops amounting to the equivalent of twelve to fourteen divisions. Hitler attacked Poland with fifty-six divisions, including nine armoured divisions, which left him with a minimum of fifty-two divisions (out of 117) with which to face the West between 1 September and the end of the month, long before France had mobilised fully, and before Britain's four divisions had crossed to the Continent. The Polish campaign was, on the evidence available to Hitler at the time, risky. But an Anglo-French attack on Germany at the very outset of the war was, in fact, impossible, and thus Hitler's decision, based upon a mixture of judgement and luck, proved to be the right one. As Churchill said, the Polish battle had been lost by Britain and France years earlier: 'In 1938 there was a good chance of victory while Czechoslovakia still existed. In 1936' – a reference to the unopposed German armed occupation of the demilitarised Rhineland in March of that year – 'there could have been no effective opposition. In 1933' – a reference to Hitler's decision, on becoming Chancellor and master of all Germany, to tear up the Versailles Peace Treaty and to walk out of the Disarmament Conference and the League of Nations – 'a rescript from Geneva would have procured bloodless compliance.'

In accordance with Hitler's plan, the Luftwaffe struck first in Poland. Its success was enormous. Within two days the Polish Air Force had been virtually annihilated on the ground of its own airfields. Despite brave and bitter resistance by the Poles, the German Army penetrated deeply into their country within a week, and by the end of the second week the Polish Army of thirty divisions had ceased to exist as an organised force. By 17 September, with Warsaw surrounded and German troops ranging beyond the River Vistula as far as Lemberg and Brest-Litovsk, the battle was effectively over. It only remained for Soviet Russia to provide the stab in the back, accomplished, also on the 17th, by Russian armies swarming across the undefended Polish frontier on a broad front. On the 18th they occupied Vilna, and at Brest-Litovsk, they met their Nazi German allies. In March 1918, during the First World War, the Bolsheviks, in breach of their agreement with the Western Allies, had made a separate peace with the Kaiser's Germany, accepting under the Treaty of Brest-Litovsk the stern and severe German terms. Now, in the same town, Nazis and Communists greeted and embraced each other like blood-brothers in scenes of sickening jubilation. The spawn of left-wing and right-wing extremism were able to forget their so-called ideological philosophies, philosophies which were diametrically opposed to each other, in a demonstration of mutual admiration and comradeship. Each had got what it wanted – for the moment – at the expense of an innocent third party. Poland had been stabbed from the front by Germany, and in the back by Soviet Russia.

The ruin and complete subjugation of Poland continued, but the incredibly courageous resistance maintained by the Poles in various undefeated pockets, notably Warsaw and Modlin, delayed the final collapse until 28 September. The resistance in Warsaw was magnificent, with all of its citizens fighting to the very last moment, and the city only fell after being pounded by days of violent bombing both by the Luftwaffe and by heavy artillery.

On 29 September, after the Soviet armies had advanced to a line agreed between Hitler and Stalin, the Russo-German Treaty partitioning Poland was finally signed. With his eastern flank secure, Hitler could now swiftly reinforce his western front strength with seasoned troops and experienced airmen. He still refrained, however, from any aggressive move in the west, taking advantage of his spectacular success against Poland to propose a new peace plan to Britain and France, convinced that both countries would welcome an opportunity to withdraw their declarations of war because, he believed, they wished to avoid a fight at all costs. In fact, Hitler had no wish to continue the war with France and Britain at this stage. His heart and eyes were set eastwards against his new and incongruous ally, and if the West could be dealt with without firing a shot, then that would best suit his ultimate plans. So it was that the 'Phoney War' part of the Second World War began its brief existence, for it did not occur to Hitler that at last the British were determined, as Churchill put it, ' ... to have his blood or perish in the attempt.'

On 28 September 1939, just one day before the signing of the Russo-German Treaty partitioning Poland, Estonia signed, under duress, a Pact of Mutual Assistance with Soviet Russia, which gave the Russians the right to garrison key bases in Estonia, and by 21 October the Red Army and Air Force had occupied these bases. Simultaneously, similar pacts were enforced upon Latvia and Lithuania, with key positions again being immediately garrisoned by Russian military forces. With Poland already partitioned, these moves barred the southern route to Leningrad, offering some security against a possible attack. Since such an attack could only come from Germany, it was clear that Russia placed little faith in the pact of mutual non-aggression between herself and Germany, known as the Ribbentrop-Molotov Pact, and which had been signed so short a time before on 21 August. The only weakness now remaining in Russia's line of defence in the north lay in the possibility of an approach through Finland, a country which, under the secret, unpublished terms of the Ribbentrop-Molotov Pact, had been allotted to the Russian sphere of interest, like Estonia, Lithuania and Latvia; Hitler had not expected

Russia to act upon these concessions either quickly or in a militaristic fashion. In October, Russia made extensive demands on Finland, which included the re-drawing of the frontier on the Karelian Isthmus to move it further back into Finnish territory, so that Leningrad, only eighteen miles from the frontier, should be out of range of possible hostile artillery. The Russians also demanded the cession of certain islands in the Gulf of Finland; concessions of territory in the Rybachiy Peninsula, including the Arctic port of Petsamo; and the leasing of Hango, at the entrance of the Gulf of Finland, for use as a Russian naval and air base. The Finns were ready to make concessions on virtually all of these demands, except that of leasing Hango, which would denude Finland of one of the major defences for its capital, Helsingfors,* and indeed would leave the strategic and national security of the country hopelessly reduced. The Finnish Government therefore refused to negotiate further, and talks broke down on 13 November. On the 28th, Molotov claimed that the Finns had fired upon Russian troops, and renounced the non-aggression pact between Finland and Russia which had been signed in 1932. On the 30th, without any declaration of war, Russian forces attacked at eight points along the 1,000-mile frontier and against the Mannerheim Line, a Finnish defensive system across the Karelian Isthmus upon which the main force of the attack initially fell, while Helsingfors was bombed by the Red Air Force on the same morning. But the big Russian bear was to receive a nasty shock.

The Soviet Government had counted upon a swift collapse of all resistance, and believed that the Red Air Force raids on Helsingfors and other cities would terrorise the Finns into early submission. In fact, between 30 November and 22 December the Russian forces were defeated and ignominiously thrown back, with heavy losses, on all fronts by the gallant and well trained Finnish Army, despite their enemy's vast superiority in numbers and weapons. In particular, the attacks on the central area of the frontier proved to be disastrous for the Russians. There the Finns holding the flanks withdrew from some of their frontier posts in the pine-forest terrain, now heavily covered with snow, in order to draw Russian columns in hot pursuit for thirty miles or so, while in the centre they held their defence lines. As the Soviet forces were drawn deeper into Finland, their columns became increasingly exposed; the Finns then violently attacked the flanks by day and by night, cutting the Russian columns to pieces and destroying their tanks with a new type of home-made petrol bomb which came to be known as the 'Molotov Cocktail'. By the end of December, with the only Russian success being

---

* Finland had been united with Sweden from the early Middle Ages to 1809, and thus in 1939 the Swedish version of Helsinki was still frequently used.

in the Petsamo area in the north, the Red Army plan for splitting Finland in two by swarming across the centre of the country had plainly failed abysmally. The attacks against the Mannerheim Line and the area immediately north of Lake Ladoga had also been repulsed by the Finns, with yet more heavy losses to the Soviet Russian forces. By the beginning of 1940 the fighting all along the Finnish front had virtually ceased, leaving the Finns victorious, at least for the time, over the huge Russian aggressor – a small, determined and courageous nation had given the 'Russian thugs' a bloody nose. On 1 February 1940, however, a vast new Russian offensive was mounted, backed with armour, heavy artillery, and aircraft. Successive assaults breached the Mannerheim Line by the 17th, and on 12 March the Finnish Government was forced to accept the terms dictated by Soviet Russia. All fighting ceased at 11.00 hours on the 13th. But if the Russians were finally successful, their initial failures were looked upon with scorn by Hitler and his generals. Finland had exposed the feebleness of the Red Army and though in the end she was forced to cede large areas of her territory, yet she had still managed to remain an independent state.*

During this same period, plans were being developed by Germany for the invasion of Denmark and Norway. On the 3 October 1939, Grand Admiral Erich Raeder, the Commander-in-Chief of the German Navy, submitted a memorandum to Hitler entitled 'Gaining of Bases in Norway', in which he drew attention to the opinions of the Naval Staff on the possibility of obtaining bases in that country as a result of combined German and Russian pressure. The aim being to improve the German strategic and tactical situation in terms of both naval and air operations. Raeder also emphasised the grave disadvantages to Germany should the British occupy Norway, which would result in Britain being able to control the approaches to the Baltic, to outflank German naval operations, and to end any German hopes of maintaining pressure on Sweden for industrial co-operation. Hitler was impressed by all these considerations, but hoped that an instrument could be found whereby a German occupation could be achieved by Norwegian request. Such an instrument did indeed exist, at least potentially. At the beginning of 1939, Alfred Rosenberg, a Nazi philosopher who was also something of a foreign affairs expert to the Nazi Party, had made contact with the leader of the extremist, Nazi-modelled National Unity Party of Norway, a former soldier and Minister of War, Major Vidkun Quisling. Through

---

* The war had cost Finland about 25,000 dead and 45,000 wounded out of forces that never totalled more than 200,000 men. Russian dead alone amounted to some 200,000 men, with an unknown, though certainly larger, number of wounded. By the time the 'Winter War' ended the Soviet Union was employing 45 infantry divisions, 4 cavalry divisions, and 12 armoured groups against the Finns.

Rosenberg and the German Naval Attaché in Oslo, contacts with Quisling were re-established in the autumn of 1939, and he agreed to co-operate with the Nazis, and to his Party's activities being linked with secret German plans for a take-over of Norway. On 14 December 1939, Quisling and his assistant Hagelin, visited Berlin by arrangement with Rosenberg and Raeder, bringing with them a detailed plan for the overthrow of the Norwegian Government and the occupation of Norway by 'friendly' Germans. In the afternoon of 16 March 1940, Hitler held a military Conference at which a date – 9 April – was provisionally decided upon for the invasion of Norway. Simultaneously with the planning of the Norwegian escapade, preparations for the battle for France had also been put in hand, with typical Teutonic efficiency, and by the end of March all was ready for the mobilisation of the mighty German war machine.

On 9 April 1940, Denmark was invaded by German troops and swiftly overrun. Also on the 9th, southern Norway was invaded and by the afternoon of the same day Oslo was occupied and Vidkun Quisling, under the protection of the Germans, was demanding that power of government should be surrendered at once. King Haakon and his Cabinet refused and withdrew to Hamar, some 100 miles north of Oslo. The Norwegian Army was quickly mobilised, but the war in Norway was over before it truly began, despite landings at several points north of Bergen between 14 April and the beginning of May of a hastily formed British Expeditionary Force with its modest Air Component, and of French troops as well. These landing points included Alesund, just south of Molde, which for a few weeks became a British base, Namsos, Mosjöen, Bodo and Harstad. The King and his Government were quickly forced to withdraw from Hamar even further north, to the British base at Molde. Then, on 29 April, they were embarked in HMS *Glasgow* to Tromso, and at the beginning of June they were finally evacuated from there to England, when the desperate situation in France forced the Allies to abandon their puny, if gallant, efforts to preserve Norway from Nazi rule. The speed with which Hitler's forces had overrun Norway was the result of remarkable feats of both strategy and tactics, the tactics even encompassing political infiltration ahead of the invasion; the campaign, politically and militarily, was an example of German thoroughness.

Now, as Britain was soon to learn, France would suffer in her turn.

CHAPTER XIV

France Collapses

From September 1939 through to the beginning of May 1940, there was an unrealistic 'war' in France, a war uninterrupted by any threat of battle. The squadrons of the Air Component flew a massive number of hours on reconnaissance, undertaking vertical and oblique overlap photography of vast areas of Northern France and along the Belgian and German frontiers without any enemy interference, and without ever crossing the German frontier. The photographic mosaics built-up from these reconnaissance flights were used to reconstruct up-to-date maps for the Army, including maps of the terrain of the Siegfried Line, a German defensive network along the Franco-German frontier, and the areas to be covered were allocated according to the positions of the different wings of the Air Component. Nothing that happened was anything like the war conditions that had been anticipated, but the calm was soon to be shattered by the storm.

At dawn on 10 May 1940, the German assault on the West was launched.

The plan, as it was conceived, almost certainly emanated from Hitler. It depended for its master stroke upon a major thrust between Luxembourg and Malmédy, south of Liège – difficult country which included the narrow strip of heavily wooded terrain in the Ardennes – towards and across the River Meuse at Sedan, thus breaking through the centre of the Allied armies. This strategy ran contrary to the old, pre-First World War, Schlieffen Plan, which formed the original blueprint for the 1940 attack but which had been based on a strong right wing in the north making a turning movement to fold back the Allies from the coasts of Belgium and France. In the teeth of considerable opposition, General

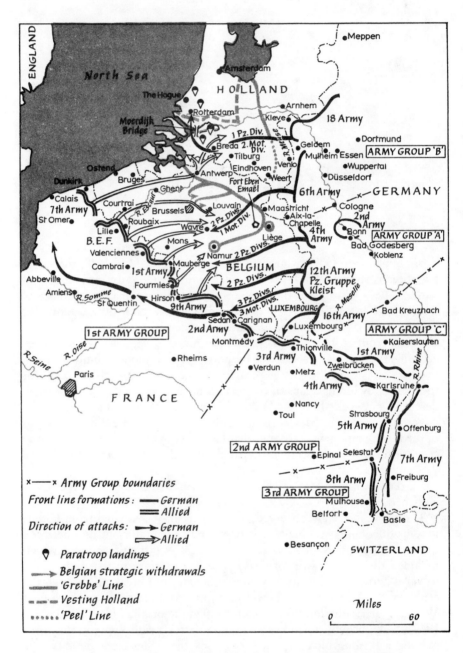

German and Allied Plans for the Western Front, 1940

Erich von Manstein, Chief of Staff to Army Group South, who had made a study of the proposed invasion schemes and who considered that adherence to the Schlieffen Plan would be fatal, produced a new plan which the Führer upheld, and which was put into operation. The Germans had foreseen that the Allied strategy would be based upon the assumption that there would be no direct attack on the Maginot Line (which extended along the German frontier from the Swiss border, near Basle, up to Montmédy on the southern end of the Luxembourg frontier) but that instead the attack would be by invasion through neutral Holland and Belgium. The Germans correctly assessed that, in order to counter this threat, the French Army and the British Expeditionary Force would thrust up through Belgium to a defensive line running from Antwerp, around Brussels, through Louvain, Namur, and Dinant, incorporating the Belgian Army in their combined forces when, as was inevitable, that army was forced back from the Belgian frontier with Germany. The Germans assumed, again correctly, that in the centre the Allies would depend upon the natural defence of the Ardennes terrain, and that their military strength would therefore be weak in this area. On these assumptions, Hitler's plan, so much in line with von Manstein's thinking, would enable the Germans to breach the link between the Allied armies lying on the line of the River Dyle and the left flank of the Maginot Line, a breach that would run from Antwerp to the northern end of the Maginot Line itself. Then, using Panzer divisions in conjunction with other forces to break through in the Sedan area, outflanking the Allies from the centre and driving towards the west coasts to cut them off from their southern bases, the Germans would be able to bottle up the main strength of the French, British, and Belgian armies against the sea. Success, of course, also depended upon the German Army being able swiftly to neutralise Holland, through which a northern thrust would be made, and upon its having the strength to compress the French and British back into Northern France. This compression would be achieved by attacks from the north, and by holding up any Allied retreat to the south of the Rivers Aisne and Somme with the forces they could pour through the central gap in the Allied lines in the Sedan area. These forces would also exercise a pincer movement by driving swiftly through to the coast at Abbeville and St Valéry-sur-Somme.

It was a bold plan, and once Hitler had forced it through against the initial prejudices of the Army General Staff, who preferred text-book-approaches to strategy and who considered the Schlieffen Plan-based scheme to be sounder, it was elaborated upon considerably by the General Staff and turned into a detailed operation. By 10 May 1940, Germany had undoubtedly profited by the absence of any military activity on its Western Front since the outbreak of war on 3 September

1939. During the Polish campaign there had been a bare fifty-two divisions available for other operations in the west, but these had been enough at the time, due to the total lack of military preparedness on the part of France and Britain. Now, with Poland subdued, with Hitler's pact with Stalin enabling him to reduce his forces in the east to a bare minimum, and with the expansion of the armed forces during the quiescent eight months of the Phoney War, Germany had 155 divisions, of which ten were Panzer divisions. Of these divisions she was able to deploy 126, plus the ten Panzer divisions (2,690 tanks, 1,000 of them being heavy tanks) in the onslaught against France. And in addition to the armour in the field, Germany had 800 tanks in reserve. Ranged against this formidable force were 103 divisions, of which ninety-four were French and nine British, although in the event of Belgium and Holland becoming involved, these 103 divisions could be supplemented by twenty-two Belgian and ten Dutch divisions, making a total Allied force of 135 divisions. The armoured strength of France and Britain , however, left much to be desired. Of the 3,000 tanks that France had available, some 500 were attached to units in the course of formation and training, and a large number were of obsolete design and were therefore held in reserve. Moreover, those that were deployed were mostly light tanks. The BEF had only 310 tanks in France, 100 of which were light infantry tanks. But the greatest superiority of the German armour emanated from the highly efficient organisation of the Panzer forces themselves, deriving from practical military application in the Spanish Civil War, the invasions of Austria and Czechoslovakia, and the campaign in Poland. These experiences had also taught the Panzer divisions to operate in close conjunction with the Luftwaffe's dive-bombers, and thereby to develop devastating tactics in co-operation.

During the night of 9/10 May the German Army began its invasion of Luxembourg, Holland and Belgium, without any declaration of war upon those countries. The invasion was preceded by widespread air attacks on the airfields, communications, and headquarters of the Western Allies, and of Holland and Belgium.

And, also on 10 May, Hitler gained a new adversary. Neville Chamberlain, faced with impending disaster in Norway and the worsening situation elsewhere in Europe, resigned as Prime Minister of Britain, and Winston Churchill became the new Premier. There was in truth little that Churchill could do to influence the events of the next few weeks, for the die was already cast. But at least Britain now had at the helm a man who could take the difficult decisions necessary in the disasters that were soon to follow, and take them decisively. Amongst those he immediately brought into his Cabinet was Anthony Eden, who became Secretary of State for War.

Shortly after 05.30 hours on Friday 10 May, the BEF was alerted and the squadrons of the Air Component moved to their advanced headquarters and aerodromes, with orders to undertake immediate reconnaissance to determine the main lines of the German advance. The orders to the Hurricane fighter squadrons were to provide air cover for the Blenheims and Lysanders during their operations, and defence cover for the Air Component aerodromes and its headquarters, just to the west of Arras. The Luftwaffe's opening blitz on this first day was not very successful, however, and the nine airfields of the Air Component and the AASF which did come under attack suffered little damage and scarcely any losses of aircraft on the ground. By contrast, the Hurricanes took a tremendous toll of the enemy. Indeed, the fighter squadrons of the Air Component and the AASF were at full stretch throughout the day protecting the forward movement of the BEF, covering reconnaissance aircraft, and defending bases. But, later on the 10th, the outlook was less rosy. While the French armies and the BEF were moving as planned into Belgium, reconnaissance revealed that the Germans had launched an airborne attack on key sectors of the Dutch frontier, on the Albert Canal bridges in Belgium, and at the Belgian Fort Eben-Emael, which lay just south of Maastricht. Little did anyone realise on this day that these assaults were not just limited to strategic advantages, but were also designed as a feint to cover the main weight of the German offensive, which was to be through the Ardennes. Then, in the afternoon, it was learned that the Fairey Battles of the AASF had attacked a German column advancing through Luxembourg, but even so the Allied Command did not at this stage appreciate that this was the prelude to a major attack through the Ardennes which was to be the lynch-pin of the German strategy. The attacks by the Battles had been made in two waves, one in the morning and one in the afternoon. Disastrously, of the thirty-two aircraft despatched, thirteen failed to return.

Throughout the morning of the 11th, the Air Component Blenheims flew repeated reconnaissance sorties over the Maastricht area to establish the strength of the German advance. The enemy was reported to have captured some bridges over the Albert Canal west of Maastricht before the Belgians had had time to demolish them, and it was soon confirmed that the Germans were crossing the canal on some of these bridges and driving on in the direction of Brussels. Aircraft losses on these reconnaissance sorties were high and the information gleaned was therefore sparse, but it appeared that the Belgian Army was already in retreat and falling back towards the chosen Allied line of defence, a line which was reached by the advancing French and British on 12 May. In fact, by the 12th the first phase of the plan of the Supreme Commander of the Allied Forces in France, the French General Gamelin, had been completed. The French Seventh Army had reached Antwerp, and had occupied the Walcheren Islands and South Beveland in Dutch territory. Seventeen Belgian divisions, after retreating from the Albert Canal, had fallen back to their prescribed positions between the right flank of the French Seventh Army at Antwerp and the left flank of the BEF at Louvain, the latter having by now reached its position along the River Dyle between Louvain and just south of Wavre. The French First Army had moved up to a line from the right flank of the BEF down to Namur, and the French Ninth Army was ranged between Namur and Charleville-Mézières, north-west of Sedan. The French Second Army had filled the gap in front of Sedan down to Montmédy and the left flank of the Maginot Line. 12 May therefore provided some good news, limited though it was, and only gleaned through reconnaissance by the Air Component squadrons. But such good news was quickly followed by bad. The AASF Battles and Blenheims had suffered disastrous losses at the hands of swarms of German fighters in the Maastricht-Tongres area, where raids had been made against the enemy advance. On 10 May there had been 135 AASF bombers serviceable; by the evening of the 12th there were only 72. If there was any cheer to be had at this stage, it was because the Hurricanes, although heavily outnumbered, were putting up a magnificent fight against the Luftwaffe's Messerschmitt 109 and 110 fighters, as well as against the Heinkel 111 and Stuka bombers.

In the early evening of the 12th Vitry-en-Artois, the advanced airfield for the Air Component's No. 52 Wing, suffered its first major air attack. Fortuitously, some Hurricanes based at Vitry were returning from providing fighter cover for No. 52 Wing Blenheims which had been on reconnaissance. The fighters immediately plunged into a furious battle with the German bombers and their escorting Me109s and 110s, while the Hurricanes still on the ground 'scrambled' at near-miraculous speed to join the fray. For those on the ground it was a cheering sight to see the Hurricanes wheeling in the sky as they engaged the enemy at varying heights rarely above 2,000 feet. Ten enemy aircraft were shot down for the loss of one Hurricane, the pilot of which parachuted safely to earth with only minor injuries. The Germans broke off the engagement and fled to their lines, but a number of Blenheims and Hurricanes under service were destroyed on the ground, a loss that could be ill-afforded.

On the 13th Vitry and Arras were under constant air attack, as were other military centres in northern France. Moreover, the roads leading southwards from the Allied front had become choked with civilian refugees with lorries, cars, horses and bicycles pulling carts, prams and push-carts, all loaded with personal possessions. Mostly these were Belgians, but the French in these northern areas were also getting out fast. The chaos on the roads hampered all military movements, and was made

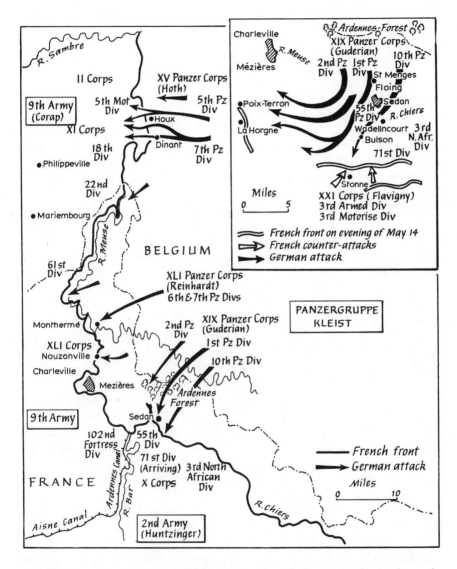

The German Approach to the River Meuse and (inset) the Breakthrough at Sedan. All along this sector the Germans broke through the weak French defences with ease.

worse by German fighters flying low above the traffic and spraying it with their front guns. The sight, when the aircraft had gone, was appalling: mothers still hugging their mutilated and dead children, and dead relatives being transported away to hoped-for safety somewhere in France. But far worse, in many ways, was the information pouring in of German advances all along the Allied front, and in particular of the thrust through the Ardennes at Sedan. By the night of the 13th the Germans had established themselves on the west bank of the River Meuse on either side of Sedan and Dinant, yet, despite both British and French air reconnaissance reports that this break-through was by major forces with massive armoured support, the Allied armies were still undecided whether the weight of the enemy advance would in fact be through Maastricht towards Brussels, or through the Ardennes against the left of the Maginot Line. The idea that perhaps the Germans might punch their way across the Meuse and then turn westwards to the coast in the rear of the Allies, did not occur to the French or British High Commands until too late.

Nor was all well elsewhere. By the evening of 13 May the Dutch Air Force had been virtually destroyed and, with the situation in Holland now desperate, Queen Wilhelmina and her Government embarked on a British destroyer for England. On the following day, the 14th, Rotterdam was devastated by a brutal and senseless bombing attack by the Luftwaffe. Within hours Holland capitulated, the surrender being signed at 11.00 hours on 15 May.

During the 14th, 15th, and 16th the Air Component and AASF airfields were under constant – mostly low-level – air attack, including dive-bombing. They also endured front-gun strafing by German fighters when, on rare occasions, these were able to disengage themselves from the defending Hurricane force, now increased by two extra squadrons brought from England to reinforce the Air Component fighter force. These were additional to the four reinforcing squadrons which had already been despatched on the 10th and 11th for protection of AASF and Air Component bases, and for escort duties with the BEF bomber and reconnaissance aircraft. The valour of these Hurricane pilots was fantastic, fighting as they did against odds of as much as three and four to one; indeed, it was their skill and courage which enabled the rest of the British air forces to carry on with their unenviable job with some degree of success. But it could not last, and everyone knew it. Immense damage was being done to the aerodromes, Blenheims and Hurricanes were frequently destroyed on the ground, casualties to both flying and ground crews were becoming unsustainable, and serviceability of aircraft was beginning to suffer from shortage of spares. Moreover, on the 15th, the German Panzer forces and their support troops, instead of turning the left flank of the Maginot Line after their break-through in the Sedan area and their crossing of the River Meuse, had swung north-westwards to the west coast, in accordance with Hitler's plan to cut off the Allied armies from the south and to bottle them up against the coast north of the Somme. In these engagements the French Ninth Army, which had been meant to cover the front from Namur through Dinant to Sedan, was routed, as was the French Second Army covering Sedan down to Montmédy. On the same day, 15 May, the French Seventh Army, which had moved up to Antwerp and into South-West Holland on the 11th and 12th, was now in retreat. With Belgium's seventeen divisions also in retreat, the BEF was forced to fall back from its forward position in order to conform.

The Luftwaffe's destruction of Rotterdam on the 14th had revealed a ruthless attitude to civilian life and property. As a result, there was considerable pressure for the British to give up their useless leaflet raids, in which RAF bombers dropped millions of leaflets over Germany urging the population to throw out Hitler and sue for peace. Instead there was now a powerful demand from the new War Cabinet and from the French for the Royal Air Force to undertake bombing raids against the Ruhr towns, regardless of whether such raids would endanger civilian life. German air superiority had so paralysed the French ground forces that some diversion of the enemy's bombers from their present objectives was imperative. Drawing off the enemy's fighters to defend the homeland against bombing raids was expected to deter the German bombers from their attacks, since they would no longer have adequate fighter cover. On 15 May, therefore, the decision was taken to use RAF Bomber Command as a strategic bombing force, but as the French had virtually no modern bombers, their possible contribution was not taken into account. In fact, the French Air Force had by now almost ceased to exist.

The decision to bomb German towns settled another tenuous argument. The French had been demanding ten more fighter squadrons, over and above the ten Hurricane squadrons already in France, but Air Chief Marshal Sir Hugh Dowding, the Commander-in-Chief of RAF Fighter Command, resolutely opposed the transfer of any more squadrons (there were already ten AASF and thirteen Air Component squadrons in France). He was afraid that British bombing of the Ruhr and other German towns would attract reprisal raids and he wanted to be ready to defend Britain effectively against such attacks. If the drain of fighters to France continued, Dowding visualised his forces being 'bled white and in no condition to withstand the bombing attack which will inevitably be made on this country as soon as our powers of resistance fall below a level to which we are already perilously close.' By the grace of God, he won his point.

On the night of 15/16 May, ninety-six Wellington, Whitley and Hampden bombers of Bomber Command took off to bomb objectives east of the Rhine. Seventy-eight aircraft were directed against oil plants, although only twenty-four claimed to have found them. Then, on the 17th, it was decided to change the decision to bomb targets in Germany in favour of bombing attacks against the German armoured divisions and infantry which had broken through the French lines and crossed the River Meuse. From then onwards Bomber Command's efforts were divided between objectives east of the Rhine and targets in the land battle area. Results from both forms of activity were poor. The military targets on the Meuse and other break-through areas were totally unsuitable for night bombing, and the industrial haze of the Ruhr baffled crews' identification of their targets, since they had no suitable night navigation and target-finding equipment at this stage of the war. The result was that during the next few nights Bomber Command achieved none of its objectives. Industrial damage was negligible and no delay was inflicted on the advance of the German Army; indeed, not a single German fighter or bomber was diverted from the attacks on the Allied armies.

By the 16th, the AASF bases astride the River Aisne were threatened and had to be withdrawn southwards. At mid-morning on the 17th, with Arras under constant air attack and the Air Component bases in danger of being surrounded by the German advance, Air Component HQ instructed all its squadrons to withdraw westwards to Component aerodromes near the coast north of Abbeville. The Headquarters itself retreated to Boulogne.

Many sorties were flown by all squadrons of the Air Component on the 18th, and with the information coming from these squadrons it was evident that the situation had become desperate. The Panzers which had broken through at Sedan were continuing their advance at a staggering pace, and there was absolutely no sign of any opposition to their progress. By evening they had passed Peronne and St Quentin, and were approaching Amiens, moving along the line of the Somme. Further north, the Germans had already passed Brussels and had broken through the French and Belgian lines at many points, driving towards Cambrai, Arras, Mons, Ghent, and Antwerp. The BEF had been driven back to the River Scheldt and, although intact as a fighting unit, was fast falling back to the coast. In fact, the entire Allied armies were being systematically bottled up between the River Somme and the Scheldt. What French reserves there were south of the Rivers Somme and Aisne seemed incapable of making any impression on the German drive to the coast, now heading in the direction of Abbeville and St Valéry-sur-Somme. Indeed, the French appeared to have little stomach for battle, and the Belgians were clearly ready to surrender at any moment – which they did ten days later, on 28 May.

In the early afternoon of the 19th all Air Component units were ordered

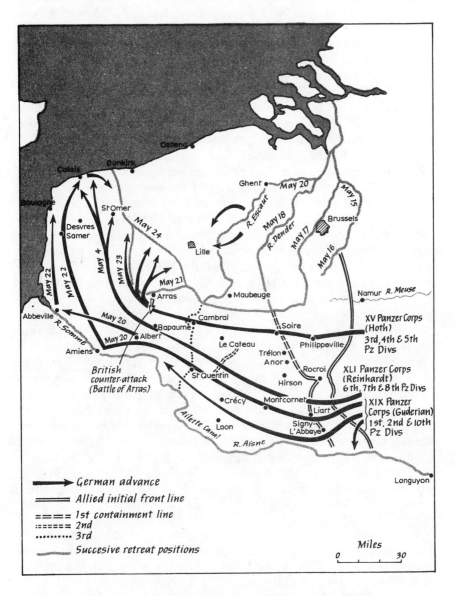

Calais
Dunkirk
Ostend
Ghent May 20
Boulogne
St Omer
Desvres May 24
Samer
May 4
May 23
May 22
May 22
May 27
Arras
May 20
Cambrai
May 20 Albert
Bapaume
Abbeville
R. Somme
Amiens
Le Cateau
St Quentin
British
counter-attack
(Battle of Arras)
Crécy
Montcornet
Liart
Laon
Signy-
L'Abbaye
R. Aisne
Ailette Canal
Brussels
May 15
May 16
May 17
May 18
R. Escaut
R. Dender
Lille
Maubeuge
Namur R. Meuse
Soire
Philippeville
Trélon
Anor
Rocroi
Hirson
Longuyon

XV Panzer Corps
(Hoth)
3rd, 4th & 5th
Pz Divs

XLI Panzer Corps
(Reinhardt)
6th, 7th & 8th Pz Divs

XIX Panzer
Corps (Guderian)
1st, 2nd & 10th
Pz Divs

German advance
Allied initial front line
1st containment line
2nd
3rd
Succesive retreat positions

Miles
0   30

The Panzer thrust to the Channel, 15-23 May 1940

to destroy immediately the codes and cipher books in their possession. Later, units were advised that Air Component Headquarters were being evacuated forthwith to Hawkinge in England and that all squadrons were to fly to appointed British bases without delay; the Hurricane squadrons received their evacuation orders separately. By the evening of the 21st only a few Lysanders of No.4 Squadron assigned to GHQ were left in France. The evacuation of the Air Component was carried out in such haste that most of its equipment and stores fell into enemy hands, the loss of Hurricanes in France being particularly grievous. In all 261 of these fighters had operated with the Air Component, of which only 66 returned to England – 75 had been destroyed in action and 120 damaged machines could not be repaired in time to be flown back to England. The cost of ten days' operations in France was 195 Hurricanes, something like a quarter of Britain's entire strength in modern fighters at that time.

By the 20th the Germans had reached Abbeville and St Valéry-sur-Somme, thus cutting off the routes south across the Somme, and by the 21st they had surrounded Arras and were moving up towards Boulogne, driving the BEF, the French First Army and the Belgian divisions up against the coast in the area of Dunkirk, Boulogne and Calais. By now it was evident to Winston Churchill, so recently appointed Prime Minister, that the British forces were in grave danger of being cut off, unable to escape from the German military net. He therefore ordered the Admiralty, at a War Cabinet meeting held on 20 May to assemble 'as a precautionary measure' a large number of small vessels in readiness to proceed to ports and inlets on the French coast to evacuate the troops, should it become necessary to do so. Vice-Admiral Sir Bertram Ramsay, Commanding Dover, was given operational control of this exercise, which went by the code-name 'Operation Dynamo'. It was planned, if the need arose, to evacuate the army from Calais, Boulogne and Dunkirk. Thirty craft of passenger-ferry type, twelve naval drifters and six small coasters were allocated initially, and on 22 May forty Dutch schuits which had taken refuge in British ports were requisitioned to add to the force; these were manned by naval crews for the task. In addition, many small privately owned craft and small ships volunteered for the rescue plan between the 25th and 27th, providing a substantial if amateur force to add to the official rescue team.

On 22 May Arras fell, and the BEF began its withdrawal to the coast, and by the 25th the last of the Allied troops in Boulogne had been evacuated by sea. On the 28th the escape of the BEF to the coast hung in the balance, the Germans having overrun Calais and Gravelines and thrust between the BEF and the Belgian forces, now heading towards the coast to the north of Dunkirk – that day the Belgian Army surrendered. At 18.57 hours on the evening of the 26th 'Operation Dynamo' was put into action, and the first troops were brought back to England from Dunkirk that evening. Then, on the morning of the 27 May, measures were taken to increase the 'fleet' of small craft for what was by now clearly going to be an emergency evacuation of both the BEF and as many French troops as possible. Forty motor-boats, some of them river craft, were assembled during the day and were joined by lifeboats from liners, Thames yachts, fishing boats, lighters, barges and pleasure craft – virtually anything, in fact, that could float on the water and carry some soldiers, however few. By the night of the 27th all these boats were ploughing their way across the Channel to Dunkirk, returning with rescued troops.

The miraculous evacuation of Dunkirk went on until 14.23 hours on 4 June under constant German artillery fire and bombing and strafing attacks by the Luftwaffe. When the last boat sailed back to England 338,226 men of the BEF and 26,175 French soldiers had been rescued. The German attempt to capture the entire force of the BEF had been thwarted, thanks to the resource and courage of the Royal and Merchant Navies, and of ordinary amateur sailors with their little pleasure boats, which for the occasion had been turned into men-of-war. Nevertheless, the entire operation could have been brought to nought but for the Royal Air Force. The pilots and aircraft of Fighter Command dominated the skies over the area, fighting at all heights above and below clouds, and Bomber Command continually attacked the German forces. As Churchill said:

> ... There was a victory inside this deliverance, which should be noted. It was gained by the Air Force ... This was a great trial of strength between the British and German Air Forces. Can you conceive a greater objective for the Germans in the air than to make evacuation from these beaches impossible, and to sink all these ships which were displayed almost to the extent of thousands? Could there have been an objective of greater military importance and significance for the whole purpose of the war than this? They tried hard, and they were beaten back; they were frustrated in their task. We got the Army away; and they [the Germans] have paid fourfold for any losses which they have inflicted. All of our types and all our pilots have been vindicated as superior to what they have at present to face ... May it not also be that the cause of civilisation itself will be defended by the skill and devotion of a few thousand airmen.

The last sentence was to prove most prophetic.

After Dunkirk, and in order to support French units still fighting south of the Somme but remorselessly being driven back to the Seine, British troops were landed in Normandy on 7 June, where they joined those

British units which had eluded the German trap in the north. Within days the Allied resistance was crumbling, and by 9 June the Germans had reached the lower reaches of the rivers Seine and Oise and were threatening Paris. On the 14th Paris fell, and the French Government fled to Bordeaux. A new government was formed under the aged Marshal Pétain, who was determined to sue for a separate armistice and peace with Hitler, regardless of what his ally, Britain, wanted. By 16 June General Weygand, who had replaced General Gamelin as Commander-in-Chief of the Allied Forces in France, had become the Minister for National Defence in Pétain's administration. Weygand held the view that all was over for France, and to this Pétain was quick to react. On the 17th he asked Hitler for an armistice, and ordered all French forces to cease fighting without bothering to communicate his actions and intentions to the British. During the night of the 17th/18th, therefore, the withdrawal of British troops was begun from Cherbourg, Brest, St Nazaire and other western ports. By 16.00 hours on the afternoon of the 18th the last ship had left the shores of France and 136,000 British troops and 20,000 Polish soldiers had been safely evacuated.

On 22 June 1940, French representatives signed an armistice accepting all the German terms. The formal signing took place in the same railway carriage at the Rethondes crossroads in the forest of Compiègne where, on 11 November 1918, the Germans had been humiliated. Now France also was humiliated.

Royal Air Force losses of aircraft in May and June 1940 had been serious, and every operational command had suffered heavily. The AASF lost 229 aircraft, the Air Component 279, Fighter Command 219, Bomber Command 166, and Coastal Command 66; out of this total of 959 aircraft lost, 477 were fighters. Against this, the Luftwaffe lost a total of 1,284 aircraft in the same period. The British Army's losses in men were remarkably low considering the conditions, but although the evacuation of Dunkirk and, later, from Normandy and Brittany, saved the bulk of our forces, the losses of equipment and arms were disastrous.

On 18 June, in a speech to the House of Commons and to the nation, Winston Churchill finished his survey of the grave situation with these immortal words:

> What General Weygand called the Battle of France is over. I expect that the Battle of Britain is about to begin. Upon this battle depends the survival of Christian civilisation. Upon it depends our own British way of life, and the long continuity of our institutions and our Empire. The whole fury and might of the enemy must very soon be turned upon us. Hitler knows that he will have to break us in this island or lose the war. If we can stand up to him, all Europe may be free and the

life of the world may move forward into broad, sunlit uplands. But if we fail, then the whole world, including the United States, including all that we have known and cared for, will sink into the abyss of a new Dark Age made more sinister, and perhaps more protracted, by the lights of perverted science. Let us therefore brace ourselves to our duties, and so bear ourselves that, if the British Empire and its Commonwealth last for a thousand years, men will say, 'This was their finest hour'.

Part 2

SURVIVAL

CHAPTER XV

Britain Stands Alone

On 4 June 1940, Göring's deputy, Generaloberst Erhard Milch* undertook a reconnaissance of the Dunkirk area in his personal aircraft, even before the very last boats of the British evacuation fleet had departed from the coastal waters of France. In surveying the ruins left after the flight of the British Expeditionary Force, he was amazed to see the prodigious quantities of war equipment which choked the roads leading to Dunkirk and the beaches, and which littered the beaches themselves. Tanks, guns, vehicles and other military equipment had been abandoned; indeed, the arms of the British Army in France had been left behind almost in their entirety. What had crossed the Channel back to England, Milch decided, was a completely disarmed army.

The rapid progress across France which had followed Dunkirk and which had led to the final evacuation of the remaining British south of the rivers Somme and Seine on the night of 17/18 June, convinced Milch that an immediate onslaught on Britain should be made while the island's defences were clearly disorganised, and while the Royal Air Force was licking its wounds and endeavouring to re-form. On 18 June he went to see Reichsmarschall Göring at the German Command Headquarters at Sovet in Belgium, in order to present his plan for an immediate attack upon southern England. He proposed that all available paratroops and airborne forces which remained operational after the battles of Belgium, Holland and France should be despatched at once to capture key fighter aerodromes on the south coast such as Manston, Tangmere,

* Later Generalfeldmarschall Erhard Milch, State Secretary in the German Air Ministry and Armaments Chief of the German Air Force.

Westhampnett, Gravesend and Hawkinge. The airborne attacks were to receive 'artillery' support from Stuka dive-bomber formations, which in turn were to have aerial cover from Me109 fighter squadrons. As soon as the airfields had been taken over they were to be reinforced by ordinary ground troops lifted in by Ju52 transports in second and third waves; these aircraft would also maintain supplies of ammunition whilst further troops and supplies were ferried across the Channel in sea-going transports. The air support was to be provided by Luftflotte (Air Fleet) 2 under Feldmarschall Albert Kesselring, and by Luftflotte 3 under Feldmarschall Hugo Sperrle. It was a bold plan which might well have succeeded, since Britain's ground defences were almost non-existent at the time, and the Royal Air Force, Fighter Command in particular, were near to a state of complete exhaustion.

Milch's plan did not differ greatly from the provisional plans for the invasion of Britain which were already being prepared by the German High Command under the code-name *Seelöwe* – 'Operation Sealion'. The timing, however, was significantly different. Hitler was confident that Britain would be prepared to sue for peace so soon as France was subdued, and he wanted to allow time for such peace approaches to be made before exerting military pressure. If he could avoid further conflict with the British then he could turn his wholehearted attention to the destruction of his hated ally, the Soviet Union; with that accomplished there would be nothing to stop him dominating all Europe and perhaps even the United States of America. Milch's admirable plan was therefore met with 'amazement' by Göring, and turned down as being 'untimely'. The British public was left incredulous at the failure of hordes of German bombers, paratroops and airborne forces to descend upon them in a furious onslaught whilst the country was virtually defenceless, stunned by the collapse of France.

The Germans' hesitation was to prove vital to Britain's survival. That survival could now only be achieved by RAF Fighter Command, which had performed magnificently in the Battle of France but which had lost many aircraft it could ill-afford, and whose pilots desperately needed a rest. Apart from giving aircraft production units a chance to replace losses and to build fighters in excess of planned output in June, July and August – actual output for June was 446 fighters against 292 planned, July was 496 against 329, and August 476 against 282 – the breathing space enabled a modification of cardinal importance to be introduced into all Hurricane and Spitfire aircraft. It had always been assumed that air combat would take place at medium and low altitudes and within a maximum height of about 16,000 feet, whereas in fact it was discovered during the days of the Battle of France and Dunkirk that although attacks on enemy bombers took place within the 16,000 feet ceiling, aerial combat with escorting fighters was invariably at heights in excess of 20,000 feet. At these heights the performance of the German Me109, with its variable-pitch three-bladed constant speed airscrew, was markedly superior to that of the Hurricane and Spitfire, which were only fitted with two-pitch propellers – fine pitch for take-off and coarse pitch for cruising. The variable-pitch constant-speed propellers automatically adjusted to varying engine speeds, thus improving the aircraft's performance at all heights, but in Britain to date they had only been allocated to bomber production lines.

In June, at the request of the engineer officer at RAF Hornchurch, Flight Lieutenant McGrath, the de Havilland Aircraft Company sent a team of experts to Hornchurch to carry out a trial conversion of a No. 65 Squadron Spitfire to take a variable-pitch, constant-speed propeller. The results were startling. An extra 7,000 feet was added to the service ceiling of 31,900 feet, and the aircraft gained greatly improved manoeuvrability and speed at height, and far better take-off and climbing performance. On 22 June, two days after the de Havilland test pilot, E. Lane-Burslem, had reported success, the company received a verbal order direct from Fighter Command to convert all Hurricanes and Spitfires as a matter of the utmost urgency, giving priority to Spitfires. De Havillands agreed to proceed without waiting for Air Ministry and Ministry of Aircraft Production official sanction and paper-work, and immediately began conversions at twelve fighter stations simultaneously, with a programme for completion of all Spitfires by 20 July. On 24 June, conversion kits were coming out at the rate of twenty per day, quickly increased to provide a further twenty per week to the Supermarine Company for modification of production-line Spitfires before delivery to the squadrons. As soon as the de Havilland engineers arrived at each fighter station, picked teams of NCOs and fitters carried out conversions under supervision, continuing independently after completing two or three under the watchful eyes of the de Havilland men. By 20 July all Spitfires had been fitted, but still the German onslaught had not begun. By 15 August when the real weight of the German air offensive was launched as a prelude to 'Operation Sealion', the invasion, 1,051 Spitfires and Hurricanes had been modified. Now they were ready to take on – and defeat – the pride of Germany's fighter force, the Me109, at high altitude, and to bring slaughter to the enemy bomber forces.

But even worse than the aircraft problems was the shortage of fighter pilots, a shortage made more acute by the losses in France and over Dunkirk. Air Chief Marshal Sir Hugh Dowding, C-in-C Fighter Command, had preserved some of his fighter force intact by refusing to commit the many extra squadrons demanded by the French when their own squadrons turned out to be either non-existent, or equipped with aircraft whose performance was so hopelessly inadequate that they could not survive against the German Air Force. But despite refraining from committing any Spitfire squadrons to the Battle of France, Dowding's force was still desperately undermanned for the task which he knew must lie ahead. His predicament was appreciated by Churchill who, on the collapse of France, immediately issued instructions to the Admiralty and the Air Ministry that all trained pilots who were suitable for fighter duties should be transferred to Fighter Command as a matter of extreme urgency. The Admiralty responded magnificently, handing over on 6 June forty-five partially trained Fleet Air Arm pilots for completion of training on Hurricanes and Spitfires. Thirty more were added before the end of the month, bringing the total to seventy-five, which included seven ex-RAF Volunteer Reserve (RAFVR) pilots who had been attached to the Fleet Air Arm. Ten of these naval pilots were recalled in July for service in the Mediterranean, but the remaining fifty-eight were to fight throughout the Battle of Britain, with great distinction but heavy loss, eighteen being killed in the summer and autumn of 1940 in defence of their country. Coastal Command transferred some of its best pilots to the fighter force, as did Bomber Command, and other welcome additions came from Canada, South Africa, Rhodesia, Australia and New Zealand. Some Belgian, French Czechoslovakian and Polish pilots who had managed to escape to England also swelled the ranks of Fighter Command.

To compensate, at least in part, for the shortage of pilots and aircraft, Watson-Watt's 1935 brain-child*, RDF, surrounded the south and eastern shores of Britain in a chain of twenty stations from west of the Isle of Wight to north of the Tees. These stations could detect and plot the movement of aircraft at distances as great as 100 miles, determine their altitude, and identify friend from foe by means of an instrument, fitted to all British aircraft, known as IFF – 'Identification Friend or Foe' – which was triggered into transmitting an identification signal when in the coverage of the RDF Chain transmissions. Because of this capability in detecting approaching enemy aircraft and formations, calculating their direction of approach, speed and height, the fighter squadrons could be conserved on the ground instead of patrolling, and be despatched and vectored to intercept the enemy at the appropriate time and distance from the shores of Britain. Since there was a comprehensive system of communications linking the RDF stations to Fighter Command's central operations room, which in turn was linked to the squadron bases, the fighters could be 'scrambled' at a moment's notice for direct interception of the enemy. The system did, in fact, enable Fighter Command to

* See Chapter X.

employ its limited force in a most efficient manner, thus counterbalancing to a considerable extent the shortage of aircraft and crews.

The rest of the ground defences were not in such good fettle, however. Before the war the Chiefs of Staff had recommended the provision of 4,000 anti-aircraft guns, and at the beginning of 1940 a reassessment of ground defence requirements had put the figure at 8,000 guns. But by the beginning of August 1940 just before the German onslaught, Anti-Aircraft Command possessed only 2,000 guns. The balloon barrages, a system whereby industrial areas were surrounded by tethered balloons designed to cripple low-flying aircraft, were also inadequate in numbers, but in any case they were inadequate for other reasons – the Germans soon fitted cable-cutters to the wings of their bomber aircraft, or simply bombed from above the barrages. The number of searchlights in readiness for night attacks was closer to requirements, although even these were below the level desirable for effective defence. Guns and searchlights were particularly vital in the event of a German switch to night attacks, for the Hurricanes and Spitfires could not provide the protection needed against this form of aerial offensive. The scientists had, however, been at work on this problem, having already commenced urgent development of an RDF equipment for installation in night-fighter aircraft, such as the Bristol Blenheims and Beaufighters, which would enable their crews to 'see' the enemy in the dark. Research into this device, which was known as AI (Air Interception), had begun at the end of 1939 at St Athan in Wales, where a team of Ministry of Aircraft Production scientists was working on various applications of airborne RDF to assist fighters, bombers and Coastal Command's anti-submarine aircraft.

The AI development which was being undertaken by Drs Lovell* and Hodgkin† was moved in May 1940 to Worth Matravers in Dorset, where an establishment known as the Telecommunications Research Establishment (TRE) was set up after bringing various RDF research elements from different parts of Britain under one control. At Worth Matravers the AI project continued under Lovell and Hodgkin and the overall direction of Dr P.I. Dee,‡ whose group became responsible for all RDF airborne equipment. Again, the question was whether the programme for the development of AI would produce a working system

* Later Sir Bernard Lovell, Kt, OBE, LLD, DSc, FRS, Professor of Radio Astronomy at the University of Manchester; Director of the Nuffield Radio Astronomy Laboratories, Jodrell Bank.

† Later Sir Alan Hodgkin, OM, KCB, MA, DSc, FRS, Nobel Prize for Medicine 1963; President of the Royal Society 1970-1975; John Humphrey Plummer Professor of Biophysics, Cambridge.

‡ Later Professor P.I. Dee, CBE, FRS, Head of the Department of Natural Philosophy at the University of Glasgow.

in time for defence against a night offensive. Survival against a day or night offensive now depended upon time, and the amount of time available in which to reach a state of readiness depended upon Hitler's patience in waiting for the capitulation of Britain which he believed to be imminent after the fall of France.

After Dunkirk there had been rumours, especially in neutral Eire, of a widespread movement in Britain to oust Churchill, and of general unrest at the prospect of continuing a war which could bring destruction to vast areas of the country. These rumours encouraged Hitler to believe that Britain would soon ask for an armistice, and the reports were helped on their way by the British Secret Service, which deliberately allowed traitorous and pacifist elements to send their messages to Germany through the neutral embassies in the UK and via Dublin. Even the United States was convinced that the end was nigh for Britain, and the US Naval authorities anxiously asked whether ammunition for the Royal Navy and materials for repair of its ships should be sent across the Atlantic to America. Indeed, the US went even further, proposing that the British Fleet should be ready to withdraw to American waters. To counter such alien thoughts of capitulation Churchill telegraphed Lord Lothian, the British Ambassador in Washington, on 22 June saying: 'There is no warrant for such precautions at the present time.' Two days later, concerned about the US lack of confidence in British survival, Churchill cabled W.L. Mackenzie King, the Canadian Prime Minister, asking him to speak with the President of the United States, Franklin D. Roosevelt. Part of this cable read:

> ... there is no question of trying to make a bargain with the United States about their entry into the war and our despatch of the Fleet across the Atlantic should the Mother Country be defeated ... I have good confidence in our ability to defend this island, and I see no reason to make preparation for or give my countenance to the transfer of the British Fleet. I shall never enter into any peace negotiations with Hitler, but obviously I cannot bind a future Government which, if we were deserted by the United States and beaten down here, might very easily be a kind of Quisling affair ready to accept German overlordship and protection. It would be of help if you would impress this danger on the President ...

On 28 June Churchill followed up his brief cable of the 22nd to Lord Lothian with a longer and more explicit telegram:

> No doubt I shall make some broadcast presently, but I don't think words count for much now. Too much attention should not be paid to eddies of United States opinion. Only force of events can govern

them. Up till April they were so sure the Allies would win that they did not think help necessary. Now they are so sure we shall lose that they do not think it possible. I feel good confidence we can repel invasion and keep alive in the air. Anyhow, we are going to try. Never cease to impress on the President and others that if this country were successfully invaded and largely occupied after heavy fighting some Quisling Government would be formed to make peace on the basis of our becoming a German Protectorate. In this case the British Fleet would be the solid contribution with which this Peace Government would buy terms. Feeling in England against United States would be similar to French bitterness against us now. We have really not had any help worth speaking of from the United States so far. We know the President is our best friend, but it is no use trying to dance attendance upon Republican and Democratic Conventions. What really matters is whether Hitler is master of Britain in three months or not. I think not. But this is a matter which cannot be argued beforehand. Your mood should be phlegmatic. No one is down-hearted here.

On 30 June, a week after the signing of the Franco-German armistice, Göring issued his general order for the air offensive against Britain in readiness for Hitler's command to prepare the way for 'Operation Sealion'. The German Air Force task, code-named '*Adlerangriff*', 'eagle-attack', was to be the responsibility of Luftflotte 2, based in Holland, Belgium and North-East France under Kesselring; Luftflotte 3 in North and North-West France under Sperrle; and Luftflotte 5, based in Norway and Denmark under General Hans-Juergen Stumpff. Together their resources amounted to some 3,500 aircraft and, with 75 per cent serviceable, they could rely on having at least 250 dive-bombers, 1,000 long-range bombers and 1,000 escorting fighters. Göring stated that during the air offensive it would be necessary for the three Luftflotten to co-ordinate their attacks as closely as possible, especially in respect of targets and timing. The distribution of duties between Luftflotten 2, 3 and 5 would specify not only targets, but also times and dates of attack so that, in addition to the most effective results being achieved from the bombing, the defending British forces would be split up and dissipated over wide areas. The order went on to say:

(A) The war against England is to be restricted to destructive attacks against industry and Air Force targets which have weak defensive forces. These attacks under suitable weather conditions, which should allow for surprise, can be carried out individually or in groups by day. The most thorough study from maps of the target and its surrounding area and the parts of the target concerned, that is the vital points of the target, is a pre-requisite for success. It is also stressed that every effort should be made to avoid unnecessary loss of life amongst the civil population.

(B) By means of reconnaissance and the engagement of units of smaller size it should be possible to draw out smaller enemy formations and by this means to ascertain the strength and grouping of the enemy forces. After the initial attacks have been carried out and after all forces are completely battleworthy, the task of the Luftwaffe will be:

(a) to attack the enemy air forces, its ground organisations, and its supporting industry, in order to provide the necessary conditions for a satisfactory overall war against enemy imports, provisions and defence economy, and at the same time to provide the necessary protection for those territories occupied by ourselves.

(b) to attack importing harbours and their installations, importing transports and warships, in order to destroy the English system of replenishment. Both tasks must be carried out separately, but must be carried out in co-ordination one with another.

As long as the enemy air force is not defeated the prime requirement for the air war is to attack the enemy air force on every possible opportunity by day or by night, in the air or on the ground, without consideration of other tasks.

In short, Göring's plan of campaign was to sound out Britain's defences by using small bomber formations escorted by fighters, and then to throw the full weight of the Luftwaffe against the Royal Air Force in a bid to destroy it, its resources, and the British aircraft industry. Harbours and port facilities were also to be obliterated in order to cut off vital imports from abroad. It was an ambitious plan, but it had worked in Poland, Belgium and Holland, so why not against Britain?

In fact, Göring had made a mistake, underestimating the quality, skill and courage of RAF Fighter Command, a vastly better equipped and trained force than had faced the Germans in their offensive against Poland, or even in the Low Countries and France, where Fighter Command had by no means been fully committed. Moreover, he was unaware of the secret and ever-watchful RDF Chain surrounding Britain's southern and eastern shores, which enabled Fighter Command to follow the German Air Force's every move, and to deploy its defending fighters in the most efficient manner.

Göring was so convinced that Britain would quickly sue for peace after the Luftwaffe had been unleashed against her, that he took little interest in the various invasion study papers that the High Command had prepared and submitted to Hitler on 26 June. He had misjudged Hitler's intentions, however, as became evident when, on 2 July, the Führer issued his preliminary directive for the invasion of England. The directive called for detailed planning at High Command level and, as a result, Göring found that although the Luftwaffe's prime objective was still to be the destruction of the Royal Air Force, his original planning and target selection had now to be co-ordinated with the invasion requirements of the Army and Navy. What Hitler made clear in his instructions was that Germany had every intention of invading Britain if she did not sue for peace quickly or if the preliminary bombing did not bring about her collapse. In fact, Britain was to be subdued first by the defeat of the Royal Air Force and then, if this did not produce pleas for an armistice, by a seaborne attack and invasion.

The first Luftwaffe operations over England were, in fact, flown during June, beginning on the night of the 5th/6th when some thirty aircraft attacked airfields and other objectives near the east coast. Further attacks were made on the following night, again on a small scale, and there was then a lull until 17 June, when the French asked for an armistice. From that date onwards small forces of German aircraft ranged over England every night in scattered and ineffective fashion. From the point of view of the Germans this nightly activity was designed to give crews training and experience in night operations, and at the same time to intimidate the British population, although it failed in the latter. Daylight activity, however, which was to form the heart of the German offensive, was not resorted to until the beginning of July, and even this was on a modest scale, partly because weather hampered operations during the first eight days of the month, but more so because Hitler was still not ready to give up his cherished hopes of peace with Britain on his terms, without having to force the issue by mounting a full-scale military attack.

On 16 July Hitler issued his preliminary Directive No. 16 for 'Operation Sealion'. Three days later, on the 19th, he made a speech to a specially convened session of the Reichstag in which he reviewed 'the events unique in history' which lay behind the making of modern Germany, and expressed his 'gratitude to our magnificent soldiers'. He also appealed 'once more and for the last time to common sense in general' an appeal which was in effect an offer of peace to Britain in exchange for her surrender. In this speech he said:

> The programme of the National Socialist movement, in so far as it affected the future development of the relations of the Reich with the rest of the world, was simply an attempt to bring about a revision of the Treaty of Versailles, as far as possible by peaceful means. Germany's demands for this revision will probably one day be regarded by posterity as extremely reasonable. In practice all these demands had to be carried through contrary to the will of the

Franco-British rulers. For years we were able to effect this revision without war. It finally appeared that international co-operation might lead to a peaceful solution of the remaining problem. The agreement to this end signed in Munich in 1938 was not only not welcomed in London and Paris, but was actually condemned as a sign of weakness. Now that that peaceful revision threatened to be crowned with success, the Jewish capitalist warmongers saw their pretext for realising their diabolical plan for war vanish into thin air ... If Mr Churchill and the rest of the warmongers had had but a fraction of the responsibility towards Europe which inspired me they would never have begun their infamous game. It was only due to the European and non-European bodies, in their war interests, that Poland rejected my proposals which in no way affected her honour or existence ... It took only 18 days to beat Poland. Then on the 6th October, 1939, I addressed the German people for the second time during this war. I appealed to the heads of the enemy States and to the nations themselves. At the same time I addressed this appeal to the rest of the world, although I feared that my words would not be heard ... For this peaceful proposal of mine I was abused. Mr Chamberlain spat upon me in the eyes of the world, and Mr Duff Cooper and the other political warmongers declined even to mention peace or to work for it.

After reviewing the events of the war from September 1939 to the fall of France, emphasising how it had been his own military plan which had resulted in the humiliating defeat of the Low Countries and France, he evaluated Germany's present strength. The Army, he said, was stronger than ever before. So also was the Air Force. Vital raw materials such as coal and iron were available in almost unlimited quantities, and there were 'tremendous possibilities presented by the acquisition of enormous spoils of war and the exploitation of the territory acquired.' After stating that German-Russian relations were now on a secure basis as a result of the recent treaty of friendship, the Führer went on to say:

Only a few weeks ago Mr Churchill said he wanted war. Only a few weeks ago he started air raids on civilians on the pretence of bombing military objectives. I have ordered hardly any reprisals, but that does not mean that this will be my only reply. We know full well that our reply, which will come one day, will bring people endless suffering and misery. But not, of course, to Mr Churchill, who will be in Canada. Mr Churchill ought for once to believe me when I say that a great Empire will be destroyed – an Empire which it was never my intention to destroy or harm. If this struggle continues it can only end in the annihilation of one of us. Mr Churchill thinks it will be Germany. I know it will be Britain. I am not the vanquished begging

182

for mercy. I speak as a victor. I can see no reason why this war must go on. We should like to avert the sacrifices which must claim millions. It is possible that Mr Churchill will once again brush aside this statement of mine by saying that it is merely born of fear and doubt of victory. In that case I shall have relieved my conscience of the things to come.

During the days following Hitler's speech, diplomatic representations to Britain to agree to an armistice and to seek peace with Germany were made through Sweden, the Vatican, the USA and Eire. As the German Chargé d'Affaires in Washington had attempted to communicate proposals for peace negotiations to the British Ambassador, Churchill cabled Lord Lothian on 20 July, instructing him that on no account should he reply to the message from the German representative in Washington – it should be treated with the contempt it deserved. The approaches to the British Embassies in Sweden and Eire were also ignored, as were those from the Vatican. Then, on the night of 22 July, the Foreign Secretary, Lord Halifax, brushed aside Hitler's 'summons to capitulate to his will' in a BBC wireless broadcast to the nation. He contrasted Hitler's view of Europe with the picture of Europe for which Britain was fighting, and declared that 'we shall not stop fighting until Freedom is secure.'

Finally, on 3 August, the King of Sweden made a personal appeal to Churchill to accept Hitler's offer of peace without further delay, and so end the war. The appeal was prompted by the fact that Sweden felt herself to be in peril, threatened by the German occupation of Denmark and Norway and by the Russian occupation of Finland. The Swedes were therefore anxious that the war should not be prolonged for fear of Sweden herself being occupied, and they did their utmost to seek cordial relations with Hitler. Churchill's reply was blunt:

On October 12, 1939, His Majesty's Government defined at length their position towards German peace offers in maturely considered statements to Parliament. Since then a number of new hideous crimes have been committed by Nazi Germany against smaller States upon her borders. Norway has been overrun, and is now occupied by a German invading army. Denmark has been seized and pillaged. Belgium and Holland, after all efforts to placate Herr Hitler, and in spite of all the assurances given to them by the German Government that their neutrality would be respected, have been conquered and subjugated. In Holland, particularly, acts of long-prepared treachery and brutality culminated in the massacre of Rotterdam when many thousands of Dutchmen were slaughtered and an important part of the city destroyed.

These horrible events have darkened the pages of European history with an indelible stain. His Majesty's Government see in them not the slightest cause to recede in any way from their principles and resolves as set forth in October, 1939. On the contrary, their intention to prosecute the war against Germany by every means in their power, until Hitlerism is finally broken and the world relieved from the curse which a wicked man has brought upon it, has been strengthened to such a point that they would rather all perish in the common ruin than fail or falter in their duty. They finally believe, however, that with the help of God, they will not lack the means to discharge their task. This task may be long; but it will always be possible for Germany to ask for an armistice, as she did in 1918, or to publish her proposals for peace. Before, however, any such requests or proposals could even be considered it would be necessary that effective guarantees by deeds, not words, should be forthcoming from Germany which would ensure the restoration of the free and independent life of Czechoslovakia, Poland, Norway, Denmark, Holland, Belgium, and above all France, as well as the effectual security of Great Britain and the British Empire in a general peace.

Now the die was cast. Hitler knew that Britain would never capitulate, and that military defeat of the island nation was the only means of finishing the war in the west. He hoped that it would be achieved by an air offensive alone since he and even his generals, but particularly his admirals, regarded an invasion attempt in the face of an undefeated British Navy as putting the German Army at severe risk. Churchill, however, had rejected all his offers of a peace negotiation, and so the Führer ordered the German Air Force to proceed with its offensive with a view to an invasion being undertaken in mid-September. The Battle of Britain was about to begin.

'There was nothing to stop him imposing his will on the people . . .' Hitler addressing 120,000 storm-troopers at Nürnberg in the 1930s.

(Inset) A demonstration by the German Sudeten Party in Czechoslovakia, 1938. The Nazi uniform was banned, but the Party was secretly financed from Germany.

Hitler greeting Mussolini at the Brenner Pass in 1938. The Italian leader's compliance allowed the Nazis to take over Austria in March of that year.

The Anschluss. Left to right: Himmler, General Keitel and, beside Hitler, Dr von Seyss-Inquart, the Nazi puppet who took over as Austrian Chancellor.

The 'Men of Munich', who between them settled the fate of Czechoslovakia on 29 September 1938: (left to right) Chamberlain, Daladier (French Prime Minister), Hitler, Mussolini, and Count Ciano (Italian Foreign Minister, and Mussolini's son-in-law).

'Peace in Our Time' was to last for under a year: Chamberlain at Heston Aerodrome, waving the paper bearing Hitler's signature, 30 September 1938.

Reichsmarschall Hermann Göring, Hitler's deputy and head of the Luftwaffe throughout the war. Göring had been the last commander of the crack von Richthofen fighter squadron during the First World War.

Hitler with Dr Josef Goebbels, the Nazi Minister of Enlightenment and Propaganda from 1933-45. Despite his outward optimism, Goebbels's private diary recorded the shattering physical and psychological effects of the Allied bombing raids.

The author (right) with Dr Albert Speer, the former Nazi Minister of Armaments and Munitions, at the latter's house in Heidelberg in 1972. Speer provided considerable evidence of the effectiveness of the Allied bomber offensive, and believed that it was a crucial factor in the German defeat.

The RAF College, Cranwell, in 1933. The old Cadets' Mess and Quarters are in the foreground, with the familiar New College under construction in the background.

(Top) The author, as a Cranwell cadet, with an Avro 504N in 1932. Despite the age of its design (it had served in the First War), the 504 was the RAF's initial flying-training aircraft from 1927 until 1934.

(Inset) The Avro Tutor, successor to the 504 as the initial flying-training type.

'A force of obsolete wooden biplanes'—Armstrong-Whitworth Siskin IIIAs in 1932.

Hawker Hart light bombers in 1934, one of the several variants of the Hawker Fury fighter, and among the last open-cockpit biplanes to be delivered to the RAF.

Westland Wapitis patrolling over the North-West Frontier of India in 1935. The RAF achieved considerable success with this method of 'imperial policing'.

The revolutionary Fairey Monoplane at Cranwell in 1933, before its record non-stop long-distance flight from Cranwell to Walvis Bay, South-West Africa. It covered the 5,431 miles in 57 hours and 25 minutes.

Equally revolutionary was Fairey's massive Night Bomber, later renamed the Hendon when it entered service, which brought about a radical change in the concept and design of the RAF's bombers.

The Handley Page Hampden which, with the Whitley and the Wellington, bore the brunt of the early raids over Germany. The aircraft was a disappointment, having a small bomb-load and restricted range, and its defensive armament was poorly sited.

The Vickers Wellington, built on the Barnes Wallis-developed geodetic-construction principle, was able to carry a reasonable bomb-load and to absorb a considerable amount of battle-damage, but was still not really up to the task of carrying the war, nightly, to Germany.

The Hawker Hurricane, the first of the RAF's 'modern' eight-gun fighters bears a distinct resemblance to its ancestors, the Fury series biplanes. Hurricanes bore the brunt of the fighter action in both the Battle of France and the Battle of Britain.

The four-engined Avro Lancaster which, with the Short Stirling and Handley Page Halifax, also four-engined, superseded the unsatisfactory twin-engined bombers in the strategic bomber offensive. The cupola for the H_2S scanner is clearly visible beneath the fuselage.

The interior of an RDF early-warning station in 1940. Information about incoming German raids was passed from these stations to the Fighter Command Groups, which would send up fighters to intercept the enemy.

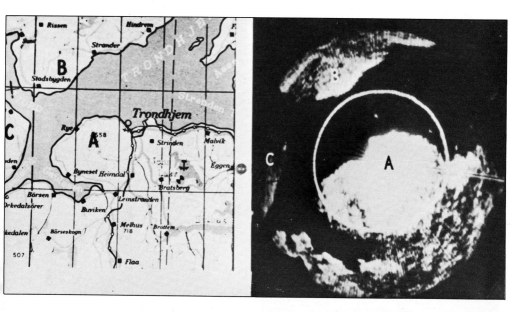

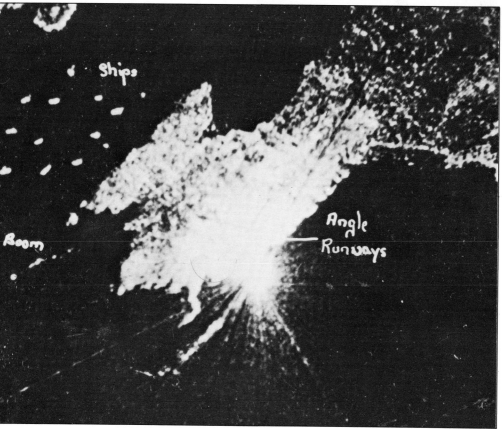

The RDF aids to navigation and blind-bombing played a considerable part in the bomber offensive. The picture shows (left) a map of the Trondheim area of Norway; on the right, a photo of the 'picture' of the same area as it appears on an H_2S cathode-ray tube. The circle is the bombing ring, and the line running from the centre to the right of the picture is the aircraft's heading.

The remarkable results obtained with the later marks of centimetric H_2S—photo by the author of a MkVI ($1\frac{1}{4}$-cm K-band) H_2S tube, showing a detailed 'map' of Milford Haven.

(Top left) Lord Renwick of Coombe, who (as Sir Robert Renwick) by 1942 had overall responsibility for the development and production of all ground and airborne radar systems.

(Top right) The author (as a Group Captain) in 1943, when he was Chief Radar Officer to the C-in-C, Bomber Command.

The Operations Room at Bomber Command HQ, High Wycombe; the author (left) with Air Vice-Marshal Saundby, Deputy C-in-C and Harris's right-hand man.

(Top) Flight Lieutenant (later Wing Commander) E. J. Dickie, who, as a member of the staff of the RDF Department, did considerable work with the navigational and blind-bombing devices for the bombers.

(Left) Dr A. C. B. (now Professor Sir Bernard) Lovell, who was responsible, under Dee, for the development of H_2S.

Dr (later Professor) P. I. Dee, who headed the group at TRE responsible for the development of most of the RDF navigational and blind-bombing aids.

Left to right: Saundby, Air Marshal A. T. Harris, C-in-C, Bomber Command, and Air Commodore R. Harrison examining bomb-damage photographs in 1942, not long after Harris had taken over the Command.

The powers behind the Allied strategic air offensive against Germany, photographed at Harris's official residence, 'Springfield', in 1943. Left to right: General H. H. ('Hap') Arnold, Commanding General of the US Army Air Forces; Harris; and Brigadier-General Ira C. Eaker, commanding US Eighth Bomber Command.

Arnold (left) with Air Chief Marshal Sir Charles (later MRAF Lord) Portal, Chief of the Air Staff, at the Quebec Conference in August 1943.

The Yalta Conference, February 1945. Churchill, Roosevelt and Stalin with Eden (behind Churchill) and Molotov (behind Stalin). The Conference had a profound effect on the post-war world, and also upon the direction of the air offensive against Germany.

In March 1945, Montgomery's Twenty-First Army Group made an amphibious assault crossing of the Rhine. Bomber Command's raids crushed German defences and casualties to the Allies were consequently light—so calm was the area that Churchill, Field-Marshal Sir Alan Brooke, the CIGS (centre) and Montgomery were able to enjoy a picnic lunch beside the river in peace.

Air Chief Marshal (later Marshal of the RAF) Sir Arthur Harris, C-in-C Bomber Command from 1942 until the end of the war. He died in April 1984, just a few days before his 92nd birthday.

CHAPTER XVI

The Battle of Britain

Daylight activity by the GAF (German Air Force) from 10 July to 10 August was concentrated primarily against sea-going convoys in the Channel and those taking a route west of Ireland. These attacks on shipping carrying essential supplies to Britain were supplemented by raids on coastal ports, including Falmouth, Plymouth, Weymouth, Portland, Southampton and Dover, and supported by aerial mine-laying at night. In terms of ships sunk the daylight attacks were only moderately successful, the total lost amounting to some 40,000 tons – almost the same tonnage was sunk as a result of mine-laying by night, and this with far smaller losses of aircraft. However, the flying effort forced upon Fighter Command by the daylight attacks was very large, amounting to some 600 sorties a day during what was a very testing phase for the Command's limited resources of pilots and aircraft. Since the fighter escorts with the convoys were of necessity small, a handful of Spitfires and Hurricanes were invariably in aerial combat with German formations of 100 or more aircraft, outnumbered by three or four to one. It says much for the skill and courage of the fighter pilots that during this period they shot down 227 German aircraft for the loss of 96. One factor which contributed towards the defending fighters' success was the withering fire-power of the Spitfires and Hurricanes with their armament of eight machine-guns.

On 4 June, Dowding's force amounted to 446 operational aircraft after Fighter Command's losses of 477 aircraft during the Battle of France and the Dunkirk evacuation; the latter figure included the losses of those Hurricanes which had been attached to the Advanced Air Striking Force and the Air Component of the British Expeditionary Force. By 13

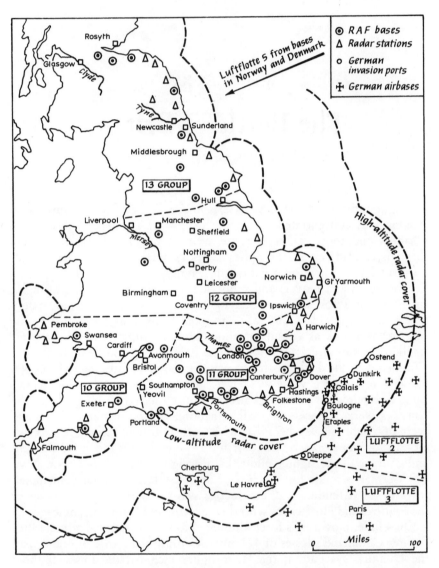

RAF and Luftwaffe Dispositions for the Battle of Britain and the Blitz, July 1940-May 1941

August Fighter Command had made a remarkable recovery and Dowding was able to dispose 704 operationally serviceable aircraft, of which 620 were Hurricanes and Spitfires backed by 289 reserves of the same aircraft. Even so, when the Air Staff reviewed the strategic consequences of the fall of France they concluded that Fighter Command needed at least double this strength to survive a German onslaught from the air. As there was no hope of procuring this number of aircraft in the near future, Britain had to rely on the quality of its fighter pilots, on the RDF Chain, and on the organisation of Fighter Command to defeat the enemy in the face of what were clearly going to be the most enormous odds. And the time for that battle had now come.

On 6 August Göring told his Luftflotten commanders that 'Operation Sealion' was to be launched during the first two weeks of September, and that the *Adlerangriff* was to start on the 13th. The real Battle of Britain was about to begin.

At the outbreak of the battle, RAF Fighter Command consisted of four Groups: No. 13 Group, with headquarters at Newcastle-on-Tyne and its squadron bases covering the east coast from Catterick in North Yorkshire to Wick in Scotland; No. 12 Group, with Headquarters at Watnall near Derby and its squadron bases so disposed as to cover the east coast from north of the Humber down to south of the Wash, as well as the industrial North and Midlands as far south as Cambridge; No. 11 Group, with its headquarters at Uxbridge and its squadron bases protecting London, and the south and east coasts from Swanage to the Thames Estuary and East Anglia to just south of Norwich; No. 10 Group, with headquarters at Box in Wiltshire and its squadron bases covering the south-west coast, Wiltshire and the Bristol Channel area.

In the initial stages of *der Adlerangriff*, Nos. 11 and 10 Groups took the brunt of the attack from Luftflotten 2 and 3, which had been ready at dawn on 13 August to open the air battle which, as Göring saw it, was to destroy the Royal Air Force and crush Britain. In the morning the opening raids were reduced, due to weather, to attacks on Eastchurch, and RAF Odiham, but in the late afternoon the full force of the two Luftflotten was directed at Portland, Southampton and Sheerness, and at RAF aerodromes in Hampshire and Kent. In all, the Germans flew 1,485 sorties – Southampton, in particular, suffered the most serious damage when large fires were started in the warehouses and docks. In all, however, the 13th was a victory for Fighter Command which, in 700 sorties, shot down 45 German aircraft for the loss of only 13. One of the notable discoveries of this day was the vulnerability of the Ju87 Stuka dive-bombers. In the late afternoon, No. 609 Squadron from Middle Wallop spotted a formation of Stukas below preparing to attack their aerodrome. Half of the escorting Me109s were already being engaged in combat by Hurricanes of No. 238 Squadron, also from Middle Wallop, and thirteen 609 Squadron Spitfires promptly dived through five Me109s shooting down one on the way, and proceeded to attack the Stukas from out of the sun as they began their dive upon the aerodrome. Within seconds nine of the dive-bomber Stukas were streaking to the ground in flames. One pilot from 609 Squadron was reported as having said during his intelligence interrogation that he had been sad to have missed the 'Glorious Twelfth' that year, 'but the glorious thirteenth was the best day's shooting I ever had!'

A similar fate befell the Stukas in the following days and Göring was forced to concede that his precious dive-bombers, so successfully employed in Spain and against Poland and Holland, could never survive against Britain's modern fighters.

On the night of the 13th, the Germans, pursuing their plan to destroy British air power, began nightly attacks on aircraft factories. On the first evening they had some success when their bombers from Kampf-geschwader 100, a bomber group which specialised in night operations, hit the Nuffield factory at Castle Bromwich, which was making Spitfires, with eleven high-explosive bombs. This success appeared to be a lucky chance, for during the rest of August attacks on the Bristol Aeroplane Company at Filton, the Westland Aircraft Company at Yeovil, Rolls-Royce at Crewe, and the Gloster Aircraft Company at Hucclecote, Gloucestershire, were a dismal failure, KG100 failing to drop its bombs within even five miles of the targets. This inaccuracy at night continued until the Germans put into use their newly developed blind-bombing aids, known as *Knickebein* and *X-Gerät**, but these did not become operational until late October.

After the intense fighting of 13 August, GAF operations were more subdued on the 14th, but Fighter Command was kept active with scattered raids over the west and north-west, and attacks on RAF stations at Manston, Tangmere, Andover and Middle Wallop, amongst others. The score for the day was nineteen German aircraft shot down for the loss of eight British.

15 August, however, was to see the heaviest fighting of the entire battle, when Luftflotte 2 attacked the south-east, Luftflotte 3 the south, and Luftflotte 5, based in Norway and Denmark, was brought in for the first time to operate against the north-east. The plan was to engage the British fighters from the south-west to the north-east, thus stretching their resources beyond their capacity to mount an effective defence on such a vast front. In this way Göring reckoned that his bomber forces would be able to attack and wreck RAF Stations and other vital targets

* These systems are described in the next chapter.

188

with comparative impunity. It was perfect weather for the assault, with a ridge of high pressure over the British Isles giving clear sunny weather and only slight broken cloud over the Channel.

The first attack was made against the south-east. At 11.29 hours a formation of some fifty Ju87s, escorted by the same number of Me109s, crossed the coast between Dover and Dungeness, with RAF Hawkinge and Lympne as their targets. No. 54 (Spitfire) Squadron from Hornchurch and No. 501 (Hurricane) Squadron from Gravesend met the force, attacking the Stukas from out of the sun and engaging the escort fighters in furious combat. At Lympne hits were scored on the sick-quarters and several other buildings, but the most serious damage was that done to water and power supplies, which were cut off as a result of direct hits on installations. Even so, the aerodrome was fully serviceable again within forty-eight hours. At Hawkinge the damage was less, with one hangar hit and a small barrack block destroyed. The most serious consequences of the raid were the temporary shut-down of the RDF stations at Rye, Dover and Foreness due to power failure caused when the electric mains were hit. The enemy, however, paid dearly and was driven off with severe losses; into the bargain, another German formation of fighters only was driven back before it could reach the British coast.

While the Channel remained the scene of repeated alarms, constantly forcing 11 Group to put up intercepting patrols, there followed an attack which was to prove the most dramatic of the day. Banking on surprise and ignoring the capabilities of the RDF Chain (a feature of Britain's defences which the Germans still regarded as of no real value), Luftflotte 5 launched two simultaneous attacks in the north-east. At 12.08 hours No. 13 Group Operations Room received its first warning of the approach of enemy aircraft. The RDF plot indicated that they were opposite the Firth of Forth at a range of nearly a hundred miles, heading south-west and numbering thirty-plus. Given such early warning, 13 Group's fighter squadrons were scrambled in ample time to be put in an excellent position for interception. No. 72 Squadron (Spitfires) was the first to intercept, thirty miles out beyond the Farne Islands, and reported that the enemy, far from numbering some thirty aircraft, consisted of sixty-five He111 bombers and thirty-four Me110 fighters. Nothing daunted, 72 Squadron sailed into the formation from the flank, one section attacking the fighters and the rest engaging the bombers, taking the Germans completely by surprise, inflicting heavy losses amongst the Heinkels, and splitting the formation into two parts. One of these parts was savagely mauled by 79 Squadron Spitfires before it reached the coast north of Sunderland, and the other half was engaged by Hurricanes of Nos. 605 and 607 Squadrons and Spitfires of No. 41 Squadron just off

Sunderland. The Messerschmitt escorts, short of petrol and out-manoeuvred by the Hurricanes and Spitfires, turned back and fled for their bases in Norway. The He111s, after dropping most of their bombs in the sea, also turned and ran for home. Not a single factory or airfield was hit, the only damage being to twenty-four houses in Sunderland.

Meanwhile, a hundred miles to the south, an unescorted formation of fifty Ju88s was detected heading towards Scarborough. Spitfires from No. 616 Squadron were the first to engage the enemy ten miles off Flamborough Head, and they were quickly joined by 73 Squadron's Hurricanes. Together their attacks resulted in the destruction of several of the enemy, but the bulk of the Ju88s succeeded in crossing the coast, some turning north to bomb Bridlington, where houses were hit and an ammunition dump was blown up, the others attacking RAF Driffield, a bomber station in Yorkshire, where they damaged four hangars and destroyed ten Whitley bombers on the ground. By 14.20 hours the last of the German aircraft had turned for home, having demonstrated their impotence to operate successfully by day without a heavy Me109 escort in the face of the fighting superiority of the Hurricanes and Spitfires.

In the afternoon, as the raids in the north ceased, the third great operation of the day began, with attacks against the RAF stations at Manston, Martlesham Heath and Eastchurch, and against the RDF stations at Dover, Rye, Bawdsey and Foreness, although these achieved little success. At Rochester on the Thames Estuary, however, the Germans had better luck when they hit the Pobjoy and Short Brothers aircraft factories, causing loss of output for several weeks. Then, between 17.00 and 17.20 hours, the south-coast RDF stations detected some 250 aircraft from Luftflotte 3 approaching the Hampshire and Dorset coasts. Eight Fighter Command squadrons were 'scrambled' in time to begin interceptions before the enemy force crossed the English coastline. All told, 150 Spitfires and Hurricanes, the largest force so far put up by Fighter Command to meet one attack, engaged the enemy in fierce battles off Portsmouth and Portland. The Germans suffered substantial losses, and many were beaten back before they could cross the coast, while those that did cross were relentlessly pursued and harried over the southern counties. So small was the proportion of bombers to escorting fighters, due to the successes already achieved by Fighter Command, that the damage on the ground by bombing was minimal. Only at Middle Wallop, attacked in the late afternoon for the third day running (earning it the name 'the tea-time Wallop'), was any success gained, but even so, the damage to two hangars was small. No. 609 Squadron's Spitfires got off the ground before the dive-bombing started, shot down several of the Ju88s as they bombed, and harried the surviving stragglers out to sea.

These attacks were followed by yet a further approach to our shores at

18.15 hours of more than seventy aircraft plotted in the region of Calais and heading for the coast between Dover and Dungeness. Fighter Command scrambled four more squadrons, followed by another four and a half, as the enemy penetrated inland. Some of the Luftwaffe aircraft were intercepted over Folkestone and Maidstone and forced to run for home, but one formation of Me110s carrying bombs and escorted by Me109s reached Croydon. Here they were engaged by Hurricanes of 32 Squadron from Biggin Hill and 111 Squadron from Croydon, who shot down several of the enemy. But the Germans managed to bomb not only Croydon and West Malling airfields, but also the Rollason and Redwing aircraft factories, causing severe damage. Even so, the Redwing plant started up on a new site within twenty-four hours.

Once daylight operations on 15 August were over, the Germans continued their activity by night, employing some seventy bombers in scattered raids on Birmingham, Boston, Kirton, Beverley, Southampton, Crewe, Yarmouth, Harwich, Bristol and Swansea. These attacks were, however, even less effective than the daylight raids. But what had been effective was the superb defence provided by Fighter Command on that day. A total of 1,786 sorties had been flown by the Germans against England – 520 bombers and 1,266 fighters – on the 15th, yet the damage caused had been very small. By contrast, Fighter Command, in 974 sorties, had shot down seventy-five of the enemy for the loss of thirty-four of their own aircraft, in which seventeen pilots were killed while sixteen escaped with wounds. Practically every available German fighter had been used in an attempt to destroy the British fighters in the air while ground facilities were wrecked by bombing, but in the event the bombing was a dismal failure, and the German losses were far heavier than had been expected. The day's events had lasting effects on the conduct of the Luftwaffe's future operations. Luftflotte 5 was largely withdrawn from Norway and Denmark, most of its bombers and some of its fighters being transferred to bolster Luftflotte 2 in Holland, Belgium and Northern France, while what was left was confined to reconnaissance duties and limited night operations. Fighter Command's spirited opposition in the north, and in the south and south-east, forced the battle to be concentrated in the south and south-east, where heavier bomb loads could be carried over the shorter ranges, and where the Me109s could carry sufficient fuel to provide effective escort duties. Moreover, from the 15th onwards the Me109s were allowed less freedom, being ordered to stay close to the bomber formations at all times. This was a complete negation of the original plan to use them to bring the RAF to combat over a wide area and at points of the GAF's choosing, thereby dissipating the RAF's effectiveness. Now the German fighters had to sit and wait for the attack to come to them.

Another sign of Fighter Command's victory on 15 August could be found in Göring's instruction issued after the German losses had been assessed, losses which were multiplied by the wounded and dead amongst the crews of damaged aircraft that managed to reach base. In future, only one officer was to fly with any one crew; experienced men were now at a premium, and the GAF could no longer afford to lose more of its highly trained officer class than was absolutely necessary.

On the 16th, 17th and 18th the daylight raids continued, with the Germans losing 119 aircraft – seventy-one on the 18th alone – to Fighter Command's forty-nine aircraft, in which eighteen pilots were killed and thirty-one escaped to safety by parachute. The 18th was another significant victory for the British fighters, and, moreover, their success was acknowledged by the fact that Göring decided to withdraw the Ju87 dive-bombers from future operations, thus reducing his bomber force by a third. The Stukas had proved to be sitting ducks for the Spitfires and Hurricanes, and losses had been high in both aircraft and crews.

Bad weather from 19 to 23 August reduced the German activity considerably, giving Fighter Command a much needed respite, but on the 24th the Luftwaffe roared into action again and throughout the rest of August and early September it continued its raids in great force. As a result of the new German tactics, by which the escorting fighters stayed close to the bombers, squadrons of ten or twelve Spitfires and Hurricanes now found themselves engaging between twenty and forty bombers protected by as many as a hundred fighters. By sheer force of numbers the Germans were able to break through the defences. Thirty-three such raids were made in this two-week period, of which twenty-three were successfully directed at fighter aerodromes, and Fighter Command Group HQs, and other nerve-centres of defence. By 6 September the damage inflicted was having a serious effect on the RAF's fighting efficiency because of dislocation of telephone links between Fighter Command, the RDF stations and the Command's Group Operations Rooms and aerodromes. The general dislocation of the ground organisation needed to handle the Command's squadrons was, in fact, becoming a matter for grave concern.

And British losses were rising to unsustainable levels. In the two weeks following 24 August Fighter Command lost 277 aircraft against German losses of 378, but the RAF's loss of 103 pilots killed and 128 seriously wounded amounted to a quarter of all those available. Casualties had in fact become so high that fighter pilots were no longer being trained in sufficient numbers to meet wastage rates, while even the transfer of Bomber and Coastal Command pilots to Fighter Command pilots, who, after a short conversion course, joined in the fray, failed to fill the gap. Indeed, by 6 September there were no fresh squadrons to replace the tired and battered fighter units that were in action. Then, just as Fighter Command reached the point when it could no longer sustain the losses in men and aircraft incurred in fighting on such a wide front in protection of its aerodromes, Sector Stations, RDF stations, and the ports and harbours in the south-west, south and south-east, Göring switched his entire attack to London. While this meant that the capital was now to absorb the greatest weight of the raids, it also meant that Fighter Command could concentrate Nos. 11, 10 and 12 Groups in defence of a limited area, and could thereby take the opportunity of making some recovery from having had to operate at full strength over all of the south, the south-east and the Midlands.

On 1 September the RAF Photographic Reconnaissance Unit (PRU) had spotted enemy barges moving in large numbers along the South Beveland and Terneuzen-Ghent canals towards the sea, and during the next few days concentrations of barges began to build up at Ostend and Flushing. On 31 August there had been 18 invasion barges in Ostend port; on 2 September the number had increased to 70, on the 4th to 115, and on the 6th to 205. During the same week the few barges at Flushing increased by 120, at Dunkirk by 34, and at Calais by 53, and every day processions of barges, transports, motor-boats, tugs and trawlers had been spotted by high-flying PRU Spitfires, the vessels moving southwards and westwards, hugging the coast, making for the enemy-occupied Channel ports. On the evening of 6 September, after the Combined Intelligence Committee had studied the interpretation of the PRU photographs, they decided that these massive movements must mean that an attempted invasion was imminent. Invasion Alert No. 2 – 'attack probable within the next three days' – was therefore issued. In fact, heavy bombing of the concentrations of barges in the canals and of barges and shipping in the Channel by Bomber Command, and constant shelling of the invasion ports by the Navy, coupled with the undiminished activity of the British fighters, led the German Naval Staff to record on 1 September:

> The enemy's continuous fighting defence off the coast, his concentration of bombers on *Seelöwe* embarkation ports, and his coastal reconnaissance activities indicate that he is now expecting an immediate landing ... The English bombers, however, and the mine-laying forces of the British Air Force are still at full operational strength, and it must be acknowledged that the activity of the British forces has undoubtedly been successful ...

The German Naval Staff immediately reported, that owing to counter-action against the invasion fleet by the Royal Air Force and Royal Navy, preparations for 'Operation Sealion' could not be completed by 15 September. Hitler therefore postponed D-day to the

21st, and accepted the proviso that ten days' notice must be allowed, meaning that the next preliminary order must be issued on 11 September.

On the 10th, with the mounting success of Bomber Command's attacks, a further postponement was called for and the date was put off until the 24th. On 14 September, Admiral Erich Raeder, C-in-C of the German Navy, expressed the view that 'The present air situation does not provide conditions for carrying out the operation as the risk is still too great.' He recommended that air attacks on England, particularly on London, should be intensified and continued without interruption, in the hopes that a decisive defeat could be achieved in this manner – Göring could risk his beloved Luftwaffe, but Raeder was not prepared to risk his fleet. As he had feared, within a few days the Germans were to witness the consignment of more and more German shipping to the bottom of the Channel, including a third of the total force of 1,910 invasion barges.

On Saturday, 7 September, the GAF began the switch of its operations to concentrate on London.

The day started peacefully enough, but in the late afternoon the RDF stations detected a number of German formations heading in the direction of Kent and Sussex. 11 Group's reaction was to concentrate on protecting vital fighter aerodromes, as it had in the past few weeks, and 12 Group sent three squadrons from Duxford to assist, in particular to guard North Weald aerodrome. At 17.00 hours the first wave of bombers, covered by a massive fighter escort, flew up the Thames, raining down HE (high-explosive) and incendiary bombs on Woolwich Arsenal, power stations, the docks at Thameshaven and at West Ham. Soon a huge area of warehouses and dock installations was a mass of flames. The enemy formations were fiercely attacked by No.257 (Hurricane) Squadron and No. 19 (Spitfire) Squadron from Northolt and Duxford, ably assisted by the newly formed No. 303 (Polish) Squadron. Then, while the enemy's first wave was fighting its way back to base, constantly harried by Fighter Command, three fresh formations headed in towards Dover, and were promptly engaged before they had crossed the coast. As the German aircraft steadily converged on the London dock area they were again attacked ruthlessly by fighters, but the sheer weight of numbers enabled them to get through and to inflict appalling damage in London's dockland. The GAF had a price to pay, however. The twenty-three squadrons of Spitfires and Hurricanes which had been scrambled in defence destroyed forty enemy aircraft for the loss of twenty-eight. Moreover, many German aircraft staggered back to base damaged and carrying many wounded among their crews.

For London there was no respite. From 20.00 hours that night until 04.00 hours the following morning 250 German bombers kept up their attacks, easily identifying targets by the lurid glow of a hundred or more dockside fires. Between them they dropped 300 tons of HE and 13,000 incendiaries, more in fact, than had been dropped during the daylight hours. The battle was now not only against the Royal Air Force but also against the British people; the people, however, could take it, none better than the Londoners. They proved themselves a hardy breed, meeting the onslaught without fear, standing in the streets to cheer the British 'Fighter Boys' as the Hurricanes and Spitfires roared into action in a display of 'dog-fighting' that outmatched anything cooked up by Hollywood. And the 'Fighter Boys' now began to dominate the air by day.

On 8 September the Luftwaffe sent 100 aircraft in an attempt to repeat their success of the day before, but they were driven off before causing any real damage. On the 9th an attack by a somewhat larger force was again repelled, and on the 11th, after a pause due to bad weather, a number of enemy bombers got through to London but achieved no concentration and caused little damage. On the 12th and 13th cloud made any major raids impossible, although single aircraft on the 13th managed to score hits on the Admiralty, the War Office, and Buckingham Palace. One of the enemy bombers crashed outside Victoria Station after being literally rammed in the heat of battle by an incensed Sergeant R. Holmes of No. 504 (Hurricane) Squadron, who had already shot down two Dornier 17s and was out of ammunition. He miraculously survived his suicidal attack, successfully baling out and making a parachute descent to land on the roof of a house in Chelsea, from which he rolled into a dustbin, to the amazement of the occupant of the house.

15 September* brought a massive attack upon London just as its population was enjoying Sunday lunch. As 240 German bombers and their fighter escorts assembled over France, they were detected by the RDF stations, and by 13.00 hours all available British fighters had been scrambled to meet the threat. Repeatedly throughout the afternoon attack after attack was thrown against the capital – by the end of the day 1,000 German bombers had been launched against London. Constantly engaged by Fighter Command's Hurricanes and Spitfires, flown with considerable gallantry by a force of somewhat 'devil-may-care' pilots, few of the enemy penetrated to the heart of London, and the damage sustained was relatively light. But the GAF took a beating which made that day, as it turned out, the turning point of the battle. They lost fifty-six aircraft to Fighter Command's twenty-six, and many more aircraft which reached base were severely damaged, with more of their aircrews killed or wounded. After this, enemy aircraft activity was greatly reduced for more than a week.

The last of the major daylight raids came on 27 September, when three

---

* This day has since come to be known as 'Battle of Britain Day'.

attacks were made on London and one on the Bristol Aircraft Company at Filton. The Bristol factory escaped damage and London suffered hardly at all, but the Luftwaffe again took a beating – forty-five aircraft shot down against Fighter Command's loss of twenty-eight. On the 30th, in a series of smaller raids and diversions, the Germans lost another forty-seven aircraft to a British loss of twenty.

It was the end of Göring's hopes of defeating Britain by destroying the Royal Air Force. The Luftwaffe was now forced to switch to night bombing, a form of offensive for which they were neither trained nor adequately equipped. British losses in pilots and machines had been far less than those of the GAF, and, contrary to Göring's belief, the gross wastage of Hurricanes and Spitfires from all causes from the beginning to the end of September had at all times remained below the replacement rate. From 10 July to 1 October Germany's aircraft losses amounted to 1,733, against Fighter Command's loss of 915.

On 12 October the invasion was called off by Hitler, at least for the year 1940, and was finally abandoned completely on 13 February 1941. There were ample reasons: unfavourable weather; an unresolved conflict between the German Army, which demanded a landing on as wide a front as possible, and the German Navy, which believed that it could only protect a landing on a narrow front; and, above all, the defeat of the Luftwaffe by the Royal Air Force in the battle for command of the air over the Channel and Southern England.

CHAPTER XVII

The Night Offensive

At the beginning of June 1940, radio monitors operated by the Intelligence Branch of the Royal Air Force detected signals in the 30-megacycle band emanating from Western Germany. Coincidentally, a mysterious message with the code-name 'Willi Knickebein' – literally 'Willi Crooked-leg' – was picked up. It referred to transmissions on 30 megacycles from Cleve in West Germany and, in addition, gave the latitude and longitude of a position which proved to be that of Derby, where the Rolls-Royce works were situated. This information, coupled with the discovery of a Lorenz blind-landing equipment in a shot-down KG100 bomber of a complexity far exceeding that of the standard Lorenz apparatus, led Dr R.V. Jones,* Deputy Director of Intelligence Research at the Air Ministry, to become suspicious that the Germans might be developing a radio beam system for blind-bombing. Jones immediately reported his beliefs to Professor Lindemann, Churchill's personal scientific adviser and formerly Jones's Professor at Oxford University. Lindemann, in turn, reported the matter to Churchill, giving his opinion that such a system could probably be jammed or interfered with in a way that would render it ineffective, provided that the system could first be fully investigated from the air and the ground. On 17 June, further confirmation of the development of a blind-bombing system using a radio beam came from the interrogation of the crews of shot-down German bombers. Churchill immediately convened a special meeting,

---

* After the war he became Professor R.V. Jones, CB, CBE, FRS, Professor of Natural Philosophy at the University of Aberdeen.

which was held in the Cabinet Room on 21 June and attended by senior members of the Air Staff, the Ministry of Aircraft Production, and certain scientists, including Lindemann and Tizard, to hear Jones's report on the subject.

On 18 June, at Jones's instigation, steps had been taken to investigate the 30-megacycle transmissions from the air in order to establish whether they took the form of radio beams similar to the Standard Beam Approach (SBA) beams coming into use with the RAF for blind-landing at night or in fog. The unit chosen to undertake this work was the Blind Approach Technical & Development Unit (BAT & DU) at Wyton in Huntingdonshire. Interestingly, it was known that the Standard Telephone and Cable Company of Great Britain, which manufactured the SBA system, and the Lorenz Company of Germany were both wholly-owned subsidiaries of the International Telephone and Telegraph Company in the USA.

At 22.00 hours on the night of 21 June, the day on which Churchill had held his special meeting, an Avro Anson of the BAT & DU piloted by Squadron Leader R.S. Blucke,* the unit's CO, took off from Wyton on a second attempt to locate a beam emanating from Cleve in West Germany and passing over Derby in England. The aircraft was equipped with an American wireless set covering the 30-megacycle band, a set similar to the type then used by US pilots. The set was operated by Corporal Walker,† a peacetime radio enthusiast and a member of the RAF Volunteer Reserve. Soon after take-off Walker was twiddling his knobs and listening for a signal that would indicate a transmission associated with a radio beam.

A beam is a radio transmission so directed that it produces a flight path for an aircraft to follow. It is rather like the beam from a searchlight or lighthouse, its narrowest point being at the source of the transmission, gradually widening as the distance increases from the source. The beam being a radio one, however, is followed with the ears and not the eyes. The pilot knows when he is following the path of the beam because he hears a continuous buzzing note in his earphones, produced by the aircraft's receiving equipment picking up the beam's signals. This is termed the equi-signal zone. One side of this zone is indicated by an interrupted note, the note being a long blast with a pause between each blast. This side of the beam is known as the 'dash area' – the further the aircraft is away from the equi-signal zone, the longer the duration of the gap between the dashes. The other side of the beam is indicated by short notes or blasts, and is known as the 'dot area'. As with the dash area, the

* Later Air Vice-Marshal R.S. Blucke, AOC No. 1 Group, Bomber Command.
† Later Flying Officer Walker.

198

further away the aircraft is from the equi-signal zone, the longer the duration of the gap between the dots. The closer the aircraft approaches to the equi-signal zone, the shorter the gap between the dots or dashes until, on the very edge of the zone, the tones become blurred almost into one continuous note. These dot and dash areas are the guide to finding one's way to the equi-signal zone; they are also the warning to a pilot flying along the beam that he is straying to the left or right of his course.

It was not long before Walker picked up strong clear signals on 30 megacycles consisting of dashes at a rate of sixty per minute. This was encouraging and Blucke, who could hear the transmission in his earphones, headed north, confident that he was near the equi-signal zone. He was right. Twenty miles north of Wyton the dashes changed into a continuous note, indicating that the aircraft was in the beam. With great skill he now investigated the beam. He found it to be only half a mile wide with very clearly defined dot and dash edges, and by keeping close to one edge of the equi-signal zone he found that he could fly along the beam and maintain course with an accuracy to within 100-200 yards. Now came the matter of locating the beam's direction. His navigator, having confirmed the aircraft's position from a D/F fix, now plotted the path of the beam. Sure enough it extended towards Western Germany in one direction and over Derby in the other direction, and one notable feature was the narrowness of the beam at so great a distance from its source.

When Blucke landed back at Wyton he immediately telephoned a report of his findings to HQ Fighter Command, whence it was passed to Jones at the Air Ministry, who in turn advised Lindemann of the satisfactory results of the flight. Lindemann promptly informed Churchill.

The Prime Minister took immediate action, supporting Lindemann's and Jones's proposal for the formation of a radio-countermeasures unit as a matter of the first priority. Without delay, therefore, No. 80 Wing was formed under Wing Commander E.B. Addison,* with its HQ at Radlett in Hertfordshire. 80 Wing's task was to devise methods of jamming the German beam transmissions or of disrupting their effectiveness in some other manner. On the air side, BAT & DU was expanded, and its HQ and its aircraft were moved to Boscombe Down. Whitleys were added to its Ansons, and plans were made to re-equip the unit with Wellington bombers. Blucke was promoted Wing commander, remaining in command of a greatly enlarged unit which now had added to its strength a number of operational bomber crews. The unit's new task was to track down all beam transmissions emanating from Germany and

---

* Later Air Vice-Marshal E.B. Addison, AOC No. 100 Group, Bomber Command.

German-occupied territory and, in co-operation with No. 80 Wing, to check the effectiveness of any countermeasures applied to the *Knickebein* system. Both BAT & DU* and No. 80 Wing came virtually under the direct control of Churchill.

Within a very short time, BAT & DU had established that the German *Knickebein* system consisted of a beam directed over the chosen target and along which an aircraft could guide itself. A second beam from another site was so directed as to intersect the first beam at the point at which bombs should be released in order to hit the target, thus making blind-bombing a simple matter of listening for the signal at the intersection of the two beams. By early August new beams emanating from Dieppe and Cherbourg had been located and the transmitting stations identified and pin-pointed, and during July and August it had become clear that the Germans were calibrating their beams on targets in the north, the Midlands and the south-west, concentrating on large industrial centres. At the same time they were testing the system with single bomber aircraft of KG 100. During this period, ironically, BAT & DU were using special radio sets to follow every beam heard over England back to its source, while No. 80 Wing was developing an ingenious method of bending the beams. By transmitting dots and dashes from their own hastily designed transmitters, locked in such a manner to the enemy transmissions that they filled in the gaps between the dots and dashes on either side of the enemy beam, one vast equi-signal could be created. Then further dots and dashes could be superimposed on top of this falsified equi-signal zone either to the right or left of the original beam. With cunning this could be done so that a beam which had been directed onto, say, Liverpool, could be so diverted that the German bombers flew to the west of their target and dropped their bombs in the Irish Sea instead of on the city. It was during the German tests of their secret blind-bombing method that No. 80 Wing perfected its system of beam-bending, with BAT & DU aircraft flying along the enemy beams to check the effectiveness of the countermeasures. By the middle of September 80 Wing was ready to cause the maximum disruption of *Knickebein*, just in time for the German switch to a night offensive. This was most fortunate, since there was as yet no adequate air or ground defence against night bombing attacks; moreover, BAT & DU had established that the German system was accurate to within a square mile, and was therefore an excellent device for area bombing.

BAT & DU crews were, however, sceptical about how long beam-bending would confuse the Germans. They were of the opinion

* The author, as an Army Co-operation pilot out of work since the fall of France, was posted to BAT & DU on 22 July 1940.

that the enemy crews, for whom they had a considerable respect, would quickly detect the loss of quality in the tone of the signal when in the effective area of the countermeasures, because the German beams had a very strong and pure signal. While this loss of quality might be taken for ineffective jamming, a pilot would almost certainly note any change of course indicated by his compass and would therefore become suspicious of the reliability of the beam. He would then rely on his compass and ignore the beam, because once his aircraft had settled on to a steady course and was making good the calculated track for the target, it would be easy for him to maintain that track accurately for a considerable distance. It was also felt that interference with the cross-cutting beam, which was so set up as to give the indication of the point of bomb release, would also be ineffective because this beam could be switched on just before the time of attack to make a cut at a predetermined position which could be decided upon shortly before take-off.

As a result of this scepticism Squadron Leader H.E. Bufton* devised an ingenious method for bombing the beam transmitters at night, using the beam itself as a blind-bombing aid. The method was based on two fundamental facts: first, that a beam transmitter produces a beam in diametrically opposite directions, the two beams forming a straight line, as it were, with the transmitter at the middle point of that line; second, that a 'cone of silence' exists directly above the transmitter, so that if the beam is followed towards its source the continuous buzzing note suddenly stops when the aircraft is over the transmitter and then, almost immediately, starts again as the back beam is entered. Bufton's procedure was to fly down a beam until the transmitter was reached and, shortly after entering the back beam, to execute a 30-degree alteration in his course to port or starboard and maintain this for 90 seconds. He would then make a fixed-rate turn, measured on the aircraft's turn indicator, through approximately 180 degrees until the back beam was re-entered with the aircraft now heading in the opposite direction. The time taken between the moment of re-entering the beam and passing over the cone of silence was noted on a stop-watch. The wind speed and direction having been carefully estimated during the flight down the front beam, the pilot could now calculate how many seconds should elapse after re-entering the back beam before releasing a stick of bombs to fall right across the transmitting station. The procedure was then repeated, but this time bombs were released at the correct moment. In order to test this system, many dummy runs were made over the Boscombe Down SBA transmitter, which had the same characteristics as the German *Knickebein*.

---

* Later Group Captain H.E. Bufton, DSO, DFC, OC No. 109 (Pathfinder) Squadron, No. 8 Group, Bomber Command.

The British adhered to beam-bending as a countermeasure until it became evident that the Germans were no longer being fooled in the target area, and were only relying on the beam up to the point where its direction appeared to be at variance with the compass. Even then, the beam and its cross-cut were still of immense value to the Luftwaffe crews up to the near vicinity of the target, and it was therefore decided to resort to bombing to neutralise the German beams. The first attack was made on the night of 13/14 November against the Cherbourg transmitter, and succeeded in putting the transmitter out of action for two days. BAT & DU maintained its offensive using only a handful of aircraft to effect breakdowns in the transmissions during critical hours for the German crews. The enemy reacted swiftly and Göring ordered extra defences to be provided for the transmitters, including anti-aircraft guns sited along the lines of the beams on either side of their transmitters, and balloons along the approach to the transmitters. With considerable audacity, the BAT & DU crews continued with their attacks, despite having to fly a gauntlet of flak and balloons for night after night. It was not long before the *Knickebein* system became totally discredited because of its lack of reliability in the face of beam-bending and the bombing of the transmitters, but the Germans had by now produced a variation of greater sophistication.

Known as *X-Gerät*, the new German system comprised a very narrow beam intersected by three beams near the target. The first intersecting beam gave aircraft flying down the main beam a general warning of approach to the point of bomb release, the second gave imminent warning, and the third indicated the moment at which the bomb-aimer should activate a device which automatically released the bombs at the correct moment. This system was more difficult to jam and not so easy to locate for bombing. *X-Gerät* had its disadvantages for the Germans, however, since unlike *Knickebein*, the airborne equipment was not fitted in all aircraft, but only in the He111s of KG 100. As a result, KG 100 employed the system in a pathfinding capacity, with some considerable success until effective jamming apparatus was developed by No. 80 Wing at the beginning of 1941, and BAT & DU found ways of locating and bombing the transmitters most of which used the same sites as the *Knickebein* ground apparatus. But despite successful countermeasures to German bombing aids, the real answer to the night offensive had to be the actual destruction of bombers in the air, as had been the case in the Battle of Britain. But AI, the night-fighter airborne RDF, was still not sufficiently developed to act as an effective deterrent to the enemy's bombing force.

From the night of 7/8 September to the night of 12/13 November the Germans concentrated their main night offensive on London, largely on the orders of Hitler, who was furious at the failure of the daylight raids to bring about a British surrender. Göring, equally vindictive because of the RAF's failure to lie down and die, fully supported his Führer in this decision to destroy Britain's capital and seat of government as a reprisal for continued defiance of the might of Nazism.

During this period there were only ten nights when, according to German reckoning, Luftwaffe attacks did not amount to the scale of major raids; that is to say, when less than 100 tons of HE were dropped in a single night. Normally, an attack extended throughout the hours of darkness, maintaining a minimum force of 150 bombers, and an average force of 300. London, covering as large an area as it does, required very much larger bomb-loads to create extensive disruption and destruction, and few of the German bombers carried much more than a ton of bombs each. Unless the GAF could succeed in destroying key points such as power stations, gasworks and railway communications, its task was doomed to failure; in fact it displayed little or no capability to bomb so accurately and selectively. Göring, however, was confident of success, and wrote in an Order of the Day issued to his crews on 18 October:

> ... you have, above all in the last few days and nights, caused the British world-enemy disastrous losses by uninterrupted, destructive blows. Your indefatigable, courageous attacks on the heart of the British Empire, the city of London with its $8\frac{1}{2}$ million inhabitants, have reduced British plutocracy to fear and terror. The losses which you have inflicted on the much vaunted Royal Air Force in determined fighter engagements are irreplaceable ...

But it was not to be long before Göring and the Luftwaffe discovered that they had sadly underestimated the tenacity of the British people and the power of the RAF.

By mid-November, when the Germans gave up the idea of bringing about a British surrender by crushing London, over 13,000 tons of HE and nearly 1,000,000 incendiaries had been dropped on the capital. Since London was so close to the enemy's bomber bases in occupied Holland, Belgium and Northern France, the German crews had no need of their beams for locating the city. By the time the enemy switched from the intensive bombing of the capital to attacks on the industrial centres in the rest of Britain, the London docks had taken the worst pounding. The railway system had suffered too, but the great bulk of traffic was uninterrupted, except for short periods. Houses, places of business, shops and administrative buildings, including hospitals, had all suffered, but Londoners still turned up for work, almost as if nothing had happened, although cars and buses were often forced to make back-street detours in order to skirt streets blocked by rubble from wrecked buildings. Even the suburban railways were quick to find a way around damaged or blocked routes into the city. Despite the 13,000 civilians killed and the 20,000 injured during September and October alone, the population remained defiant, and showed no signs of failing morale.

More than 12,000 night sorties were flown by the GAF over Britain during this period, nearly all of them over London. From the British point of view, however, what was disappointing were the small losses suffered by the enemy. From 7 September to 13 November only eighty-one enemy aircraft were brought down, of which anti-aircraft guns claimed fifty-four, night-fighters only eight, and the balloon barrage four. The remaining fifteen crashed due to their own technical failures or as a result of a combination of anti-aircraft fire and night-fighter attacks. Given the enemy's first-line strength of 1,400 long-range bombers and an aircraft production rate of 300 per month, this loss rate of 0.7% of 12,000 sorties was so small that it was easily sustainable. What Britain still needed was a destruction rate closer to that inflicted on the Luftwaffe by Fighter Command in the earlier daylight battles.

The new phase of the German offensive began on the night of 14/15 November with a massive attack against Coventry, code-named 'Moonlight Sonata'. There was a full moon that night, and visibility was excellent. The raid was led by the He111s of KG100 acting as pathfinders and using, for the first time, their latest radio-aid system, *X-Gerät*, to help them locate the target and mark it, saturating the area with incendiaries in order to start as large a conflagration as possible to guide the main force. KG100 crossed the English coast at Lyme Bay at 18.17 hours, using the beams from the Cherbourg transmitter, and arrived over Coventry at 20.15 hours. The main force was already en route for the target from different directions, one stream approaching from across the Norfolk and Lincolnshire coasts, one crossing between Selsey Bill and Portland, and the third crossing the coast between Selsey and Dungeness. The total force employed was 437 bombers, and the attack was maintained until 06.00 hours in the morning – 394 tons of HE, 56 tons of incendiaries and 127 1,000-pound parachute mines were dropped on the city. The damage was extensive. Twelve important aircraft factories and nine other major industrial units were also affected by damage to general utilities such as water supplies, gas mains and telephone cables. Fortunately, only one electricity plant was hit. The disorganisation to transport was another serious handicap, all railway lines in and out of the city being blocked, and all road traffic having to be diverted around the outskirts of the built-up area. The loss of 500 retail shops created problems in the distribution of food, and on the aesthetic side, the beautiful and historic Coventry Cathedral was destroyed by blast and fire. A new verb had been added to the dictionary of war – 'to Coventrate'.

Recovery from the devastation and its attendant disorganisation was, however, surprisingly swift. All railway lines except one were re-opened and operating by the 18th. Unexploded bombs were speedily defused and removed, and within a few days an excellent transport service to take employees to their places of work and to evacuate the homeless was in action. Although 300 people had been killed and 800 seriously injured morale was unshaken and, like the citizens of London, those of Coventry remained defiant.

On the nights of the 15th/16th and 16th/17th London was again the target, as though to remind the city that it was not to be wholly spared from continued attention. Then, on 17/18 November, Southampton was attacked, followed by three nights of major raids against Birmingham under the code-name 'Umbrella'. In the last week of the month the GAF struck at Southampton, London, Liverpool, Bristol and Plymouth, and in December Manchester and Sheffield were added to the list of towns suffering major raids. 1940 closed with an incendiary attack on London on 29 December, in which extensive damage was caused to buildings almost entirely by fire. But in none of these raids was the destruction so effective as to bring about a disastrous disruption to production, or to have a permanent effect upon the ability of the nation to prosecute the war with vigour, and with confidence in final victory.

As the old year passed on and the new began, the German attacks were substantially reduced by bad weather. In November 6,000 sorties had been flown against Britain, in December 4,000, but in February the number declined to 1,200. However, during this period – November 1940 to the end of February 1941 – only seventy-five enemy aircraft were shot down out of more than 12,000 sorties made against Britain, and of these the anti-aircraft guns claimed two-thirds and the night-fighters one-third. These were disappointing figures, but better defence measures were about to come into operation.

The airborne RDF equipment known as AI had recently become operational in Blenheim night-fighters. It was, in effect, a miniature version of the equipment used in the RDF stations which watched for the enemy approaching the shores of Britain. AI transmitted pulse signals which, when they 'hit' an enemy aircraft, were bounced back to the night-fighter's receiver, where they were displayed on a cathode-ray tube. The equipment not only showed the presence of the enemy ahead, but measured its distance away up to about one and a half miles; once the night-fighter was on the tail of the enemy bomber it could close to a firing distance of a few hundred yards and shoot it down without actually seeing it. Experience, however, indicated that AI, which effectively enabled the night-fighter to 'see' the enemy in a limited field of vision and at limited range, could never be really effective unless there existed a highly efficient control organisation on the ground to guide a fighter to an opportune position in relation to an enemy bomber. In daylight, this positioning was done by the ground RDF stations, but since visual range in daylight is so great, getting the fighters to within five miles of a German intruder, or even further away, was good enough to ensure interception. At night, however, it was necessary to place a fighter no more than one and a half miles from, and directly behind, its quarry. By the beginning of 1941, TRE had developed an RDF ground system for this purpose which went by the name of Ground Controlled Interception (GCI).

The principle of GCI was no different from that of ordinary RDF location, except that a beam of transmitted signals was used which was narrow in azimuth and which, by being rotated, searched over a large area. Anything that the beam passed across indicated its presence by its echo and then, when the beam passed across it again, indicated its fresh position, and so on. Actually, the beam 'illuminated' any object within range once every second, since it rotated at 60 rpm. The indicator employed a radial timebase on the cathode-ray tube, instead of a linear one, which meant that instead of the object's distance being measured on a calibrated straight line across the tube, the screen had the appearance of a clock face with only one hand, the time-base being the hand. This time-base of fluorescent light revolved at the same speed as, and synchronous with, the rotating beam, and any echo from an aircraft illuminated by the beam appeared on the tube when the time-base swept over it, its distance being indicated by its distance from the centre of the tube along the line of the time-base. Since the beam rotated, the echo was only an instantaneous one, showing only during the fraction of time that the object in the air was being illuminated. On the next round of illumination the echo appeared on the tube a little closer or a little farther away, or a little to either side of its first position, depending on the speed and direction of the target aircraft, the amount of displacement on the time-base representing the distance the aircraft had travelled in one second. To make it easier to watch the progress of the echo, a screen with slight afterglow properties was used, so that the echo remained visible on the screen after the beam had ceased to illuminate the object, but just faded before the object was illuminated again. Since the beam was rotating constantly through 360° the bearing of the object was always relative to the source of the beam, that is, to the centre of the cathode-ray tube. Thus, with the tube orientated for true north, if an echo first appeared on the rotating time-base when this finger of light was just passing through the point due west as marked on the periphery of the tube, the echo's bearing would be 270° true from the source of the beam.

As with the normal RDF Station, the RDF identification equipment carried in night-fighters, IFF (Identification Friend or Foe), gave a special kind of echo when illuminated on the GCI screen which could be instantly identified. Thus, with an enemy echo and a friendly echo showing on the same tube, it was relatively easy to direct a fighter by radio until it was on the tail of the intruder. The whole process appeared on the screen in the GCI station with continual presentation of the change in the relative positions of the two aircraft; in fact, the ground controller had an accurate moving picture of the night-fighter he directed and the enemy he wished to destroy. The controller could therefore quite easily guide his intercepting aircraft into a position where the enemy was dead ahead at, say, a distance of one mile. The night-fighter's crew could then switch on the AI set and 'see' instantly the image of the enemy – all that remained was to close in and open fire.

By March 1941, with GCI established and working, and with the changeover in five of the six night-fighter squadrons in Fighter Command from Blenheims to Beaufighters, which were greatly superior for AI night interceptions, the Command's fortunes underwent a quite dramatic change. The eight non-AI equipped Hurricane and Defiant squadrons allocated for night operations also added to this change for the better as a result of their increased experience, and because they too derived assistance from GCI. Göring's night offensive was no longer to be cheap and easy. In February the enemy losses were only four by fighters and eight by guns, but during March night-fighters shot down twenty-two enemy bombers and the anti-aircraft guns seventeen. In April the score rose to forty-eight for the fighters and thirty-nine for the guns, and in the first two weeks of May the loss-figures began to be really serious for the GAF; ninety-six bombers were shot down by night-fighters, thirty-two by the AA guns, and ten crashed from causes unknown. This amounted to a loss rate of 3.5% of the total enemy night sorties for two weeks of the month, a considerable improvement upon the figure for the period from September 1940 to the end of February 1941, a bare 0.7%.

By February 1941, the German High Command was becoming increasingly critical of what had been achieved by the Luftwaffe. The doubts expressed by Feldmarschall Keitel and General Jodl about the efforts of Göring's air fleets were powerfully reinforced by those of Admiral Raeder, and at a conference on 4 February all three jointly expressed their opinion to Hitler that the GAF's attacks had neither crippled British production nor shaken British morale. Raeder emphasised that Britain's truly vulnerable points were her dependence on imports and her shortage of shipping space; German air strategy should therefore be concentrated on exploiting these weaknesses.

The defeat of Britain was now becoming a matter of urgency. Hitler regarded his pact of mutual non-aggression with Russia as a tactical move in a game of political chess, and never as a basic reorientation of his policy towards the Communist East – indeed, he cynically referred to the pact as his 'Moscow misalliance'. The war against the Soviet Union had merely been postponed in his programme of world domination while he subjugated Britain and the rest of Western Europe first. With the failure to defeat the British decisively in 1940, the decision facing the Führer in February 1941 was not whether or not he was going to war with the Soviet Union, but whether that war should be embarked upon before or after the conclusion of hostilities with Britain. Hitler chose the first alternative, almost certainly in order to deprive Britain of what might turn out to be her last possible European ally. He feared that Russia would be ready to turn on her Nazi ally the moment it appeared that Germany was losing the war with Britain, or that the war was reaching a stalemate. To strike first against what he believed to be an incompetent military nation was therefore now in Germany's best interests, he reasoned and the German High Command was accordingly instructed to be ready to move against Russia by May/June of 1941. Still anxious to bring Britain to her knees, or at least to render her incapable of offering any serious threat to Germany during a Russian campaign, Hitler supported Raeder, Keitel and Jodl and ordered a blockade of Britain to be exercised jointly by the German Navy and the GAF. Whilst the U-boats dealt with British ships at sea, Göring's bombers were now to concentrate primarily on destroying Britain's shipyards and sea ports. Checking the activities of the Royal Air Force by attacks against the air armaments industry was to take second priority, and bombing for the purpose of achieving defeat by fear was to be abandoned.

Between the night of 19/20 February and 12 May 1941, the GAF mounted sixty-one raids, using more than fifty bombers on each raid. Seven of these were against London, in particular the docks, five against Birmingham, two against Coventry, and one against Nottingham. The remaining forty-five raids were on ports, including Portsmouth, Plymouth, Bristol and Avonmouth, Swansea, Merseyside, Belfast and Clydeside, all of which were heavily and repeatedly bombed. On the east coast Hull received several attacks, Sunderland had one big raid, and Newcastle suffered two major raids. In addition there were numerous minor raids and a number of attacks on shipping, as well as constant aerial mine-laying. On the night of Friday 18 April Portsmouth received its heaviest attack, and Plymouth was subjected to four grim nights from the 20th/21st which completely wrecked the greater part of the city. April also witnessed the greatest weight of bombs dropped on London – 876 tons on the night of the 16th/17th, and 1,010 tons on the night of

Saturday 19th. Then, on the night of Saturday 10 May, came the last onslaught on London, when the capital was treated to a final 700 tons of HE and incendiaries. In terms of damage it was the most disastrous raid of all, but it was also the last raid of the 'Blitz', as this period of bombing had come to be known. High-explosive bombs crashed down with regular and sickening concussion, reducing to rubble all that they hit; incendiaries fell in thousands, so that soon the entire sky reflected the deep red stain from more than two thousand fires that spread across the city. Because of severe damage to 150 water mains, coupled with the low tide in the Thames, the fire brigades were unable to extinguish the fires, and by 06.00 hours on Sunday morning hundreds were still burning out of control. Five docks and seventy other key targets, most of them factories, were hit and disrupted or put out of action for weeks. All but one of the main railway stations were blocked, and through routes were not fully operational again until early June. More than 3,000 people were killed or injured. Even Whitehall felt the impact. The House of Commons was hit by HE and incendiaries and so severely damaged that it was out of action for years, and had to be rebuilt and restored after the war before it could be used again.

It was indeed a night of terror but, for the British, it was also a night for exultation. Thirty enemy bombers were brought down during the raid, most of them the victims of GCI and the night-fighters. For the Germans it was a devastating loss, amounting to 15% of the total sorties flown.

The level of losses in May could no longer be sustained by the GAF now that Hitler had taken the decision to invade the Soviet Union in the very near future. By the middle of June two-thirds of the Luftwaffe's strength had been withdrawn to Germany's eastern frontier with Russia, and had established its HQ at Posnan. On 22 June 1941 Hitler began his invasion of the Soviet Union without any declaration of war. A respite in which to recover had at last arrived for Britain.

The German air offensive against Great Britain had achieved some success. Aircraft production had been seriously disrupted both by direct damage, and by the enforced dispersal of aircraft production units away from major industrial centres – it was not until late February 1941 that output approached the level of August 1940. The steel and ship-building industries had also suffered major setbacks, and communications and power supplies had frequently been so damaged that they had created adverse conditions for manufacturing plants. With the bombing of ports and their associated warehouses stocks of food and of vital oil supplies had been destroyed. 600,000 men had been tied down on military and civil defence duties. 43,381 civilians had been killed and 50,856 seriously injured, a total of 94,237 civilian casualties inflicted between June 1940 and the end of May 1941. Yet the offensive had failed to be a great strategic victory for Germany. Although damage was widespread throughout Britain its effect on industrial production had never proved crucial, and disruption had never been more than temporary.

For the Germans, the result was a serious blow. Göring's much-vaunted GAF had suffered heavily, and had been discredited and defeated at the hands of the Royal Air Force; above all, it had failed in its task of subduing Britain. Hitler was now committed to war with Russia, while his western front remained unsecured. It was the beginning of the end.

CHAPTER XVIII

The Battle of the Atlantic

The Battle of Britain and the Blitz were not the sole tactics employed by Hitler in his attempts to defeat the one country still defying the efforts of Nazi Germany to dominate the entire continent of Europe. Throughout the aerial assault on the British Isles the enemy had steadily developed his long-range blockade by the use of his navy.

Until the German invasions of Norway and Denmark in the spring of 1940, followed by the rapid occupation of the Lowlands and France, the war at sea had gone steadily in Britain's favour. Germany's overseas commerce had been brought to a standstill by a successful blockade mounted by the Royal Navy, and the enemy's surface-raiding cruisers and U-boats had been held firmly in check. Indeed, by the time of the disastrous Norwegian episode the Royal Navy had accounted for one-third of the German Navy's cruisers and nearly one-half of its destroyers. But after the fall of France Britain had become desperately vulnerable to the tactics of a blockade herself, dependent as she was on sea communications with her Empire overseas and on the shipment of essential supplies from these countries and from the United States. With the French, Belgian and Dutch ports being gained by the Germans, and with the loss of the support of the French Fleet, the Royal Navy's task had been made infinitely more difficult. Then, when Italy joined the war on Germany's side, the Royal Navy gained the added problem of contending with the threat presented by the Italian fleet in the Mediterranean. Even closer, there was another potential threat to Britain's trade routes since the Republic of Ireland had assumed a policy of neutrality under its Head of Government, Eamon de Valera, with

211

some feelings of sympathy towards the German cause.

Churchill was well aware of the unsatisfactory situation between Britain and Eire which had existed just prior to the war. Nominally a Dominion, with the King still signing Letters of Credence for the appointment of its representatives to other countries, Eire under de Valera had declared itself independent and neutral, although while wishing to be accepted as such, she had nonetheless requested from Britain consignments of arms of various kinds at cut-rate prices! At the beginning of 1938 de Valera had begun negotiations with the British Government for the renunciation of all British rights to occupy for naval purposes the two southern Irish ports of Queenstown (Cobh) and Berehaven, and the naval base on the west coast at Lough Swilly. On 25 April 1938, when Germany was becoming a visible threat, an agreement effecting such a renunciation had been signed. Churchill, still 'in the wilderness' at that time, had been horrified. When, in 1922, as Colonial and Dominions Secretary, he had dealt with the Irish Settlement, he had far-sightedly reached an agreement with the new-born Republic of Ireland that these ports should remain available for use by the Royal Navy, since they were essential to the protection of Britain's Atlantic shipping routes in the event of war. The reason why Berehaven and Queenstown were essential was easy to understand, for they fulfilled the need for fuelling bases from which the Navy's destroyer flotillas could range westwards into the Atlantic, to hunt down U-boats and to protect incoming convoys as they approached their ports of destination in the narrowing sea-lanes. Lough Swilly was ideally situated for the similar purpose of protecting the approaches to the Clyde and the Mersey. To abandon the use of these port facilities meant that the Navy's flotillas would have to start in the north from Lamlash and in the south from Pembroke Dock or Falmouth, thus decreasing their radius of action by more than 400 miles.

Virtually the entire parliamentary Conservative Party, except for a handful of Ulster members, had supported Neville Chamberlain, the then Prime Minister, in ratifying the 1938 agreement ceding the Irish ports, as had the Labour and Liberal oppositions. Churchill, who had opposed the agreement with the support of Brendan Bracken, commented that 'A more feckless act can hardly be imagined – and at such a time'. In his speech to the House of Commons he had said:

> ... You had the rights; you have ceded them; you hope in their place to have goodwill strong enough to endure tribulation for your sake. Suppose you have not. It will be no use saying, 'then we will retake the ports'. You will have no right to do so. To violate Irish neutrality should it be declared at the moment of a Great War may put you out

of court in the opinion of the world, and may vitiate the cause by which you may be involved in war ... You are casting away real and important means of security and survival for vain shadows and for ease.

On 8 December 1940, Churchill, having inherited, from the moment he became Prime Minister on 10 May, everything that, before the war, he had warned against, had addressed a letter to Roosevelt, the American President. This letter was in the way of a report upon the situation in Europe and an exposé of the prospects for 1941 now that the Battle of Britain had been won by a narrow margin, and the night Blitz, although not yet won, was being contested with some success and with every hope of the Germans being defeated in the night skies as they had been during the day. Churchill had reported with 'candour and confidence' because he was convinced, he said, that the vast majority of American citizens believed 'that the safety of the United States as well as the future of our two Democracies and the kind of civilisation for which they stand are bound up with the survival and independence of the British Commonwealth of Nations. Only thus can those bastions of sea-power upon which the control of the Atlantic and Indian Oceans depend be preserved in faithful and friendly hands.' The control of the Pacific by the United States Navy and of the Atlantic by the British Navy were indispensable, he averred, to the security and trade routes of both the USA and Great Britain, and 'the surest means of preventing war from reaching the shores of the United States'. He warned that it would take three to four years to convert industry from peacetime to wartime purposes, and that saturation point was reached when the maximum industrial effort that could be spared from civil needs had been applied to war production. Germany, he said, had reached that point by the end of 1939; Britain and its Empire were about half-way through the second year, and the United States, he calculated, was nowhere near as advanced as Britain, despite the immense programmes of naval, military and air defence only just started in America. Although the USA was not as a nation contemplating entry into a European war, Churchill had gone on to claim that it was the British duty in the common interest, as well as for Britain's survival, 'to hold the front and grapple with the Nazi power until the preparations of the United States are complete ... Therefore I submit with very great respect for your good and friendly consideration that there is a solid identity of interest between the British Empire and the United States while these conditions last.'

Churchill had continued by explaining that Britain was unlikely to be able 'to match the immense armies of Germany in any theatre where their main power can be brought to bear'. By the application of sea and air power she could, however, meet the enemy armies successfully in many regions, and thus prevent the German domination of Europe from spreading to other vital areas, such as Africa and Southern Asia, while Britain built up its military land forces. Shipping and safe sea routes were now the priority, not men. 'Even if the United States were our ally instead of our friend and indispensable partner, we should not ask for a large American expeditionary army,' he wrote. What was needed now was concentration on munitions and supplies, and on an increase in the number of destroyers already placed at the disposal of the Royal Navy by the USA. He emphasised that the danger of Britain 'being destroyed by a swift, overwhelming blow has for the time being very greatly receded,' a reference to the defeat of the German Air Force in the Battle of Britain.

> In its place there is a long, gradually maturing danger, less sudden and less spectacular, but equally deadly. We can endure the shattering of our dwellings and the slaughter of our civil population by indiscriminate air attacks, and we hope to parry these increasingly as our science develops, and to repay them upon military objectives in Germany as our Air Force more nearly approaches that of the enemy. The decision for 1941 lies upon the seas.

It was in shipping and the power to preserve sea routes from attack, particularly across the Atlantic Ocean, that the crux of the whole war would be found in 1941. If, on the other hand, Britain could move the necessary tonnage, civil and military, to and fro across the seas indefinitely, then '... it may well be that the application of superior air-power to the German homeland and the rising anger of the German and other Nazi-gripped populations will bring the agony of civilisation to a merciful and glorious end.'

Churchill had then gone on to Britain's shipping losses. In the five weeks from the end of September 1940 to 3 November, total losses had amounted to 420,300 tons, and from the beginning of June 1940 to the end of the year over 3,000,000 tons of British, Allied and neutral merchant shipping had been sunk by the enemy. Of this tonnage, 59 per cent had been sunk by the German U-boats, and the remainder by the long-ranging, four-engined Focke-Wulf Fw200 Condor aircraft, surface raiders and mines. The estimated tonnage needed to maintain the war effort at full strength was 43,000,000 tons per month, Churchill wrote, but in September 1940 actual tonnage had only reached 37,000,000 tons, and 38,000,000 tons in October. 'Were this diminution to continue at this rate,' he added, 'it would be fatal unless, indeed, immensely greater replenishment than anything at present in sight could be achieved in time.' Without the assistance of the French and United States Navies, and with the Germans in occupation of all ports around the northern and west coasts of France, the Royal Navy was now suffering a severe restriction further aggravated by Eire's intransigence. 'We are denied the use of the ports or territory of Eire in which to organise our coastal patrols by air and sea. In fact we have now only one effective route of entry to the British Isles, namely the Northern Approaches, against which the enemy is increasingly concentrating, reaching ever further out by U-boat action and long-distance aircraft bombing.' Apart from the need for ships to hunt down raiders and to escort convoys, Churchill emphasised that:

We should also then need the good offices of the United States and the whole influence of its Government, continually exerted, to procure for Great Britain the necessary facilities upon the southern and western shores of Eire for our flotillas, and, still more important, for our aircraft working to the westward into the Atlantic. If it were proclaimed an American interest that the resistance of Great Britain should be prolonged and the Atlantic route kept open for the important armaments now being prepared for Great Britain in North America, the Irish in the United States might be willing to point out to the Government of Eire the dangers which its present policy is creating for the United States and itself.

Seven days earlier, on December 1940 Churchill had drawn the attention of the Chancellor of the Exchequer, Sir Kingsley Wood, to the subsidies being paid by Britain to Eire's agricultural producers. He requested Wood to advise how these subsidies could be terminated and what retaliatory measures could be taken in the financial sphere by Southern Ireland, 'noting that we are not afraid of their cutting off food, as it would save us the enormous amount of fertilisers and feeding-stuffs we have to carry into Ireland through the de Valera-aided German blockade ...' The Chancellor's reply had prompted, on 13 December, a letter from Churchill to Roosevelt as a follow-up to his letter of the 8th. In it, the Prime Minister had emphasised that Britain was so hard pressed at sea that she could no longer undertake to carry 'the 400,000 tons of feeding-stuffs and fertilisers which we have hitherto convoyed to Eire through all the attacks of the enemy'. This tonnage was needed, he said, for Britain's own supplies and, he added, Britain did not need the food which Eire had been supplying, at a heavy cost. It was necessary for Britain to concentrate on essentials and the Government proposed to let de Valera know of this decision. De Valera would

of course have plenty of food for his people, but they will not have the prosperous trading they are making now ... We also do not feel able in present circumstances to continue the heavy subsidies we have hitherto been paying to the Irish agricultural producers. You

215

[Roosevelt] will realise also our merchant seamen, as well as public opinion generally, take it much amiss that we should have to carry Irish supplies through air and U-boat attacks and subsidise them handsomely when de Valera is quite content to sit happy and see us strangled.

Not once during the war did de Valera and his Government offer the hand of friendship to Great Britain; by contrast, 183,000 volunteers from Eire fought on the Allied side. It was only after the Germans bombed Dublin, on the night of 30 May 1941, that the Government of Eire displayed any visible disenchantment with Hitler and his Nazi Germany. Ironically, this bombing was inadvertent, arising from British 'beam-bending' interference with German pathfinding equipment, causing the Luftwaffe's pathfinding aircraft to deviate from their course in an attack on Liverpool and Merseyside and to mark Dublin, on the other side of the Irish Sea, in error. The follow-up aircraft were also duly led astray, and they too successfully bombed the neutral Irish capital.

The appalling weather conditions which had heralded 1941 and hampered the activities of the German U-boats and Focke-Wulf Condors proved, if only temporarily, that an ill wind can blow some good. In January and February there was a notable decline in Allied shipping losses, but that situation was to be short-lived. On 30 January Hitler, in a speech in Berlin, had announced that 'In the Spring our U-boat war will begin at sea, and they [the British] will notice that we have not been sleeping. And the Air Force will play its part, and the entire armed forces will force a decision by hook or by crook.' On 24 February Hitler was sufficiently confident of victory to prophesy that the war with Britain would be over in sixty days. Certainly the next two months seemed to justify his optimism about victory, if not within his time-scale, as the German offensive at sea reached its climax. New ocean-going U-boats and powerful reinforcements of Fw200s and He111s, backed by the surface-raiding pocket-battleship *Admiral Scheer*, the battle-cruisers *Scharnhorst* and *Gneisenau*, and the heavy cruiser *Admiral Hipper*, comprised the main German task force for the throttling of Britain's sea-routes and the consequent denial of the supplies she so desperately needed to survive and continue the fight. In March sinkings reached 532,000 tons and in April 644,000 tons; of the latter losses, 296,000 tons were dispatched to the bottom of the sea by the Fw200s and He111s alone.

The intensive German campaign at sea was, however, foreseen by Churchill, and occasioned his 'Battle of the Atlantic' directive of 6 March 1941, which played an absolute priority on the defeat of Germany's blockade tactics. After stating that, in view of various German statements, Britain must assume that the Battle of the Atlantic had begun, he said that

'The next four months should enable us to defeat the attempts to strangle our food supplies and our connection with the United States'. He then went on to detail priorities, which included taking 'the offensive against the U-boat and the Focke-Wulf wherever we can and whenever we can. The U-boat at sea must be hunted, the U-boat in the building yard or in dock must be bombed. The Focke-Wulf and other bombers employed against our shipping must be attacked in the air and in their nests.' He gave extreme priority to fitting ships with equipment to catapult or otherwise launch fighter aircraft against bombers attacking the convoys – 'Proposals should be made within a week.' Then, from the point of view of air defence, he emphasised that measures for building up the strength of Coastal Command in order to cover the North-Western Approaches, and for the support of Coastal Command on the east coast by Fighter Command and Bomber Command, must be pressed forward with overriding priority. Other measures included increasing the anti-aircraft armament of ships and the crews to man the guns, while merchantmen were to be armed to the teeth. A speed-up was demanded from all departments involved in repair and refitting of damaged ships, both merchant and naval, which had by now accumulated in British ports as a result of enemy attacks. 'By the end of June this mass must be reduced by 400,000 tons net ... Labour should be transferred from new merchant shipbuilding which cannot finish before September, 1941, to repairs. The Admiralty have undertaken to provide from long-distance projects of warship building up to 5,000 men at the earliest moment, and another 5,000 should be transferred from long-distance merchant shipbuilding.' The directive covered other instructions to the various Ministries, including a demand to the Minister of Labour to increase the force employed on ship-repair, shipbuilding and dock work by at least another 40,000 men.

The most controversial aspect of Churchill's directive was that pertaining to the strengthening and support of Coastal Command. In February of 1941 he had given priority to the build-up of Bomber Command, foreseeing that the bomber was then the only weapon that could take the war to the German homeland (and would be so for a long time to come), a condition essential for ultimate victory. But now, with the Battle of the Atlantic directive, the Admiralty saw the opportunity of increasing its hold over air strategy by whittling down Bomber Command to the advantage of Coastal Command, which it could in some measure control. Bomber Command, which had earlier in the war been plundered for support of the ill-fated British Expeditionary Force in France, was again plundered. Seventeen squadrons consisting of 204 long-range aircraft, with their crews, were diverted for duties with Coastal Command, never to be returned to Bomber Command. Added to this blow was the fact that all replacement crews for these squadrons were drawn from Bomber Command Operational Training Units (OTUs). It was only due to the new Chief of the Air Staff (CAS), Air Chief Marshal Sir Charles Portal,* and his Deputy Chief of the Air Staff (DCAS), Air Vice-Marshal Harris, that a greater run-down of Bomber Command was resisted. These two men had been associated with each other in their service careers over a number of years, and both were convinced of the necessity for a powerful strategic air offensive against Germany if victory was to be gained. Neither, however, underestimated the menace of the U-boat and bomber offensive against British shipping and, in turn, the disaster to Britain that a successful German blockade would bring about.

In a minute to the CAS dated the 2 February 1941, Harris wrote of a Joint Intelligence Sub-Committee Report on the possibility of a German invasion.

> In the Summary of Conclusions it is stated that Germany's only hope of obtaining victory this year is by successful invasion of this country.
>
> I do not agree with this, and I consider that within the next few months, and certainly before the end of this year, we shall encounter a vast and perhaps vital increase in the extent and effectiveness of air or other attack against shipping. I am convinced that Germany's plan to win the war against us is, as it always has been in my estimation, to blockade these isles with every weapon and resource at her disposal and to bomb us fortissimo crescendo ...

Where Harris differed with the Admiralty about the protection of British shipping was in the method. He was of the firm opinion that patrolling the North-Western Approaches and other sea-lanes with bomber aircraft, in the hopes of sighting a submarine and attacking it, was a complete waste of time and effort. Such, however, was the Admiralty's interpretation of the reference in Churchill's directive to support by Bomber Command, and which had resulted in seventeen bomber squadrons being diverted to duties with Coastal Command. By studying the statistics of the Whitley aircraft of Coastal Command's No. 502 Squadron over the six months from October 1940 to March 1941, Harris found that on 144 sorties only six submarines had been sighted, four attacked with claims of one or possibly two sunk, for the loss of eleven aircraft and twenty-nine personnel. In the same period there was only one – and that inconclusive – report of a Focke-Wulf sighting. Taking into account the hours flown, he deduced that it had taken 250

---

* Later Marshal of the Royal Air Force the Viscount Portal of Hungerford, KG, GCB, OM, DSO, MC. From February, 1939, he was Air Member for Personnel until he took up his appointment as C-in-C Bomber Command on 3 April 1940. He remained as CAS until the end of the war.

flying hours per submarine sighting. In a note to the CAS detailing these figures, Harris wrote:

> It all boils down to this – are we going Navy fashion to disperse our entire resources attempting to cope defensively with the problem at its outer fringes – an immense area – or are we going Air War fashion to concentrate upon attacking the kernel of the problem at the centre? There is no possible comparison in effectiveness as between the two methods and, furthermore, if we adopt the first how the Boche will laugh! 20 submarines and a dozen Focke-Wulfs providing complete anti-aircraft defence for the whole of Germany!

During Portal's time as C-in-C Bomber Command, Harris had already demonstrated with No. 5 Group's Hampden aircraft the effectiveness of aerial mine-laying around the enemy's ports. Now, at the Air Ministry, both men were convinced that sea-mining from aircraft, direct bombing attacks on dockyards, ports and Focke-Wulf bases and, above all, bombing of industrial areas and factories involved in the production of submarine parts and in their assembly, were the best methods of defeating any attempted blockade.

Although Portal's absolute resistance to the idea of the new long-range four-engined Halifax bombers, now about to come into service, being allocated to Coastal Command was successful, the transfer of the seventeen squadrons – mostly of Blenheims and Whitleys – went ahead. On the subject of further support by Bomber Command in the Battle of the Atlantic. Portal's views again prevailed. While the reinforced Coastal Command directed its efforts against U-boats at sea by patrolling vast areas by day and by night, using RDF search equipment known as Anti-Surface Vessel (ASV), Bomber Command intensified its aerial sea-mining operations against German and German-occupied ports, and its bombing of German naval bases and the Focke-Wulf bases at Stavanger and Bordeaux. Some of the weight of the bombing fell upon the German homeland, but instead of being directed against the Ruhr, Berlin and various oil targets, which had previously been preferred, it was now launched against Hamburg, Kiel and Wilhelmshaven. The shift from inland industrial areas brought no relief to Germany, for the truth was that the bombing of inland targets had been a dismal failure, due to lack of adequate navigational and target-finding aids. Germany had suffered scarcely at all. Bomber Command's efforts against south-west Germany, including the Ruhr, between May 1940 and May 1941 were mainly wasted, 49 per cent of the bombs falling in open countryside and much of the remainder, although dropping on built-up areas, falling in very scattered patterns and completely missing selected aiming points.

Sea-mining from the air and attacks on coastal targets proved much more fruitful – and of vital importance to the defeat of Germany's blockading campaign. The Channel ports received major attention when the German heavy cruiser *Admiral Hipper*, which had already docked at Brest for refuelling after raiding convoys in the South Atlantic, was joined there on 22 March by *Scharnhorst* and *Gneisenau*, the two battle-cruisers having returned to refuel after raiding convoys in the North Atlantic. The success falling to these ships had been less than the Germans had originally anticipated, largely because of the presence with the convoys of British battleships like *Ramillies, Rodney*, and *Malaya*, which heavily outgunned the surface raiders. Since the German High Command had instructed that their ships should not be put at risk, the commanders of the surface raiders were unable to operate as effectively as they might otherwise have done. Now, with the three German cruisers sheltering in Brest, Bomber Command proceeded to hem them in with highly effective sea-mining and constant bombing of the port, the plan being to prevent them from operating on the high seas again.

In the same weeks Royal Navy destroyers achieved an outstanding success against U-boats, sinking five, including those of the three famous U-boat commanders, Prien, Schepke and Kretschmer. Prien's U.47 was sunk with all hands on 8 March by the destroyer *Wolverine*, and U.99 and U.100, commanded by Schepke and Kretschmer, were sunk, again with all hands, on the 17th. It was a success which profoundly influenced the course of the battle; Churchill remarked of the episode that 'the first round of the Battle of the Atlantic may be said to have ended in a draw'.

Hitler's hopes of a quick victory by blockading Britain would soon suffer a death blow.

Bismarck, Germany's newly completed battleship, mounting eight 15-inch guns and built regardless of pre-war treaty limitations, was one of the most heavily armoured ship afloat. Her 45,000-ton displacement exceeded that of Britain's newest battleships by some 7,000 tons, and her speed was at least equal to that of her opposite numbers in the Royal Navy: 'You are the pride of the Germany Navy,' Hitler exclaimed when he visited her in May 1941. A revised German naval plan was now formulated. *Bismarck* was to move into the North Atlantic accompanied by the new 8-inch gun cruiser *Prinz Eugen*, there to be joined by *Scharnhorst* and *Gneisenau* from Brest. The presence of *Bismarck*, reputed to be more than a match for anything afloat, would enable any escorting British battleship to be successfully engaged while the battle-cruisers wrought havoc among the ships in the convoys.

This plan was, however, frustrated by Bomber and Coastal Commands. On 28 March, six days after *Scharnhorst* and *Gneisenau* had docked in Brest, a PRU Spitfire confirmed their presence there and in the next few days, in addition to intensive mining. Bomber Command despatched some 200 bombing sorties against the port. Although no direct hits were scored on the battle-cruisers, an unexploded 250-pound bomb caused *Gneisenau* to be removed from dry dock to the outer harbour on 5 April, where she was detected by another PRU Spitfire. At first light on the morning of the 6th, four Beaufort torpedo-bombers of No. 22 Squadron, Coastal Command, set off to attack *Gneisenau*. Only one Beaufort, piloted by Flying Officer Kenneth Campbell, located the target in the heavy haze. Penetrating the outer harbour he quickly spotted the cruiser lying in the inner harbour alongside one of the shore quays. Flying between flak-ships at mast level, through a hail of withering fire, he skimmed over the mole on *Gneisenau*'s seaward side and launched his torpedo at a range of 500 yards. His aircraft was immediately shot down, with the loss of all its gallant crew, but the torpedo found its mark, piercing *Gneisenau*'s stern beneath the water-line; eight months later, her starboard propeller was still under repair.*

The crippled battle-cruiser was re-docked for repairs on 7 April, only to suffer further injury on the night of the 11th/12th, when Bomber Command scored four direct hits and two near misses, causing damage to one of the gun turrets, to the gunnery control room, and to living quarters, and killing or wounding many of the vessel's crew. *Scharnhorst* was more fortunate, escaping any direct damage, but her refitting programme was seriously delayed because of the destruction of dock facilities. With continued mine-laying and bombing by Bomber Command the two battle-cruisers were now confined to port for the foreseeable future, and the enemy's ground design for a powerful attack on North Atlantic shipping was frustrated. *Bismarck* and *Prinz Eugen* would now have to undertake the task of surface-raiding the Allied convoys on their own.

On 20 May, the British Naval Attaché in Stockholm advised the Admiralty that a Swedish warship had reported sighting *Bismarck* and *Prince Eugen* passing through the Kattegat, and on the following day both ships were spotted near Bergen by a PRU Spitfire. Bad weather now hampered air operations and the two German ships were temporarily lost until, in the late afternoon of the 23rd, the British cruisers *Norfolk* and *Suffolk*, on patrol in the ice-bound stretch of water between Iceland and Greenland known as the Denmark Strait, independently sighted *Bismarck* and *Prinz Eugen* approaching from the north, skirting the edge of the ice in a patch of clear weather. The battle-cruiser HMS *Hood*, Britain's largest and fastest capital ship despite having been built in 1920, in company with the new battleship *Prince of Wales* and six destroyers, had

---

* Flying Officer Campbell was posthumously awarded the Victoria Cross. The other members of the crew were Sergeants J.P. Scott, W. Mullis, and R.W. Hillman.

left Scapa Flow soon after midnight on the 22nd. With the news of the sightings by *Norfolk* and *Suffolk, Hood* and *Prince of Wales* immediately shaped their course to intercept the enemy west of Iceland, while other naval forces were ordered by the Admiralty to proceed to stations to protect convoys in or approaching the vicinity. At dawn on 24 May, HMS *Hood* engaged the enemy, opening fire at 05.52 hours with her 15-inch guns at a range of about 25,000 yards. *Bismarck* and *Prinz Eugen* replied at once, and *Hood* suffered a hit which started a fire that spread at alarming speed, soon engulfing the entire midships. *Bismarck* was also hit, although not by *Hood*, but at 06.00 hours, after *Bismarck* had fired her fifth salvo, *Hood* literally blew apart, and within a few minutes she had disappeared beneath the waves with the loss of all but three of her crew of more than 1,400 men. *Prince of Wales* continued the unequal fight, scoring hits which pierced *Bismarck*'s fuel-oil tanks and caused her to reduce speed, but, damaged and now heavily outgunned, the British battleship had to break off the engagement. She had, however, inflicted enough damage to force *Bismarck* to make for port for repairs. Vizeadmiral Günther Lütjens, the Fleet Commander who was on board *Bismarck*, chose to try to seek refuge in the French port of Brest. Late that night, as the great battleship steamed southwards alone (*Prinz Eugen* having earlier slipped away under cover of darkness to the south for Brest), the chase for *Bismarck* began.

When *Prince of Wales* broke off her action, British cruisers had continued to shadow the enemy raider. During the night Fairey Swordfish torpedo aircraft from the carrier *Victorious* attacked *Bismarck*, hitting her with one torpedo which caused negligible damage, but now the appalling weather conditions favoured the German ship, and for a while all contact with her was lost. Then, on 26 May, after many hours had passed without a sighting of the enemy, a Consolidated Catalina flying-boat of No. 209 Squadron, Coastal Command, made contact. Unluckily, after breaking cloud only a quarter of a mile away from *Bismarck*, the flying-boat was hit by the German's anti-aircraft guns and had to return to base. But another Catalina, this time from No. 240 Squadron, soon re-established contact, and proceeded to shadow the ship. By now it was too late for the British ships involved in the chase to intercept their quarry before she reached waters within range of the German bombers based in Brittany. It was therefore decided to make an aerial attack in an endeavour to destroy *Bismarck* before she could reach Brest, and Swordfish from the aircraft-carrier HMS *Ark Royal* were detailed for the task. Fifteen of the elderly biplanes took off at 14.30 hours but, because of bad weather, mistakenly attacked the cruiser HMS *Sheffield*, fortunately without damage. Fifteen more Swordfish took off just after 19.00 hours on the evening of the 26th, and by 21.30 hours they had successfully completed their mission. Two torpedoes had struck hard and true and *Bismarck*, although still afloat, was almost completely out of control, her steering gear badly damaged. The British shadowed her throughout the night, and five destroyers harried her with gunfire and torpedoes. The battleship HMS *Rodney*, which had been on her way to the USA for a re-fit, had been recalled to join the fray, and at 08.47 hours on the morning of 27 May, in company with the flagship, HMS *King George V*, she opened fire, followed a minute later by *King George V*. Soon most of *Bismarck*'s guns were silent, a fire was blazing amidships, and she was listing heavily to port. *Rodney* now turned across the German ship's bow and, at a range of 4,000 yards, pumped in heavy fire from her 16-inch guns. By 10.15 hours all of *Bismarck*'s guns had fallen silent, and the ship lay wallowing in the heavy seas, a flaming, smoking ruin. At 10.40 hours, the cruiser HMS *Dorsetshire* having delivered the *coup de grâce* with her torpedoes, the great battleship, the pride of Hitler's navy and the most powerful capital ship of her time, heeled over and sank. With her died more than 2,000 men of her crew, including the Fleet Commander, Vizeadmiral Lütjens, and the ship's commander, Kapitän Lindemann.

A magnificent example of co-operation between the Royal Navy and the Royal Air Force had, in a matter of weeks, put paid to Hitler's hopes of winning the Battle of the Atlantic, and of thereby defeating Britain. By July 1941 Churchill's directive of 6 March, which had given absolute priority to the Battle of the Atlantic, had been lifted, and priority was switched back to the build-up of Bomber Command.

Part 3
THE STRATEGIC AIR OFFENSIVE AGAINST GERMANY

CHAPTER XIX

Prelude to the Bomber Offensive

At the outbreak of war, Bomber Command had consisted of a front-line force of thirty-three squadrons comprising 480 aircraft, a figure pitifully below that of 990 first-line bombers, backed by 200 per cent reserves, which had been planned in 1936/37 by the Joint Planning Sub-Committee of the Chiefs of Staff in their 'Appreciation of the Situation in the Event of War Against Germany in 1939'.* In the last month of peace the strength had been fifty-five squadrons, but when the war started Air Chief Marshal Sir Edgar Ludlow-Hewitt,† the C-in-C, wisely withdrew twenty-two squadrons from the front line to cover initial war wastage and to provide for the urgent needs of operational training. Ten of the remaining thirty-three operational squadrons were immediately despatched to France to form the Advanced Air Striking Force. These squadrons were equipped with the obsolescent single-engined Fairey Battle, which had a puny 1,000-pound bomb-load and was slow, ill-defended, and so short-ranged that it was incapable of reaching targets in Germany from England. The remaining twenty-three squadrons in England were, however, equipped with rather better material, six operating with twin-engined Bristol Blenheims, and the remainder with twin-engined Whitleys, Wellingtons and Hampdens. The last three types were all slower than the Blenheims, but were capable of carrying much larger bomb-loads to a far greater range.

In contrast, Germany had a medium-range force of some 1,500

* See Chapter X.
† Air Chief Marshal Sir Edgar Ludlow-Hewitt, KCB, CMG, DSO, MC, C-in-C Bomber Command from 12 September 1937 to 2 April 1940.

bombers which was fully capable of reaching all vital targets in Britain when operating from bases in Holland, Belgium and Northern France. By a miracle, however, the Germans did not launch an offensive against those three countries immediately war was declared, and thus they could not immediately hurl a *Blitzkrieg* against Britain – after sweeping through the Low Countries and France they still refrained from mounting an immediate aerial assault. Those months of phoney war proved vital to the modest build-up of Bomber Command, to the training of crews for operational conditions, and to the improvement, though limited, of technical requirements of operational aircraft such as armament, armour-plating in cockpits, navigational facilities, and many other minor but important fittings necessary to efficient night operations. Also, with the first experiences of operating under night conditions came the recognition that such navigational facilities as were available, or were even planned for the future, were utterly inadequate for an effective night offensive. And a night offensive it had to be, with Germany's vital targets at such long range and to be reached only via the heavily defended hostile territory over which the attacking bombers would have to fly.

In 1940, the only truly successful British night operations were the aerial sea-mining undertaken by No. 5 Group's Hampdens in moonlight conditions, night attacks on enemy invasion barge concentrations, and night bombing of coastal ports in enemy-occupied territory and of the northern German ports of Hamburg, Bremen, Kiel and Wilhelmshaven. The latter were not entirely successful, but even less so were the raids on inland targets such as Berlin, the Ruhr, and various oil targets.

Portal, who had succeeded Ludlow-Hewitt as C-in-C Bomber Command on 3 April 1940, was well aware of the parlous state of the Command's resources. He was also one of the few senior commanders, in any of the Services, who believed that a successful strategic bombing offensive against the German homeland was an essential element to the winning of the war. Harris, his ablest Group Commander at the time, believed even more ardently that a powerful bombing offensive against Germany was crucial for victory. Indeed, Harris went further; he was convinced that the war could be won by Bomber Command alone, once its strength and equipment had been brought up to a standard that he considered would be possible by the beginning of 1942. Both men worked with dedication to strengthen Bomber Command in those early years.

On 25 October 1940 Portal had been appointed Chief of the Air Staff in place of Air Chief Marshal Sir Cyril Newall,* being succeeded at

* Air Chief Marshal Sir Cyril Newall was CAS from 1 September 1937 until 24 October 1940. Later Marshal of the Royal Air Force Lord Newall, GCB, OM, GCMG, CBE, AM Governor-General of New Zealand.

Bomber Command by Air Marshal Sir Richard Peirse.* No sooner had Portal taken over as CAS than he brought Harris into the Air Ministry as DCAS, the appointment dating from 25 November. This was, perhaps, predictable. Portal had first met Harris at Worthy Down in 1927 when he was commanding No. 7 Squadron and Harris No. 58 Squadron. Both units were equipped with Vickers Virginia night-bombers, twin-engined, open cockpit biplanes. There had been a friendly rivalry between the two commanders as to who would produce the most efficient squadron, Harris having already raised No. 58 from being a very mediocre unit to its position as probably the most skilled night-bomber squadron in the RAF by the time Portal had arrived to take over command of No. 7 Squadron. Both men had formed a tremendous respect for each other during this period of their Service lives. After Worthy Down days they had kept in touch, although, until the war, they never served closely together again, except for a brief period in 1934 when Harris took over from Portal as Deputy Director of Plans at the Air Ministry. It was in the post of DD Plans, from July 1933 to June 1937, that Harris, then a Group Captain, continued Portal's early efforts to develop an effective role for bomber aircraft in any future war, and to determine the kind of aircraft and aircraft performance that would be needed to undertake such a role. Both men had foreseen the problems of waging a bombing war against an enemy like Germany from an island base such as Britain, and with the rise of Hitler Germany had increasingly seemed the most likely opponent. To mount a strategic air offensive against such a distant enemy demanded the capability to carry large bomb-loads over great distances, unless continental allies could be relied upon to provide advanced airfields. Neither Portal nor Harris believed in the ability of France or the Lowlands to survive a German invasion, and they therefore plumped for a force capable of carrying very large bomb-loads to the most distant targets, under cover of darkness, from bases in England. It had not been until 1936, however, that Harris's pressure for a truly strategic bomber had begun to bear fruit and the Air Staff, urged on by the then CAS, Marshal of the RAF Sir Edward Ellington, had started to think in terms of far heavier bombers than were then in service.

From the Directorate of Plans, under Harris, and from the Directorate of Operational Requirements, under Wing Commander R.H.M.S. Saundby, had ultimately come two new aircraft specifications which had proved to be the blueprints for the twin-engined Avro Manchester, the four-engined Handley-Page Halifax and Short Stirling, the Manchester

---

* Air Marshal Sir Richard Peirse, KCB, DSO, AFC, was C-in-C Bomber Command from 5 October 1940 to 21 February 1943. He was succeeded by Harris.

effectively becoming the prototype for the famous four-engined Avro Lancaster. Harris and Saundby were therefore the two men largely responsible for the planning and development of the giant bombers which, in the end, would comprise the force that Harris commanded as C-in-C Bomber Command from February 1942 until the end of the war, with Saundby as his Senior Air Staff Office (SASO) and, later, his Deputy C-in-C. Close contact between Portal and Harris, however, did not occur again until 1940 when Portal himself was C-in-C Bomber Command and Harris one of his Group Commanders, but from then onwards it continued until the end of the war.

The conviction held by Portal and Harris, and indeed by Ellington, that war would take to the air and that it could only be won by a concentrated bomber offensive against Germany was, ironically, to be supported by Generalfeldmarschall Erhard Milch, then State Secretary in the German Air Ministry, in a speech to a meeting of Gauleiters on 6 October 1943. Milch said of the British, employing the unusual expression '*Die Engländer*', which can be construed as a mark of respect:

> They have already in the years 1936/37 considered the development of four-engined bombers. The *Engländer* planned right from the beginning to use these bombers by night and not by day, because the speed and height of these planes were not suitable for daylight attacks in the face of our day fighter defence ...
>
> The type of planes the *Engländer* has are of different performances. There are three main types. The best is the Lancaster, the worst the Stirling, and then there is the Halifax. These are the three types which are frequently mentioned in the German reports of planes shot down over German territory ... Germany has certainly not observed this method of war well enough and has not been able to disturb the build-up of the forces of the *Engländer* ... The attempt in our country to construct four-engined planes was started in 1934 and continued in 1935 and 1936, but on the basis of a tactical decision of the authorities in charge, this was given up in 1937 in favour of twin-engined planes ...
>
> It is regrettable that this development [four-engined bombers] which we started, and which seemed to be fruitful, was not continued and was abandoned in order to have available a great number of planes as soon as possible. The two-engined planes were preferred because they could be constructed quicker and more easily.

Equally ironic was the fact that the British politicians concerned, except Churchill and a few of his followers, were from 1934 to 1936 also advocating smaller, twin-engined light bombers because they were cheaper to make than four-engined aircraft, and greater numbers could be produced in less time. These politicians believed that the deterrent to attack would be found in numbers of aircraft, regardless of the fact that such aircraft would be useless for retaliatory attacks against an enemy such as Germany. But the then CAS, Ellington, consistently opposed such a view, and relentlessly supported the design and construction of the four-engined bombers which were to come into service at the outset of 1942. By 1936 he was winning his battle, and the Directorate of Plans was receiving his unqualified support; barely in time, as events were to prove.

Now, on 9 July 1941, with priority no longer being given to the Battle of the Atlantic and with the German invasion of the Soviet Union launched, a new directive from the Air Staff was sent to the C-in-C Bomber Command. It advised Peirse that a comprehensive review had been made of Germany's political, economic and military situations, and that this had revealed that the weakest points in the enemy's armour lay in the morale of the civilian population and in the inland transportation system, the latter weakness arising from the very considerable extension of German military activities due to the Russian escapade. The directive went on to state: 'I am to request that you will direct the main effort of the bomber force, until further instructions, towards dislocating the German transportation system and to destroying the morale of the civil population as a whole, and of the industrial workers in particular.' It was signed by Air Vice-Marshal N.H. Bottomley, for the Air Staff. Bottomley had taken over from Harris as DCAS when, in June, the latter had been promoted Air Marshal and, at Portal's instigation, sent to the USA, where he was to lead a mission to speed up the delivery of military stores and equipment which the RAF had already ordered or was hoping to acquire from America. Harris was a logical choice, since he had led the peacetime purchasing mission to the USA in 1938, but he had been reluctant to go, having set his heart on obtaining a command.

It was this new directive, ordering that Bomber Command be turned onto targets deep in Germany, which led to the revelation that the bomber crews were unable to find even a given town in the dark, let alone undertake precision night attacks. Worse still, it quickly became apparent that the Command was even incapable of area bombing with any degree of success. Inaccurate navigation was the primary cause, followed by inaccurate bombing when the target was, on rare occasions, correctly located.

Recognition of Bomber Command's problems was essential if any successful offensive against Germany was to be mounted. Portal and his Air Staff were anxious to build up a force of 4,000 heavy bombers, the number estimated as being that required to maintain a powerful enough strategic offensive to bring about the defeat of Germany within a year. Even with every possible priority, however, the completion of such a force was inconceivable before 1943/44 at the very earliest. Admittedly, by the middle of 1941 Wellington bombers were coming off production at a fast rate and the new four-engined bombers, Stirlings, Halifaxes and Lancasters, capable of carrying greatly increased bomb-loads, were due to come into service at the beginning of 1942. In fact, the Command's bomb-carrying capacity was slowly becoming adequate for effective bombing, while its ability to deliver bombs to the right place remained hopelessly inadequate. It was this poor performance throughout the second half of 1941 which mitigated against Portal's hopes of receiving the priorities he needed to fulfil his vision of a first-line strength of 4,000 bombers, or indeed even 1,000, by 1943/44. Not surprisingly, the lack of success achieved by the bombing effort against Germany throughout the second half of 1941 rendered the Government reluctant to commit itself to so great a concentration of effort upon one means of winning the war. Even the very survival of Bomber Command was now in question, despite the fact that in this force lay – and would continue to do so for a long time to come – the only means of carrying the war into the heart of Germany, thereby giving some help to Britain's new Russian ally, and providing time for the Army to recover from its disastrous losses of 1940 and 1941.

The process of recognition of the bombing problem had, in fact, begun. At TRE a revolutionary device known as 'Gee', designed to enable an aircraft's navigator to determine his exact position easily, quickly and with a high degree of accuracy, had reached that stage of development when it was ready for operational trials. The system had originally been developed as an aid to landing an aircraft 'blind', but its greater potential had been rapidly recognised by the scientists developing it under R.J. Dippy. Gee had the major advantage that it required no transmissions from the aircraft itself, transmissions which would give away its position to the enemy. The system consisted of three ground transmitters situated widely apart and transmitting pulse signals simultaneously. The centre station acted as the 'master' and the other two as the 'slaves', the pulse signals from the slaves being synchronised to those from the master. The Gee apparatus in the aircraft received these pulse signals, measured the difference in time of receipt between each slave's pulses and the master's, and thereby determined the aircraft's distance from the master and one slave and from the master and the other slave. In effect, this meant that the aircraft lay on a line of constant path difference between the master transmitter and one slave, and on another between the master and the other slave, the point of intersection of these two lines indicating the aircraft's exact position. Special maps were designed with many lines of constant path difference drawn upon them, like a lattice network, so that the readings from the aircraft's Gee receiver

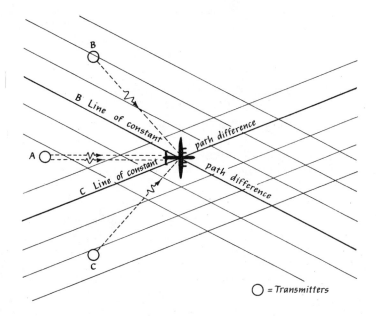

The Gee fix

could be readily plotted. The system could also be used in reverse by setting up on the aircraft's Gee receiver the readings of the point to which the pilot wished to fly, and then homing on that point by following the guiding indications on the receiver's cathode-ray tube. The system, although going a long way towards solving Bomber Command's navigational problems, had two major drawbacks: its range from the ground stations, and therefore from the shores of England, was limited to approximately 350 miles, which brought the Ruhr and parts of Western Germany within range, but left important but more distant targets beyond its range; second, the signals from the transmitters could be interfered with over Germany, thus reducing the effective range of the system still further. It was estimated that the Germans could be employing interfering techniques within six months of a receiver from a shot-down aircraft coming into their hands.

Gee was not the only revolutionary device under development – or consideration – at TRE, but at the time it was the most advanced in development, and by April 1941 it was ready for installation in some Bomber Command Wellingtons. By August, sufficient aircraft of No. 115 Squadron, based at Marham in Norfolk, had been equipped to allow operational trials to be undertaken. At TRE, Dr A.C.B. Lovell, who, with Dr Alan Hodgkin, had been responsible for the development of the night-fighter's AI equipment, had considered the idea of fitting the bombers with equipment which could receive a 'picture' of the terrain over which the aircraft was flying from the reflections of pulse signals directed at the ground. What Lovell had in mind was a device that would enable aircraft to be navigated accurately without seeing the ground, and to bomb an unseen target with precision. While crude efforts using modified 1½-metre AI equipment had been encouraging, it was the emergence of the centimetric techniques, developed for AI in the second half of 1940 and during 1941, that gave real impetus to Lovell's ideas. Even so, no serious attention was given to the subject because, at the time, Bomber Command did not accept the view that the bombers were failing to devastate the targets they were supposed to be attacking. The idea that bombs were not being dropped in the right place was quite unacceptable to the C-in-C, his staff and his Group Commanders. There was, however, one exception among senior RAF officers – Saundby, now the newly appointed Senior Air Staff Officer to the C-in-C, having been Assistant Chief of the Air Staff (Technical) at the Air Ministry until the end of November 1940. He was far from confident that the bomber was succeeding in its task, and recognised that the aircraft needed infinitely better navigational and target-finding equipment if Bomber Command was to be a viable strategic weapon.

Saundby was not quite alone in his views. Another who did not believe in the efficacy of Bomber Command in 1941 was the Prime Minister's scientific adviser, Lord Cherwell, the former Professor Lindemann. Cherwell was a champion of the bomber, and supported the view that even if a bomber offensive could not, on its own, bring about the defeat of Germany, a sustained and devastating bombing campaign against the enemy's cities of industrial and political importance was an essential prelude to victory. He also believed that the enemy's means of production could be disrupted not only by destroying factories, but also by intimidating workers and shattering their morale; he regarded installations producing material for military requirements, and their associated workers and their homes, as legitimate targets in war. By the middle of 1941, however, he had become convinced that the bomber force was not sufficiently large to destroy Germany quickly, and that even if it were, it would prove incapable of delivering its bomb-loads with the required accuracy. Cherwell therefore decided that he must have evidence of the true accuracy, or otherwise, of bombing before he could know how to help Bomber Command to become an effective weapon of offensive warfare.

Given all the facilities available to Cherwell, and his influence with Churchill, he was able to set in motion a most searching enquiry into the bombers' performance. In the first half of August, Mr Butt, a member of the War Cabinet Secretariat, examined 650 photographs taken during June and July at night from aircraft on their bombing approach runs to their targets. Half the photographs purported to have been taken at the time of bomb-release on the aiming-point, and the other half had been taken independently of bombing, but named the position in the target areas which was believed to have been photographed. In all, the photographs related to forty-eight nights, twenty-eight targets, and one hundred raids, and Butt also studied summaries of operations, plotting reports and various other pertinent operational documents. His statistical conclusions were disquieting, to say the least:

1. Of those aircraft recorded as attacking their target, only one in three got within five miles.
2. Over the French ports, the proportion was two in three; over Germany as a whole, the proportion was one in four; over the Ruhr, it was only one in ten.
3. In the Full Moon, the proportion was two in five; in the New Moon it was only one in fifteen.
4. In the absence of haze, the proportion is over one half whereas over thick haze it is only one in fifteen.
5. An increase in the intensity of AA fire reduces the number of aircraft getting within five miles of their target in the ratio three to two.
6. All these figures relate only to aircraft recorded as attacking the target; the proportion of the total sorties which reached within five miles is less by one third. Thus, for example, of the total sorties only one in five got within five miles of the target, ie within the seventy-five square miles surrounding the target.

In short, many of the aircraft then credited with attacking a target successfully had, in fact, dropped their bombs in open country. But Peirse, as C-in-C Bomber Command, and the Command in general, were critical of the Butt Report and, living in a fool's paradise, were convinced that it painted a picture that was much too gloomy.

Cherwell was of a different opinion. He told Churchill that however inaccurate Butt's figures and findings might be, they were sufficiently striking as to emphasise the supreme importance of improving the Command's navigational methods. The Prime Minister was persuaded to give a real priority to the development of RDF to meet Bomber Command's navigational and bomb-aiming needs. Cherwell had played his cards well, and his timing had been excellent. The Gee trials, begun in the first half of August when Butt was assessing the results of his enquiry, had been highly successful, indicating that the system was remarkably accurate within its range of 350/400 miles, and could therefore be employed as a means of navigating aircraft unerringly to targets within this range, at night and regardless of visibility conditions. Its value as a blind-bombing device was, however, questionable, although it seemed likely that it would produce far better bombing results than those which the Butt report had highlighted. Since one aircraft had been lost on the trials, Portal wisely took the decision to prohibit any further flights over enemy territory until a substantial force could be equipped with Gee, and the crews properly trained in its use.

Cherwell, well aware of other RDF aids to navigation and bombing which were languishing in retarded development at TRE for lack of Bomber Command interest and, therefore, of any form of priority, moved quickly once Churchill had backed the development of these scientific aids. After consulting Portal, he engineered the appointment of Sir Robert Renwick* to co-ordinate the research, development and production of all RDF aids for aircraft. Renwick already had the major task of 'progressing' the production of the new four-engined bombers due to come into service at the beginning of 1942; it seemed most appropriate, therefore, that he should also handle the new RDF devices which would equip these bombers.

Renwick assumed his new duties in October 1941. He recognised immediately, as had Cherwell, that he would need in the Command Headquarters an organisation to plan and co-ordinate the training of servicing personnel for these new systems, and of navigators to operate the airborne equipment. Moreover, he was convinced – again, like Cherwell – that the successful development of aids to navigation and bombing would require a close liaison between Bomber Command and TRE, in order to make certain that operational requirements were properly understood by the scientists, and to ensure that their designs were suitable for efficient production and capable of being maintained in serviceable order, under operational conditions, by RAF technical personnel. Renwick discussed these matters with Saundby, the SASO, with whom he had had close contact when the latter had been at the Air Ministry as Assistant Chief of the Air Staff (Technical). Saundby was, above all others in Bomber Command, absolutely intent upon improving the bomber's capabilities by modern techniques, for he had recognised that the bombing arm could never fulfil its true role in war until it had at its disposal aids to night navigation and blind-bombing far in advance of

---

* Sir Robert Renwick, Bt, had formerly been Chairman of the London County Electric Supply Company. He had been brought into the Air Ministry and Ministry of Aircraft Production by Lord Beaverbrook the then Minister of Aircraft Production, and then became Controller of Communications, Air Ministry, and Controller of Communications Equipment, Ministry of Aircraft Production. After the war he was raised to the peerage, as Lord Renwick of Coombe. He died in September 1973.

those that had been available to it in 1939. Furthermore, during his time as ACAS(T), he had gained an insight into TRE's developments in RDF for night-fighters and for the ship- and submarine-hunting aircraft of Coastal Command, and was aware that this scientific establishment was also working on ideas for helping the bombers. As a result of the discussions between Saundby and Renwick, it was decided to form an RDF Department within Bomber Command HQ at High Wycombe, under the command of a Wing Commander reporting directly to the SASO. The author of this book was the officer selected for this new appointment, having served in France with an Army Co-operation squadron in 1939 and 1940, and then with the BAT & DU, the specialist unit which had been charged with the task of investigating from the air the German blind-bombing beam system, and later, of bombing the enemy transmitters blind, using the Germans' own beams as guides for the target approach and bomb-release point. Early in 1941 he had been appointed to the Directorate of Operational Requirements at the Air Ministry to progress the development, production and introduction of RDF aids to the Commands, and in this last appointment he had been involved with the introduction of Gee into Bomber Command for the operational trails. He was therefore known to both Saundby and Renwick, and already had experience of TRE and its latest activities. In December 1941 he moved to High Wycombe to take up his new post.

Despite Bomber Command's apathy, TRE had not been idle. When, however, the results of the Butt Report had become known to the scientists, revealing the critical failure of the night-bombing effort, the Establishment became a hive of activity in the interests of Bomber Command. On the last Sunday in October 1941, Lovell and his superior Dr P.I. Dee, had been looking at a centimetre AI equipment set up on the high ground above Swanage at Leeson Girls' School, where TRE was now based, when they suddenly realised that the downward angle at which, on the cathode-ray tube, they were viewing echoes in the direction of the Isle of Wight was not appreciably different from the downward angle from an aircraft viewing towns or coastlines at long range. As has been said earlier, Lovell had already formulated ideas about the possibilities of terrain identification using $1\frac{1}{2}$-metre AI equipment, but now, with 10-centimetre equipment, the possibilities of seeing towns and coastlines on a cathode-ray tube in an aircraft were immeasurably increased. Dee immediately arranged for two of his assistants to fly in a Blenheim fitted with a helical-scanning 10-centimetre AI with the scanner adjusted to give a depressed forward angle of view, the initial flight taking place on 1 November. The results were highly encouraging, and demonstrated that a centimetre airborne RDF equipment could give discreet returns from certain ground areas such as rivers, towns, coastlines

237

and lakes, quite distinct from the general ground returns that showed on the tube. Responses on the tube were, however, comparatively numerous, and it was evident that many were emanating from objects other than towns – a landing screen (a screen set up to warn incoming aircraft of the approaching end of the runway) near Salisbury, for example, gave a particularly strong response, as did the aerodrome and camp at Boscombe Down, and other military camps on Salisbury Plain. But the response from the town complex at Bournemouth was impressive, and indicated the potential of the new development.

A.P. Rowe,* TRE's Chief Superintendent, impressed by the evidence in photographs taken of the cathode ray tube during the test flight, and realising the importance of the discovery, agreed to Dee's suggestion that a special group should be set up within the latter's division under Lovell to concentrate on centimetre RDF to be employed by Bomber Command in an offensive role. Without waiting for the issue of an operational requirement from the Air Ministry, Lovell and his team immediately began work on designing a system which would assist bomber aircrew with navigational and bombing problems, the resulting airborne RDF device coming to be known as 'H₂S' after Cherwell had christened it 'Home, Sweet Home'. It was based on the same principal as radio-location, in that it depended upon the fact that very high-frequency radio waves travel in straight lines and, in the same manner as light, are reflected back in varying degree from suitable surfaces, and that these reflections, commonly called 'echoes', can be picked up by a receiver and relayed to a cathode-ray tube on which they show as spots of light. Since, with H₂S, the transmissions and their resulting echoes were extremely rapid, the picture presented to the operator would constantly record the features of the ground which the equipment scanned and over which he was flying. By using a rotating aerial array (or 'scanner', as it was called), and by directing the beam of transmissions downwards and revolving it through 360 degrees, the features recorded would be those all around and underneath the aircraft. Moreover, by using a plan position indicator (PPI), where the time-base revolves, as in the GCI equipment, like a clock hand, the aircraft's position would be shown as the centre of the cathode-ray tube with the ground features below being displayed around that centre. This concept was Lovell's, arising from his imaginative approach to the problems which confronted a navigator at night. The 'picture' on the tube was not expected to be a replica of a map or of the detailed landscape which the eye normally sees; rather, it would appear as a series of spots of light of varying degrees of brightness. These had to be

---

* A.P. Rowe, CBE, later Vice-Chancellor of the University of Adelaide, Australia. He died in 1976.

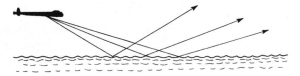

H2S beam strikes water. Energy is reflected away from aircraft

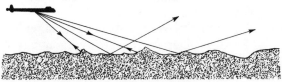

H2S beam strikes land. Some energy is reflected back to aircraft

H2S beam strikes built-up area. Much energy is reflected back to aircraft

Effects of different surfaces on H$_2$S

understood, of course, but they would be comparable to the map picture and could be correctly interpreted. There would be three distinct types of response on the cathode-ray tube: water would be represented by a dark shadowy effect, ordinary land by a lighter response, and a town by a bright area. The representations would correspond to the general shape and size of the objects seen, so that a large town, for instance, would be distinguishable from a small one. In particular, the contrast between land and water would be very sharp because land would give an appreciable echo whereas water would reflect back very little signal; coastlines and inland waterways were therefore expected to show up very clearly and be easily identifiable. With H$_2$S, in fact, it was hoped that the navigator in a bomber could have a continuously moving picture of the country over which he was flying up to any range, since the system would be carried in the aircraft itself, and would be self-contained and independent of any ground stations.

H$_2$S was soon to be developed into an accurate bombing device, due in large measure to the co-operation between Lovell's group and Bomber Command's newly formed RDF Department, but it was not to become available for installation in bombers, even in limited quantities, before the end of 1942. It was Gee that was to be the mainstay of successful bombing during 1942, and by February the first ten squadrons in Bomber

Command to be fitted with the device were ready for operations, complete with crews trained in its use; with RDF operators established at the ground stations of the first Gee chain, and with mechanics trained to service the airborne equipment at the squadron bases. Of these squadrons five operated twin-engined Wellingtons, two were equipped with four-engined Stirlings, two with four-engined Halifaxes, and one with four-engined Lancasters, providing the Command with some 200 Gee-equipped bombers.

For the nations still opposing Nazism, 1941 was to end with a disastrous series of events. On Sunday 7 December Japan, without any declaration of war, attacked and destroyed the greater part of the US Pacific Fleet at its anchorage in Pearl Harbor in an unprecedented air raid. On the same day the Japanese bombed Hong Kong and Singapore, and launched invasions of Malaya, the Dutch East Indies, and other Far Eastern countries. Then, on the 10th, they successfully attacked and sank two of Britain's major warships off Malaya, the battleships *Prince of Wales* and *Repulse*. On the 8th Britain formally declared war on Japan, and on the same day Germany and Italy declared war on the USA, now at war with Japan. What had started with the invasion and crushing of Poland was now truly a world war.

Japan's intervention in the war dramatically changed the situation in the line-up of opposing forces, and demanded of the Allies an urgent reassessment of their future strategy and tactics. Within days of the Pearl Harbor episode, Churchill left England for Washington, accompanied by Beaverbrook, the Minister of Aircraft Production, Admiral Sir Dudley Pound, the First Sea Lord, Field-Marshal Sir John Dill, formerly Chief of the Imperial General Staff, and Portal, the Chief of the Air Staff. The party sailed on the battleship HMS *Duke of York*, disembarking at Hampton Roads and flying on to Washington to arrive on the evening of 22 December. The meetings that followed became a matter of resolving strategic issues, and of determining how best to achieve Allied co-operation in order to conduct the war effort in the most effective manner, one immediate result being the setting-up of the Combined Chiefs of Staff Committee in Washington. What became quickly evident, however, was that America would need time to put its military forces into a state of real readiness before it could make a cogent contribution to the prosecution of the war. This in itself emphasised the necessity for Britain to find the means to carry the war into Germany without further delay, in order to prepare the way for an invasion of Europe at some time in the future when America could provide a viable force to join with a resuscitated British Army. Only Bomber Command could provide such action and, ironically, it was in large part due to Japan that the bomber offensive suddenly received powerful backing.

Thanks to Cherwell, the Butt Report, and TRE, the ingredients for the success of such an offensive were there. What the Command now needed was a highly competent and dynamic leader.

In the first week of January 1942, during the visit to Washington, Portal persuaded Churchill that a much more aggressive C-in-C was required for Bomber Command and that the man for the job was unquestionably Harris. Churchill agreed and the decision was taken to have Harris, still on the mission in the USA, returned to England to take over from Peirse. On 10 February Harris sailed for home from Boston in the armed merchant-cruiser *Alcantara*.

Two days later, on 12 February, while Harris was on the high seas, the German battle-cruisers *Scharnhorst* and *Gneisenau*, accompanied by the heavy cruiser *Prinz Eugen*, slipped out of Brest and, in daylight, successfully passed up the Channel and through the Straits of Dover. The three ships had in fact left Brest just before midnight on the 11th, taking the Admiralty completely by surprise – no one had imagined that the Germans would be so audacious as to run the gauntlet of the batteries at Dover by day. Motor torpedo-boats, destroyers and torpedo-carrying aircraft all attacked, without success until, finally, Bomber Command was ordered to despatch a force of bombers after the ships had successfully passed through the Straits into the North Sea. The weather was appalling, and the attack was a complete and costly failure. Of 242 aircraft despatched, only 39 succeeded in finding the ships in the mist and rain, 188 did not see a thing, and 15 failed to return to base. Later that evening, however, both *Scharnhorst* and *Gneisenau* were heavily damaged by mines previously laid by Bomber Command in the narrow sea lanes of the North Sea approaches to the Channel. *Gneisenau* just made it to Wilhelmshaven, there to beach herself, and *Scharnhorst* limped her way to Kiel. Churchill judged the ships' escape as 'an episode of minor importance', but it was an inauspicious event for Bomber Command. Those opposed to an aggressive bombing policy against the German homeland – chiefly the Admiralty and certain politicians – used the episode to attempt to prove that bombing the more distant targets in Germany could never succeed when even a short-range target such as Brest had survived numerous bombing attacks during 1941, allowing the German surface raiders to escape to safety.

February 1942 brought other mortifying days. On the 15th Singapore fell to the Japanese, and in the Western Desert Rommel and his Afrikakorps stood triumphant over the British Army in Libya. Indeed, the new Grand Alliance between Britain and the USA was in danger of being stillborn. In Bomber Command now lay the only means by which Allied strategy could move from the defensive, which spelt ultimate disaster, to the offensive, which offered a chance of eventual victory.

Two days in February would lighten the gloom, although it would only be in the future that such would be recognised. On the 14th, an Air Staff directive authorised the Command 'to employ your effort without restriction, until further notice, in accordance with the following directions'. These directions gave the priorities for targets to be attacked in Germany, the introduction of Gee being given as the reason for mounting the offensive:

> TR 1335 [Gee] will confer upon your forces the ability to concentrate their effort to an extent which has not hitherto been possible under the operational conditions with which you are faced. It is accordingly considered that the introduction of this equipment on operations should be regarded as a revolutionary advance in bombing technique which, during the period of its effective life as a target-finding device, will enable results to be obtained of a much more effective nature.

The estimated time before the full use of Gee over Germany would be impaired by jamming was given as six months. It was therefore emphasised in the directive that the Command should strike with full force during this period, in order to destroy Germany's capacity and will to make war, and to 'enhearten and support the Russians' while they were maintaining so effectively their counter-offensive against the German armies.

The second date was 22 February, when Air Marshal A.T. Harris took over as C-in-C Bomber Command, just seven weeks before his fiftieth birthday.

CHAPTER XX

The Offensive Opens

It was no enviable task that faced Harris when he took up his appointment. He knew that he would have to chalk up successes swiftly if he was to receive backing for a greatly increased bomber force, and yet the force at his disposal at the outset was lamentable. Excluding five squadrons of light bombers, unsuited to operations over Germany, he had forty-four squadrons of which only thirty-eight were actually operational – a far cry from the 68 bomber squadrons, consisting of 990 first-line aircraft backed by 200 per cent reserves, which it had been planned in October 1934 would be available by 1939. Of the forty-four squadrons only fourteen were equipped with the new four-engined heavy bombers, the Stirlings, Halifaxes and Lancasters, the rest still operating with the old Wellingtons, Whitleys and Hampdens, which carried much smaller bomb-loads, had less range, and were slower. The total of serviceable aircraft with crews was 378, of which only 69 were heavy bombers, and 50 aircraft in the force were light bombers, which were suitable only for making harassing attacks on the enemy's airfields in Belgium and France. All this meant that Harris had an average force of 250 medium and 50 heavy bombers until such time as the Command's resources could be expanded. In fact, while the total of aircraft in the Command numbered some 600, he could only count on a normally available force of about 300 serviceable aircraft with crews with which to begin his long campaign against the industrial cities of Germany.

Things were not quite as bad as they seemed, however. 200 of the available aircraft had been fitted with Gee, including all the four-engined heavy bombers, and all aircraft coming off the production lines for

Bomber Command were also equipped with Gee during manufacture. Moreover, Saundby had already organised trials with Gee over England to determine the best tactical methods of attack when using the new system, and the results had been very encouraging. These trials, known as 'Crackers I' and 'Crackers II', had taken place on the nights of 13 and 19 February, the aircraft dropping flares instead of bombs. The trial on the 13th had brought to light certain inaccuracies caused by poor operation of the ground stations due to inadequate monitoring facilities, insufficient telephone links between the monitor station and the transmitting stations, and lack of supervision of the operators by responsible officers. By the time of the second trial on the 19th all these problems had been ironed out, and Gee showed promise of radically improving the effectiveness of the bomber.

On 25 February 1942, three days after Harris had assumed command, Sir Stafford Cripps, the Lord Privy Seal, made an extraordinary speech in the House of Commons when winding up a two-day debate on the war situation. It appeared that he had chosen his time deliberately in order to embarrass and discourage the new C-in-C of Bomber Command from the start. Referring to the policy of using heavy bombers against Germany, which had been raised by 'a great number of Members', he stated that 'a number of Honourable Members have questioned whether, in the existing circumstances, the continued devotion of a considerable part of our effort to the building up of this Bomber Force is the best use that we can make of our resources'. He reminded the House that this policy was initiated at a time when Britain was fighting alone against Germany and Italy, and that bombing seemed to be the most effective way of taking the initiative against the enemy. He was hardly correct in this statement. Such bombing as there had been in 1940 and 1941 had been almost entirely against invasion ports, U-boat and other German naval bases, and the Focke-Wulf aerodromes, all in connection with preserving the country from invasion and from the crippling effects of a blockade. Cripps went on to say:

> Since that time we have had an enormous access of support from the Russian Armies, who, according to the latest news, have had yet another victory over the Germans, and also from the great potential strength of the United States of America. Naturally, in such circumstances, the original policy has come under review. I can assure the House that the Government are fully aware of the other uses to which our resources could be put, and at the moment they arrive at a decision that the circumstances warrant a change, a change in policy will be made.

The Russian victories referred to were in fact little more than a greater resistance to the German invasion than had been expected, for the real German offensive, which nearly eliminated the Soviet Union, was yet to come. The reference to US potential was true, but any significant contribution from this quarter could not be expected in 1942; indeed, it was well into 1943 before American help began to make any marked impression on the fortunes of the Allies. Cripps's speech was, in fact, ill-informed, even downright mischievous. The best that can be said is that his pacifist ideals and his intense dislike of exposing civilian populations to the horrors of a bombing war blinded him to the realities of the true situation, and made him forget that civilians all over Europe had been and were still being subjected to German bombs, shells and bullets, and to the ruthless behaviour of their invading armies. Even his own countrymen had had to suffer, and were still to suffer, attacks by bombing.

The Cripps speech transferred the doubts about the wisdom of a strategic air offensive from the confines of discussions between the Chiefs of Staff, members of the War Cabinet and the Ministries, to speculation in Parliament, the country at large and, inevitably, the press. The effect was not only disturbing in Britain but also in America, where the Lord Privy Seal's statement was published in full in the *New York Times*. The idea that the British Government had lost confidence in the principle of a bomber offensive as a means of weakening Germany's ability to carry on the war – a view that had been expressed so strongly by Churchill and the British Chiefs of Staff at the Washington conference only a few weeks earlier – was clearly damaging. The CAS and the Royal Air Force delegation in Washington feared that Cripps's speech would have an adverse effect upon American views on the best methods of conducting the war. Furthermore, it was felt that the speech as reported would strengthen the hands of those Americans who favoured concentrating on the war against Japan, rather than against Germany, and might well have an adverse effect upon American production of heavy bombers.

There was now a paramount need for Harris to succeed in the offensive from the very first, and both he and Saundby, his SASO, were acutely aware of the fact.

From the moment he took over, Harris had been well briefed by Saundby who, keenly conscious of the Command's present weaknesses, could nevertheless visualise its potential once its strength had been substantially increased with the new four-engined aircraft, and its efficiency vastly improved by the introduction of the revolutionary RDF aids to navigation and blind-bombing, of which the first was Gee. Having been associated with TRE in his time at the Air Ministry, Saundby was well aware of the other devices which already showed much promise in development, and he had recognised the necessity for

--·-- International boundaries
at the outbreak of war

Range circles are measured
from Lincoln

NORWAY

OSLO

Stavanger

North

Sea

DENMA

EIRE

Jurby

UNITED
KINGDOM

Doncaster
Manby
Lincoln

Syerston
Newton
Lichfield
Marham
Mildenhall
Newmarket

King's Lynn
Gt.Yarmouth
East Harland

LONDON

Flushing

Zeeland

Ostend
Bruges
Dunkirk
St Omer
Boulogne
Berthune
Abbeville
Bruneval
Billancourt
Arras
Albert
Amiens
Sedan

Calais

Eindhoven
Hingene
Lille
Gembloux
Malmédy

BELGIUM

Aachen

Koblenz
Trier
Lutterade
Kreuznach

Rotterdam

HOLLAND

Ibbenbüren

The Ruhr
See Inset

Wilhelmshaven

Emden

Osnabrück

Sylt
Hornum

Fle
Kiel
Brunsb
Lübec
Bremer

Wenz
Rote
Heme
Diephol
Ha

Brun
Bielefie
Paderb

Kassel
Eschwege
Cologne
Wesseling
Neuwied
Frankfurt
Mainz
Worms
Mannheim
Oppau
Karlsruhe
Offenburg

Wetzlar
Fu
Limburg
Hanla
Ascha
Darmsta
Stutt
Mur

Cherbourg

Brest

Lorient

St Nazaire

Loire

200 miles

300 miles

Poissy
Villacoublay

Gennevilliers
PARIS
Villeneuve

Dombasle

Saarfels

400 miles

FRANCE

BERNE

SWITZERLAND

La Pallice
La Rochelle

500 miles

Bay of
Biscay

Bordeaux

600 miles

Turin

IT

700 miles

Rhine

Ems

Ranges of Principal Bomber Command Targets

246

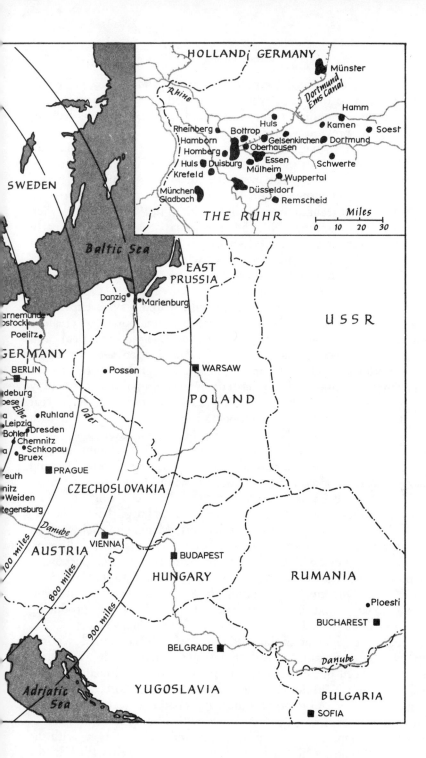

THE RUHR

HOLLAND
GERMANY
Münster
Rhine
Dortmund Ems Canal
Hamm
Huls
Kamen
Rheinberg
Bottrop
Soest
Hamborn
Gelsenkirchen
Dortmund
Homberg
Oberhausen
Huls
Duisburg
Essen
Schwerte
Krefeld
Mülheim
Wuppertal
München Gladbach
Düsseldorf
Remscheid

Miles
0   10   20   30

SWEDEN

Baltic Sea

EAST PRUSSIA

Danzig
Marienburg

arnemunde
ostock
Poelitz

USSR

GERMANY

BERLIN

Possen
WARSAW

deburg
ese
Elbe
Ruhland
POLAND
Oder

Leipzig
Dresden
Bohlen
Chemnitz
Schkopau
Bruex

reuth
PRAGUE
nitz
Weiden
CZECHOSLOVAKIA
Regensburg

Danube

VIENNA

100 miles
800 miles
900 miles

AUSTRIA
BUDAPEST

HUNGARY
RUMANIA

Ploesti
BUCHAREST

BELGRADE
Danube

Adriatic Sea

YUGOSLAVIA
BULGARIA

SOFIA

intensive training of crews if both the new aircraft and the new RDF aids were to be used to the best advantage. He had therefore prepared the ground for such training in the Command's OTUs, despite lack of backing from his previous C-in-C.

Harris and Saundby were not unknown to each other. In 1923 and 1924 Saundby had been one of the flight commanders in No. 45 Squadron in Mesopotamia when Harris had been the squadron commander; it was this squadron, then equipped with Vickers Vernons, that had developed some of the earliest techniques in night bombing. In 1926 and 1927, when Harris was commanding No. 58 (Virginia) Squadron, an early night-bomber squadron of the UK-based air force, Saundby had again been one of his flight commanders. Later when, before the war, Group Captain Harris had been Director of Plans at the Air Ministry, Saundby, then a Wing Commander, had been Director of Operational Requirements. So it was that two men with shared service experience over a number of years were now together again, poised to create a formidable team. Harris was forceful, forthright, practical and determined, and once he had made up his mind upon a course to be followed nothing could hold him in check, although he always studied carefully the views and advice of his staff. He was no politician. Saundby had a brilliant technical brain, was an excellent tactician, had great imagination and, although far from being a politician, was blessed with an able sense of diplomacy. It was an admirable combination.

The Directive of 14 February had given Bomber Command four primary targets in the Ruhr areas, Essen, Duisburg, Düsseldorf and Cologne, and three alternative targets, also within Gee range, Bremen, Wilhelmshaven and Emden. In addition, there had been a list of further alternatives which lay outside Gee range, Hamburg, Kiel, Lübeck, Rostock, Berlin, Kassel, Hannover, Frankfurt, Mannheim, Schweinfurt and Stuttgart. All these targets were important industrial areas, although Berlin had been included, according to the Directive, for the purpose of maintaining 'the fear of attack over the city and to impose ARP measures'. The Directive also mentioned, as an additional commitment, the Renault factory at Billancourt, near Paris, which was producing armaments and motorised vehicles for the German military forces.

Although Gee coverage of the southern areas of Britain and down into France was not yet available, only the Eastern Chain (as it was called) having so far been put into operation, Harris chose the Renault factory for his first strike. Without Gee the Bomber force was forced to depend upon good weather and good visibility, and upon new tactics devised by Saundby during the 'Crackers' exercises with Gee. These consisted of using a flare-dropping force to mark and illuminate the target, with the main force dropping a liberal load of incendiaries mixed with HE, the last to include a maximum quantity of 4,000-pound bombs. The chances of success against the Renault factory were greater than they were against a target deep inside Germany, and that certainly influenced Harris's choice for his first blow of the new campaign.

On the night of 3/4 March, just ten days after Sir Stafford Cripps's disturbing statement, the factory was attacked in entirely favourable weather conditions. The bombing was concentrated and the devastation was impressive, including nearly 25 per cent of the machine-tools destroyed or damaged and many others rendered useless because of the destruction of buildings. Buildings containing designs, blueprints and records were burnt to the ground, 722 vehicles ready for delivery were wrecked, and office and ancillary buildings for stores were damaged or completely demolished. The death toll, however, was remarkably low, a result which had been hoped for, since there was no wish to harm the French population. Out of 3,000 workmen on duty, only 5 had been killed, although several others, with their families, had unfortunately also been killed in neighbouring houses. Of 235 bombers despatched, 223 had reached the target (according to photographs taken from the aircraft during the bombing runs), and these had dropped 461 tons of bombs. The raid had lasted just under two hours and had achieved a concentration of 121 aircraft per hour over the target, a concentration that all previous British bombing raids had failed to achieve by a wide margin.

This Renault raid was a notable success, and provided a much-needed boost to the morale of the bomber crews as well as enhancing Bomber Command in the eyes of the public. But Harris and Saundby were well aware that this attack was no real test of the Command's ability to destroy, at a much greater range, the heavily defended targets within Germany itself. They knew that the inevitable trial of strength had yet to be faced – and the sooner it was faced, the better.

Using Gee on operations for the first time, three raids were launched against the Ruhr on the successive nights of 8/9, 9/10, and 11/12 March, with Essen as the principal target. The first attack was undertaken by 211 aircraft, of which 82 were equipped with Gee. The Gee-equipped aircraft were divided into a flare force dropping sticks of twelve bundles of three flares each to light up the target, and an incendiary force of fifty aircraft dropping a full load of incendiaries. The Gee force was followed by a main striking element carrying full loads of HE bombs, including many 4,000-pounders. Night photographic evidence indicated that the majority of the Gee aircraft had passed close to their target area, and reports from crews were favourable. Even so, PRU coverage on the next morning showed that the raid had been only partially successful. On the second night, the 9th/10th, the same tactics were employed, but the attack went astray because a Stirling, hit by anti-aircraft fire, jettisoned its incendiaries over Hamborn on the run-in to Essen. The result was that many of the following aircraft released their bombs on the fires that had been started in Hamborn, instead of proceeding further to Essen, where the Krupp armament works was the main aiming-point. The third raid, on the 11th/12th was essentially a failure because the main bomber force was led astray by an unexpected decoy conflagration near Rheinberg. Nevertheless, damage in Essen resulting from these raids was appreciably greater than anything which had previously been achieved, and included damage to engineering works, railway centres and houses. The Krupp factory was virtually untouched, however, although by good luck the Thyssen steel works at Hamborn had received numerous direct hits on the second night from bombs released on the fires caused by the jettisoned incendiaries from the unfortunate Stirling.

Without delay, Harris and Saundby had the causes of the partial failure of these raids investigated by Group Staffs, the Headquarters Operations Staff, and the Bomber Command RDF Department, which consisted of both specialist navigators and RDF technical officers, a number of whom had had experience on operations – one, Flight Lieutenant E.J. Dickie,* had been one of the first Gee navigators in No. 115 Squadron when this squadron had undertaken Gee trials over Germany in August 1941. It was established that although the flare force on all three raids had, with the aid of Gee, dropped its markers in the right places, a large part of the main bombing force had arrived after the flares had gone out. In addition, the incendiary force had dropped its loads over too wide an area to achieve the concentration necessary for real success. The interesting aspect of these investigations was the discovery that the inaccuracy was principally one of bombing short of the target, and that the pattern of bombing was consistent with the statistical error to be expected for Gee at that range.

On 13 March Harris despatched a letter to Churchill on the subject of these initial Gee raids, the latter having requested an immediate report on the results. Harris's letter was his first, in his capacity as C-in-C Bomber Command, to the Prime Minister, and it marked the beginning of a remarkably close relationship, one which was to secure the continued existence of Bomber Command throughout the war, and to ensure the growth of the strategic bomber offensive against Germany. The letter read:

Prime Minister,
You asked me for a comparison between the weight of attack in the

---

* Later Wing Commander E.J. Dickie. After the war he became Deputy Director of Control and Navigation Development at the Ministry of Transport and Civil Aviation.

Coventry Blitz and the weight of attack in our first Gee operation on Essen.

Coventry:
430 aircraft dropped 400 tons of bombs in 1 night. (It was a 1 night Blitz).
Of this total, 220 dropped 183 tons of bombs on Coventry itself.

Essen:
401 aircraft dropped $657\frac{1}{2}$ tons of bombs in 3 nights. I hope, however that no official comparison will be made between these two weights of attack as indicating that Essen has as yet been taking Coventry's medicine.

The analysis of the whole operation, together with the plotting of night photographs, which I have just been able to have completed for a conference with my Group Commanders this afternoon, shows that there was no worthwhile concentration on the exact target of Essen. There were various reasons for this – technical, tactical and training – many of which could possibly not have been anticipated and needed clarification by practical experience to be impressed upon us. These lessons have, I hope, now been absorbed and we are in process of perfecting the method as fast as we can within the limitations of crews, aircraft and weather. Nevertheless, we are all enthusiastic as to the utility and efficiency of the Gee method ...

The crews are enthusiastic, especially with the result of the second night's operation on Essen, and the gain so far is not only an excellent means of navigation and especially homing, but that the number of aircraft effectively bombing within the immediate neighbourhood of the selected target was far greater than on similar types of operation prior to the coming of Gee.

A.T. Harris

On the same day that Harris despatched his letter to Churchill the fourth Gee raid was planned, this time against Cologne. The RDF Department had expressed the view that perhaps the incendiary force aircrew had placed insufficient reliance on the Gee equipment when they had released bomb-loads in the previous Gee attacks, resulting in loads being released by crews when they thought they were over the target, rather than when Gee indicated that they were over the target. Saward, the Wing Commander RDF, proposed to Saundby that the aircrew should be given definite instructions about bomb-release using the new equipment, and this was agreed. The Cologne attack took place on the night of 13/14 March, the Gee aircraft again being divided into a flare-dropping and an incendiary force, followed by the main striking force. On this occasion instructions were issued to squadrons that all Gee aircraft were to approach the target from west to east along a specific Gee path, using the homing technique, and to release their flares 'blind' when the equipment indicated that the bomb-release point had been reached. The incendiary aircraft were instructed to approach along the same Gee path, but to drop their loads visually if the Rhine, running through the east side of the town, was sighted, or 'blind' on the Gee indications if the river was not sighted. It was a moonless night, and visual sightings were expected to be difficult.

The Cologne raid was far more successful than the first three against Essen. The night photographs taken with bombing* showed that over 50 per cent of the aircraft claiming to have attacked had hit the city, and PRU photographs taken after the raid quickly added confirmation of the success. These disclosed that the Franz Clouth Rubber Works, covering an area of 480 by 350 yards, had been almost completely destroyed by fire; 300 by 250 yards of the railway workshops in the Nippes marshalling yard had been razed to the ground; and the Chemische Fabrik and adjacent factory buildings in the Cologne suburbs had been totally devastated. In addition, substantial damage had been caused by direct hits on thickly built-up areas, and on the Humbolt Deuts submarine diesel engine works.

On 24 March, Harris again wrote to Churchill to report on the outstanding results of the Cologne raid. After giving the Prime Minister further details of the earlier raids on Essen, resulting from daylight reconnaissance photographs which had revealed that the damage to Essen and Hamborn had been much greater than had at first been thought, he went on to enthuse about the successful outcome of the Cologne raid. 'It seems probable', he wrote, 'that over fifty per cent of the aircraft claiming to have attacked actually hit Cologne. Evidence over the last seven months shows that under similar weather conditions with no moon we should normally expect to get only ten per cent of the force on the target.' He went on:

> You will note from the attached report on Cologne that day photographs amply confirm the claim that very serious damage was occasioned during the attack. German broadcasts and reports from German sources in Ankara alike confirm that we did a lot of damage and killed plenty of Boche.
>
> We hope that we have further improved the methods and to produce still better results in future.
>
> The crews are enthusiastic over Gee. They increase their skill in

---

* Flares were carried in the bomb-bays with the bombs, as were cameras – both were triggered at the moment of bomb-release, the flares providing illuminations.

using it on every trial. Technical shortcomings in the equipment are being overcome. We are on a good thing.

The RDF Department, however, was disappointed with the result, even though it had been so much better than anything yet achieved against a German town. The total force of 120 aircraft had been impressive and, apart from a considerable number of incendiary bombs, it had dropped the substantial load of 97 tons of high explosive. But to inflict extensive damage it seemed that what was needed was more like 970 tons, yet if there were sufficient aircraft to deliver such a load the question was how to find the time in a single night to put them across the target. Concentration in time over a target was still being based on the principle of a maximum of 100 aircraft per hour, the Renault raid at the beginning of March having achieved a record 121 aircraft per hour. The RDF Department concluded that the crux of achieving much greater concentrations lay in accurate navigation and quick target-location; so accurate and so quick, in fact, that search would be unnecessary and all aircraft would fly in towards the target, cross and bomb it, and fly straight on beyond the far side, all travelling in the same direction in a thick, concentrated stream. With Gee providing the very accurate navigation which it had already demonstrated on operations, it was realised that a force of bombers could be so concentrated in time and space because Gee enabled the aircraft to maintain, as laid down in the plan for an attack, the correct track to the target area and to keep to exact times along that track and at the target. Saward and Dickie concluded that it would be perfectly easy and safe to concentrate 120 Gee aircraft over a target such as Cologne in a period of fifteen minutes. Saward discussed the matter with Saundby, who scratched away with a pencil on his blotting-pad, periodically peering over the top of his half-moon spectacles while the theory was expounded to him. Removing his spectacles and chewing the ends of the side-pieces, Saundby finally commented: 'So you want one hundred and twenty Gee aircraft to attack a target like Cologne, and you want all these aircraft to be concentrated over the target in a quarter of an hour?' At length he rose from his chair and sailed majestically into Harris's office, followed by his Wing Commander RDF. Saundby explained the proposal to his C-in-C, going into the advantages of concentration: saturation of defences, shortened time spent by aircraft in the target area and therefore reduced risks of losses, and the overwhelming effect on the ARP and fire services of the total load of incendiary and HE being dropped in a very short space of time. The proposal appealed to Harris, and he asked Saward what sort of concentration he thought could be achieved in one hour if the majority of the bomber force was equipped with Gee. Saward gave it as his opinion that, if the target was within Gee range and all aircraft were so equipped, well over 500 aircraft could be packed into an hour's raid.

Before the end of March, an experiment in concentration was attempted against Cologne, when 120 aircraft attacked the town in twenty minutes with great success and without the loss of a single aircraft. The timing proved to be well-nigh perfect, a significant feature being that each aircraft arrived back as its base within a few minutes of its estimated time of arrival. Day photographic reconnaissance revealed that Cologne had sustained considerable damage, and that this had been confined to one area of the town around the aiming-point. But the real importance of this experimental raid was that it provided proof that, with good navigational aids, very considerable numbers of aircraft could be concentrated successfully over a target in a short space of time. The age of saturation raids was in sight.

Churchill, who was now under pressure from the Admiralty to order the diversion of bomber squadrons to anti-submarine duties, was pleased with the results of the new offensive, for they provided him with a reason to support bombing in preference to submarine patrolling. He also received unexpected backing from Roosevelt at this time. In a letter to Harry Hopkins* dated 12 March 1942, Churchill had expressed his concern at the extent of tanker sinkings west of the 40th meridian and in the Caribbean Sea, areas protected by US anti-submarine patrols. He suggested some rearrangement of convoy escort duties, between the Royal and US Navies, and hoped that Roosevelt could withdraw a few destroyers from the Pacific to provide additional escort forces until more British anti-submarine corvettes, nearing completion, came into service. Roosevelt indicated American co-operation in a cabled reply, but in a follow-up letter, dated 20 March, he wrote:

> Your interest in steps to be taken to combat the Atlantic submarine menace as indicated by your recent message to Mr Hopkins on this subject impels me to request your particular consideration of heavy attacks on submarine bases and building and repair yards, thus checking submarine activities at source and where submarines perforce congregate.

The wording was reminiscent of Harris's when, in a minute to the CAS (quoted earlier) dated 20 March 1941, exactly a year before, he had written on the subject of the submarine menace: '... are we going Navy fashion to disperse our entire resources attempting to cope defensively with this problem at its outer fringe – an immense area – or are we going

---

* Harry Hopkins was President Roosevelt's adviser and close confidant, and became the faithful and perfect channel of communication between Roosevelt and Churchill. Although without public office, he was capable of taking decisions of the highest consequence, and the strength of the Anglo-American alliance owed much to his efforts.

Air War fashion to concentrate upon attacking the kernel of the problem at the centre?' The views on bombing which Harris had expressed to Hopkins and Roosevelt when he was in America in 1941 had clearly taken root.

Churchill's reply to the President, dated 29 March, was well timed, for it was written on the day after Bomber Command had made by far its most sensational attack of the war, raiding the Baltic port of Lübeck with enormous success. The reply stated: 'In order to cope with U-boat hatchings we are emphasising bombing attacks on U-boat nests, and last night we went to Lübeck with 250 bombers, including 43 heavy. Results are said to be best ever. This is in accordance with your wishes.' The Prime Minister went on to say that in view of the heavy sinkings still occurring on the US side of the Atlantic (that is, west of the 40th meridian), the Admiralty was pressing for the diversion of six bomber squadrons to anti-submarine patrol duties. His view, he said, was:

> On merits I am most anxious to meet their wish. On the other hand, the need to bomb Germany is great. Our new method of finding targets is yielding most remarkable results. However, our bombing force has not expanded as we hoped ... Just at the time when the weather is improving, when Germans are drawing away flak from their cities for their offensive against Russia, when you are keen on bombing U-boat nests, when oil targets are especially attractive, I find it very hard to take away those extra six squadrons from Bomber Command, in which Harris is doing so well.

Both Roosevelt's letter and Harris's initial success with Bomber Command had, in fact, strengthened Churchill's resolve to give the bombing offensive a fair trial.

The Lübeck raid, which had taken place on the night of 28/29 March, was so successful that it even overshadowed the raids on the Ruhr which had been made earlier in the month. At that time of year the Baltic ice was beginning to break up, so that Lübeck, an old port, would soon come into full use, supplying the military requirements of the German armies in North Russia and in Scandinavia; it would also be open for the import of iron ore and other strategic materials from Sweden, a major supplier to Germany. In addition, the town housed important industries, military depots and a training centre for submarine crews. The form of attack was similar to that employed against Essen and Cologne, except that the incendiary content of the bomb-load was far greater, since the town consisted of many old wooden buildings and houses and was thus highly vulnerable to fire. The night of the raid was moonlit, and visibility was excellent. The target was well beyond Gee range, but even so the device proved a great asset, for it enabled accurate navigation to be maintained over the greater part of the route. 234 aircraft were despatched, not 250 as Churchill, with poetic licence, had written to Roosevelt, and these dropped some 300 tons of bombs, of which 144 tons were incendiaries. The town was literally ablaze when the last aircraft headed for home.

Photographic reconnaissance revealed that 200 acres of built-up area in the island city had been completely devastated, including 1,500 houses, the Town Hall and municipal buildings, the gas and electricity works, and the tram depot. South-west of the island, in the suburb of St Lorenz, 65 acres of built-up area had been completely destroyed, and to the north-east, in the suburb of Marli, a 4,000-pound bomb had destroyed ten large houses and partially destroyed forty-five others over an area of $5\frac{1}{2}$ acres. The Drager works, which made oxygen apparatus for submarines and aircraft, had been obliterated, as had numerous other industrial concerns. But the greatest devastation was in the old town and the docks, where it was so extensive that no goods could be sent through either the town or the port for more than three weeks, and the effectiveness of the port was reduced for many months longer.

The German reaction is best summed up by Goebbels's diary entry for 30 March:

This Sunday has been thoroughly spoiled by an exceptionally heavy air raid by the RAF on Lübeck. In the morning I received a very alarming report from our propaganda office there, which I at first assumed to be exaggerated. In the course of the morning, however, I was informed of the seriousness of the situation by a long distance call from Kaufmann. He believes that no German city has ever before been attacked so severely from the air. Conditions in parts of Lübeck are chaotic.

Then again, on 4 April, he recorded:

The damage is really enormous. I have been shown a newsreel of the destruction. It is horrible. One can well imagine how such an awful bombardment affects the population. Thank God it is a North German population, which on the whole is much tougher than the Germans in the south or the south-east. Nevertheless we can't get away from the fact that the English air raids have increased in scope and importance; if they can be continued for weeks on these lines, they might conceivably have a demoralising effect on the population.

Churchill was delighted with the raid's success, and once the PRU information had been interpreted by the Photographic Interpretation Section of Bomber Command and made available to him, he expressed his satisfaction in another letter to Roosevelt, dated 1 April 1942:

Only the weather is holding us back from continuous heavy bombing attacks on Germany. Our new methods are most successful. Essen, Cologne, and above all Lübeck, were all on the Coventry scale. I am sure it is most important to keep this up all through the summer, blasting Hitler from behind while he is grappling with the Bear.

But Churchill was still concerned about the losses at sea, and conscious of the Admiralty's continued pressure for the diversion of Bomber Command aircraft to anti-submarine patrol duties. What he hoped for was a strong indication, if not actual proof, that the bomber offensive could forge ahead while at the same time provide an effective counter to the German U-boat campaign which, although now operating on a reduced scale since the latter half of 1941, was still a menace. Portal was also concerned that anti-submarine activities should not result in the waste of bombers on useless patrols. He preferred the tactics of air mining, and the bombing of ports housing U-boats, factories making parts, and dockyards assembling these craft. When there had been a meeting with Churchill in the last week of March to discuss the U-boat problem, Portal had asked Harris for a brief on Bomber Command's mining activities, in particular the mining of the western French ports, which were nests for U-boats operating in the Atlantic and along other sea routes important to Britain. His request was dated 23 March, and Harris's reply the 24th.

In his memorandum, Harris detailed past results from the beginning of mining operations in 1940 up to 31 December 1941. The total number of mines laid from the air during this period came to 2,669, of which 1,757 had been laid by Bomber Command's No. 5 Group Hampdens, and 812 by Coastal Command aircraft. The number of enemy ships known to have been lost to this method was 98, representing a gross tonnage of 211,360 tons. 27.2 mines were therefore laid per known ship lost, but Harris argued that for every known loss at least one unknown enemy ship had probably also been sunk. He based this assumption on more than 300 wrecks shown on German wartime charts made available through British Intelligence. Making allowances for losses due to normal marine risks, British wrecks resulting from Dunkirk, and direct sinkings from aerial attacks by Coastal Command and other forces, he reckoned it was reasonable to claim 200 ships sunk by Bomber Command's mining efforts. This figure was reinforced by a study of the known losses in the 60 minefields laid by air, which showed that sinkings varied between nil and 8 in each minefield, except for one where the known losses were 24. This field was under continuous observation from neutral Sweden, and was therefore the only area from which precise results could be obtained.

On the subject of U-boats, Harris wrote that during the first five months of 1941 the building yards of north-west Germany had been the main targets and that the effect of the attacks had been a marked slowing-up in the rate of launching and completing of U-boats, delays varying from two to six months. One raid on Wilhelmshaven, carried out in January 1941, had been so successful that U-boats under construction there had spent eighteen months on the slips instead of the normal eight. At Emden, three U-boats had been reported damaged beyond repair, and Harris wrote that a recent report, dated 3 March 1942, 'states that the heavy raids on this port during the winter have caused havoc to shipping and particularly mentions the fact that a new submarine was destroyed on the eve of its departure.' At Kiel, there had been similar delays to launchings, and the same was the case in Hamburg and Flensburg. All of this, Harris emphasised, had been achieved by Hampden aircraft, which could only carry one mine. Now, however, he had put in hand the conversion of all Bomber Command aircraft to be able to carry mines as well as bombs and, he wrote,

> since the Stirling and Lancaster can carry six apiece and the Halifax and Wellington two, the vast increase in potential effort becomes apparent. With these new facilities in mine-laying I anticipate in average weather, which frequently gives opportunities for wholesale mine-laying when nothing else of profit can be done, no particular trouble or serious interference with the bomber effort in laying 800-1,000 mines a month.

He went on to say that his aim now would be to lay 500 to 1,000 mines in the approaches to Lorient, St Nazaire, La Pallice, the Gironde River, Quiberon and St Jean de Luz. This form of attack, he asserted, with the bombing of shipyards and marine factories, would prove to be the best way of dealing with U-boats and other types of shipping.

Portal was now able to convince Churchill that the bombing offensive against Germany, which included in its target priorities dockyards where submarines were assembled and industrial centres where submarine parts and related equipment were manufactured, coupled with a programme of greatly increased mining from the air, provided the best contribution that Bomber Command could make to counter the U-boat war. With the Prime Minister convinced, the Command was therefore protected against any incursions into its strength by the Admiralty. But more bombing successes were urgently required in order to keep the support for the bomber offensive from flagging, as well as to strike back at the enemy.

Before April was over Harris and Saundby had added another highly effective attack to the growing list of Bomber Command 'successes'. On four consecutive nights (23/24, 24/25, 25/26, and 26/27 April), the town of Rostock on the Baltic coast – even further away than Lübeck and with a busy port being used for supplies to the Russian front and for importing vital materials from Sweden – was, by standards at that time, heavily bombed. As a target it was rather more important than Lübeck, for apart from its substantial port facilities, Rostock housed major submarine building yards and a large Heinkel aircraft assembly plant. The weather was perfect on all four nights, with a near-full moon, and Gee again proved an invaluable aid to accurate navigation over most of the route. Just over 500 sorties were flown and 305 tons of incendiaries and 442 tons of HE were dropped. The damage was formidable. The Turkish Ambassador in Berlin told his government that the 'Neptune Shipbuilding Yard and the Heinkel factory have been completely destroyed from end to end'. Photographic reconnaissance confirmed the Ambassador's statement and revealed that more than 70 per cent of the city had been devastated, port installations had been wrecked, and all services had been disrupted. Later Intelligence reports disclosed that over 100,000 people had been rendered homeless.

Goebbels was furious. On the 26th he wrote: 'It has been, it must be admitted, pretty disastrous ... The Führer arrived in Berlin at noon ... he is in extremely bad humour about the poor anti-aircraft defence at Rostock which caused him endless worry.' Then, on 27th April: 'Last night the heaviest attack yet launched had the seaport of Rostock once again as its objective. Tremendous damage is reported. During the morning hours no exact estimate can be made, as all long-distance communication with Rostock has been interrupted.' On the 28th, after the fourth successive raid, he wrote: 'The air raid last night on Rostock was even more devastating than those before. Community life there is practically at an end ... The situation in the city is in some sections catastrophic.' Two days later Goebbels received the official reports about the conditions in Rostock. 'Seven-tenths of the city,' he wrote, 'have been wiped out. More than 100,000 people had to be evacuated ... At Rostock there was, in fact, panic.'

The cost to Bomber Command was twelve aircraft lost, 2.4 per cent of the force employed.

Other raids were made against German towns during April, including Essen, Dortmund, Hamburg, Kiel and Cologne, but none with the same ferocity and success as those against Rostock. Lübeck and Rostock had proved that a small, relatively undefended town could be seriously disrupted by a concentrated attack by between 200 to 500 aircraft. Lübeck had received the attention of 234 aircraft and 300 tons of bombs in one night, and Rostock 521 aircraft and 747 tons of bombs spread over four nights. Harris and Saundby now wondered what would be needed to achieve similar results against a major Ruhr town, or a large seaport such as Hamburg; certainly it would require far greater numbers of aircraft than Bomber Command could muster in April 1942.

The arrival in England at the end of February of the advanced echelon of the United States Eighth Air Force, which was in fact the nucleus of that force's Eighth Bomber Command, had provided no solution to the shortage of bomber aircraft and crews then available for operations. The opportunities for co-operation were there, not least because US Eighth Bomber Command was headed by Brigadier-General Ira C. Eaker, a firm friend of Harris. The acquaintance had first been made in 1938, when Harris had been in America on a buying mission and Eaker was on US General H.H. Arnold's Air Staff in Washington, and it had been renewed when Harris had again been in Washington in 1941, as head of the RAF Delegation. Despite this, however, it was to be some months before the American bombing force was in a position to undertake operations against the enemy; indeed, its first Boeing B17 Flying Fortresses did not arrive in England until 1 July 1942, and its first operational mission was not flown until 17 August of that year, against a relatively easy target in France. Moreover, the American aircrew had been trained exclusively for daylight operations.

Thus Bomber Command had to discover, from its own resources, the means to produce the force that its leaders were now convinced it required for saturation raids against major German targets – no easy task.

CHAPTER XXI

'Operation Millennium'

The first ten weeks of Harris's command had seen a profound change in the success of the bombing of Germany, compared with earlier operations. But it was clear to Harris and Saundby that Bomber Command required two cardinal items if it was to produce destruction by bombing on a scale large enough to be decisive. Gee's accuracy of track and time-keeping enabled bombers to be marshalled over England in large forces, and to be concentrated both along the fly-in route and across the target itself, giving greater protection against flak and fighters by saturating the defences. Concentration over the target also increased the extent of damage, quite apart from the improvement in accuracy of bombing by Gee, by stretching ARP facilities beyond their capacity to cope effectively with fires. Another advantage of Gee was that it assisted the aircraft to return to and land at their bases with a minimum of crashes over home territory; in the past the casualty rate to aircraft and crews returning from raids had been high, due to being lost or to difficulties in landing. Gee was extremely accurate over England, and was of considerable assistance in guiding aircraft not only to base but also right down to actual landing, but its range was still limited to some 350 miles, which restricted the number of targets it could cover. Moreover, it was estimated that Gee would only be free from jamming over enemy territory for little more than six months from its first use on operations, which would further restrict the number of possible Gee targets. Thus the Command had a vital need for a system, independent of ground stations and with unlimited range, to provide more accurate navigation and more precise target-finding and bombing, and to allow for attacks on all the important targets in Germany, regardless of distance. Bomber Command's requirement was for a large enough force of heavy bombers to carry the size of bomb-load essential to making any real impression on the Ruhr, and on towns such as Bremen, Hamburg, Hannover, Frankfurt, Stuttgart, Mannheim, Kassel, Munich, Nürnberg and Berlin.

At TRE, solutions to the problems of navigation and blind-bombing at all ranges were now well in hand. Lovell and Dee had already begun development of the revolutionary RDF system for bombers known as H₂S, and by the end of 1941 this development work was proceeding apace, operating on 10 centimetres. In January and February of 1942 the first experimental models, which were crude in the extreme, were demonstrated in the air to Saward and Dickie. From February to September, when H₂S reached the initial production stage, it was Dickie who collaborated with Lovell and his team, guiding development along lines that would provide a bomber's navigator with the presentation of H₂S information in the most useful form. This presentation included a picture on the cathode-ray tube, known as the Plan Position Indicator (PPI), having a true north presentation to conform with a map and a finger of light constantly indicating the heading of the aircraft, and an alterable scale to provide a 30- to 40-mile view of the area all around the aircraft for navigation, or an enlarged and more detailed 10-mile view for bombing purposes. In fact, with Dickie's guidance and Lovell's ingenuity, H₂S was soon able to give a moving map-like picture to the navigator for general navigation, and an enlarged image for target location and blind-bombing purposes; in addition, the system incorporated a very accurate RDF altimeter. While the picture on the earliest models was not an exact replica of a map and had therefore to be interpreted, coastlines did represent an almost perfect pattern of what was indicated on a map. The close co-operation between Lovell's group at TRE and the RDF Department at Bomber Command was soon to pay handsome dividends.

On 28 April, Saward and Dickie made flights in Blenheim V.6385, which had been equipped with an experimental H₂S incorporating these navigating and bombing facilities. They were greatly impressed by the system's performance, and reported to Saundby that its potential was considerable. Bomber Command therefore pressed for speedy completion of the development of the new device and for its introduction into all heavy bombers at the earliest possible date. H₂S faced an initial problem, however, in the type of output valve that it employed. The demonstrations on 28 April had been made with a set using a klystron, which was too low-powered to provide a reflected signal strong enough to ensure a picture of sufficient detail for towns to be identified, and covering an adequate area around the aircraft's position to allow accurate

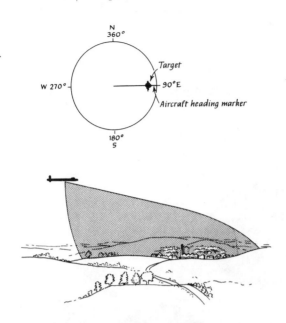

Response from built-up areas as displayed on early H$_2$S sets

navigation. What was needed was the newly developed output valve known as the magnetron, which was capable of giving much greater power output, resulting in a stronger reflected signal and, therefore, improved range and definition. The magnetron, however, was highly secret, being the real success behind the RAF night-fighters' latest 10-centimetre AI equipment and the GCI system. As a result, there was substantial opposition to its use in any equipment which would be flown over enemy territory, and thus might fall into enemy hands.

H$_2$S had a firm backer in Lord Cherwell, however, who exerted his influence on Churchill. While this did not bring about a sudden decision on the magnetron, it did result in the Prime Minister taking an active interest in the system, and in pressure from him to progress its full development with all speed. On 6 May 1942, in a letter to the Secretary of State for Air, Sir Archibald Sinclair, he wrote:

> I hope that a really large order for H$_2$S has been placed and that nothing will be allowed to stand in the way of getting this apparatus punctually ... I have heard Sir Robert Renwick mentioned as a man of drive and business experience who has already rendered valuable service in connection with Gee. Perhaps you might think he is a good man for this purpose ...

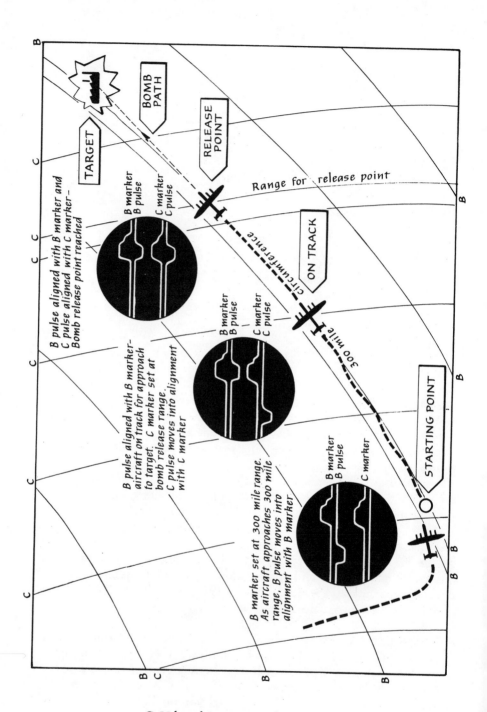

G-H bombing approach to target

In fact, Sinclair had already put Sir Robert Renwick in charge of all RDF aids to bombing and navigation – largely at Cherwell's instigation. Renwick's list now included not only Gee and H_2S, but also two other new devices, Oboe and GH. Oboe was a precision system whereby an aircraft could be tracked over a target by two ground stations in England and then instructed when to release its bombs so that they would fall within 100 yards of the selected target. Although its range was limited to 300 miles, this was still enough to cover important Ruhr targets. Its other limitation was that only one aircraft at a time could be operated across the target by one pair of ground stations, which meant that the system could only be used for target-marking tactics. GH was the reverse of Oboe in that the aircraft instrument measured its distance from two RDF stations in England, tracking itself over the target by measurement from one and determining its bomb-release point by its distance from the other. It had an important advantage over Oboe in that up to eighty aircraft could operate on the system simultaneously from one pair of stations, and any number of targets could be attacked at the same time. It was also highly accurate, and could achieve results similar to those attainable by Oboe. In the spring of 1942, however, H_2S and Oboe were insufficiently advanced in development for there to be any hope that they would be available for operational use much before the beginning of 1943; GH was even further behind in development.

Harris and Saundby were well aware of these new systems, for they insisted on being kept well briefed by the RDF Department. The C-in-C also pressed hard for greater priority to be given to their development, not only by constantly raising the matter with Portal, but through his growing contacts with Churchill as well, particularly during the Prime Minister's frequent weekend visits to Chequers, only a few miles away from Bomber Command headquarters. But both Harris and Saundby knew that these revolutionary developments could not improve the effectiveness of the bombing offensive for some time to come, and at this stage Harris therefore concentrated on building up the size of his force. To do this in the face of a very considerable opposition to the strategic bombing policy needed a dramatic raid that would be so successful in terms of its size and results that it would bring howls of anguish from the Germans and capture support for Bomber Command from a delighted British public. From such a raid Harris also wanted proof that his Command could achieve industrial destruction on a decisive scale, provided that sufficient aircraft could be put on to a target in one attack. The bombing of Lübeck and Rostock had proved that small, relatively undefended towns could be seriously disrupted by concentrated attacks employing some 200 to 500 aircraft. What Harris and Saundby were now aiming for was a vastly bigger force attacking in one raid.

The trial Gee raid on Cologne late in March had proved that far larger numbers of aircraft could be concentrated against a target in the period of one hour than had previously been believed possible. In the Cologne operation 120 aircraft had been successfully concentrated into an attack lasting twenty minutes, and the time-scale had not presented any difficulties; indeed, it was believed that, given a large enough Gee force, the numbers could have been safely doubled. By April the number of aircraft fitted with Gee had increased and by late May it was expected that at least 400 aircraft would be equipped, which meant that most of the Command's front-line strength would have Gee by that time. That strength was not great enough for Harris, however. He had set his mind on a raid using 1,000 aircraft.

In fact, at the beginning of May the Command did have a force of 1,000 bombers, if the aircraft (and their crews) from Operational Training Units and the Heavy Conversion Units (HCUs)* were included in that total. The OTU crews were only partly trained, but the more advanced of them had already had some night operational experience dropping leaflets over France, and there would also be scratch crews for some OTU and HCU aircraft available from group and station headquarters staffs. To use all of these crews presented many dangers, however. If losses on a single, vast operation were very high, particularly amongst OTU and HCU crews, then the Command's reserves would be placed in jeopardy and the whole programme of training and expansion might be wrecked. But Harris knew that, set against this risk, the advantages of a successful raid with 1,000 aircraft against a major German industrial town would be very great. Saundby who, in the first week of May, had made a study of the possible availability of aircraft for a mammoth strike, told Harris that by drawing aircraft from the OTUs and HCUs and having them manned only by instructor crews and more experienced pupil crews, it would be possible to raise more than 700 bombers and at the same time minimise the risks inherent in using the majority of pupil crews. To meet the shortfall of 300 aircraft, he proposed that outside help should be sought from Coastal and Army Co-operation Commands. During the past twelve months more than 200 aircraft and operationally experienced crews had been transferred from Bomber Command to Coastal Command for anti-submarine and anti-surface vessel patrols; these aircraft and crews were ideally suited to take part in the vast raid now envisaged.

Given that 1,000 aircraft could be raised for such a colossal experiment, it was obvious that a full moon and good weather would be essential.

* At the HCUs, crews from squadrons formerly equipped with twin-engined aircraft, or from OTUs, underwent conversion courses that equipped them to operate the four-engined bombers.

The next full-moon period was from 26 to 31 May, and the one after that from 22 to 27 June. Plainly, if this incredible plan was to be put into action soon, then the choices of date were limited. With great boldness, Harris decided to launch the operation at the end of May, and immediately sought support from Portal. The latter was readily persuaded that a raid of this magnitude would, if successful, not only damage the enemy, but would also bring powerful backing from official sources and public alike for the expansion of the bomber force, since it would prove that by bombing, Germany could be effectively attacked, and that therefore Britain's Russian ally could be directly assisted. Portal also foresaw that such an attack would demonstrate how Germany's overall strategic effort could be seriously impaired by industrial disruption and the need to disperse military resources to defend the homeland. He therefore promised to seek Churchill's blessing for the venture, and agreed that Harris should also see the Prime Minister in order to explain his plan.

Harris visited Chequers on the Sunday after his interview with Portal, the latter having already advised the Prime Minister of the proposal. Churchill listened with immense interest to Harris as he expounded his plan, and received with great enthusiasm the idea of a raid by 1,000 aircraft that would be concentrated into so short a space of time – ninety minutes – thus saturating defences while suffering losses estimated as being not greater than 5 per cent.* Harris told him that the target he planned to attack would be either Hamburg or Cologne, since both cities had water close by to help identification, and both were within Gee range. In actual fact, Hamburg was just outside Gee range, but it was the target that Churchill most favoured because it was a major German naval port and an assembly base for U-boats.

By Monday 18 May Harris was ready with a detailed plan for the 1,000-bomber raid, to be made either against Hamburg or Cologne, the final choice of target having to depend at the last minute on the weather forecast. Cologne was, in fact, the Command's favoured target, being well within Gee coverage, the unanimous advice from Saundby, Air Commodore Harrison,† Group Captain Elworthy,‡ and Saward having been: 'Stay within Gee coverage. Go to Cologne.' The total number of Gee-equipped aircraft now topped 500, including 100 HCU

---

* A 5-per cent loss would amount to 50 aircraft and up to 350 aircrew.
† Air Commodore R. Harrison was the Deputy Senior Air Staff Officer.
‡ Group Captain S.C. Elworthy was Group Captain operations. After the war he became Marshal of the Royal Air Force Sir Charles Elworthy, GCB, CBE, DSO, MVO, DFC, AFC, Chief of the Air Staff and Chief of the Defence Staff. Later, as Lord Elworthy, he was Governor of Windsor Castle until he retired to his home country of New Zealand.

four-engined heavies which had been modified and fitted by the RDF Department's teams of mechanics on squadron stations, so that 50 per cent of the possible force was now Gee-equipped. It was important to have the greatest assistance that Gee could provide; moreover, the experimental raid on Cologne in March supplied a useful blueprint for detailed planning.

On the morning of the 18th, Harris had a meeting with Portal at the Air Ministry during which he outlined the details of the plan, and explained that to realise a force of 1,000 aircraft he needed 250 to 300 to be supplied by other Commands. He also told Portal that he was considering undertaking two such raids within the coming full-moon period, explaining that if the first raid was a success and losses were low, then with such a force already marshalled, it should be used at least a second time, given favourable conditions.

Portal advised Harris by letter on 19 May that the Prime Minister warmly approved of the 'Thousand Plan' and that, after consulting with the First Sea Lord, he (Portal) believed that there would be no objection to the idea of Coastal Command co-operating by providing 250 aircraft, unless it had special operations planned at the time. Portal went on to tell Harris to proceed on the assumption of co-operation, and to consult directly with the C-in-C Coastal Command. In addition, he suggested that the C-in-C Fighter Command should be asked to provide intruder fighter attacks against enemy aerodromes, and North Sea sweeps in protection of returning bombers. Lastly, he recommended that approaches be made to Army Co-operation Command and to Training Command for possible help, and ended with the words: 'Please let me know before the operation is actually staged so that I can tell the Prime Minister.'

Letters were prepared by Saundby on the 20th, in conjunction with the Operations, RDF and Intelligence Staff, which set out the details of the Thousand Plan. These were despatched to Coastal, Army Co-operation, Fighter and Training Commands, and to the AOCs of the five operational Bomber Groups and the Bomber Operational Training Groups, and contained a request from Harris for the maximum contribution that could possibly be made. The intention behind the raid was expressed in blunt terms: '... to annihilate one of Germany's main industrial centres by fire.'

On the 21st, Air Chief Marshal Sir Philip Joubert de la Ferté, C-in-C Coastal Command, promised to provide 250 aircraft, the greatest single contribution needed to attain the figure of 1,000 bombers. Army Co-operation Command offered nothing, but Air Marshal Sir William Welsh, C-in-C Flying Training Command, offered four aircraft and crews, while Fighter Command promised maximum support with harassing attacks on enemy fighter aerodromes and with North Sea sweeps in protection of the bombers. Then, on the 26th, with the raid planned for the night of 27/28 May, or the first night within the same full-moon period that would provide suitable weather conditions, the Admiralty intervened, ordering the C-in-C Coastal Command that under no circumstances were aircraft and crews from his force to take part in the operation. It was vicious timing, and it reduced the overall size of the raid to some 800 aircraft.

A Herculean last-minute effort to raise the extra aircraft and crews from within Bomber Command itself saved the day. The weather helped, for it was not until the night of the 30/31 May that it was sufficiently good for the attack to be undertaken. By that time, by dint of indefatigable effort in the groups and squadrons to make more aircraft serviceable, and by raising many 'scratch' crews from group and station staffs, the figure reached 1,046 aircraft, of which 1,042 were from Bomber Command alone and 4 were from Training Command. The Admiralty's last-minute torpedo had brought some good – the 'Thousand Plan' was now entirely a Bomber Command affair.

At 09.10 hours on Saturday morning, 30 May, Harris entered the Operations Room for his planning conference, accompanied, as usual, by Saundby. With a characteristic hunch about his shoulders, he walked slowly but deliberately to his desk. After handing his cap to his PA he sat down heavily in his chair and leant back to allow the meteorological synoptic charts to be placed on the desk in front of him. Behind him stood Saundby and, in a half circle, the Deputy SASO, representatives of the Operations staff and the RDF Department, and the Command's Senior Intelligence Officer. Not a muscle moved, and no sign of an expression stirred the C-in-C's face while the forecast for the next twenty-four hours was outlined to him by the Meteorological Officer, Mr Magnus Spence, who, as he finished reading, stood up straight and rather precisely clasped his hands in front of his short, stocky figure.

Harris moved at last. Slowly he pulled an American cigarette carton from his pocket and, flicking the bottom with his thumb, selected the protruding Lucky Strike. He lit the cigarette and then drew from his right breast pocket a short, chunky cigarette holder. Never taking his eyes off the charts, he deliberately pressed the cigarette into the end of the holder, which he then grasped firmly between his teeth. He continued to stare at the charts. Slowly his forefinger moved across the map, over the continent of Europe until it came to rest on a town in Germany. The pressure on his finger bent back the end joint and drove the blood from the top of his finger nail, leaving a half circle of white. He turned to Saundby, his face still expressionless.

'The Thousand Plan – tonight.'

His finger pressed on Cologne as he spoke.

The Command staffs worked all day under the expert guidance of Saundby, who was responsible for the detailed planning and the tactics to be adopted. Times for waves of target-marking squadrons were worked out in detail so as to fit intricately and precisely into the general pattern of the whole attack, in order that the target should be constantly lit by flares throughout the raid. Incendiary forces and high explosive forces were interwoven to create the greatest possible conflagration, and aircraft routeing was carefully selected in relation to the latest information on enemy defences. Concentration points and times were calculated in detail so that the waves of bombers arriving from all parts of England should finally merge into one mammoth stream of destruction. The lattice lines along which the Gee aircraft were to make their bombing approach were carefully selected, and the exact Gee co-ordinates where the routes of these aircraft should join the bombing approach line were indicated. The approach was to be made from west to east with the Gee aircraft of Nos. 1 and 3 Groups opening the attack with flares and a full load of incendiaries. Neumarkt, in the centre of the old city, was the aiming point. The 367 aircraft of the OTUs and HCUs were to follow this incendiary attack with incendiary and HE loads, using the fires started by the Gee aircraft as their guide. The last wave was to consist of all the available four-engined heavy bombers of Nos. 4 and 5 Groups, amounting to just over 200 Gee-equipped Lancaster and Halifax aircraft carrying HE and incendiaries – their attack would be packed into a fifteen-minute final crescendo. The whole attack over the target was to last precisely ninety minutes.

By 17.30 hours all the squadrons knew that they were to take part in the greatest aerial offensive the world had ever seen. In every bomber briefing room in Great Britain there was an air of excitement as the crews assembled for their final instructions. As Commanding Officers called for silence, announcing that they had a special signal from the C-in-C to all his aircrews, there was an expectant hush; then, as the words were read from the message sheet, the silence became electric:

The force of which you form a part tonight is at least twice the size and has more than four times the carrying capacity of the largest Air Force ever before concentrated on one objective. You have an opportunity therefore to strike a blow at the enemy which will resound, not only throughout Germany, but throughout the world.

In your hands lie the means of destroying a major part of the resources by which the enemy's war effort is maintained. It depends, however, upon each individual crew member whether full concentration is achieved. Press home your attack to your precise objective with the utmost determination and resolution in the foreknowledge that if you individually succeed, the most shattering and devastating blow will have been delivered against the very vitals of the enemy. You are a thousand strong. Let him have it – right on the chin.

The raid on Cologne, code-named 'Operation Millennium', was an outstanding success. 898 aircraft claimed to have identified and attacked the target, dropping 1,455 tons of bombs of which 915 tons were incendiaries and 540 tons HE, for a loss of forty aircraft, representing 3.8 per cent of the total force despatched. The results, compared to any previous attack against German towns, were prodigious: over 600 acres of built-up area were completely destroyed and more than 250 factories were devastated or seriously damaged; 200,000 people had to be evacuated from the city; power, gas and water supplies, communications, and travelling facilities were all severely disrupted. The full extent of the damage could not be assessed by photographic evidence for several days because of the huge pall of smoke that hung over the city up to a height of 15,000 feet. For Cologne it was a catastrophic raid. Overnight, the whole concept of the bomber as an offensive weapon had been revolutionised, and Germany had been staggered by a crippling blow to one of her major industrial cities in a raid lasting just one hour and a half.

Göring could not believe the first fantastic reports to come from Cologne. Albert Speer,* who at that time was Germany's Minister for Armaments and War Production told the author that he had been with Göring at the Veldenstein Castle in Franconia when the news of the weight of the attack was reported to the Reichsmarschall by his adjutant. According to Speer, Göring had shouted: 'Impossible! That many bombs cannot be dropped in a single night! Connect me with the Gauleiter of Cologne.' An incredible telephone conversation had then taken place between Göring and Gauleiter Grohe, in which the former said that the information from the Cologne Police Commissioner was a 'stinking lie'. After Grohe had confirmed the bad news, Göring had replied: 'I tell you as Reichsmarschall that the figures cited are simply too high. How can you dare to report such fantasies to the Führer?' He was quickly to learn, however, that Cologne really was in a state of chaos – his promise that the German Air Force would never let the enemy attack the Fatherland

---

* Before the war Albert Speer had been an eminent young architect and consulting engineer, and had been responsible for the design and construction of numerous important public buildings in Germany. In February 1942, he was unexpectedly appointed to the key post of Armaments Minister by Hitler after the former Minister, Fritz Todt, had been killed in an aircraft accident. After the war Speer was sentenced to eighteen years in Spandau jail for war crimes, and was released on 1 October 1966. In the 1970s, the author spent many days with him at his home in Heidelberg when researching material for his biography of Harris. Speer died in 1981.

had, overnight, worn remarkably thin. Speer said that Göring just could not accept, at first, that such a blow could fall on a German town.

The tremendous success of 'Operation Millennium' made headlines on both sides of the Atlantic, and drew forth congratulations both from the USA and the Soviet Union. Harris and Saundby had proved that a major city could be seriously devastated with a heavy enough attack, and that defences could be saturated by employing a large concentration of aircraft. Public and official support for the expansion of Bomber Command was now assured.

Churchill recognised this remarkable feat of arms, perhaps as great as any in Britain's history of Britain, with a message to Harris:

> I congratulate you and the whole of Bomber Command upon the remarkable feat of organisation which enabled you to despatch over 1,000 bombers to the Cologne area in a single night, and without confusion to concentrate their action over the target in so short a time as one hour and a half. This proof of the growing power of the British Bomber Force is also the herald of what Germany will receive, city by city, from now on.

'Operation Millennium' was a turning point in the war.

CHAPTER XXII

The Bomber Offensive Develops

As has been said, by the middle of 1942 the development of RDF aids for improving navigation and target-location at night and from above cloud was proceeding well. There was, however, a growing opinion at the Air Ministry that a specialised target-finding force should be created by bringing together a number of squadrons under the command of one man, and creaming off from the bomber Groups their best crews to man the squadrons and sustain their losses. The idea was supported by Portal, but bitterly opposed by Harris. Portal's support was influenced by a report by Mr Justice Singleton on 'The Bombing of Germany', dated 20 May 1942, which had been prepared in accordance with instructions from Churchill issued on 16 April. The Singleton Report reviewed the results of the German bombing of Britain from August 1940 to June 1941 and concluded that its effect had been very serious, and would have been even more so had it continued beyond June and had it been intensified; this, despite the fact that the offensive had been ill-directed and the tonnage of bombs dropped had been small compared to the weights discharged by Bomber Command in the first few months of 1942. The report went on to indicate what could be achieved against Germany in the future by an increased weight of attack, citing the raids on Lübeck and Rostock as examples. But Singleton noted the problems of navigating to and finding targets in the Ruhr and other non-coastal areas. His examination of attacks on the Ruhr led him to conclude that the bomber force needed more and far better scientific aids to navigation and target-location if the greater weight of bombs carried was to be of any real value. If the means of getting to, finding and accurately bombing the industrial inland towns of Germany could be provided, then Singleton had no doubts as to the importance of a strategic air offensive against Germany. He ended his report with a very telling paragraph:

> To sum up, I do not think that great results can be hoped for within six months from 'air attacks on Germany at greatest possible strength'.* I cannot help feeling that the six month period ought to be looked upon as leading up to, and forming part of, a longer and more sustained effort than as one expected to produce results within that limited time. Much depends on what happens in Russia. The effects of a reverse for Germany, or lack of success, would be greatly increased by an intensified bombing programme in the autumn and winter. Effect on morale would normally be greater at that time than it would be now. And if this was coupled with knowledge in Germany that the bombing would be on an increasing scale until the end, and with realisation of the fact that the German Air Force could not again achieve equality, I think it might well prove the turning point – provided always that greater accuracy can be achieved.

Portal recognised the Singleton Report as the first outside and impartial support for a large-scale strategic bomber offensive against Germany, but he was conscious of the emphasis on accuracy and aware that the new RDF aids, H_2S and Oboe, were unlikely to be available, even in limited quantities, until the late winter or early in 1943. He therefore felt that some means of achieving accuracy in navigation and bombing must be found as an interim measure, and a target-finding force made up of the best and most experienced crews in Bomber Command seemed to him to be the soundest solution. He also believed that the new RDF systems such as H_2S, which would be in short supply when they first became available, should initially be concentrated in such a target-finding force.

Harris, for his part, was equally aware of the Command's immediate lack of adequate scientific aids that would enable it to be fully effective as an offensive force, and he was therefore in favour of establishing target-finding methods using selected squadrons. But he was opposed to the formation of a separate Group as a kind of *corps d'élite*, with its inevitable disadvantage of upsetting morale by making the main force Groups feel inferior. Harris wanted the Groups to have their own target-finding squadrons, the underlying principle being that such squadrons should be selected for their efficient performance and good record on operations in their own Groups. He also foresaw a need, when the bomber force had become big enough to undertake more than one major raid on the same night on targets of such different content that they

* Singleton's terms of reference asked him, in considering the likely effects of bombing the enemy, to assume 'air attacks on Germany at the greatest possible strength' during the six months from May 1942.

would require different methods of attack, for the greater flexibility that would accrue if all the Groups had their own target-finding forces.

After several meetings with Portal on this contentious subject, and after the exchange of a series of nearly acrimonious letters in June, Harris was forced to agree to set up a separate target-finding force, to be called the Pathfinder Force (PFF). Having been overruled by Portal he accepted the decision with good grace, although he did not abandon his idea of creating separate target-finding squadrons in some of the Groups at a later date, when the total forces at his disposal were large enough to permit major attacks against several targets simultaneously.

The Pathfinder Force was to consist of four squadrons initially, and six squadrons ultimately, the squadrons to be provided by the four operational Groups. It was to be established in the East Anglia area, with its Headquarters at RAF Wyton in Huntingdonshire. The first four squadrons were to be No. 7 (Stirling) Squadron from 3 Group, No. 35 (Halifax) Squadron from 4 Group, No. 83 (Lancaster) Squadron from 5 Group, and No. 156 (Wellington) Squadron from 1 Group. To command the PFF, Harris selected a Wing Commander who had served under him in 1932 when he had commanded No. 210 Flying-Boat Squadron at Pembroke Dock. This was D.C.T. Bennett,* an Australian in his early thirties who had held a short-service commission in the Royal Air Force before the war and who had then joined Imperial Airways, where he became a Captain with the remarkable distinction of holding almost every licence available in civil aviation, including a first navigator's certificate, a radio operator's licence and an engineer's certificate. When war broke out he had initially taken part in the opening of the transatlantic ferry for the delivery of American aircraft to Great Britain, before joining and commanding a night-bomber squadron in 1941. In that same year he had been shot down in flames over Norway, but escaped by parachute with his crew, which he led to safety in Sweden after many adventures en route. With his persuasive tongue, he had then managed to talk his way out of Sweden and back to England. Now chosen to command the new force, Bennett was immediately promoted to Group Captain.

The formation of the Pathfinder Force coincided with the trials of H₂S to determine whether it should be finally designed to use the klystron output valve, or the highly secret magnetron. As the new force was to receive priority for the equipment of its aircraft with all new RDF aids to navigation and bombing, it was essential that Bennett should, without delay, become conversant with H₂S and the other aids that were under

---

* Later Air Vice-Marshal D.C.T. Bennett, CB, DSO, DFC, Air Officer Commanding No. 8 Group (Pathfinders). He was elected to Parliament in the Middlesbrough by-election of 1945, on a Liberal ticket.

development at TRE. Saundby therefore arranged that, after reporting to HQ Bomber Command on 3 July, Bennett should be driven down to TRE at Great Malvern, and from there to neighbouring RAF Defford, where the H_2S trials were being undertaken, on the following day. It fell to Wing Commander Saward, head of the Command's RDF Department, to drive Bennett down to Malvern and Defford and to introduce him to those concerned with the new developments. The timing was highly appropriate, since Saward was due to fly with the two different types of H_2S before reporting on the difference in performance between the klystron and magnetron versions – now Bennett would have the opportunity of assessing both for himself.

The battle over the magnetron was rapidly coming to a head. The Secretary of State for Air, Sir Archibald Sinclair, called a meeting for 15 July at which a decision on the use of the magnetron was to be taken. The first few flights with the klystron-equipped H_2S had been great failures, the range being severely limited, not more than twelve miles at best. Moreover, the signals were too weak to permit accurate interpretation of the picture on the cathode-ray screen. The first flights with the magnetron version of H_2S, however, had been as promising as those with the klystron had been disapointing; Gloucester was seen at twenty-two miles' range and Birmingham was identified at nearly thirty miles, although interpretation still needed skill. But the sharp contrast between land and water resulted in coastlines being displayed with clear definition – the River Severn was discernible almost as far as Gloucester with the Severn Bridge plainly visible. On 14 July, Saward submitted the Command RDF Department's report on the magnetron H_2S, and on the 15th Bennett's preliminary report was available, in time for Harris to make use of it at the Secretary of State's meeting, scheduled for the afternoon of the same day. Both Bennett and Saward stated that the magnetron H_2S was so superior in performance to the klystron version that the utmost pressure should be exerted to secure permission to proceed with the magnetron type and to abandon the klystron. At the Secretary of State's meeting, however, the opponents of the magnetron H_2S used the powerful argument that the enemy, having captured magnetron H_2S from a downed bomber, could so improve his night-fighter RDF equipment and ground warning system that its early revelation could prove to be the destruction of Britain's own bomber force. Cherwell and Watson-Watt were of the opinion that it would take from twelve to eighteen months to develop the magnetron from the moment one fell into German hands, and Harris argued that there was no point in keeping the magnetron in a glass case, since it might well be developed by the Germans in any case, and used against Britain first. Having made it clear that H_2S was vitally important to the success of the newly created Pathfinder Force, and that the device was only viable if built with the magnetron, Harris went on to emphasise, acidly, that he was not asking for H_2S in order to build Germany, but to destroy her. Cherwell's backing proved decisive, and the decision was made to proceed with the magnetron version of H_2S; it was agreed, moreover, that development and production should proceed on the highest priority.

With every chance of H_2S being available in sufficient quantities for use by the Pathfinder Force early in 1943, and with Oboe, the precision marker-bombing device, expected to be available by the end of 1942, Harris and Saundby now foresaw the possibility of a successful and sustained offensive against Germany. What was still needed, however, was a much larger force of bombers and crews.

The formation of the PFF produced no immediate and dramatic change in the fortunes of Bomber Command. During the first half of 1942 the Command had, in any case, been spectacularly successful in its bombing of Germany compared to the earlier period of the war, and this level of success continued throughout the remainder of the year. The 'Thousand Raid' on Cologne had been followed almost immediately by another major attack, this time against Essen, on the night of 1/2 June with 956 aircraft, including 347 from the OTUs. Cloud mixed with industrial haze had made visual identification of the target extremely difficult, with the result that the raid was a partial failure, Essen receiving only minor damage and the Krupps factory remaining unscathed, although the scattered bombing had caused heavy damage to Oberhausen and Mulheim, to the north-west and south-west of Essen. The size of the force again saturated defences, and the loss of thirty-one aircraft, 3.2 per cent, was low for the most strongly defended district of Germany.

On the night of 25/26 June another 'Thousand Raid' had been mounted, with 1,006 aircraft despatched to attack the North German port of Bremen. After the personal intervention of Churchill with the Admiralty, Coastal Command had provided 102 aircraft for the operation, the other 904 coming from Bomber Command's own resources, including 272 aircraft from the OTUs. This raid had done serious damage to the Focke-Wulf works and to the Deutsche Schiffwerke shipbuilding yards, and factories and warehouses all over the city had suffered severely. In addition, some 27 acres of the business and residential areas had been completely destroyed. Even so, the damage had not been on the scale achieved at Cologne, and the losses had proved to be higher than those suffered on the two previous large-scale attacks – forty-nine aircraft, 5 per cent of the force despatched, failed to return.

After these three major raids, only four more operations over Germany using aircraft and crews from the OTUs were undertaken in 1942. These were against Düsseldorf on the nights of 31 July/1 August and 10/11

September, against Bremen on the night of 13/14 September, and against Essen on the night of 16/17 September. The raids against Düsseldorf were highly successful, the first attack being made with 630 aircraft and the second with 476 aircraft. 300 acres in the centre of the town were completely devastated, a single 8,000-pound bomb totally wrecked the main railway station, a large area of the docks and their associated warehouses were destroyed, and thirty factories, including the Schiess-Defries and Krieger steel works and two major chemical works, were seriously damaged; in fact, the destruction was on a similar scale to that at Cologne.

The raid on Bremen was also a considerable success, but the Essen attack was effectively a failure, once more because of industrial haze and cloud. Essen was still the hard nut to crack, and the means of finding this target and of bombing it accurately had yet to come to hand.

These were not the only raids undertaken during the period June to September 1942. Bomber Command mounted attacks of more than 200 aircraft ten times in June, and in July there were ten major raids with forces of the order of 300 aircraft on each occasion. Bremen, Hamburg, Emden, Kiel, Frankfurt, Karlsruhe, Munich, Osnabrück, Aachen, as well as the Ruhr towns, all received attention at a level which, by now, was creating consternation on the part of the German authorities and fear amongst the German public. Apart from industrial and town-area devastation, the famous battle-cruiser *Gneisenau* was so seriously damaged by bombing raids on Kiel that the First Sea Lord conveyed his sincere thanks and congratulations to Harris, and confirmed that photograph reconnaissance indicated that her condition was such that she was now unlikely to be able to put to sea again for a very long time (in fact, she remained out of action for the rest of the war). And in addition to the bombing during this period, the Command laid more than 4,000 mines.

Despite this growing success, the weight of attack that Bomber Command could throw against the enemy was still insufficient to be decisive in the war against Germany, and both Harris and Saundby knew it. The Command's successes, however, had indicated that, given a large enough force at its disposal, and with adequate modern navigational and target-finding aids, it could bring about a situation whereby an invasion of Europe could be contemplated without serious losses being sustained by the land and naval forces engaged in such an enterprise. Harris himself remained confident that a complete defeat of Germany could be accomplished by bombing alone, provided that he had a greatly increased bombing force, and provided also that the Americans had a large enough day-bombing force for the combined commands to produce round-the-clock bombing on a scale similar to that achieved during the 'Thousand Raid' on Cologne. To achieve his aim of a greatly increased bomber force, Harris therefore mounted a new and vigorous offensive, but this time with his pen.

The strong personal relationship that Harris had established with Churchill during his first few months as Commander-in-Chief was truly remarkable, and unquestionably it had a profound effect upon the conduct of the war. Theirs was a friendship based upon trust in each other's judgement and respect for each other's capabilities. HQ Bomber Command at Knaphill, near High Wycombe, was close to Chequers, the Prime Minister's country residence, and Churchill, who had a penchant for going behind the backs of his Ministers and Chiefs of Staff in order to talk directly with his operational commanders and thus get a feeling of what was happening in the field, took immediate advantage of this proximity. Harris readily reciprocated, and as a result he became perhaps the most outspoken man to have the Prime Minister's ear – and, indeed, his eye, for Harris's letters and memoranda to Churchill are numerous, cogent and frequently trenchant, although he kept Portal informed at all times of his conversations with Churchill, and showed him copies of his letters and memoranda.

On 17 June 1942, shortly after the 'Thousand Raid' on Cologne, Harris sent his first powerful plea to Churchill for the expansion of Bomber Command. It took the form of a memorandum on the use of air power, and in it he wrote: 'Prime Minister, Victory, speedy and complete, awaits the side which first employs air power as it should be employed.' He asserted that Germany, entangled in the meshes of vast land campaigns on the Russian front and in North Africa and the Middle East, could no longer disengage her air power for strategic application in the west.

> She missed victory through air power by a hair's breadth in 1940. She missed then only through faulty equipment and training, and the tactical misdirection of an Air Force barely adequate for the purpose. That is a historical fact. We ourselves are now at the crossroads. We are free, if we will, to employ our rapidly increasing air strength in the proper manner. In such a manner as would avail to knock Germany out of the war in a matter of months, if we decide upon the right course. If we decide upon the wrong course, then our air power will now, and increasingly in the future, become inextricably implicated as a subsidiary weapon in the prosecution of vastly protracted and avoidable land and sea campaigns.

Harris reviewed the successes of Bomber Command in the first half of 1942 which included the vast destruction at Lübeck, Rostock and Cologne, the extensive devastation at Kiel, Hamburg and Emden, and the heavy damage inflicted upon the submarine manufacturing centre at Augsburg. In addition, he referred to the successful attacks on six or more other German towns, and on the Renault and Matford fighting vehicle construction centres in France. For good measure he threw in the fact that the Command had also taken a heavy toll of enemy shipping as a result of its mine-laying activities. 'That, and much more,' he wrote, 'has been done by less than thirty squadrons in six months. It is the only British force that has fetched a squawk out of Germany.' The immediate reaction to the successful Cologne attack, he claimed, had been to

> deprive my Command (which would be 100 per cent stronger today, but for a continual series of diversions within the last six months) of a further large part of its striking power for the comparatively futile purposes of carrying paratroops in side-shows, to bolster further the already over-swollen establishments of the purely defensive Coastal Command, and further to swell the already over-large air contingent in the Middle East.

He went on to warn against the dangers of becoming involved in a Continental war and of thus having to face the vast and highly efficient German Army. This, he said, was exactly what Germany wanted, because 'once we get a footing on the Continent our last bomb will have been dropped on Germany. Thereafter the whole of our air effort will be required to bolster up our land struggle in France.' This, he maintained, would leave Germany free to ignore the defence measures of the homeland and would enable her to put everything into the land battle against the Allies. It was imperative for victory, Harris said, to abandon the disastrous policy of military intervention in the land campaigns of Europe until the enemy's cities and resources had been so reduced by bombing as to make Germany's further prosecution of the war an impossibility. This, he insisted, was 'the only course offering a quick victory; it is the only course which can bring any ponderable aid to Russia in time.'

He finished his memorandum by stating:

> This war will end as an air war fought on direct lines, and in no other manner, no matter what happens elsewhere, or when or how. We are now at the crossroads, opportunity knocks at our door; that knock will grow fainter and fainter as the months go by.

After reading this memorandum, Churchill asked Harris to produce a more comprehensive note on the role and work of Bomber Command, and to include a detailed summary of the Command's contribution to the anti-submarine campaign. With Saundby's help this document was completed and submitted to Churchill on 28 June 1942, having been seen and approved by Portal. On 6 July, Churchill requested his Personal Secretary to ask Harris whether he had any objection to his paper being printed and circulated to the War Cabinet on the Prime Minister's authority. Harris agreed, provided that Portal was made aware of the intention in advance of circulation. The paper was duly issued on 24 August as a War Cabinet document under the title 'Note by Air Marshal Sir Arthur Harris, KCB,* OBE, AFC, on the Role and Work of Bomber Command'.

The document was a reiteration of Harris's previous memorandum to Churchill, except that it contained a more detailed review of the strength of Bomber Command and its successes to date. It also included appendices detailing the allocation of air resources, the Command's combined bombing and mining effort, and the effort directed solely against naval targets. The last appendix was an impressive assessment of Bomber Command's contribution to the anti-submarine campaign.

In the concluding paragraphs of the document, paragraphs 17 and 18, Harris assessed the Command's use:

To sum up, Bomber Command provides our only offensive action yet pressed home directly against Germany. All our other efforts are defensive in their nature, and are not intended to do more, and can never do more, than enable us to exist in the face of the enemy. Bomber Command provides the only means of bringing assistance to Russia in time. The only means of physically weakening and nervously exhausting Germany to an extent which will make subsequent invasion a possible proposition, and is therefore the only force which can, in fact, hurt our enemy in the present, or in the future secure our victory. It is the only type of force which we shall ever be able to bring directly against Japan.

Finally, it is apparent that an extraordinary lack of sense of proportion affects outside appreciation of the meaning, extent and results of Bomber Command's operations. What shouts of victory would arise if a Commando wrecked the entire Renault factory in a night, with a loss of seven men! What credible assumptions of an early end to the war would follow upon the destruction of a third of Cologne in an hour and a half by some swift moving mechanised force which, with but 200 casualties, withdrew and was ready to repeat the operation 24 hours later! What acclaim would greet the virtual destruction of Rostock and the Heinkel main and subsidiary factories by a Naval bombardment! All this, and far more, has been achieved by Bomber Command; yet there are many who still avert their gaze, pass by on the other side, and question whether the 30 squadrons of night bombers make any worth-while contribution to the war.

* On 10 June 1942, after the 'Thousand Raid' on Cologne, Harris had been made a Knight Commander of the Bath.

Between 15 October 1941, and the middle of June 1942, twenty-four squadrons had been taken away from Bomber Command to 'finance' the operations of Middle East, Army Co-operation and Coastal Commands. Some of these squadrons were supposed to be only on load, but so far only one had been returned. Since March 1942, fifteen squadrons had been transferred to other Commands. Even after the Harris document was circulated as a Cabinet Paper, inroads into the strength of Bomber Command continued to be made by the Army and the Navy with apparent political support. An example of official opposition to Harris's views was provided by L.S. Amery, the Secretary of State for India, in a letter to Churchill dated 1 September 1942.

My dear Winston,

Many thanks for letting me see Harris' note on the role and work of Bomber Command. It is a fine spirited vindication of his own show, but I confess I found it entirely unconvincing as regards the main issue raised in my letter to you, namely that of the immense strategical importance of the air, not only in tactical cooperation with army and navy, but more particularly as a vital means of transport for all the services.

In Harris' view, I gather, any attempt to use the air for other purposes than bombing would mean that 'our only offensive weapon against Germany would be destroyed'. Nobody denies the immense value of the bombing of Germany as a contribution to the final result, but it is at any rate an open question whether attacking Germany (in the geographical sense) is necessarily the only, or indeed the best, offensive against Germany's armed strength ... It surely may very well be the case that the elimination of the Germans and Italians from North Africa and the effective bombing of Italy might produce even greater results in the long run than bombing Germany at this stage.

Again, Harris uses the word 'offensive' for something that is not in essence a major strategic offensive, but only part of a process – no doubt a very desirable and necessary process – of attrition. It is not an offensive in the sense of the strategic offensive that clinches great issues at decisive moments. That can only be done, under modern conditions, by the cooperation of the air with the other services and by the full utilisation of air-given mobility by the army. If Alexander now checks and drives back Rommel he could convert that to annihilation if only he were able to drop a division by air on the other side of him. Even without that I don't know how he could keep up a really sufficient rapid pursuit westwards unless his troops could be supplied by air. Again, I do not see how success in North Africa can be turned to really good account unless we are able, not only to use the Air Force with the Navy in clearing the passage of the Mediterranean and crippling Italy by bombing, but also to do what Rommel has done, namely bring over reliefs and lighter supplies by air.

Harris' note is an admirable paean of praise for Bomber Command, which no one would dream of contradicting; but it does not in fact touch the issue of how air can be used most decisively to win this war.

Yours ever,
Leo Amery

Churchill's reply to Amery was: 'I merely thought it would interest you. It does not express my views.' By this date, an invasion of North Africa by the Americans was in an advanced stage of planning, timed to coincide with a major offensive by Montgomery's Eighth Army, across the Western Desert from El Alamein to link up with the Americans in Tunisia after their drive from the Algerian landing places. The plan was fully supported by Churchill, who could not therefore give too much away to Harris at this time, although he was certainly in favour of an all-out bombing offensive against Germany at an appropriate moment. But it was Harris's next impassioned plea, dated 3 September, for overriding priority to be given to a vast bombing offensive against Germany, almost at the expense of any other military campaign then envisaged, that earned a rebuff from Churchill. Coincidentally, Harris's letter arrived two days after Amery's.

In his letter, Harris argued that the worst policy the Allies could adopt was to disperse their forces in such a manner 'as never to have sufficient for a victory in any theatre'. The key to German successes, he asserted, had been their policy of concentrating the maximum force upon a single objective at a time: 'They do not undertake any fresh commitment until they have succeeded in the previous one, and throughout they have maintained the minimum of defensive forces in those areas where they were not actually undertaking offensive operations.' (This was not quite true, for Germany had, in 1940 and 1941, abandoned its attempt to defeat Britain and taken up the cudgels against her then ally Russia instead.) After claiming that the Allies had 'lost face throughout the world by defeats all over the world', he declared that 'our sole means of winning the war will be by attack on Germany.' If Germany could be so devastated and dispirited by bombing then, he insisted, an invasion of Europe 'would be a mopping-up operation'. With great numbers of German troops tied down on the Russian Front, and with the marked air superiority that the Allies now had in Western Europe in numbers, quality, and scientific devices, the time was at last ripe for a major and sustained combined bombing offensive by the British and American bomber forces against the German homeland. He warned, however, that

283

as soon as the Germans could make withdrawals from the Russian Front as a result of a defeat of the Soviet armies, the Allies' chances of delivering decisive blows against Germany by air would progressively diminish: 'The present is, therefore, the best and, perhaps, the only opportunity that we are likely to have to strike decisive air blows against Germany.' After emphasising that he needed a strength which would permit continuous raids at night by 800 to 1,000 aircraft, with an American daylight back-up of similar numbers, Harris pleaded that the whole strategy of the use of air power should be reviewed as a matter of urgency. 'The war cannot and will not end,' he averred, until a decision in the direct air war between the Allies and Germany had been sought. 'It may end the war in our favour in a year; by no other method can we hope to end it – either way – in years.'

Churchill's reply, dated 13 September, was cool, to say the least:

> You must be careful not to spoil a good cause by overstating it. I am doing all I can to expand Bomber Command, and I set a high value on your action against Germany. I do not however think Air bombing is going to bring the war to an end by itself, and still less that anything that could be done with our existing resources could produce decisive results in the next twelve months.

On the same Sunday evening that Harris received this rebuff, he was summoned to Chequers to discuss the problems facing Bomber Command. Churchill was more amenable at this meeting, and Harris took the opportunity to impress upon the Prime Minister the fact that the RDF scientific blind-bombing systems, H_2S and Oboe, were nearly ready for operational use. It was therefore essential, he insisted, to commence the build-up of the Command without delay if full advantage was to be taken of these revolutionary devices, which, initially, would be operated by the newly formed Pathfinder Force. Churchill was well aware of the progress of the new RDF aids, having been kept informed of developments by his scientific adviser, Cherwell, a keen advocate of strategic bombing. During this private meeting, it was the prospect of a devastated Ruhr and of the destruction of Germany's major industrial seaboard towns, at which Harris confidently hinted, that encouraged Churchill to take a more active interest in priorities for the bombers, even though he was, at the time, much preoccupied with plans for Montgomery's imminent assault on the Germans in North Africa from his El Alamein positions, and with 'Operation Torch', the American invasion of North Africa by landings at Casablanca, Oran and Algiers. The priority for Bomber Command's immediate activities, however, was to remain one of support for the forthcoming North African campaign.

By the middle of October 1942, the air assault against Germany, with the exception of sea mining, was almost entirely subordinated to attacks in support of 'Operation Torch', planned for 8 November to coincide with Montgomery's drive across Libya towards Tunisia. The priority targets for the bombers were primarily in northern Italy, and Bomber Command's operations started with two raids against Genoa on the nights of 22/23 and 23/24 October, followed by a daylight attack on Milan on the 24th and a night attack on the 24th/25th. In all, there were six raids on Genoa and two on Milan in October and November, on a scale of between 70 and 90 aircraft for each attack, except for three raids on Genoa when the forces were 112, 122 and 175 aircraft. Turin received seven attacks in November and December and, of these, four were with forces of 232, 228 and 227 aircraft. This meant that Turin suffered relatively major raids and the results bore this out; the Fiat and Lancia factories were very seriously damaged, as were other smaller industrial units as well as built-up areas. Genoa, too, suffered badly in both the port and town area, but Milan was relatively undamaged, having received only two raids by 88 and 77 aircraft.

In all, 1,809 sorties were flown against Milan, Turin and Genoa between 22 October and 12 December 1942, for the loss of thirty-six aircraft, or just under 2 per cent. These were the only Italian cities open to attack from bases in England which were of any real industrial or economic value to the Axis Powers; added to this, Genoa was the greatest seaport in Italy. It was for these reasons, and for the further important reason that the bombing of northern Italy would compel the Italians to hold back their fighter aircraft and anti-aircraft guns from Tunisia at the time of the Allied invasion of North Africa, that priority was given to the bombing of these targets. Moreover, it was expected that the raids would increase the demoralisation of the Italian people, who had little stomach for a war into which they had been led by Mussolini and Hitler; indeed, after the attacks on Genoa the Italian leader even admitted that the people had 'given proof of moral weakness'. The use of Bomber Command for these raids, however, was anathema to Harris, who remained convinced that the war could only be won by destroying Germany, the real heart of the Axis, and that anything which forced the bomber forces away from that objective would only extend the war and, perhaps, lead to a stalemate and a totally unsatisfactory negotiated peace.

'Operation Torch' and the rapid advance into Tunisia that followed the American landings, combined with Montgomery's drive across the desert from El Alamein, ensured – in a perverse sort of way – the start of the combined Anglo-American bomber offensive against Germany in 1943, and its maintenance with growing strength throughout that year and up to June 1944. The hope of an invasion of Western Europe in 1943, as had been envisaged earlier under the code-name 'Operation

Round-up', was now out of the question, for the forces committed in North Africa and the Western Desert decided the grand strategy of the future. It is easy to wonder to what extent the North African escapade was a sop to Stalin's demands for a Second Front in 1942 or 1943. Stalin, of course, wanted that front to be opened in Western Europe, but for the Western Allies this could only have been attempted at grave risk, whereas the North African landing was a much safer and easier task. Its value in enabling an ultimate attack against the Axis 'underbelly' was, however, considerable, and this in turn kept German and Italian forces tied down right up to and after the Allied invasion of continental Europe on 6 June 1944. As it turned out, it took until June 1944 to build up an Anglo-American military force in England of a size commensurate with the task of landing in one of the enemy's most heavily defended areas and fighting against some of his best divisions. That time was also needed to devastate Germany from the air, to bring her to a state where her industrial capability was in jeopardy, and where air supremacy had passed firmly into the hands of the Allies. The North African invasion, therefore, set the time-scale for the final assault on Germany by ground forces and this, in turn, provided the demand for the absolutely essential prelude to any invasion of Western Europe if vast losses were to be avoided – a massive bomber offensive against Germany itself by the combined forces of RAF Bomber Command and US Eighth Bomber Command.

As much as Harris would have liked an all-out combined bomber offensive to have started in 1942, he knew it was impossible. He himself had neither a force large enough at his disposal, nor the necessary scientific navigating and bombing aids. Nor, indeed, was the US Eighth Bomber Command ready to undertake operations against Germany; in fact, it was not until 27 January 1943 that the Americans struck their first blow against Germany, attacking Wilhelmshaven by day. Nevertheless, by November 1942 Harris did at least know that the beginning of a serious combined bomber offensive against Germany was in sight.

Everything was, in fact, conspiring well to assist Bomber Command towards an effective resumption of the offensive against Germany by the beginning of 1943. No. 109 (Mosquito) Squadron had been formed and had joined the Pathfinder Force as one of two Mosquito squadrons fitted with Oboe, the new highly secret precision marking device, which had been developed by Mr A.H. Reeves* and Dr F.E. Jones† of TRE. Commanding No. 109 Squadron was Wing Commander Bufton who, as

* Reeves was formerly a research engineer of Standard Telephone & Cables, to which company he returned after the war.

† Dr F.E. Jones, MBE, PhD, FRS, FRAeS. Later Deputy Director of the Royal Aircraft Establishment.

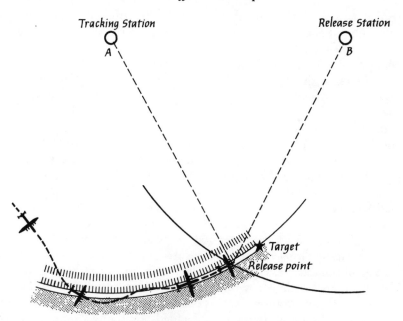

Oboe bombing approach to target

a flight commander of the Blind Approach Technical & Development Unit at Boscombe Down in 1940 and 1941, had devised a means of bombing the German blind-bombing systems known as *Knickebein* and *X-Gerät*. Among the crews of No. 109 Squadron were other former members of the BAT & DU, and thus the squadron possessed a nucleus of highly experienced 'beam' pilots.

The function of one of the two Oboe ground stations was to track the aircaft along a bombing approach path to its target. Employing RDF methods, this station constantly measured its distance from the Mosquito, and transmitted dots or dashes if the aircraft was to the left or right of its correct approach path and a continuous note if it was exactly on its bombing approach path, the distance of the target from the ground station being known. The second ground station measured the precise distance along the first station's 'synthetic' beam at which the aircraft should release its bombs in order to hit the target, and instructed the pilot accordingly. The ex-BAT&DU crews in the Mosquito squadrons, already highly experienced in beam flying, were therefore well trained for using this system.

On 26 November 1942, the Air Ministry granted permission for two pairs of Oboe ground stations to transmit continuously in readiness for the start of operations. Continuous transmission was decided upon in order to avoid the enemy associating the signals with any specific bombing attack, which might well happen if the stations only went on the air during Oboe attacks. The first Oboe flight over enemy territory did not, however, take place until the night of 20/21 December, when a test attack with six Oboe Mosquitoes from No. 109 Squadron, led by Bufton, was made against a coking plant at Lutterade in East Holland. This was supposed to be a virgin target, but photographs taken after the raid showed the area to be smothered with bomb craters greatly in excess of the number of bombs dropped by the three successful Oboe aircraft. From a calibration point of view, therefore, the raid was a failure. Other attacks took place in December and in January 1943, but it was not until 03.30 hours on the morning 16 February 1943, that the first really satisfactory calibration test was made. This attack directed against the Cadet School near St Trond in Belgium, was made by four aircraft, again led by Bufton. With the exception of several loose bombs which fell one mile from the target because of their striking each other when released in salvo, all bombs fell very close to the target, and several scored direct hits on the house, killing a sentry and a number officers and cadets. The success of the calibration test was confirmed through Intelligence sources, an agent in Belgium supplying a detailed bomb plot of the results of the raid. This plot proved that two RDF ground stations in England could guide a Mosquito aircraft, flying at 30,000 feet at a range of more than 250 miles, so that it dropped its bombs within 120 yards of the selected aiming-point. Here indeed was the target-finding and -marking system needed to ensure the accurate bombing and destruction of the vitally important Ruhr towns.

On 8 December 1942, Bomber Command received news of the next important RDF device, a device which would give the bomber accurate navigational guidance at all ranges without it being necessary for the crew to see the ground, and which would make possible reasonably accurate blind-bombing of built-up areas – the Command was advised that H_2S could be used operationally at any time after 1 January 1943. While the number of aircraft equipped with H_2S at this stage was limited, and of necessity these aircraft had to be confined to the Pathfinder Force, Bomber Command's prospects for 1943 were beginning to look good. Certainly Harris and Saundby could look back on 1942 with some satisfaction. The bombing force's capabilities had grown immeasurably, and the offensive had been immensely successful when compared with that in 1941. The Command had struck a serious blow at the German homeland, and one which, indirectly, had helped to slow the progress of the Nazi campaign against Russia. Defence requirements for German cities grew as more of her industry was threatened by the increasing bombardment, and the direct disruption of some of her military production had added to the problem. All this had been to Russia's advantage.

By the beginning of 1943, Germany's entire military situation had changed for the worse. Serious reverses had taken place in North Africa and the Western Desert, and German forces had suffered a major defeat at Stalingrad in November 1942. The advance into Russia had been halted in the closing months of 1942, and the Soviet forces had successfully launched a counter-offensive in the central Caucasus which, in late December, had won back considerable territory between the Don and the Donetz. At the beginning of 1943 the Soviet offensive was extended over an even greater stretch of the Russian southern front, resulting in further gains culminating, in February, with the recapture of Kursk, Krasnodar, Rostov, Voroschilovgrad and Kharkov. The rot in the Russian defence had at last been successfully stopped, although this might easily prove to be temporary if the German Army's supply position could be quickly restored and improved. Undoubtedly the bombing of Germany had been the main cause for the sudden interruption of the Nazi onslaught, but it was only too obvious that such a halt would not last unless the industrial productive capacity of Germany could be disrupted more completely than hitherto.

Churchill and Portal both recognised that the time had come for the beginning of the defeat of Germany by bombing.

Harris and Saundby also knew this fact and, as 1943 began, there arrived in the Command both the right scientific RDF aids, and the right team of group commanders. Air Vice-Marshal the Hon. R.A. Cochrane,* who, with Saundby, had served under Harris in Mesopotamia from 1922 to 1924, took over as AOC No. 5 Group in February 1943, and Air Commodore R. Harrison,† formerly Deputy SASO at Bomber Command, was promoted to Air Vice-Marshal and appointed AOC No. 3 Group. Bennett, commanding the Pathfinder Force, was promoted to Air Vice-Marshal, and the Force was re-formed as No. 8 Group. Air Vice-Marshal E.A.B. Rice, who had been one of Harris's station commanders in No. 5 Group in 1940, had already taken command of No. 1 Group, Air Vice-Marshal C.R. Carr was commanding No. 4 Group, and Air Vice-Marshal G.E. Brookes was commanding No. 6 (Royal Canadian Air Force) Group.

What was still required, however, was a rapid increase in the supply of the four-engined Lancaster and Halifax bombers.

---

* Later Air Chief Marshal the Hon. Sir Ralph Cochrane, GBE, KCB, AFC, C-in-C Transport Command. He died in 1978.

† Air Vice-Marshal R. Harrison, CB, CBE, DFC, AFC, was the first AOC of a bomber group, after Bennett, with operational experience in the war.

CHAPTER XXIII

The Ruhr Campaign

At the end of 1942 the CAS, Portal, produced a significant document which helped to shift the emphasis of the war effort towards strategic bombing. 'Note by the Chief of the Air Staff – an Estimate of the Effects of an Anglo-American Bomber Offensive Against Germany' and, dated 3 November 1942, it was distributed as a War Cabinet paper. It began with the statement:

> At the 137th. Meeting of the Committee (Chiefs of Staff) held on the 5th. October, I was invited to circulate a Note setting out the facts and arguments which support the Air Staff view that a heavy bomber force rising to a peak of between 4,000 and 6,000 bombers in 1944 could shatter the industrial and economic structure of Germany to a point where an Anglo-American force of reasonable strength could enter the Continent from the West.

As a yardstick for developing this appreciation, Portal took the only comprehensive record of the results of a bombing offensive that had been made thus far in the war, the analysis of the German air raids on Britain from the end of June 1940 to 30 June 1941. 'Estimates derived from the results of these attacks,' he wrote, 'are accordingly employed to forecast the effect of the very much heavier scale of bombing contemplated under the plan in question.' During the twelve months to 30 June 1941, the Luftwaffe had dropped 55,000 tons of bombs on Britain. Out of that total, 36,000 tons had been directed at industrial areas, although probably at least one quarter of that tonnage had fallen in built-up areas. These attacks had caused 41,000 deaths, and had seriously injured another 45,000 people. Nearly 350,000 houses had been rendered uninhabitable for the duration of the war, and 1,000,000 people had been displaced from their homes. In addition, there had been 2,500,000 incidents of housing damage, many of which caused the temporary displacement of the occupants, and all of which required repairs. The damage to factories, power plants, shipping, harbour facilities, and public utilities had had a direct effect upon the war effort, although the extent of that effect, Portal said, could not be assessed with any exactitude. 'Judging by contemporary standards,' he wrote, 'the German attacks were an inferior example of bombing technique. The attacks were not well planned; the Luftwaffe was only partly prepared for night operations; the effort was widespread over the country and the methods of reaching and marking targets were, on the whole, unreliable.' He added that the German raids of 1940 and 1941 had been small by comparison with the recent Bomber Command raids, and that the damage per ton of bombs dropped had been only a fraction of that inflicted by Bomber Command's large-scale concentrated attacks made with the latest target-finding methods and the techniques of mixing incendiaries with high explosives. In essence, the first main reason for the ineffectiveness of the German attacks was because they had been made on a scale far below that necessary to produce a decisive result: 'The total tonnage of bombs dropped by the Luftwaffe throughout the year amounted to less than two-thirds of the peak monthly scale of attack contemplated in this paper.' The second main reason was Germany's decision in 1941 to mount an offensive against the Soviet Union; by the middle of that year 'it was necessary for the Luftwaffe to move East for the invasion of Russia.'

Portal went on to detail the scale of attack contemplated for the Anglo-American bomber offensive, and finally summarised his conclusions:

(i) The paper assumes that an Anglo-American Heavy Bomber Force would be based in the United Kingdom and built up to a first-line strength of 4,000 to 6,000 by 1944.
(ii) Such a force could deliver a monthly scale of attack amounting to 50,000 tons of bombs by the end of 1943, and to a peak of 90,000 tons by December 1944.
(iii) Under this plan $1\frac{1}{4}$ million tons of bombs would be dropped on Germany between January 1943 and December 1944.
(iv) Assuming that the results attained per ton of bombs equal those realised during the German attacks of 1940-41, the results would include:
  (a) the destruction of 6 million German dwellings, with a proportionate destruction of industrial buildings, sources of power,

means of transportation and public utilities;

(b) 25 million Germans rendered homeless;

(c) an additional 60 million 'incidents' of bomb damage to houses;

(d) civilian casualties estimated at about 900,000 killed and 1,000,000 seriously injured.

(v) If the attacks were spread over the main urban areas the result would be to render homeless three-quarters of the inhabitants of all German towns with a population of over 50,000.

(vi) Expressed in other terms, this scale of attack would enable every industrial town in Germany with a population exceeding 50,000 to receive, in proportion to its size, ten attacks of 'Cologne' intensity.

(vii) If the attacks were concentrated on the 58 towns specified in Appendix 1,* each would receive, in proportion to its size, some 17 attacks of 'Cologne' intensity.

(viii) A concentrated attack of this character would destroy at least one-third of the total German industry.

(ix) A substantial proportion of the total industry of Germany is necessary to maintain a minimum standard of subsistence among the German People. As the German economic structure is now stretched to the limit this proportion cannot be further reduced. Consequently, the loss of one-third of German industry would involve either the sacrifice of almost the entire war potential of Germany in an effort to maintain the internal economy of the country, or else the collapse of the latter.

(x) It is hoped that our bombing efficiency will prove to be substantially better than that achieved in the German attacks of 1940-41. In that case the process of attrition will be much accelerated.

(xi) It is considered that the German defences will be incapable of stopping these attacks.

(xii) It is certain that the diversion of more and more of a waning aircraft production to the defence of Germany will heavily handicap all German operations by land, sea and air in other theatres.

(xiii) It is concluded that an Anglo-American bomber force of the size proposed could reduce the German economic and military strength to a point well below that at which an Anglo-American invasion of the Continent would become possible. This result might well be achieved before the combined force had built up to peak strength.

Portal's Note was a document of paramount importance, and was, in fact, the forerunner of the directive which emerged from the Roosevelt-Churchill-Combined Chiefs of Staff conference at Casablanca in mid-January, and received the immediate approval of Churchill and Roosevelt. It described the task of the bomber forces as follows:

* These towns were named and populations and industrial activities detailed.

Your primary object will be the progressive destruction and dislocation of the German military, industrial and economic system and the undermining of the morale of the German people to a point where their capacity for armed resistance is fatally weakened.

Within that general concept, your primary objectives, subject to the exigencies of weather and tactical feasibility, will for the present be in the following order:

(a) German submarine construction yards.
(b) The German aircraft industry.
(c) Transportation.
(d) Oil plants.
(e) Other targets in enemy war industry.

The above order of priority may be varied from time to time according to developments in the strategical situation. Moreover, other objectives of great importance either from the political or military point of view must be attacked. Examples of these are:

(I) Submarine operating bases on the Biscay coast. If these can be put out of action, a great step forward will have been taken in the U-boat war which the CCS have agreed to be the first charge on our resources. Day and night attacks on these bases have been inaugurated and should be continued so that an assessment of their effects can be made as soon as possible. If it is found that successful results can be achieved, these attacks should continue whenever conditions are favourable for as long and as often as is necessary. These objectives have not been included in the order of priority, which covers long-term operations, particularly as the bases are not situated in Germany.

(II) Berlin, which should be attacked when conditions are suitable for the attainment of specially valuable results unfavourable to the morale of the enemy or favourable to that of Russia.

You may also be required, at the appropriate time, to attack objectives in Northern Italy in connection with amphibious operations in the Mediterranean theatre.

There may be certain objectives of great fleeting importance for the attack of which all necessary plans and preparations should be made. Of these, an example would be the important units of the German Fleet in harbour or at sea.

You should take every opportunity to attack Germany by day, to destroy objectives that are unsuitable for night attack, to sustain continuous pressure on German morale, to impose heavy losses on the German day fighter force and to contain German fighter strength away from the Russian and Mediterranean theatres of war.

Whenever Allied Armies re-enter the Continent, you will afford all possible support in the manner most effective.

In attacking objectives in occupied territories, you will conform to such instructions as may be issued from time to time for political reasons by His Majesty's Government through the British Chiefs of Staff.

The directive, one of the most important of the war, was addressed to Air Marshal Sir Arthur Harris, as C-in-C Bomber Command, and to General Ira C. Eaker, as C-in-C US Eighth Bomber Command, and was received by them on 4 February 1943. In truth, it was more a statement of policy than a detailed direction to Harris about the way in which he should use his forces, and against which specific targets. But the primary object was clearly stated as being 'the progressive destruction and dislocation of the German military, industrial and economic system and the undermining of the morale of the German people to a point where their capacity for armed resistance is fatally weakened.' It was the signal for a full-scale strategic air offensive, and thus it gave support for the build-up of Bomber Command to a size commensurate with the task it had been set.

Meeting the requirements of what became known as the Casablanca Directive demanded a rapid increase in the strength of Bomber Command, both in terms of the right aircraft and of the latest RDF aids. By the end of 1942 the Short and Harland Stirling four-engined bomber, which had proved to be something of a failure, was being phased out in favour of increased production of the Avro Lancaster. In addition, there was a retrenchment of production of the Handley-Page Halifax, again in favour of increased Lancaster production. The fact was that the Lancaster had materially exceeded its performance specifications and seemed capable of accepting unending increases in its original payload. It had proved itself able to operate at heights between 22,000 and 27,000 feet, carrying a bomb-load of 8,000 pounds to Berlin and many other distant targets in Germany at a cruising speed of 240 miles per hour. By contrast, the Stirling's operational height was no more than 14,000 feet with a bomb-load of less than half that of the Lancaster, and a cruising speed of marginally over 200 miles per hour, making it very vulnerable to the enemy's anti-aircraft fire. The Halifax was slightly better in that its operational height was 18,000 feet, but, like the Stirling, its bomb-load, range for range, was half that of the Lancaster, and its cruising speed was little better than 200 miles per hour. Comparison of bomb-load, range for range, was not all of the story, however, for the Lancaster was capable of carrying 12,000 pounds well beyond the Ruhr, and, later, was able to carry the 22,000-pound 'Grand Slam' bomb, which no other aircraft in the world could carry. Now, therefore, the pressure was on greatly increased production of Lancasters to meet the necessary build-up of the bomber force, the Command's aim being, in fact, for its force to consist entirely of Lancasters except for the few Oboe Mosquitoes in the Pathfinder Force required for target-marking activities.

On the RDF front, H_2S had been used on an operational trial against Hamburg on the night of 30/31 January 1943, a small force of 148 aircraft being led to the target by Pathfinders equipped with H_2S. The ease with which the H_2S aircraft located and marked the target indicated the future promise of this device, and the H_2S crews were highly enthusiastic, reporting that they had had no difficulty in 'seeing' and identifying Heligoland, Zwolle, Bremen, the Zuider Zee, Den Helder, the East and North Frisians, Cuxhaven and Hamburg itself. One navigator was positively euphoric about the approach for dropping his marker bombs: 'I got it bang on,' he said. 'I was able to see the docks on the cathode screen like fingers of bright light sticking out into the darkness of the Elbe.' Others made the same claims, reporting that coastlines, estuaries and rivers appeared 'like a well-defined picture of a map.' After three more raids led by H_2S-equipped aircraft (on 2/3 February against Cologne, on the 3rd/4th again against Hamburg, and on the 4th/5th against Turin in Northern Italy), it quickly became evident that H_2S was more than just a target-finding and blind-bombing device. It was also an excellent instrument for night navigation at any range from base, and therefore an essential aid to all aircraft in finding the way to targets deep in Germany. The initial idea that H_2S should be limited to the PFF alone was therefore dropped, and on 21 February 1943 Saundby despatched a letter to the Air Ministry, requesting that H_2S should be introduced into all Lancaster and Halifax aircraft at the earliest possible date. In the case of the Lancaster Mk II programme, however, there was to be an exception. This version was being equipped with modified bomb-bay doors to accommodate the 8,000-pound and other, larger bombs. These modifications would not permit the installation on the underside of the fuselage of the rotating aerial scanner which was part of the H_2S system. Instead of H_2S, therefore, the Lancaster IIs, which were designated to replace No. 3 Group's Stirlings, were to be fitted with G-H, another precision blind-bombing device which, as has been mentioned earlier, was similar to Oboe but which could operate with eighty aircraft simultaneously from one pair of ground stations, and could therefore be used for direct bombing of special targets through ten-tenths cloud, or at night, without it being necessary for crews to see the target. G-H was not likely to be available until late in 1943, however, the same being the case with the Lancaster IIs.

At the beginning of 1943, with increasing numbers of Lancaster and Halifax aircraft coming into service, with H_2S and Oboe already available, even if in limited quantities, and with G-H due at the end of 1943, Bomber Command was at last beginning to take on the appearance of a viable strategic offensive force. Indeed, by the beginning of March Bomber Command had at its disposal an effective operational strength of thirty-seven heavy four-engined bomber squadrons and fourteen and a half medium twin-engined bomber squadrons, giving it a first-line strength of some 660 heavies and 300 mediums. Now, with the short nights approaching and with two Oboe Mosquito PFF squadrons ready for operations, the Ruhr campaign was about to commence.

The Ruhr was Europe's principal producing area for coal, coke, iron and steel, and the home of vast metallurgical and chemical industries; above all, it was the centre for the Krupps concern, Germany's vitally important armaments complex. The area was, in fact, a huge concentration of industry which was not only self-sufficient, but upon which much of Germany's other industrial areas – in particular industries associated with war production – depended for raw materials.

It was Essen that Harris chose for the opening of the Ruhr offensive. This devastating campaign began at 21.00 hours on the night of 5/6 March 1943, with the centre of Krupps as the aiming point. The assault had been planned with that attention to detail which characterised the Command's Headquarters Staff, led by Saundby, responsible for planning. Saundby, now Deputy C-in-C, was a brilliant tactician, and was largely responsible for the bombing successes of the Command; indeed, it was the combination of Harris as strategist and Saundby as tactician that was ultimately to bring disaster to Germany. For this attack, a force of 442 aircraft was despatched, of which 303 were heavies. The raid was led by eight Oboe Mosquito aircraft, whose duty was to drop yellow target-indicator flares along the line of the bombing approach, but finishing fifteen miles short of the target. They were then to mark the aiming point with salvos of red indicator flares in accordance with a closely calculated schedule, the first salvo falling at zero hour, the next three minutes later, the next ten minutes later, and so on until the last salvo, which was to fall at zero-plus-thirty-three minutes. Following close on the heels of the Mosquitoes was a force of twenty-two Pathfinder heavies. Their job was to maintain the yellow path of flares on the bombing approach path and to drop green target-indicators and HE on the red indicators, followed by a delay of one second before releasing their loads of incendiaries, the technique of mixing HE and incendiaries being employed to get fires started in the target area. The main force, carrying bomb-loads of one-third HE and two-thirds incendiaries, were then to bomb the red indicators, or, if these could not be seen, the green indicators.

The raid on Essen was a very considerable success, with 1,054 tons of bombs being accurately dropped in thirty-eight minutes. For the first time in the war Krupps itself was severely damaged, as were the Goldschmidt Company, the Maschinenbau Union, the power station, gasworks and the municipal tram depot. An area somewhat larger than 160 acres was laid waste, by far the greater part by fire, and 30,000 people, mostly Krupps workers, were rendered homeless. The attack was followed up by further raids on Essen on the nights of 12/13 March, 3/4 April, and 30 April/1 May. The attacks continued beyond this last date, but in the two months of March and April 1,552 aircraft bombed Essen in four raids, dropping 3,967 tons of bombs on this vitally important target. The damage was significant, and Krupps suffered so badly that production at their Essen armament complex was gravely interrupted. Following the first raid on the night of 5/6 March, Goebbels wrote in his diary:

> During the night Essen suffered an exceptionally severe raid. The city of the Krupps has been hard hit. The number of dead, too, is considerable. If the English continue their raids on this scale, they will make things exceedingly difficult for us. The dangerous thing about this matter, looking at it psychologically, is that the population can see no way of doing anything about it. Our anti-aircraft guns are inadequate. The successes of our night fighters, though notable, are not sufficient to compel the English to desist from their night attacks. As we lack a weapon for attack, we cannot do anything noteworthy in the way of reprisal.

After the raid on the night of 12/13 March, he recorded:

> Later in the evening the news reached us of another exceedingly heavy air raid on Essen. This time the Krupp plant has been hard hit ... Twenty-five fires were raging in the grounds of the Krupp plant alone. Air warfare is at present our greatest worry. Things simply cannot go on like this. The Führer told Göring what he thought without mincing his words. It is to be expected that Göring will now do something decisive.

On 10 April, Goebbels visited Essen to inspect the damage. He was greatly shocked by what he saw, and wrote in his diary:

> We arrived in Essen before 7 am. Deputy Gauleiter Schlessmann and a large staff called for us at the railway station. We went to the hotel on foot because driving is quite impossible in many parts of Essen. This walk enabled us to make a first-hand estimate of the damage inflicted by the last three raids. It is colossal and indeed ghastly. This city must, for the most part, be written off completely. The city's building experts estimate that it will take twelve years to repair the damage ...

Nobody can tell how Krupps can go on. Everyone wants to avoid transplanting Krupps from Essen. There would be no purpose in doing so, for the moment Essen is no longer an industrial centre the English will pounce upon the next city, Bochum, Dortmund or Düsseldorf.

Goebbels was right. Bochum and Düsseldorf, in company with Duisberg and Cologne, had already been heavily attacked since 1 January, and Dortmund and other Ruhr towns were to receive punishing treatment in the months to come. Between January 1943 and the end of April, Essen, Duisberg, Bochum, Düsseldorf and Cologne received the attention of 4,219 sorties dropping 10,230 tons of bombs, with Essen, Duisberg and Cologne bearing the real brunt of these attacks. The losses to Bomber Command were 163 aircraft, or 3.86 per cent, which was well within the sustainable loss rate. During the same period, which still provided long nights for longer-range targets, 2,569 sorties were flown on raids against Hamburg, Wilhemshaven, Kiel, Stettin and Bremen, with a total bombdrop of 6,310 tons for the loss of 84 aircraft, or 3.27 per cent, Hamburg and Wilhelmshaven being the most heavily attacked of these targets. Berlin received 2,888 tons from 1,515 sorties spread over five raids; losses were 70 aircraft, or 4.62 per cent. Nürnberg, Munich, Stuttgart, Frankfurt, Mannheim and Pilsen also received attention to the extent of 5,797 tons of bombs from 2,812 sorties, Nürnberg, Stuttgart and Frankfurt receiving the greatest weight of attack; losses were 133 aircraft, or 4.7 per cent, but would have been considerably less had it not been for the loss of 37 aircraft out of 327 attacking the Skida works at Pilsen on the night of 16/17 April – a loss of 11.3 per cent. In addition to all these attacks, the northern Italian towns of Milan, Turin and Spezia were quite heavily raided.

During the four months from January to the end of April 1943, Bomber Command despatched 11,910 sorties dropping 26,269 tons of bombs, for total losses of 492 aircraft, or 4.13 per cent. This was a vast increase on the 5,435 sorties flown against Germany and Czechoslovakia, dropping 6,646 tons of bombs, during the same period in 1942. The losses in that period amounted to 218 aircraft – 4.01 per cent. A straight comparison of effort is not, however, the only measure of the Command's ascendancy – the effectiveness in 1943 was far greater because of the introduction of Oboe and H_2S to the Pathfinder Force, and because of greatly improved target-marking techniques.

Apart from the bombing in the first four months of 1943, Bomber Command sowed 5,442 sea mines in 2,338 sorties for this purpose. The losses were 92 aircraft, or 3.9 per cent, but the rewards were considerable; a known toll of some 50,000 tons of shipping was taken, including two U-boats sunk and two severely damaged.

As May dawned, with the approach of the short nights, the frequency of the attacks against the Ruhr increased. The battle of the Ruhr, which had begun in March with the highly successful attacks against Essen, was now enjoined with great ferocity, with town after town being reduced to ruins under the scourge of the bomber force. Dortmund and Duisberg were half obliterated, Düsseldorf suffered nearly three-quarters destruction, Hagen, Mulheim and Wuppertal-Barmen were more than 50-per cent devastated, and Bochum and Remscheid had 83 per cent of their built-up areas destroyed before the end of the summer. One of the most shattering operations, however, was against the small and important industrial town of Wuppertal-Elberfeld. Its position in the Ruhr was such that location by night was almost impossible by visual means, even in full-moon conditions, while the town's long and narrow shape demanded a high degree of bombing accuracy to attain effective concentration. Its size, estimated by population, was slightly greater than that of Coventry, where the Luftwaffe's devastatingly successful attack on the night of 14/15 November 1940 had completely destroyed 100 acres in a raid lasting two hours. Wuppertal-Elberfeld was a town of 929 acres when on the night of 24/25 June 1943, the first Oboe Mosquitoes, leading 631 bombers of which 517 were heavies, dropped their target-indicators. Twenty minutes later 870 acres of the town lay in ruins.

One other major attack on the Ruhr undertaken in this May/June period was of special importance, not only because of its success, but also because it marked the beginning of No. 5 Group's break-away from dependence upon the Pathfinders, and its development as an independent Group with its own target-finding and -marking force and techniques.

The idea of destroying the Ruhr dams had been considered by the Air Staff before the war, for it was realised that the breaching of these dams could cause widespread industrial damage to many parts of the Ruhr. The proposal had been shelved, however, because no known bomb or torpedo could hope to collapse a concrete-encased wall of the thickness used in the construction of the Möhne and Eder dams, or an earth dam such as the Sorpe dam. In 1942, Vickers-Armstrong's leading aircraft designer, Barnes Wallis, who had designed the Wellington bomber with its ingenious geodetic construction, turned his mind to the development of bombs for specialised purposes. His first interest was the destruction of the Ruhr dams, and to this end he developed the idea of a bomb shaped like a cylinder, which could be bounced along the surface of the water from a low-level release height of about sixty feet. More ingeniously, the bomb was to be rotated before release to about 500 rpm in the reverse direction to its line of trajectory so that, when it struck the dam wall, it would 'wind' itself downwards, the gyroscopic effect of the anti-rotation keeping it close to the dam, and detonate at an appropriate depth. The effect of such a bomb, being that of an underwater earthquake, was carefully calculated by Wallis to breach a dam such as the Möhne or Eder. By February 1943 he had carried out laboratory tests and half-scale trials with a Wellington releasing a bomb into the sea at Chesil Bank in Dorset. The trials showed much promise – enough to interest Portal, who asked Harris to send someone down to Vickers to talk with Barnes Wallis about his 'bouncing' bomb. Group Captain S.C. Elworthy, the Group Captain Operations at Bomber Command, was duly despatched by Saundby to investigate the claims of Wallis for his bomb's ability to breach the Ruhr dams.

Elworthy was so impressed by the films of both the laboratory tests and the half-scale trials, and by Wallis's explanations of his ideas, that he persuaded Harris and Saundby to see the scientist as a matter of urgency. When Wallis visited Bomber Command at the end of February he convinced both Harris and Saundby so completely of the credibility of his weapon that they immediately gave their unqualified support for the project. Events now moved swiftly. The task of bombing the dams was given to Cochrane, the AOC of No. 5 Group, and authorisation was given for the formation of a special squadron for the operation, using Lancasters adapted to take the bomb and its rotation gear. The squadron was numbered No. 617, and was to become a legend of the Second World War. Within five days of its formation, on 20 March, under Wing Commander Guy Gibson, No. 617 had begun specialised training and trials for its unique task. The target date for readiness to undertake what was to be known as 'Operation Chastise' was set for 10 May.

By the 15th, all had been ready for several days. The crews, having carefully studied models of all three dams, had practised with dummy bombs off Chesil Bank until they had perfected their method of attack; the route had been chosen. On 16 May, the special 9,000-pound bouncing bombs (still warm from the filling factory, which had placed a special explosive within their skins) were fused and in position on the aircraft, ready for take-off that night. The weather forecast was favourable, and on that same evening nineteen Lancasters set off on their mission, led by Gibson, who was to use the Master Bomber technique for the first time.

The aircraft left in three waves. The first, consisting of nine Lancasters led directly by Guy Gibson, was to attack the Möhne dam and then the Eder; the second, of five aircraft led by Flight Lieutenant J.C. McCarthy, was to attack the Sorpe; and the third, also of five Lancasters, was to act as reserve should its efforts be required. All the bombers were fitted with VHF radio-telephones, as used in fighter aircraft, so that they could speak to each other as required during the attacks. Flying very low on courses carefully chosen to avoid known heavily defended areas, the first two waves crossed the coast of Holland and the Zuider Zee simultaneously. One aircraft of Gibson's formation was shot down on the way and one of McCarthy's had to return when it lost its bomb after striking the Zuider Zee through flying too low, whilst one was so badly damaged by flak en route that it too had to return to base. When his formation, now reduced to eight aircraft, reached the Möhne Lake and identified the dam itself, Gibson dived down to sixty feet to make the first attack. Under intense fire from the German defences he made his approach at 240 miles per hour. At precisely the calculated moment Pilot Officer Spafford, the bomb-aimer, released the first bouncing bomb, and a few seconds later a vast column of water rose into the air right beside the dam. The surface of the lake was so disturbed that the second attack, by Flight Lieutenant Hopgood, had to be delayed by several minutes. When he did attack his aircraft was unfortunately hit by flak and crashed, the bomb falling on the power house just beyond the dam, destroying all the telephonic communications. The next three aircraft dropped their bombs successfully and, peering through the spray that reared up into the air, Gibson soon saw that the attack had breached the dam. The water of the lake 'like stirred porridge in the moonlight', as he described it, 'rushed through a great breach'. In a few minutes, he went on,

> the valley was beginning to fill with fog ... we saw cars speeding along in front of this great wave of water which was chasing them ... I saw their headlights burning and I saw the water overtake them, wave by wave, and then the colour of the headlights underneath the water changing from light blue to green, from green to dark purple until there was no longer anything except the water bouncing down.

At the head of the three aircraft which had not yet dropped their bombs, Gibson proceeded to the Eder dam. One by one the aircraft attacked and released their bombs. One bomb hit the parapet of the dam, detonating and unfortunately destroying the aircraft which had dropped it, but the other two Lancasters were completely successful, breaching the dam in two places and sending a wall of water some thirty feet high sweeping down the valley.

The attack on the Sorpe dam was not so successful. Flight Lieutenant McCarthy's formation, already reduced from five to three aircraft because two had had to return to base without completing their mission, lost two more Lancasters to enemy defences en route to the target. This left McCarthy to attack on his own, which he did, damaging the dam in its centre but failing to breach it. Gibson* called up the three reserve

* For his part in the raid, Wing Commander Guy Gibson was awarded the Victoria Cross. He was later killed in action, on 19 September 1944.

aircraft to follow this attack, but only one succeeded in locating the dam and dropping its bomb, again without breaching the dam. Of the two aircraft which failed to find the target, one went missing, presumed shot down.

As the vast walls of water swept down from the Möhne and Eder lakes, Oberförster Wilkening, discovering that the telephones were out of action, raced to the nearest railway station on the Ruhr-Lippe line and rang up headquarters at Soest. He reported that an immense flood wave some 30 feet high was pouring from the Möhne dam down the valley at a speed of 6 yards a second. The Regierungspräsident in control of Westphalia was, however, unable to issue orders and warnings since almost all communications were disrupted, and those which were still intact only remained so for a short time as the waters from both the Möhne and Eder lakes rapidly submerged lines and put electricity supplies out of action. The floods soon spread to the bottom of the Ruhr valley and overran the district around Schwerte and Hattingen. And the disaster continued to spread. Many hydro-electric installations were destroyed, the storage power station at Bringhausen was flooded, Affoldern, Wabern and Felsberg, sixteen miles from the Möhne dam, were submerged by the raging torrents. The Eder floods inundated large areas of Kassel and the aerodrome at Fritzler was put out of action. Waterworks and purification plants all along the Ruhr were put out of action and the main railway line between Hagen and Kassel was washed away. Road and railway bridges were also swept away – the ferro-concrete bridge at Neheim was not only destroyed, but even its piles were uprooted, while the iron bridge at the same location was swept more than 100 yards down stream on the crest of the flood.

Serious as was the destruction of the hydro-electro installations and the extensive damage to industrial factories and communications, the real blow to the Ruhr was the loss of vital water. In an interview with the author, the late Dr Albert Speer, Germany's wartime Minister for Armaments Production, explained that the loss of electric power to the Ruhr was minimal because hydro-electric power represented only a small percentage of supply needs. In fact, most of Germany's electricity came from coal-fired generating stations and the Ruhr, in common with other parts of Germany, was fed on a grid system. He recorded, however, that:

What was the harm to us, was the water for the coking plants for gas, which was a key to our industrial processes in the Ruhr, and water for the cooling processes in steel production and other industry. We needed a lot of water and the Ruhr wells could not possibly supply sufficient water. If the Sorpe dam could have been breached as well it would have been a complete disaster. But it was a disaster for us anyway.

302

Referring to the rebuilding of the dams, Speer said:

> It was urgent to rebuild the dams to be able to conserve water in the
> lakes again when the rainfall would be coming in October, November
> and December, and great priority was given to this. My fear was that
> you would bomb our reconstruction work from high level and so
> prevent us storing again the water so urgently needed. This was my
> great fear, because the situation was already a disaster for us for a
> number of months.

The Ruhr offensive continued unabated throughout June and July 1943,
and, although more distant targets began to receive priority in late July
and onwards into August and September as the longer nights approached,
major bombing visits continued to be made to the Ruhr towns to
maintain the disruption of industry created by the campaign. It is
interesting at this stage to recall the comments of leading Nazi officials at
the beginning of the war. On 8 August 1939, in Essen, Göring said: 'We
will never allow a single bomb from hostile aircraft to hit the Ruhr.'
Then, in Berlin on 9 September, soon after war had been declared, he
boasted that 'First and foremost I will ensure that the enemy cannot bomb
us.' On 19 May 1941, after the last major German attack on London,
Erhard Milch said: 'Germany will never show such devastation as
England and other nations which declared war on us show today.
Germany, under the orders of the Führer, will march to final victory
without heavy loss of valuable lives and without damage being done to
war material and factories.' On 1 May 1942, Goebbels said during a
speech: 'British attacks on German cities will now once again be repaid
blow for blow. The losses of the RAF in aircraft and personnel in attacks
on occupied territory and on the Reich are such that Mr Churchill must
soon ask himself how long such operations can be sustained.'

By May 1943, however, Goebbels had changed his tune. On the 25th
he wrote in his dairy:

> The night raid by the English on Dortmund was extraordinarily
> heavy, probably the worst ever directed against a German city ...
> Reports from Dortmund are horrible. The critical thing about it is that
> industrial and munitions plants have been hit very hard. One can only
> repeat about air warfare: we are in a position of almost helpless
> inferiority and must grin and bear it as we take the blows from the
> English and Americans.

Then again on the following day:

> The fact is that the Royal Air Force is taking on one industrial city
> after another and one does not need to be a great mathematician to

prophesy when a large part of the industry of the Ruhr will be out of commission.

And on 28 Goebbels wrote:

The English wrested air supremacy from us not only as the result of tremendous energy on the part of the Royal Air Force and the British aircraft industry, but also thanks to unfortunate circumstances and our own negligence ... It seems to me that the air situation should be considered one of the most critical phases of the war and that it should be conducted quite independently of developments in the East.

The effectiveness of the Ruhr campaign as a whole was unquestionable. Even before it was over, Goebbels was convinced that British air power, in the shape of Bomber Command, was the most likely instrument of war to bring about the total defeat of Germany.

By the end of July 1943, there was a saying current in Germany: 'What is a coward?' – 'Anyone from the Ruhr who volunteers to go to the Front.'

CHAPTER XXIV

'Pointblank'

The Casablanca Directive of January 1943 had envisaged round-the-clock bombing, with night attacks by RAF Bomber Command and daylight attacks by US Eighth Bomber Command. This 'Combined Bomber Offensive', as it was termed, had, up to June 1943, largely resulted in the major offensive against the Ruhr and other towns deeper in Germany being undertaken by the RAF alone. Indeed, apart from targets in Occupied France and near the western borders of Germany, the US Eighth did not mount any significant attacks against major German towns until late in July.

The principal reason for the inability of the Americans to play their part in this early stage was lack of fighter cover. When they began operations in Europe they had been confident that their aircraft, armed with heavy-calibre 0.5-inch guns and flying in close formation, would be more than a match for the German fighters. The first few months of 1943 proved this confidence to be ill-founded, and heavy losses quickly made it clear that without fighter escort the US bomber formations were vulnerable to unsustainable losses. As long-range escort fighters were not at this stage available, and as it was evident that the German Air Force fighters were rapidly being equipped with 20-mm cannon, which fired an explosive shell and which could outrange the 0.5-inch guns, US Eighth Bomber Command had to confine much of its activity to French targets, primarily coastal ones, and to targets in Germany which were at such range as to permit fighter escort.

Bomber Command, on the other hand, in its growing strength, had been pounding Germany by night in no uncertain terms, and the highly

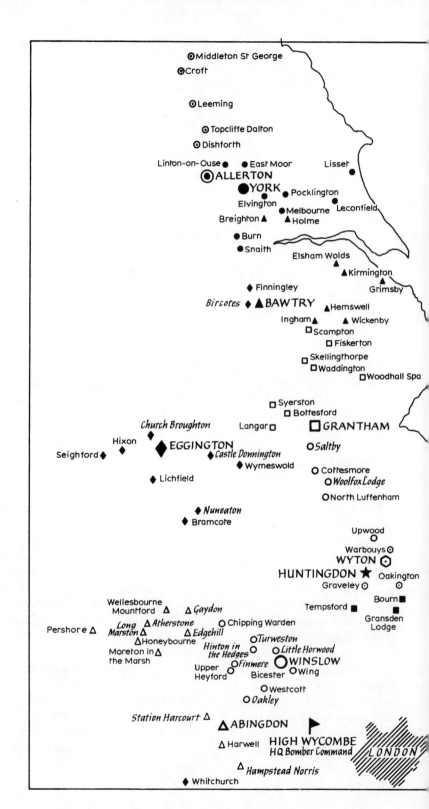

Disposition of Bomber Command, March 1943

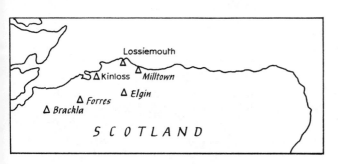

Lossiemouth
△
Kinloss △△ *Milltown*
△ *Elgin*
△ *Forres*
△ *Brackla*

S C O T L A N D

Foulsham
★ ★ Oulton
★ Great Massingham
★ Swanton Morley
★ Marham
wnham Market
ethwold ■
★ ★ ■ East Wrentham
eltwell
Lakenheath

NING
Newmarket
■ Chedburgh

■ Ridgewell

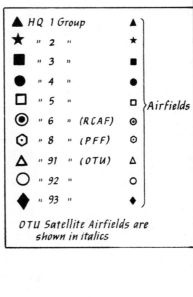

▲	HQ 1 Group		▲
★	" 2 "		★
■	" 3 "		■
●	" 4 "		●
▢	" 5 "		▢	Airfields
◉	" 6 "	(RCAF)	◉
⬡	" 8 "	(PFF)	⊙
△	" 91 "	(OTU)	△
○	" 92 "		○
◆	" 93 "		◆

OTU Satellite Airfields are
shown in italics

Miles
0   10   20   30

successful Ruhr campaign had forced the Germans to deploy increasing numbers of fighter aircraft on their western front. Speer, in a speech to the conference of Gauleiters in June 1943, referred to the serious losses in production of coal, iron, steel, crankshafts and other vital war requirements, caused by the bombing. Because of this, he explained, a decision had been taken to double the anti-aircraft defences of the Ruhr and to draft in 100,000 men for repair duties; in addition, there were to be substantial increases of day- and night-fighters for the western defence. These defensive measures made it necessary for the Allies to reconsider the priorities laid down in the Casablanca Directive. The truth was that the losses in Bomber Command had been higher in the first six months of 1943 than had been anticipated, even though they were not, as yet, unsustainable. As a result a new directive was issued to Harris and Eaker, dated 10 June 1943, which came to be known as 'Pointblank'.

After preliminaries, the directive stated:

> The increasing scale of destruction which is being inflicted by our night bombers and the development of the day bomber offensive by the Eighth Air Force have forced the enemy to deploy day and night fighters in increasing numbers on the Western Front. Unless this increase in fighter strength is checked we may find our bomber forces unable to fulfil the tasks allotted to them by the Combined Chiefs of Staff.
>
> In these circumstances it has become essential to check the growth and to reduce the strength of the day and night fighter forces which the enemy can concentrate against us in this theatre. To this end the Combined Chiefs of Staff have decided that first priority in the operation of British and American bombers based in the United Kingdom shall be accorded to the attack of German fighter forces and the industry upon which they depend.

The division of duties between US Eighth Air Force and RAF Bomber Command was then set out. Essentially, Eighth Bomber Command was given the task of destroying the German airframe, engine and component factories, and the ball-bearing industry, upon which the strength of the German fighter force depended. In addition, its task included the destruction of enemy fighters in the air and on the ground. To destroy the German aircraft industry required precision bombing of selected factories, and in this the Americans had specialised, having trained themselves to bomb in formation by day, using the most accurate bombsights which could be devised. To apply this technique in daylight, however, meant facing appalling opposition from the German fighter force, opposition that was to last right up to the end of 1943, when it was at last possible to protect the American bombers with adequate escort fighter cover. As has already been mentioned, long-range fighters were not available at this stage of the war, and as a result fighter escorts could not offer cover for more than marginal penetration into Germany. But by the beginning of 1944 the long-range, high-performance P51 Mustang, American-designed and -built and fitted with the Rolls-Royce Merlin* engine and its derivatives, began to arrive in England to undertake long-range fighter escort duties.

The 'Pointblank' Directive prescribed the tasks for RAF Fighter Command and the fighter forces of the US Eighth Air Force: 'The attack of enemy aircraft in the air and on the ground,' and 'The provision of support necessary to pass bomber forces through the enemy defensive system with the minimum cost.' The latter task, however, was not completely achievable, and would not be so until the arrival of the Merlin-engined Mustangs.

Harris and Saundby interpreted Bomber Command's task as set out in the 'Pointblank' Directive as requiring attacks against those industrial towns in which there were large numbers of aircraft component factories. These targets were mostly to the east and south of the Ruhr and, due to the short June and July nights, Bomber Command was not at first able to undertake these new operations. Instead, it concentrated on targets such as Krefeld, Aachen, Cologne-Mulheim, and the closer Ruhr targets, as well as French targets such as the Schneider Armament works at Le Creusot and the Peugeot works at Montbéliard. The results of all these raids were highly successful, and by the middle of July the Ruhr was in a desperate condition. One attack was, however, made against a target which fell into the 'Pointblank' category. On the night of 20/21 June, the former Zeppelin works at Friedrichshaven on the Bodensee (Lake Constance), which was producing RDF apparatus for German night-fighters, was attacked by 60 Lancasters of No. 5 Group with considerable effect. No Pathfinder Force aircraft were used, the Group operating entirely on its own and using its own target-finding and target-marking techniques supplied by No. 617 Squadron, which had proved its pathfinding abilities on the dam-busting raids. The aircraft flew on to North Africa after the Friedrichshaven attack, where they refuelled and bombed-up again for a raid on the Italian naval base at La Spezia on the way back to England.

Although the 'Pointblank' Directive gave priority to the destruction of the German fighters and the aircraft industry associated with their production, naval targets, particularly those involved with U-boat construction, remained high on the list of target priorities set down by the Chiefs of Staff. In July 1943, the Admiralty began to exert much

* One of the most successful aero engines of all time, the Merlin was also the principal power-plant for Hurricanes, Spitfires and Lancasters.

pressure for the elimination of Hamburg, and the city therefore became, for Bomber Command, an urgent target. Hamburg was the second largest city in Germany, with a population in excess of a million and a half, and its shipyards were the most extensive in Europe, housing many ships and U-boats under construction. The greater part of its shipbuilding yards, including the famous Blohm and Voss yards, had been given over to the building and assembly of U-boats; these yards were responsible for some 45 per cent of the total output of German submarines. Hamburg was also the largest and most important port in Germany. It contained 3,000 industrial establishments and 5,000 commercial companies, most of which were engaged in the transport and shipping business. In addition, there were major oil refineries, the second largest manufacturer of ships' screws, the largest wool-combing plant in Germany, and various manufacturers of precision instruments, electrical instruments, machinery and aircraft components. Quite apart from its vital shipbuilding activities, Hamburg was, in fact, a town of the utmost industrial importance to Germany, and as such it was, after Berlin, the most heavily defended city in Germany.

Many attacks had been made against Hamburg in varying degrees of intensity, but the damage had not been significant. It was a target which lay just outside Gee range and although the Pathfinder-led raids, using H_2S for the first time at the beginning of the year, had been reasonably successful, these had been on a comparatively small scale. But now, in July 1943, when Bomber Command was called upon to undertake 'the obliteration of Hamburg', the RDF aids at its disposal were considerable, with H_2S equipping the major portion of the main bomber force, as well as the Pathfinders. Because Hamburg was an ideal H_2S target, being a seaboard city and therefore easily identifiable from the map-like display of coastlines and rivers on the H_2S cathode-ray screen, not only could there be certainty of exceptionally accurate marking, but the main force could be sure of following up the Pathfinders with equal accuracy. Quite apart from H_2S, the entire bomber force was now equipped with the Mk. II Gee, which could use frequencies additional to those available to the Mk. I instrument, including some which greatly extended the range of Gee to well beyond that at which Hamburg lay. These frequencies were easy to jam, but they had been kept from being compromised until a special demand for their use occurred. Lastly, a device known as 'Window' was to be used. This consisted of bundles of strips of metallised paper, cut to carefully calculated lengths so that, when scattered from aircraft in large quantities in the region of the enemy's RDF detection and gun-laying systems, they would create so many signal responses that the operators would be utterly confused and unable to single out approaching aircraft.

The attack on Hamburg was more in the nature of a campaign than a series of raids, and went by the ominous code-name 'Operation Gomorrah'. Planned in meticulous detail by Saundby (now an Air Marshal and Deputy Commander-in-Chief of Bomber Command), it was a significant assault from the point of view of British and American co-operation in the combined strategic offensive. That co-operation had been called for in the Casablanca Directive of January 1943, but had not materialised until now because of US Eighth Bomber Command's inability to operate deep into German territory due to lack of fighter cover. In the case of 'Operation Gomorrah', however, the Americans, for the first time, interlaced vitally important daylight raids with the major Bomber Command attacks. Their contribution was small compared to that of the RAF bomber force, but it was the start of what, at the end of 1943, was to become round-the-clock bombing.

'Gomorrah' was planned to take place over a period of four nights, beginning on the night of 24/25 July; as Harris told his crews in a message to them just before the first assault: 'The Battle of Hamburg cannot be won in a single night. It is estimated that at least 10,000 tons of bombs will have to be dropped to complete the process of elimination ...' The route was out over the North Sea to a position exactly fifteen miles north-east of Heligoland, the point at which the bomber force was to turn in towards its target. With Gee working perfectly to these distances the accuracy of navigation was excellent and the timing precise, and aircraft concentration was therefore at its greatest. Both Pathfinder and main-force aircraft would then use H_2S to identify the coast in the neighbourhood of Cuxhaven, the River Elbe as the screen showed it unfolding as far as Hamburg and, finally, as the dock area was revealed as bright fingers of light. In thirty minutes over the target 740 aircraft out of 791 despatched rained down 2,396 tons of bombs, of which 980 tons were incendiary, the remainder being HE.

'Window' worked to perfection. The RDF-controlled searchlights waved aimlessly in all directions, the anti-aircraft gunfire was hopelessly inaccurate, and the German night-fighter controllers were thrown into complete confusion – one was heard to shout over the R/T: 'I cannot follow any of the hostiles; they are very cunning!'

In Hamburg, the results of the raid were disastrous. Goebbels described it as 'a real catastrophe ... an exceptionally heavy raid with most serious consequences for the civil population and for armaments production.' On the morning of 25 July, with the city's defences utterly disrupted, the US Eighth Bomber Command made a precision attack with sixty-eight bombers against the port and district of Wilhelmsburg, and another on the 26th with fifty-three aircraft against the Neuhoff power works. Then came RAF Bomber Command's follow up. On the night of the

27th/28th, 793 heavy bombers struck again, dropping 2,417 tons of bombs, of which 50 per cent were incendiary and the rest HE. This was followed, on the night of the 29/30, by an attack with 726 bombers dropping 2,382 tons. The final onslaught was delivered on the night of 2/3 August. On that night there was unexpectedly high cloud and severe icing conditions which resulted in only 462 aircraft out of 740 despatched attacking successfully, the remainder bombing alternative targets. Nevertheless, the bombers which did attack dropped a further 1,462 tons of bombs into what had become a blazing inferno.

For six days after the last raid it was impossible to obtain photographic assessment of the extent of the damage because of the vast pall of smoke covering the entire city, but reports from elsewhere in Europe talked of fire-storms raging through the city with temperatures approaching 1,000°C. When photographic evidence from reconnaissance became available it showed that 75 per cent of Hamburg had been razed to the ground. More than ten square miles of built-up areas had been eradicated. Shipyards, industrial plants, commercial and residential areas had been wiped out, and city services were no longer able to operate.

Goebbels wrote in his diary on 29 July, the day after the third raid:

Kaufmann, in a first report, spoke of a catastrophe the extent of which simply staggers the imagination. A city of a million inhabitants has been destroyed in a manner unparalleled in history. We are faced with problems that are almost impossible of solution. Food must be found for this population of a million. Shelter must be secured. The people must be evacuated as far as possible. They must be given clothing ... He spoke of about 800,000 homeless people wandering up and down the streets not knowing what to do.

A few days later Goebbels wrote an article in the *Völkischer Beobachter* which summed up succinctly the effectiveness of the Allied bomber offensive:

There is only one reply to massed terror raids, and that is massed counter-attacks. As long as we are not in a position to reply in kind the best we can do is to strengthen our defences ... The enemy is today attacking our morale. It is the duty of every individual to defend it. Our cities have now to stand in 1943 what Britain had to stand in 1940 ... The Government is doing everything that is humanly possible. But these measures would not suffice if the people did not supplement.

The Soviets are hammering against the doors of the Ukraine.

The British and Americans are storming Sicily and are sending out their air forces to Germany to break our morale.

In such a phase of the war, the morale of the people is a factor decisive for the outcome.

After the war, Speer, Germany's Minister of Armaments Production, wrote:

The devastation of this series of raids could be compared only with the effects of a major earthquake. Gauleiter Kaufmann teletyped Hitler repeatedly, begging him to visit the stricken city. When these pleas proved fruitless, he asked Hitler at least to receive a delegation of some of the more heroic rescue crews. But Hitler refused.

He went on to say that 'Hamburg had suffered the fate Göring and Hitler had conceived for London in 1940.'

Speer continued on the same subject:

Hamburg put the fear of God in me. At the meeting of Central Planning on July 29 I pointed out: If the air raids continue on the present scale, within three months we shall be relieved of a number of questions we are at present discussing. We shall simply be coasting downhill, smoothly and relatively swiftly ... We might just as well hold the final meeting of Central Planning in that case. Three days later I informed Hitler that armaments production was collapsing and threw in the further warning that a series of attacks of this sort, extended to six more major cities, would bring Germany's armaments production to a total halt.

In March 1972, when the author talked with Speer at his home in Heidelberg, he asked the German if he had changed his mind about the disaster that would have resulted if six major towns had suffered the fate of Hamburg. Speer replied: 'No, no, attacks like that on six such towns and we would have been finished.' But the build-up of Britain's bomber force had started too late to maintain, at this stage of the war, such an intensity of attack for any length of time. Had Churchill, Portal and Harris been heeded in earlier, pre-war days, then the Allies might well have prevailed by the end of 1943.

The casualties in Hamburg were the highest in any single town from air raids over such a short period of time. 41,800 lost their lives and 37,439 injured, many of whom subsequently died; to these figures must be added the several thousand people who were reported missing. The Police President of Hamburg described, in his report on the raids, the scenes which took place in the fire-storms in the city, and told of streets covered with hundreds of corpses: 'No flight of imagination,' he wrote, 'will ever succeed in measuring and describing the gruesome scenes of horror in the many buried air-raid shelters.' German morale was more shaken by the stories of the Hamburg attack than by any previous event in the war, even the major defeat at Stalingrad in November 1942, when the Russians threw the Germans into retreat in the central Caucasus. In Berlin, even before the capital itself was attacked from the air, there was almost complete panic – a nightly exodus from the city to surrounding towns and the open countryside demonstrated that the people now no longer believed the promises of Hitler and Göring that the Luftwaffe would never let the enemy bomb the German homeland.

Harris and Saundby had not been content with the campaign against Hamburg alone. On the night of 25/26 July, immediately after the first Hamburg raid, Bomber Command struck at Essen with an Oboe-led force of 627 aircraft out of 705 despatched, which dropped 2,032 tons of bombs on the city. On the 28th, Goebbels recorded in his diary of events that: 'The last raid on Essen caused complete stoppage of production in the Krupp works. Speer is much concerned and worried.' Goebbels and Speer were not the only ones to be shaken – on the morning after the raid, Doctor Gustav Krupp von Bohlen und Halbach took one look at the blazing remnants of his works and promptly fell down in a fit from which he never recovered.

By August, with the nights lengthening, Bomber Command was able to turn its attention to those targets deeper in Germany which were 'Pointblank' priorities. Although heavy attacks were still maintained against the Ruhr in order to prevent any major recovery from the devastating campaign of the first six months of the year, Mannheim, Nürnberg, Munich, Hannover, Kassel, Stuttgart, Frankfurt, among others, all came under heavy attack during August, September, October and November. There was, however, one major diversion from this programme, occasioned by Intelligence information to the effect that the Germans were developing rockets carrying warheads of up to a ton of HE and capable of travelling considerable distances. This information was evidence of Hitler's secret weapon, which had been suspected since as early as April 1943, and which by June was believed to be under development at a secret experimental establishment at Peenemünde on the Baltic coast. In June, photographic reconnaissance had revealed that Peenemünde was a centre for rocket research and development; film reconnaissance of the base showed what appeared to be two very large rockets at least 40 feet in length and 6 or 7 feet in diameter. Other Intelligence sources had also reported the development of a pilotless aircraft which was, in effect, an air-mine equipped with wings, a ram-jet motor, and a simple magnetic/gyroscopic guidance system. This too had been confirmed by aerial reconnaissance of Peenemünde, for the photographs had showed a launching-ramp with one of the pilotless aircraft mounted on it, ready to take to the air.

Spurred on by the Intelligence reports, the Chiefs of Staff requested Bomber Command to attack this target as a matter of urgency, and on the night of 17/18 August 597 heavy bombers were despatched to Peenemünde to undertake the task. The raid was led by Group Captain John Searby of No. 83 (Pathfinder Force) Squadron, and 571 of the aircraft despatched attacked, dropping 1,937 tons of bombs, 84 per cent being HE and 16 per cent incendiary. H_2S again played an important role in the success of this operation for, with the bombers' course lying over the North Sea and across into the Baltic, coastlines displayed on the cathode-ray screen made accurate navigation easy – Stettin was identified, and the island of Rugen, close to Peenemünde, was clearly seen on the H_2S. The bombing was so accurate that, when the raid was over the experimental station looked like a giant solitaire board. Over 600 people working there were killed, including Dr Spiel, the scientist in charge of development. Complete destruction had been requested, and complete destruction was achieved. Unquestionably the effectiveness of the raid on Peenemünde greatly delayed the German use of the V1 (pilotless aircraft) and V2 (rocket) weapons against England until a time when, however unpleasant, they were of little military significance. The invasion of Continental Europe had begun before the Germans were ready to use their secret weapons, and the V1 launching sites were overrun before they could put them into full use. Moreover, production was so set back that the flying-bombs and rockets were never in sufficient supply to have anything more than a nuisance value.

From the beginning of August to the middle of October the most heavily blasted of the Bomber Command 'Pointblank' targets were Mannheim (5,260.6 tons of bombs in three major attacks from 457, 546, and 567 heavy bombers); Hannover (8,185.7 tons from four raids of 652, 599, 457, and 349 heavies); Nürnberg (3,371.3 tons from two raids of 605 and 566 heavies); and Kassel (3,407.1 tons from two raids of 500 and 485 heavies). Three other raids which should be mentioned here were the attacks delivered against Berlin on the night of 23/24 August, when 617 aircraft out of 727 despatched dropped 1,762 tons of bombs; on the night of 31 August/1 September, when 507 aircraft out of 621 despatched dropped 1,463 tons; and on the night of 3/4 September, when 289 aircraft out of 320 despatched dropped 980 tons. In the event, however, these attacks were only marginally successful. It was clear from the three raids that the existing H_2S equipment, operating on a wavelength of 10 centimetres, provided insufficient detail on the cathode-ray tube to make it possible to distinguish aiming-points in such a vast built-up area as Berlin. What was required was the much higher resolution provided by H_2S sets operating on 3 centimetres, a system then being developed by Drs Dee and Lovell at the Telecommunications Research Establishment.

Harris and Saundby knew of this development from the Command's RDF Staff; with his eye on a Berlin campaign before the turn of the year, therefore, Harris pressed hard for 3-centimetre H_2S to be available for the PFF by November, even if only in small numbers.

The Americans, for their part, had not been idle in fulfilling the 'Pointblank' directive issued to them, although they were to suffer grievous losses until the long-range escort fighters became available at the beginning of 1944. Notable amongst their successes were two raids made against Schweinfurt by General Eaker's Eighth Bomber Command, but, again, the attacks were marred by terrible losses at the hands of the German day-fighters. Schweinfurt was the centre for a large percentage of the ball-bearing industry, an industry that was of the utmost importance to aircraft, tank and other armaments production. Other ball-bearing production centres were Steyr, Erkner in Berlin, and Cannstatt, and supplies also came from France and Italy, or were imported from Sweden and Switzerland; the Schweinfurt production was, however, far and away the most important for Germany's war effort. Lying some forty miles due east of Frankfurt and, therefore, at considerable range from bases in England, Schweinfurt's small size was such as to make it difficult to locate and hit with a night bombing assault. Consequently, the town had been included in Eaker's list of targets, since it was essentially a target for daylight precision bombing. The first attack was mounted on 17 August, when 376 Flying Fortresses of the US Eighth Bomber Command made a split raid on Schweinfurt and on an aircraft assembly plant at Regensburg, some fifty miles to the south-east. In the case of both targets the results were excellent and Schweinfurt, in particular, was badly hit. Speer told the author: 'After this attack the production of ball-bearings dropped by 38 per cent. Despite the peril to Schweinfurt we had to patch up our facilities there, for to relocate our ball-bearing industry would have held up production for three or four months.' The cost of the attack to the Americans was, however, disastrous – sixty of the Fortresses despatched were shot down, that is, 16 per cent. As a result, Eighth Bomber Command was largely out of action for several weeks.

Then on 14 October, Eighth Bomber Command made its second raid against Schweinfurt. This too was attended by catastrophic losses. As soon as the P-47 Thunderbolt escorts withdrew near Aachen, the Luftwaffe's fighters engaged the American bombers in a ruthless running combat all the way to the target and back again. Out of 291 Fortresses despatched, 60 were shot down over enemy territory, 17 were heavily damaged but reached base, and another 121 were seriously damaged. In spite of these losses, however, the attack was highly successful, Speer remarking that: 'This time we had lost 67 per cent of our ball-bearing production. It was a catastrophe.' On the other hand, the catastrophe suffered by US Eighth Bomber Command was also great. In just one week it had lost 148 bombers and their crews in four attempts, including the Schweinfurt raid, to penetrate deep into Germany without adequate fighter escorts, with the result that it was virtually grounded for many weeks.

Overall, however, the first four months of 'Pointblank' had been a success. From 1 June 1943 to the beginning of October, RAF Bomber Command had attacked Germany and its occupied territories with 23,153 sorties, dropping 67,105 tons of bombs (more than 55,000 tons on targets in Germany), for losses were 838 aircraft, or just 3.7 per cent. As a matter of interest, in the nine months from 1 January to 30 September 1943, Bomber Command had dropped 117,387 tons of bombs on Germany and laid 11,000 sea mines. But the real evidence of the initial success of 'Pointblank' came from Germany itself.

In a speech to a conference of Gauleiters on 6 October 1943, Generalfeldmarschall Erhard Milch referred to the effect upon aircraft production in Germany of the British and American bombing attacks during 1943. Milch said:

> Our supply position should be approximately 2,400 to 2,500 planes per month – the figures for various types fluctuate slightly. Unfortunately we had to suffer a decrease in the last two months due to strong attacks of the enemy on our aircraft production centres. The greater part of our factories producing fighters have been attacked by day as well as by night. The enemy has attacked, in preference, the most important supply factories so that in September we constructed 200 fighter planes less than, for example, in July, when we achieved a peak production of 1,050 fighters. This month of September we should have reached 1,300 aircraft and we would have achieved this if the destruction had not taken place. Not only has the direct destruction of aircraft factories affected us, but so also has that of aircraft components. I assume Minister Speer, as the responsible person, has already reported in detail on this question. The worries we have in this field are extremely great.

Referring to the production of all types of aircraft, he went on to say that:

> ... a total of 1,800 planes were produced in September. In the previous month, however, the number was 1,900 and in the month before that, more than 3,000. We hope, however, that we can make up for this loss providing there are no big attacks which inflict new damage.

And on the subject of components, he said:

317

How severely our supply position can at times be affected by what seems minor things, can, for instance, be seen from the attacks on —— [word indecipherable, but possibly Hannover] and on Hamburg. In both cases our metal variable pitch propellers were badly hit. We produced during this month [September] 52 of our most important types of planes, but when everything should have been according to plan in this month we were only able to deliver 4 to the front because propellers for the others were not available until ten days later. Particularly in Hamburg our production has suffered very severely, because of the loss to these factories of 3,000 skilled workers who are still missing.

Later in his speech, Milch referred to the fact that, in view of the bombing raids, priority was being given to the defence of the home country.

Before the war, Germany had developed an 8.8-millimetre anti-aircraft gun which could, it was discovered, be converted with only minor modifications into an anti-tank weapon. With its remarkable precision sight, great range and accuracy, this anti-tank version became the most effective weapon to be used against Allied armour, and the most feared; Russian tanks, especially, suffered heavy losses to the 88. From 1941 to 1943 11,957 of these guns were produced, but by the autumn of 1943 the majority had been deployed within Germany in their anti-aircraft role for the protection of cities and industrial centres against the Allied bombing, while German troops on the Eastern Front suffered for the lack of a weapon powerful enough to stop the Soviet tanks. Talking with the author in March 1972, Speer said:

> The Russians were wrong in complaining at the lack of a second front because the second front was there by your air attacks, because if we would have had at the Russian Front all these anti-tank guns – and the 8.8 was a wonderful anti-tank gun – then the losses of the Russians in their tank attacks would have been disastrous for them. The production of 8.8 to 12.8 centimetres anti-tank guns from 1942 to the end of 1944 was 19,713 guns, but only 3,172 of them went to the Army, the rest, 84 per cent, had to be diverted to anti-aircraft defence against your bombing. It is a most interesting point, because I think the damage you did by bombing was very heavy, but the damage you did by weakening the Germany Army was much more.

Using these guns to defend the homeland had other effects on the German Army besides weakening its resistance to Russian armour. The weapons had to be manned, and this use of trained soldiers, coupled with the requirement for personnel to deal with the devastation caused by bombing, absorbed 900,000 men by October 1943, troops which would otherwise have been available for the Army.

But it was not only anti-aircraft ground defence for the home front that affected the German Army. Fighter aircraft, too, had to be concentrated in defence of the German homeland, and this, with aircraft production already badly hit by the bombing, seriously weakened air support for the German armies on the Russian Front and in the Mediterranean theatre. By October 1943, the disposition of fighter aircraft available to the Luftwaffe was as follows:

	Single-engined fighters	Twin-engined fighters
Western Front	1,000	550
Russian Front	440	100
Mediterrranean	320	10

The weakening of fighter support for the German armies in the Mediterranean theatre materially assisted the Allied campaigns in North Africa and Italy. By 13 May 1943 German resistance in Tunisia had come to an end; by 17 August the Germans had been driven out of Sicily; on 1 October Naples was entered by the British 7th Armoured Division, setting the Allies on the road to the liberation of Rome. All this had been achieved with remarkably low losses for the Allies, and with very heavy losses in men and equipment for the Germans and Italians. The reduction of fighter support on the Russian Front was to prove even more disastrous for the Germans.

The Allied bombing of Germany, largely undertaken by RAF Bomber Command up to October 1943, was not just a second front but the main, the most deadly, threat. Now the Germans began to realise that such a menace must be countered if they were not to face defeat within a year or eighteen months. But, with the ever-increasing weight of Bomber Command's attacks and the swift build-up of US Eighth Bomber Command's contribution to the combined offensive – 'Round-the-Clock-Bombing' – the Germans were too late. Ultimate defeat was inevitable.

In late October and throughout November of 1943 Bomber Command continued to operate within the priorities set down in the Casablanca and 'Pointblank' directives, but with increasing ferocity as the strength of the Command grew. This strength was not just enhanced by the larger number of bombers becoming available, but also by the bomb-carrying capacity of the Avro Lancaster – much greater than that of other aircraft – which now formed the major part of the bomber force. A comparison of the tonnage of bombs dropped on Cologne in the famous 'Thousand Raid' of May 1942, with that dropped on Hannover on the night of 22/23 September 1943, illustrates this increase in load-carrying capacity. In the

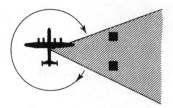 

Wide 10 centimetre beam displays two separate responses as one echo on cathode-ray tube

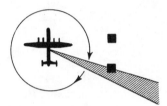 

Narrow 3 centimetre beam displays two separate responses as two separate echos

Effects achieved with wide and narrow H₂S beam widths

Cologne raid, 898 aircraft out of 1,046 despatched claimed to have identified and attacked the target, dropping 1,455 tons of bombs; in the attack on Hannover, 652 out of 711 aircraft despatched attacked and dropped the prodigious total of 2,416.1 tons of bombs on the city.

With the longest nights rapidly approaching, Harris began to set his sights on Berlin. Both he and Saundby had known for some time of the secret research work being done at TRE with experimental 3-centimetre H₂S sets which, operating on a much shorter wavelength than earlier marks, were capable of providing a far more detailed picture of vast built-up areas such as Berlin, and thus of providing the Pathfinders with more accurate location and marking of aiming-points. By September, however, the hopes of obtaining through official sources at least some 3-centimetre H₂S sets by November/December, as Bomber Command had earlier requested, had proved forlorn. As a result, therefore, Bennett of the PFF, now an Air Vice-Marshal, and Group Captain Saward of the Command RDF Staff, had hatched a desperate plan with Drs Dee and Lovell, the aim being to build six 3-centimetre H₂S sets at TRE and to have them installed in six Pathfinder Lancasters by the middle of November. Both Harris and Saundby had given their blessing to this clandestine project, the only other person 'in the know' being Sir Robert Renwick, whose unofficial help Saward had sought.

The project had started on 14 September, and by early October Dee and Lovell were well on the way with the programme, and the Command RDF Staff were already running special training courses in the maintenance of the new equipment for the Pathfinder RDF mechanics. Lovell recorded the episode in his diary:

> Backed by the enthusiasm of Bennett, Saward and their cronies, we hatched a desperate plan to equip six of the Pathfinder Force Lancasters by the end of October with an experimental X-band [3-centimetre H_2S] equipment. Arrangements were made to 'fix' the opposition, and the plan was not announced until it was already started.

('The opposition' was a reference to Ministry of Aircraft Production officials, who were invariably ready to oppose any scheme which did not go through the usual formal channels.) In the second week of October, Renwick called a meeting at the Air Ministry, the purpose of which was to advise those concerned at the Air Ministry and the Ministry of Aircraft Production that the C-in-C, Bomber Command had made a demand for a few Lancasters of the PFF to be equipped with 3-centimetre H_2S before the end of the year for certain special operations. The meeting was attended by Dee and Lovell for TRE, Saward for HQ Bomber Command, Bennett for the Pathfinder Force, and various members of the Air Ministry and the MAP. There was a certain element of humour, for only Renwick, Dee, Lovell, Bennett and Saward were aware that a programme to provide the Pathfinders with six Lancasters equipped with the new H_2S sets by the middle of November was already in full swing, regardless of the outcome of the meeting. Renwick guided the meeting with his usual skill, so that those present gave their unqualified approval to a plan for satisfying Bomber Command's urgent request.

That the clandestine programme for 3-centimetre H_2S succeeded was a result of Lovell's ingenuity and intense hard work. The very boldness of his plan inspired and stimulated everyone to work themselves to the bone, and to achieve results that they would never have believed possible under normal conditions. On 13 November 1943, the first three Lancasters equipped with 3-centimetre H_2S, JB352, JB355, and JB356, were delivered to the Pathfinder Force, and by the 17th the remaining three had been taken on the strength.

On 18 November 1943, Air Chief Marshal Sir Arthur Harris was in the Operations Room at Bomber Command HQ by 09.15 hours. Saundby had arrived a few minutes earlier, and, beckoning Saward with his finger, asked him:

'The six special Lancasters are ready?'

'Yes, sir,' Saward replied.

'Are they available for operations tonight?'

'Yes, sir.'

'Good,' Saundby muttered, and then had a word with Harris. When the weather forecast had been presented by Magnus Spence, the Command Meteorological Officer, Harris rose from his chair at the planning desk and turned to Saundby. 'Berlin Plan, Sandy – and we'll keep it going as long as we can.' He put on his cap and stalked out of the room, his face expressionless.

That night, 18/19 November, the Berlin campaign opened with an attack by 402 heavy bombers out of 444 despatched, dropping 1,590.7 tons of bombs on the city. At the same time, 352 bombers out of 395 despatched attacked Mannheim, dropping 874.4 tons of bombs, making this the first occasion on which two major raids were made against two targets deep in Germany on the same night. On the night of the 22nd/23rd 764 aircraft again attacked Berlin, dropping a massive load of 2,450 tons of bombs, of which 46 per cent were HE and 54 per cent incendiary. On the 23rd/24th 382 aircraft attacked, dropping 1,326.3 tons, followed on the 26th/27th by a force of 450 dropping 1,454.6 tons of bombs; three major night raids in one week. But Berlin was to have no respite. On the night of 2/3 December, 400 aircraft bombed the city, dropping 1,673 tons, followed, on the night of the 16th/17th, by an attack by 496 bombers dropping 1,703.1 tons, and on the 23rd/24th by 378 aircraft dropping 1,270.2 tons. The last raid in December was on the night of the 29th/30th, when 632 aircraft out of 712 despatched dropped 2,314.4 tons of bombs, 1,091.6 tons being HE and 1,222.8 being incendiary. During this December period, devastating raids were made against two other targets: on the night of the 3rd/4th 449 aircraft out of 527 despatched dropped 1,446 tons of bombs on Leipzig, causing extensive industrial damage, and on the night of the 20th/21st Frankfurt was attacked by 650 aircraft, dropping 2,196 tons of bombs.

During the first night of the new year the Berlin campaign continued, with a raid by 421 bombers dropping 1,200 tons on the city, followed on the 2nd/3rd by 383 aircraft dropping 1,125.1 tons of bombs. There were four more substantial attacks on Berlin during January 1944. On the night of the 20th/21st 769 aircraft dropped 2,402.4 tons; on the 27th/28th 536 aircraft dropped 1,738.4 tons; on the night of the 28th/29th 678 aircraft dropped 1,932.9 tons, and on the night of the 30th/31st 540 aircraft dropped 1,960.3 tons of bombs on the Third Reich's reeling capital. The penultimate major attack in the Berlin campaign took place on the night of 15/16 February 1944, when 806 aircraft out of 891 despatched dropped 2,610.1 tons of HE and incendiary in just thirty-nine minutes, and the last raid was made on 24/25 March, when 716 aircraft out of 810 despatched dropped 2,590 tons of bombs on the city. Thus closed the campaign.

From the night of 18/19 November 1943 to the night of 24/25 March

1944, 9,112 sorties were despatched in major attacks against Berlin, all four-engined heavy bombers, mostly Lancasters, except for 162 Pathfinder Mosquitoes. 90 per cent of the aircraft despatched attacked, dropping 29,341.5 tons of bombs, and total losses were 492 aircraft, which represented 5.4 per cent. From the beginning of November 1943 to the end of March 1944 26,297 sorties were flown against Germany. The total losses, including those suffered during raids on Berlin, were 1,108 aircraft, or 4.2 per cent, a figure which the Command was able to sustain. Targets in addition to Berlin which had been raided during this period were those listed in the 'Pointblank' Directive, with the addition of a few important Ruhr towns which originally had been attacked during the Ruhr campaign but which needed to be re-raided in order to prevent recuperation; 'Pointblank' targets attacked included Stettin, Magdeburg, Brunswick, Leipzig, Stuttgart, Frankfurt, and Nürnberg. Typical of the strength of these attacks were those against Magdeburg, the home of the Krupp heavy engineering works, on the night of 21/22 January 1944, when 648 heavy bombers dropped 2,205.8 tons, causing immense damage; against Brunswick, whose main industry was the assembly of Me110 twin-engined day- and night-fighters, on 14/15 February when 498 bombers dropped 2,184.3 tons with similarly disastrous results; and against Stuttgart, the home of the Bosch works and the Daimler Benz aero-engines plant, both highly important to the aircraft industry, when 598 aircraft dropped 1,988.6 tons on the night of 21/22 February, causing heavy devastation.

The Berlin campaign was, for Nazi Germany, an unprecedented disaster. Berlin was the nation's capital, and lay more than 600 miles from the Allied bomber bases, a distance which, it was presumed, placed it out of range of the Royal Air Force. It was the centre of government, and both a major industrial and a vital commercial centre. Bomber Command's sixteen attacks had been made in very poor weather conditions when the city was protected by complete cloud cover, conditions which should have reinforced Hitler's, Göring's and Goebbels's earlier promises that Berlin would never suffer a single bomb. But the concept of immunity from bombing had proved to be a myth elsewhere in the Reich, and so was now the case with Berlin. The fate Hitler had planned for London, which had been partially executed in 1940 and 1941, had been visited upon Berlin in full: just over 5,400 acres of the city had been laid waste in those winter months from November 1943 to March 1944.

Goebbels's diary covering this period is a continuous cry of horror at the effects of the bombing. He describes the destruction in the government administrative area, the damage to the Reich Chancellery, and the utter desolation in the Wilhelmplatz and the Potsdamer Platz.

Devastation is again appalling in the Government section as well as in the western and northern suburbs ... The State Playhouse and the Reichstag are ablaze ... Hell itself seems to have broken loose over us. Mines (4,000- and 8,000-pounders) and bombs keep hurtling down on the government quarter ...

This was written in the early hours of the morning of 24 November, while the night's attack was still in progress. On the 25th, referring again to that raid and to the previous attacks, he wrote: 'Conditions in the city are pretty hopeless ... About 400,000 people in Berlin are without shelter.' On the 26th: 'I visited the Reich Chancellery. It looks terrible.' On the 27th: 'The punishment Berlin took has shaken Speer considerably.' In his diary entry for that same day, Goebbels described the major attack delivered on the night of the 26th/27th:

In the early evening attention was naturally focussed on the question of a possible air raid ... And then things started. Once again a major attack descended upon the Reich capital. This time it wasn't the centre of the city that was the target as much as the suburbs of Wedding and Reinickendorf ... the important thing was damage to industry. The news that the Alkett plant [a major producer of guns and tanks] was on fire was especially depressing. Alkett is our most important factory for the production of field artillery. There we produce one half of our output of these guns ...

On 28 November, referring to the same raid, he wrote:

This time the munitions industry was especially hard hit. The Alkett works received a blow from which they won't recover easily. At Borsig's, too, there was tremendous destruction. It must be remembered that Borsig produces a large percentage of our gun output and has 18,000 employees.

And his diary entry for the following day reads:

The Berlin munitions industry is still in bad shape. Alkett is almost completely destroyed and, worst of all, valuable and irreplaceable tools and machines have been put out of commission. The English aimed so accurately that one might think spies had pointed their way.

Yet even heavier bombing was to come in December, January and February, building to a last crescendo on the night of 24/25 March 1944.

In the first six raids alone, 46 factories were destroyed and 259 were seriously damaged. Swiss diplomatic and intelligence reports* compiled

---

* The author obtained access to these reports, covering the period from 22 November 1943 (report No. 1886) to 31 December of the same year (report No. 2223), and from 1 January (report No. 1 for 1944) to 4 April 1944 (report No. 588).

at the time, covering the period from November 1943 to March 1944, detail the damage, particularly that to industrial and commercial sections of Berlin. Among other things, these reports describe the disastrous damage to Siemens Werke, Siemens und Halske, Siemens und Schuckert-Fabrik in Siemensstadt, and to the Spandau factory of Siemens-Schuckert AG. The Siemens electrical combine, the biggest in Germany, manufactured cables, aircraft instruments, electrodes and carbons for searchlights, and various military electronic components and equipment. The report for 17 December 1943 concludes that the damage to Siemens und Halske and Siemens-Schuckert was calamitous: 'The war economic significance of the exceptionally disastrous destruction can hardly be overlooked. The Berlin factories have unfinished armament orders valued at nearly 300 million Reichsmarks.' The report for 27 December listed forty-five factories covering a variety of industrial production, including precision engineering, electrical instruments, chemicals, locomotives, aero-engines, tanks, described as having been employed solely on the manufacture of war equipment but now entirely or partially destroyed. The 30 December report adds another eight manufacturing companies to the list, while the reports through January 1944 and February list many more factories where destruction had occurred or damage had been disastrous; these include such names as Daimler-Benz, AEG, Lorenz, Borsig AG, BMW, Dornier, Heinkel and Telefunken. In addition, they detail the substantial damage to railway stations, rolling stock and marshalling yards, gasworks, electricity power plants, commercial offices, shops, houses and apartment houses, and the fact that 1½ million people in Berlin had become homeless.

The Swiss did not think that Germany would collapse as a result of the bombing of Berlin, but it is clear that they were of the opinion that the Allied bombing throughout 1943, followed by the bombing of the capital, was the beginning of the end of Germany.

Albert Speer, in an interview with the author, emphasised the disruption to many industrial plants engaged on war production in the capital and its suburbs, including the Erkner plant, the most important manufacturer of ball-bearings next to Schweinfurt, which was heavily hit. Speer added that the destruction of the administrative and government buildings was a grave embarrassment, but he did not believe that the bombing of Berlin alone could have resulted in a sudden collapse of Germany. He was, on the other hand, of the opinion that the campaign contributed to the downfall of Germany, and made yet more demands for defences which detracted from the nation's ability to meet the needs of the Army on all fronts. According to Speer, production for defence needs was well below what was necessary for efficient protection of the Fatherland, at a time when the German Army also required greatly increased supplies of military hardware if it was to return to the offensive on all fronts which was essential for survival. By the spring of 1944, however, with a new front soon to open if the Allies invaded France, the bombing had forced Germany into a desperate defence of her own homeland, a defence which her leading military men knew to be unsustainable.

'Pointblank' – culminating in the Berlin campaign and in the sudden increase of US Eighth Bomber Command's activity because of long-range fighter support having become available at the beginning of 1944 – had largely completed its task by the end of March. Now the combined British and American bomber forces were to be employed in support of 'Operation Overlord' – the invasion of Europe.

CHAPTER XXV

'Overlord'

Planning for 'Overlord', the code-name for the invasion of Western Europe, had been started in April 1943 when Lieutenant-General F.E. Morgan was appointed Chief of Staff to the Supreme Commander of the Allied Forces, although a candidate for the latter post had not at that time been selected. By July, General Morgan and his Staff had drawn up a preliminary outline plan for the invasion, which had duly been considered by the Joint Chiefs of Staff at their conference held in Quebec in August. There the plan had been approved, and instructions had been issued for its further development to cover detailed planning for the Allied naval, land and air forces.

Operations planned for the Allied air forces were divided into four phases. The first was the strategic bombing of Germany in accordance with the Casablanca Directive of January 1943, and with the 'Pointblank' Directive of June 1943, as a result of which the emphasis of strategic bombing had been turned on to the German aircraft industry. The second phase called for concentration on targets associated with the immediate preparations for the invasion itself, such as railway centres, coastal defence batteries, harbours and airfields, particularly those within 150 miles of Caen and in the areas of Brest and Nantes. Flying-bomb and V2 rocket sites were not then included in the list of targets, since little was known of Hitler's secret weapons at the time. The third phase would place the bomber forces in support of the actual invasion, and included the protection of the sea and land forces during the voyage across the Channel, and when the armies were ashore. The fourth called for continuation, following successful landings, of attacks on airfields, harbours, railway centres and other communications, and for a return to the strategic bombing of Germany. These four plans covered the requirements of General Sir Bernard Montgomery, who was to command all land forces in the initial stages of the invasion and who had asked for railways to be denied to the enemy up to 150 miles from the beach-head, and for complete air cover during both the landings and the establishment of the beach-head.

On 15 November 1943, Air Chief Marshal Sir Trafford Leigh-Mallory was appointed Air Commander-in-Chief of the Allied Expeditionary Air Force, consisting of RAF Fighter Command, the Second Tactical Air Force (RAF), and the US Ninth (Tactical) Air Force, over all of which he had sole control. RAF Bomber Command and the US Eighth Air Force with its Eighth Bomber Command remained at the disposal of the Combined Chiefs of Staff. It was soon apparent to Leigh-Mallory that the air forces available to him for the invasion of Western Europe were entirely inadequate to undertake phases two and three of the air plan. Without the control of heavy bombers he knew he could not hope to attack and immobilise the large number of targets listed as being essential to success, in particular the railway centres and harbours. These views he expressed forcibly and, since he was of the opinion that both the RAF's heavy bombers and those of the US Eighth Bomber Command would have to be used, he planned accordingly.

By the end of the year, the Supreme Commander of the Allied Forces in Europe had been selected. On 16 January 1944, US General Dwight D. Eisenhower took up his new post as Supreme Commander, and on the 20th Air Chief Marshal Sir Arthur Tedder was appointed his Deputy. Eisenhower had been in command of the Allied landings in North Africa in 1942, known as 'Operation Torch', and the successful co-operation between the British and American forces in the last stages of the North African campaign, and in the invasions of Sicily and Italy in 1943, owed much to his skill as a commander, while the credit for the liaison between the Allied air forces in this Mediterranean theatre belonged to Tedder. With Montgomery appointed to command all land forces in the initial stages of the invasion, following his enormously successful campaign in the Western Desert, the top team for 'Overlord' was well chosen, and its members already acquainted with each other.

Eisenhower and Tedder were soon to be confronted by Leigh-Mallory's insistence on the need for massive support for the invasion from the combined British and British-based American heavy bomber forces, and at the same time by resistance from Harris and General Carl Spaatz, commanding the US Strategic Air Forces in Europe, to the use of these forces for operations other than the strategic bombing of Germany. Harris and Spaatz were concerned about the effect upon Germany of easing strategic bombing in favour of an almost exclusively tactical role for the bomber forces in support of the invasion. They drew attention to the vast amounts of German manpower and production locked up in defence measures, and they warned of the considerable resources of fighters, anti-aircraft guns and other defence material for the protection of the homeland that would instantly be released if the bombing of Germany was discontinued.

In the middle of January 1944, as a result of the views expressed by Harris and Spaatz, the CAS, Portal, held a meeting with the two commanders to review the progress of the combined bomber offensive, 'with particular regard to the short period remaining before the preparatory phase of Overlord.' In their report of this meeting, Harris and Spaatz stated:

1. We are convinced that the ultimate objective of the Pointblank plan should remain as stated in the Casablanca Directive and that first priority should continue to be given to the attack upon the G.A.F. fighter forces and the industry on which they depend. The reduction in the German fighter strength is in fact an essential prerequisite to progress towards the ultimate objective of the Pointblank plan and is a vital requirement in creating the conditions necessary for Overlord.
2. We are agreed that the best possible use should be made of the time remaining before Overlord by concentrating our attack upon the most important of the key installations in the German fighter aircraft industry. We consider that first priority should accordingly be given to the following:
   Single engine fighter airframe and component production.
   Twin engine fighter airframe and component production.
   Ballbearing industry.
   Owing to the requirements of the tactical situation and the uncertain weather in this theatre it will also be necessary to attack other targets from time to time, so as to cause the enemy to incur wastage of fighter aircraft in operations and to maintain pressure on him by attacking other industrial areas selected where possible from those in the Combined Bomber Plan. We do not think that priority should be given to the attack of Axis oil refineries. The enemy oil situation has recently been examined by economic experts and as a result we are convinced that there would be no justification for diverting our effort from the G.A.F. fighter industry in order to attack oil installations.
3. Considerable progress has already been made both by U.S. Strategical Air forces in Europe and by R.A.F. Bomber Command

in pursuance of the Pointblank plan. Besides the destruction of airframe factories in the successful attacks carried out by the 8th. Air Force (U.S.), considerable damage has been done to aircraft and component factories in the night attacks of Bomber Command, notably in Hamburg, Berlin, Leipzig, Kassel and Stuttgart. Now that the larger industrial areas have been so severely damaged and Overlord is imminent the concentration of Bomber Command's effort on to the remaining most vital targets so far as is practicable is justified, and has been ordered.

At paragraph 5, two other objectives which lay outside the main 'Pointblank' Directive were mentioned. The first of these was Berlin. It was agreed that 'it is most important that both R.A.F. Bomber Command and 8th. Air Force (U.S. Eighth Bomber Command) should carry out attacks on Berlin whenever weather and tactical considerations are suitable for it, but are unsuitable for attacks on vital elements of the German fighter industry ...' The second objective was the bombing of 'Crossbow' targets. 'Crossbow' was the code-name given to the flying-bomb and V2 rocket sites situated in Northern France and Belgium, close to the Channel coast.

The present importance of attacking Crossbow targets [the report stated] arises from the necessity of ensuring the security of our base for Overlord [the South of England]. Attacks on Crossbow targets have been placed high on the list for the tactical bombers of the Allied Expeditionary Air Force, and the U.S. 8th. Air Force has also been asked to carry out attacks ...

The co-ordination between commands was then reviewed, the significant decision here being that the combined bomber offensive would continue to be controlled by the CAS, acting on behalf of the Combined Chiefs of Staff.

On 20 January 1944, the Chiefs of Staff advised the Joint Staff Mission, Washington, of these decisions by coded message OZ 332. Agreement was received and the C-in-C Bomber Command, and the Commanding General, US Strategic Air Forces in Europe, were instructed accordingly in a new directive, AX 621, dated 17 February.

This directive made no mention of railway targets, but Leigh-Mallory still pressed his case for the use of heavy bombers to execute a comprehensive plan of disruption and dislocation of those parts of the French and Belgium railway systems which were vital to the German's military lines of communication. This plan had been prepared by the Allied Expeditionary Air Forces Bombing Committee, which was chaired by Air Commodore E.J. Kingston-McCloughry, an Australian, and which included Professor Solly Zuckerman* and Mr R.E. Brant, who had a considerable knowledge, acquired before the war, of the French railway system. The plan had, in fact, been prepared by Zuckerman and Brant. The targets selected for attack were those with extensive repair and maintenance facilities, for it was Zuckerman's and Brant's contention that destruction of such facilities was the best way of disrupting the railway system. By the beginning of March the committee had drawn up a list of seventy-five railway targets which were, effectively, the major maintenance and repair centres in Belgium and Northern France. Eisenhower and his Deputy, Tedder, immediately supported the railway plan, which came to be known as the 'Transportation Plan', and convinced Portal of its necessity. The CAS lost no time, and on 4 March a directive was issued to Harris headed 'Targets for attack by Bomber Command in moonlight periods prior to Overlord'. After the preliminaries, the directive stated:

> To provide for the final detailed planning of Overlord and in order to contribute materially to the requirements of Overlord during periods when Pointblank night operations are not practicable, attacks should be carried out against the following railway objectives using a ground marking technique.

There followed a list of six railway targets – Trappes, Aulnoye, Le Mans, Amiens-Longeau, Courtrai and Laon. These attacks would be in the nature of a trial to test Bomber Command's ability to undertake what amounted to precision bombing at night.

On the night of 6/7 March, within two days of receiving his order for the trial raids on transportation targets, Harris despatched 267 heavies against Trappes, a major railway centre just to the south-west of Paris. 263 aircraft attacked, dropping 1,256 tons of bombs with devastating effect. The results were staggering. Every track in the up-reception and the down-sidings was put out of action by the concentration of bomb craters, and the western exit was rendered completely impassable. Engine sheds and rolling stock were also severely damaged; indeed this rail centre was put out of action totally for one month. On the night of 7/8 March Bomber Command followed this attack with a raid against Le Mans with 200 aircraft, and again with 212 aircraft on the 13th/14th, dropping 925.1 tons and 959.7 tons, all HE. On the nights of the 15th/16th and 16th/17th it was the turn of Amiens, when 125 and 117 aircraft dropped 605.2 and 542.9 tons of HE; on the 23rd/24th Laon

---

* Later Lord Zuckerman, OM, KCB, Chief Scientific Adviser to the Defence Secretary, 1960-66.

received 306.4 tons from 72 aircraft; on 25th/26th 182 heavies struck at Aulnoye, dropping 809.1 tons; on the 26th/27th Courtrai was attacked with 102 heavies dropping 474 tons; and on the 29th/30th an additional target, the Paris-Vaires marshalling yards, was bombed by 76 aircraft which dropped 310.9 tons. With the exception of the railway centre at Laon all the attacks caused extensive damage and disruption, and Paris-Vaires, Trappes, Amiens and Courtrai were brought to a complete standstill. In fact, these raids were so successful that the Transportation Plan was approved, and on 15 April Tedder issued, on behalf of the Supreme Commander, a complete list of seventy-nine railway targets to be attacked by Bomber Command and the US Strategic Air Forces in Europe, thirty-seven being allotted to the RAF force and forty-two to US Eighth Bomber Command. An eightieth target was added to the list later.

On 14 April 1944, following a decision by the Combined Chiefs of Staff, RAF Bomber Command and the US Strategic Air Forces in Europe were placed under the direction of General Eisenhower, and on 17 April, just a few days after the allocation of railway targets between Bomber Command and US Eighth Bomber Command, Eisenhower issued his first official directive to the two strategic air forces. The instruction to Bomber Command read:

> In view of the tactical difficulties of destroying precise targets by night, RAF Bomber Command will continue to be employed in accordance with their main aim of disorganising German industry. Their operations will, however, be designed as far as is practicable to be complementary to the operations of the USSAF [United States Strategic Air Forces]. In particular, where tactical conditions allow, their targets will be selected so as to give the maximum assistance in the aims of reducing the strength of the German Air Force, and destroying and disrupting enemy rail communications. A list of targets chosen to achieve these objectives, and showing the relative priorities will be adjusted from time to time in accordance with the situation.

Although the Transportation Plan was put into effect immediately after Bomber Command's successful trial runs in March, there was concern by May that the French population in the areas of railway centres under attack was at severe risk. This resulted in Churchill raising the matter in the War Cabinet, and then consulting Roosevelt. In a message to the American President, sent by diplomatic bag and dated 7 May, he wrote:

1. The War Cabinet have been much concerned during the last three weeks about the number of Frenchmen killed in the raids on the railway centres in France. We have had numerous Staff meetings

with our own Officers and I have discussed the matter with Generals Eisenhower and Bedell Smith.* There are great differences of opinion in the two Air Forces not between them but criss-cross about the efficacy of the 'railway plan' as a short term project. In the end Eisenhower, Tedder, Bedell Smith and Portal all declare themselves converted. I am personally by no means convinced that this is the best way to use our Air Forces in the preliminary period, and still think that the G.A.F. should be the main target. The matter has been discussed in very great detail on the technical side and it would not be wise to dismiss lightly the arguments for or against.

2. When this project was first put forward a loss of 80,000 French civilian casualties, included injured, say 20,000 killed, was mentioned. The War Cabinet could not view this figure without grave dismay on account of the apparently ruthless use of the Air Forces, particularly of the Royal Air Force on whom the brunt of this kind of work necessarily falls, and the reproaches that would be made upon the inaccuracy of night bombing. The results of the first, say three-sevenths of the bombing have however shown that the casualties to French civil life are very much less than was expected by the Commanders, in fact Air Chief Marshal Tedder has now expressed the opinion that about 10,000 killed, apart from injured, will probably cover the job.

3. I am satisfied that all possible care will be taken to minimise this slaughter of friendly civilian life. Nevertheless the War Cabinet share my apprehensions of the bad effect which will be produced upon the French civilian population by these slaughters, all taking place so long before Overlord D. day. They may easily bring about a great revulsion in French feeling towards their approaching United States and British liberators. They may leave a legacy of hate behind them. It may well be that the French losses will grow heavier on and after D. day but in the heat of battle, when British and United States troops will probably be losing at a much higher rate, a new proportion establishes itself in men's minds. It is the intervening period that causes me most anxiety. We are of course doing everything in our power by leaflets etc., to warn the French people to keep clear of dangerous spots, and this may prove beneficial in the remaining interval. However, both on technical and political grounds, which latter are very gravely involved, the War Cabinet feel very great distress and anxiety.

4. Accordingly they ask me to invite you to consider the matter from the highest political stand-point and to give us your opinion as a

---

* US Lieutenant-General Walter Bedell Smith, Eisenhower's Chief of Staff.

matter between Governments. It must be remembered on the one hand that this slaughter is among a friendly people who have committed no crime against us, and not among the German foe with all their record of cruelty and ruthlessness. On the other hand we naturally feel the hazardous nature of Operation Overlord and are in deadly earnest about making it a success. I have been careful in stating this case to you to use only the most moderate terms, but I ought to let you know that the War Cabinet is unanimous in its anxiety about these French slaughters, even reduced as they have been, and also in its doubts as to whether almost as good military results could not be produced by other methods. Whatever is settled between us, we are quite willing to share responsibilities with you.

Copies of this message went to King George VI and to the Foreign Secretary, Eden, among others.

Roosevelt's reply also came by diplomatic bag, and was dated 11 May:

1. Replying to your 669 [the number of Churchill's message], I share fully with you your distress at the loss of life among the French population incident to our preparations for Overlord.
2. I share also with you a satisfaction that every possible care is being and will be taken to minimize civilian casualties. No possibility of alleviating adverse French opinion should be overlooked, always provided that there is no reduction of our effectiveness against the enemy at this crucial time.
3. However regrettable the attendant loss of civilian lives is, I am not prepared to impose from this distance any restriction on military action by the responsible Commanders that in their opinion might militate against the success of Overlord or cause additional loss of life to our Allied Forces of Invasion.

And so the Transportation Plan continued. By D-Day, 6 June 1944, RAF Bomber Command had attacked all of the 37 railway targets allotted to it; 8,800 sorties had been flown and 42,000 tons of bombs dropped, with devastating results. When D-Day dawned 21,949 British and American aircraft had attacked 80 railway targets, dropping 66,517 tons of bombs and bringing a terrible paralysis to the railway network of the Région Nord. The degree of success was categorised by three classes, 'A', 'B', and 'C'. 'A' class targets were those which had been so badly destroyed that no further attacks would be required until the enemy had undertaken vital repairs. 'B' class targets were those which had been severely damaged but which still possessed a number of installations which were intact – these would therefore require a further visit. 'C' class signified that little or no damage had been inflicted. Of the eighty targets which had been attacked, fifty-one were 'A' class, twenty-five 'B' class, and four 'C' class; of the thirty-seven targets attacked by Bomber Command, twenty-two were placed in class 'A' and fifteen in class 'B'. In addition, the Saumur railway tunnel was completely blocked by the effects of nineteen 12,000-pound bombs dropped by 5 Group's dam-busting No. 617 Squadron on 8 June, two days after D-Day. This attack was so successful that the Germans never succeeded in clearing the line.

The execution of the Transportation Plan had a considerable effect on the movements of German troops well before any Allied landings were made. Such trains as still ran moved slowly and were forced to make long detours around the devastated areas. With no freedom of movement for troops and materials in a large part of Belgium and France, it had become virtually impossible for the enemy to marshal troops quickly for any decisive counter-attack when the invasion was launched. For the Allies, the plan had proved to be an outstanding success.

The forebodings that had troubled Churchill and some members of the War Cabinet about the reactions in France proved to be ill-founded. The railway-centre raids caused no resentment. The destruction wrought by the bombing, which sent locomotives and rolling stock hurtling into the air, and tore huge craters in the ground over which the rail networks ran, twisting the tracks into a tangled mass of useless metal, was to the French population the first sign of their coming liberation from the Nazi heel; their unanimous comment was: '*Il le fallait*' – 'It had to be done'. There was, however, another reason for the lack of adverse reaction from the French population – civilian casualties were far fewer than even the most optimistic estimates put forward by Tedder. In assessing the likely effects of the bombing, Churchill had been influenced by Harris, who believed that although Bomber Command could certainly destroy the targets allocated, the accuracy of night bombing was not great enough to guarantee that there would be no 'overspill' of bombs falling outside the immediate target area. In fact, Harris had been over-cautious. Since the targets were situated comparatively close to the southern and eastern Gee chains and Oboe stations, they fell within areas of high Gee and Oboe accuracy, with the result that the precision of Bomber Command's raids matched, and even surpassed, that of the Americans' daylight bombing.

The success of the attacks on French railway targets during March and April resulted in demands for Bomber Command to be used against other pre-invasion tactical targets, such as coastal batteries, defence works and 'Crossbow' sites. In the case of battery and defence-work targets, it was not possible to concentrate exclusively on the area of the planned landings because of the need to keep the enemy guessing as to the actual location of the invasion. For every coastal battery or defence work bombed in the intended invasion area, therefore, at least two were bombed elsewhere, a total of 14,000 tons of bombs being dropped on these targets. Then, on the night of 5/6 June, a few hours before the invasion started, 1,136 aircraft of Bomber Command, mostly heavies, dropped another 5,267 tons of high explosive on the coastal batteries covering the beaches where the invasion forces were due to land. Opposition was effectively silenced, and Allied casualties were as a result unexpectedly low. Also attacked during the pre-invasion period were many purely military objectives, such as depots, tank parks and ammunition and ordnance centres.

Other pre-invasion tasks fell to the tactical air forces of the Allied Expeditionary Air Force under Leigh-Mallory, among the most important being assaults by the Second Tactical Air Force (RAF) against the enemy's radar stations, and the programme of rail- and road-bridge destruction by the US Ninth (Tactical) Air Force. The bridge attacks were highly successful, and by D-Day eighteen out of twenty-four bridges over the Seine between Rouen and Paris had been completely breached, and the remainder blocked. In addition, twelve other road- and rail-bridges over the Rivers Oise, Meuse, Moselle, Escaut and Loire, and over the Albert Canal, had been severed or blocked, a total weight of 5,370 tons of bombs being dropped from 5,209 sorties. The Second Tactical Air Force's radar-station programme, undertaken by rocket-firing Typhoons* and Spitfires, also met with considerable success. Other attacks by both the US Ninth and the RAF Second Tactical Air Forces were made against enemy airfields within a 150-mile radius of Caen, and by D-Day the Allied air forces had attained virtually complete air superiority over Western France and Belgium.

In addition to its bombing activities, Bomber Command had one special task on D-Day. During the planning stages of 'Overlord', the desire had been expressed for some form of 'spoof' invasion against one or more parts of the French coast of Normandy running from Varreville, a point almost opposite the town of Montebourg on the Cherbourg peninsula, eastwards to Ouistreham on the mouth of the River Orne. Dr Robert Cockburn of TRE suggested the dropping of 'Window' (the metallic strips which had been used to such good effect during the devastating Hamburg raids in July 1943) to confuse the German early-warning radar systems. The idea was to cut the strips to the correct lengths and widths to simulate the responses on the enemy's radar that

---

* The Hawker Typhoon, powered by a Napier Sabre engine, was a fast, strongly built fighter with outstanding agility at low altitude. For this last reason it was in widespread use as a ground-attack aircraft, its chief weapon being eight wing-mounted rockets.

would be produced by approaching ships. The problem was to drop the strips from aircraft in such a manner that they would appear to be a vast invasion fleet moving towards the French coast at a speed of no more than 5-7 knots; furthermore, the operation was to take place in the dark. Wing Commander Dickie, the senior navigator in the Command's RDF Department (now re-christened Radar Department), conceived the ingenious idea of achieving the effect of this slow forward speed by utilising G-H in conjunction with Gee. G-H was the new blind-bombing device which had Oboe accuracy, but which had the advantage over Oboe that it could be operated by eighty aircraft simultaneously from one pair of ground stations – Oboe could only handle one aircraft at a time from one pair of ground stations. G-H had only recently been introduced into No. 3 Group's Lancaster II aircraft, and Dickie had been responsible for the programme for training the navigators in its use. The 'Overlord' planning committee had proposed a 'spoof' invasion from Newhaven towards the region of Boulogne, an area of such short range from the Gee and G-H ground stations that the accuracy of navigation with the combined system could be expected to be a matter of a few yards. Dickie therefore suggested that rows of aircraft should fly on elliptical courses, tracking on G-H and using Gee for turning points, each circuit taking each row of aircraft slightly further forward than its last circuit, and slightly further forward than the preceding row of aircraft. The forward turning points of the elliptical courses for each row of aircraft were to be pre-determined Gee fixes, and it was at these points that each row was to drop its 'Window' and then turn in order to perform the next elliptical course. The Gee fixes for each row of aircraft were so calculated that the throwing-out of every batch of 'Window' would occur at a small distance ahead of the previous batch, just far enough to produce the impression of a speed of approach of 5-7 knots.

The idea was tested out in No. 3 Group, and proved to be workable. Dickie then worked out a similar scheme for a 'spoof' operation between Southampton and Cap d'Antifer, using Gee for both the tracking and the turning and dropping. Both schemes were approved, and received the code-names 'Operation Glimmer' and 'Operation Taxable'. 'Glimmer' was carried out by No. 218 (G-H) Lancaster Squadron of No. 3 Group against the Boulogne area, and 'Taxable' by No. 617 Lancaster Squadron of No. 5 Group against the Cap d'Antifer area. Both operations began soon after dusk on 5 June and continued steadily throughout the night. On the sea beneath the bombers, accompanying ships used much gunfire and, near dawn, simulated the sounds of dropping anchors and other suitable noises, all produced by gramophone records and loud-speakers. The illusion was remarkably effective and undoubtedly much confusion was created, causing the Germans to make initial diversions of troops and tanks, held in reserve until the invasion site was known, to the wrong areas.

Once the Allies were ashore and the enemy was fully apprised of the area of the real invasion, he immediately began to move his reserves to the battle zone. For the bulk of these he proceeded to use what railways he had at his disposal, and Bomber Command was therefore allotted the task of disrupting these movements, once more making its heavy night attacks on railway targets. Guided by Gee and Oboe, these raids were so successful that, within three days, all movement by rail had been brought to a standstill. Rail attacks now became even more extended, going as far afield as Amiens, Arras, Douai and St Pol, with the other Allied air forces also being used, so that by the end of July the Allied Expeditionary Air Force, the US Eighth Bomber Command and RAF Bomber Command had between them dropped 34,500 tons of bombs on traffic targets. Bomber Command's contribution was no less than 23,000 tons, or two-thirds of the total.

During the latter part of June and in July and early August, Bomber Command followed even more closely the role of tactical support to the Allied armies, for Leigh-Mallory now decided to try using the heavies as an artillery prelude to those areas to be assaulted by the ground forces. A trial of this form of softening-up the enemy was first undertaken against Villers-Bocage on the 30 June, when 258 heavies dropped 1,176 tons of HE, with great effect. Then came the first real application, against Caen on 7 July, when Bomber Command dropped 2,363 tons just before the infantry attack went in. When the Allied forces eventually reached the city they found many German troops, still dazed and helpless from the consequences of the bombing, wandering about aimlessly in a complete mental stupor. The bombing also had its disadvantages, however, because the destruction was so great and the craters so numerous that the speed of the advancing British armoured vehicles was hampered to a considerable degree. Nevertheless, more and even heavier attacks of this nature were made in support of the ground forces to assist them in making a rapid break-out from the beach-head, the bombing being undertaken by both RAF and US Eighth Bomber Commands. Caen, St Lô, Caumont and Falaise figured in this deadly new form of artillery barrage, which finally brought despair to the German commanders. The effectiveness of the bombing in direct support of the Allied armies is best expressed by Field-Marshal Günther von Kluge, who, early in July 1944, had been brought from the Russian Front to take command of the German armies facing the Allied invasion. In a letter to Hitler, dated 21 July, he said that there was no form of strategy which could counterbalance the effects of the Allied bombing other than withdrawal from the battlefield. He wrote:

The psychological effect of such a mass of bombs coming down with all the power of elemental nature on the fighting forces, especially the infantry, is a factor which has to be taken into very serious consideration. It is immaterial whether such a carpet catches good troops or bad. They are more or less annihilated and, above all, their equipment is shattered.

This letter covered a report by Field-Marshal Erwin Rommel, who had commanded the famous Afrikakorps in the Western Desert campaigns, which expressed the same opinion.

Direct support of the Allied armies was not the only contribution that the air forces made towards a successful invasion. The bombing of Germany throughout 1943 and early 1944, before Bomber Command was placed under the direction of Eisenhower, made a vital contribution to success. Moreover, between 1 January 1943 and 30 June 1944, the Command laid 25,249 sea mines which resulted in the loss to the Germans of some 175,000 tons of shippping, a not inconsiderable help to preparations for the launching of 'Overlord'. In addition, from the beginning of 1944 to 18 July, 9,800 sorties were undertaken against the flying-bomb and V2 rocket sites, 36,000 tons of bombs being dropped to good effect.

By early September 1944, Eisenhower's Allied forces had overrun France. They reached Brussels on 3 September, Antwerp on the 4th, Liège on the 8th, crossed the River Meuse and reached Luxembourg on the 10th, pierced the Siegfried Line south of Aachen on the 12th, won bridgeheads over the River Moselle at Nancy and just south of Metz on the 16th and, a few days earlier had linked up in south-west France with the Sixth Army Group, which had advanced from its landing on the south coast of France in the region of Cannes. By the middle of September the Germans were in retreat; the flying-bomb and V2 rocket sites were in the hands of the Allies, except for some in Holland which were soon to be overrun; and the advance to the borders of Germany was soon to begin. Between 1 April and 30 September 1944, while Bomber Command had been under Eisenhower's control, it had despatched 82,411 sorties against enemy targets, of which 90 per cent were at the request of Supreme Headquarters, and these aircraft had dropped the prodigious total of 304,072 tons of bombs.

On 14 September 1944, the Combined Chiefs of Staff agreed at their conference in Quebec to the withdrawal of the Strategic Bomber Forces from the Supreme Commander's control, and placed RAF Bomber Command once again under the direction of Portal, the Chief of the Air Staff, while the US Strategic Air Forces returned to the control of Arnold, the Commanding General of the US Army Air Forces in Europe.

The British and American Bomber Commands were once more to concentrate on the duties of the strategic offensive, the form of warfare for which they had been designed. They had, however, proved themselves to be an essential element in a tactical operation in support of ground forces, an element which had ensured minimal losses to the Allied armies in a military campaign fraught with difficulties, and which could have cost hundreds of thousands of lives but for the intense bombing support.

CHAPTER XXVI

Onward to Victory

The withdrawal of the Strategic Air Forces from Eisenhower's command in September 1944 came about partly because the invasion forces had swiftly overrun France, Belgium and Luxembourg, and were therefore less in need of direct heavy bomber support. More importantly, Portal recognised that, with the Allied armies now firmly established on the Continent and well on their way to the Rhine and the frontiers of Germany, it was essential to return to the onslaught on German industry to prevent any recovery that might assist the enemy to mount a viable counter-attack. In particular, he regarded the oil industry as a first priority, oil being essential to the continued operation of Germany's armed services. Portal had in fact revised his views on oil from those which he had stated in his report at the beginning of the year when reviewing the progress of the combined bomber offensive with Harris and Spaatz. At that time he had recorded: 'We do not think that priority should be given to the attack of Axis oil refineries. The enemy oil situation has recently been examined by economic experts and as a result we are convinced that there would be no justification for diverting effort from the G.A.F. fighter industry in order to attack oil installations.' At the beginning of September, however, when submitting the case for the resumption of the strategic offensive and for the return of control of the strategic bomber forces to himself and General Arnold, he wrote:

> It has become abundantly clear over the past months that the enemy is faced with an increasingly critical situation in regard to his oil supplies. To exploit his difficulties fully it is essential that the attack of his oil resources be pressed home at maximum intensity and on the widest

scale possible. Any relaxation in the tempo of our attacks against his oil installations will provide opportunity for rehabilitation and dispersal. On the other hand, a successful campaign against enemy oil at this time may well have repercussions upon the enemy's ability to fight on the French, Italian and Russian fronts which may prove decisive.

In his submission, Portal recognised that there were continual and rapid changes in the strategic situation, and that it could become necessary at any time 'to apply the whole of the strategic bomber effort to the direct attack of German morale'. At the same time, while acknowledging the the probable continuing requirements of Eisenhower for support of the land battles, he believed that these calls would be on a scale much reduced from those during the previous six months. He therefore assured the Combined Chiefs of Staff that the Supreme Commander must be given first priority for any emergency requirements of the land battle.

With the adoption of Portal's suggestions for the Strategic Air Forces by the Combined Chiefs of Staff at Quebec on 14 September 1944, a new directive was issued to RAF Bomber Command and to the US Strategic Air Forces in Europe. It began with the instruction that the overall mission would be the progressive destruction and dislocation of the German military, industrial and economic systems and the direct support of land and naval forces of the Allies. Then followed the priorities:

First Priority.
    (i)   Petroleum industry, with special emphasis on petrol (gasoline) including storage.
Second Priority.
    (ii)   The German rail and waterborne transportation systems.
    (iii) Tank production plants and depots.
    (iv) MT production plants and depots.

The directive also stated that, as a result of past raids against the German aircraft industry and against the maintenance and operational facilities of the German Air Force, the effectiveness of German air power had been greatly reduced. Furthermore, the combined strength and operational efficiency of the Allied air forces had increased so dramatically that it was no longer considered necessary to regard the Luftwaffe, and its supporting industry, as primary objectives for attack.

Included in the directive was a statement to the effect that direct support of the land and sea operations remained a continuing commitment, and that when weather or tactical conditions were unsuitable for operations against specific primary objectives, attacks should be delivered against important industrial areas.

Oil installations were essentially precision targets. Although RAF

Bomber Command has proved itself capable of precision bombing both before and during the invasion, its targets had all been at short range and within the area of high Gee, Oboe and G-H accuracy. The oil targets, on the other hand, were mainly in the Ruhr, although with some even as distant as Eastern Germany and Czechoslovakia. However, the tremendous advances of the Allied armies through France, Belgium and Luxembourg, and the planned drive through Holland, had enabled mobile Gee, Oboe and G-H stations to be set up on the Continent, greatly increasing the number of targets in Germany to fall within their range of high accuracy. Moreover, this accurate coverage was constantly being improved as advantage was taken of every further military gain, to which was added the bonus of the rapidly reducing area of enemy territory over which the bombers had to fly in order to reach targets in Germany. With refuelling bases on the Continent now available to escort fighters, this was especially advantageous to the US Eighth Bomber Command, whose day bombers could now have fighter cover ever deeper into Germany.

In October, November and December Bomber Command's attacks on oil targets and the Ruhr industrial towns were on an unprecedented scale. In daylight on 14 October Duisburg was fiercely assaulted by 957 aircraft out of 1,013 despatched, dropping 4,401.1 tons of bombs, of which 3,573.7 tons were HE and 827.4 were incendiary. The raid was led by No. 3 Group (G-H) Lancasters acting as target-locators. That night, the 14th/15th, 913 aircraft out of 1,005 despatched again attacked Duisburg, dropping 4,381.9 tons of which 3882.9 were HE and 499 tons were incendiary, the raid again being led by No. 3 Group (G-H) Lancasters. Only fifteen aircraft were lost on the first raid and six during the night attack – twenty-one in all. In this twenty-four-hour period, during which there was an additional attack on Duisburg/Hamborn by 50 aircraft dropping 292.1 tons, a total of 9,075.1 tons of bombs were dropped on the city and its outlying factory areas. Such a concentration of devastating bombing had never been seen before, not even during the days of the Ruhr campaign in 1943; beside the Duisburg attacks, even the vast Hamburg raid of July 1943 almost paled into insignificance. A comparison of figures speaks for itself; in four raids spread over ten days, Hamburg was attacked by 2,721 aircraft and received 8,657 tons of bombs, and 87 aircraft went missing; in three raids spread over twenty-four hours, Duisburg was attacked by 1,920 aircraft and received 9,075.1 tons of bombs, and only 21 aircraft went missing. A further measure of the magnitude of the Duisburg raids may also be obtained by a comparison with the bombing of London during the Blitz in 1940 and 1941, when less than 10,000 tons of bombs were dropped on the city by the German Air Force. The damage to Duisburg was catastrophic, both in industrial and residential areas.

Other major raids were made against Ruhr towns during this period, including Cologne, Essen, Düsseldorf and Dortmund, and, outside the Ruhr, against such towns as Münster, Brunswick, Stuttgart, Karlsruhe, Munich and Ludwigshaven. Essen suffered two particularly heavy attacks in the last week of October when, on the night of the 23rd/24th, 945 aircraft out of 1,055 despatched dropped 4,522.1 tons of bombs, mostly HE, and on the 25th, when in a daylight raid 740 out of 771 aircraft despatched dropped 3791.1 tons of bombs, again mostly HE. Photographic reconnaissance revealed that the town was now almost completely destroyed, and that hardly a building in the Krupps Works had escaped severe damage or destruction.

In the case of the Ruhr oil targets, No. 3 Group's G-H Lancasters performed magnificently. The Meerbeck synthetic oil plant at Homburg was bombed at the end of October, as also was the synthetic oil plant at Bottrop and the Leverkusen chemical works. These three attacks were made in daylight, the bombs being released from above ten-tenths cloud, with the aircraft relying entirely upon their G-H instruments. Accuracy was so great that the targets were extensively damaged. In November, the oil plants at Wanne Eickel, Dortmund, Castrop-Rauxel, Gelsenkirchen/Nordsten, Kamen, Homberg-Meerbeck, Sterkrade, Bottrop, Wesseling, Harburg and Scholven-Buer were all heavily attacked; by the end of November attacks against synthetic oil plants in the Ruhr were temporarily suspended because all of them had been rendered inactive. Raids were now made upon certain benzol and oil plants outside the Ruhr. On the night of 6/7 December, Merseburg/Leuna, one of the two largest synthetic oil plants in Germany, was successfully raided and put out of action by 460 aircraft dropping 1,841.6 tons of bombs – it was not before mid-January 1945 that this plant could expect to return to production, and then only to 25 per cent of its previous output. Equal in size to the Leuna plant was Pölitz, which was heavily damaged in a raid on the night of 21/22 December by 182 Lancasters from No. 5 Group, led by No. 617 Squadron, dropping 724 tons of bombs.

November and December also saw many demands for Bomber Command's support of the Allied armies, demands which were promptly and effectively met. These operations included the obliteration of Düren, Jülich and Heinsberg to assist the US Army offensive, and Kleve and Emmerich to clear the way forward for the British Second Army. Another military request came from Montgomery for the destruction of the Walcheren fortress in the Scheldt Estuary, in order to assist his Twenty-First Army Group in the capture of the vitally important port of Antwerp. The Navy, too, added its demands, which included attacks on port areas and shipping at Ijmuiden in Oslo Fjord, Gdynia in Poland, and on various E-boat and submarine pens. The most significant naval request was for the sinking of the *Tirpitz*, sister ship to *Bismarck* and Germany's last remaining major warship, which was then sheltering in Tromsö Fjord. *Tirpitz* had, on earlier, separate, occasions, been damaged by the Navy, the Fleet Air Arm and Bomber Command, and had been put out of action for a considerable period by the most recent raid. With the Navy's fear that she was about to return to duty, and thus pose a menace to supply routes essential to the successful continuation of the Allied advances in Europe, the *coup de grâce* was requested. On 12 November twenty-nine Lancasters of Nos. 617 and 9 Squadrons from No. 5 Group, led by Wing Commander J.B. Tait of No. 617 Squadron and each carrying a 12,000-pound 'Tallboy' bomb, attacked in clear weather and good visibility from between 13,000 and 16,000 feet. Twelve bombs fell inside the torpedo net defences and three direct hits were scored, including one which penetrated the deck near the bridge and split open the ship's port side. Other bombs fell across the ship, causing her to capsize. Photographic reconnaissance on the next day revealed her lying upside-down, with her hull just visible above the surface of the water. Thus ended ingloriously the career of one of the largest and most heavily defended battleships of the war – *Tirpitz* displaced 45,000 tons, 10,000 tons more than a British King George V Class battleship. Losses to Bomber Command during the raid were nil, and all aircraft returned safely to base with the exception of one Lancaster which landed in Sweden. The Tallboy bombs which sank *Tirpitz* had been developed by Barnes Wallis, creator of the dam-busting bombs, and were designed to penetrate extreme thicknesses of armour and other protective material. They had previously been used with great success against submarine pens and other such massively protected targets.*

On 16 December 1944, Field-Marshal von Rundstedt mounted his famous counter-attack against the Allies through the Ardennes, in weather that made all air operations virtually impossible. Due to extensive and thick fog, which was spreading not only over the battle area but also over bases in France, Belgium and England, the Allied air forces were forcibly grounded and, despite urgent calls from Eisenhower's headquarters for tactical support, were unable to respond – with the exception of RAF Bomber Command. The first tactical support priority was for an attack on Trier, a centre for the concentration of the enemy's supplies and armour, called for on the 19th as a matter of the utmost urgency. Bomber Command responded immediately by sending a force of G-H Lancasters from No. 3 Group, despite shocking visibility conditions at the Group's bases and the fact that the target was compeletely covered by fog. Bombing blind with the aid of G-H, the

---

* Another exceptionally heavy device developed by Barnes Wallis, and carried by the long-suffering Lancaster, was the 22,000-pound 'Grand Slam', the 'earthquake bomb'.

aircraft achieved an outstanding success, and the assault was repeated on the 21st, using a greater force of G-H Lancasters. The two raids created havoc amongst the Germans, and drew from Eisenhower his immediate congratulations to Harris in a signal despatched by Tedder:

> The Supreme Commander has asked me to convey his congratulations, to which I add my own, on the magnificent performance of your Command in its attack on Trier on 19th December. The decision to take-off despite increasing fog at Base, and the determination of crews to reach and hit the target, whatever the weather, illustrate once again how ready is the response of the Royal Air Force to the needs of the battle on the ground. Please convey to all who had a part in the planning and execution of this operation the Supreme Commander's appreciation and congratulations.

Harris replied:

> Very many thanks for the generous message from the Supreme Commander, which has been passed to all concerned. You can count on us in any weather short of the impossible.

When Eisenhower saw the reply from Harris he wrote upon it: 'Goddamnit, they have already achieved the impossible.'

Despite the atrocious weather conditions in the Ardennes, Bomber Command continued to attack fog-bound targets with No. 3 Group's G-H Lancasters until the weather cleared on 24 December. Then, in mightier force, the Command lent its weight in answer to all Eisenhower's requests for support, until von Rundstedt's offensive – known as 'the Battle of the Bulge' – petered out in the middle of January 1945, as the Allied ground forces recovered from their initial surprise and began to take the initiative.

In his book *Inside the Third Reich*, Albert Speer, who visited the battle front at this time, described how he experienced one of the night air attacks while he was talking to General Sepp Dietrich, who commanded an SS armoured force in the Bastogne area. Speer was listening to Dietrich's description of the hopelessness of the situation when:

> As if to illustrate our helplessness our nocturnal talk was interrupted by a low-level attack from huge four-motored bomber formations. Howling and exploding bombs, clouds illuminated in red and yellow hues, droning motors, and no defence anywhere – I was stunned by this scene of military impotence ...

The despair of Dietrich and Speer was understandable. Von Rundstedt's initial success in the Ardennes was being thwarted by Bomber Command and was turning into a disaster, despite the cover of bad weather which had kept all other air forces glued to the ground. Following the Trier raids on 19 and 21 December, although fog continued to interrupt air operations over large parts of Northern Europe, Bomber Command maintained its support of the Allied forces in great strength. During the week ending 31 December the Command flew 4,106 sorties, dropping 14,000 tons of bombs on the enemy's troop concentrations, supply lines and reinforcements. German reinforcements for the Ardennes offensive had to use railways running west out of Cologne, Bonn, Koblenz and Bingen, and attacks were therefore made by Bomber Command on the marshalling yards at Nippes, Gremberg, and Kalk in Cologne; at Mosel and Lutzel in Koblenz; and at Rhedt, Bonn, München-Gladbach, and Troisdorf. In addition, troop concentrations and armour at St Vith and at Houffalize (Dietrich's headquarters) were subjected to devastating bombardment. For von Rundstedt, it spelt the beginning of the end of his desperate counter-offensive, which had been designed to stem the British and American advance by cutting their west front in two, and driving the German forces, behind their Panzer spearhead, through to capture Antwerp and cut off Allied supplies.

Bomber Command's performance in the last quarter of 1944 was, indeed, dramatic. In October it despatched 17,562 sorties and dropped 61,204 tons of bombs, in November it despatched 15,008 sorties and dropped 53,022 tons, of which 14,312 tons were dropped on oil targets; in December, despite adverse weather conditions, it despatched 15,333 sorties and dropped 49,040 tons of bombs, of which a considerable tonnage was again dropped on oil targets, notwithstanding the heavy priority demands for operations in support of the Allied armies, all of which were met. By the end of February 1945, Bomber Command had dropped the prodigious total of 62,339 tons of bombs on oil and benzol plants, to which it added another 24,298 tons in March and April, while extending its range far beyond the Ruhr to oil targets such as Brux and Zeitz in Czechoslovakia. It is interesting to note that the 62,339 tons of bombs dropped by the end of February had been directed against thirty-six oil and benzol plants in ninety-five attacks. In the case of the benzol plants, small and difficult to hit, and based mostly in the Ruhr, only No. 3 Group with its G-H Lancasters could find and destroy these targets; this they did regardless of weather and visibility conditions, such was the accuracy of G-H and the skill of crews using this remarkable radar device. For the longer-range oil targets, the credit was shared by No. 5 Group, with its own target-finding force, and by the Pathfinder Force leading other main-force squadrons, both Groups using the new 3-centimetre H_2S.

Although oil remained a high priority during the first three months of 1945, new demands were made upon Bomber Command by Eisenhower for support of the advancing Allied armies, including requests for the destruction of various cities in order to create chaos in those areas which were soon to be overrun by the British, American and Russian armies. In January 1945, the Chiefs of Staff, with victory in sight, were of the opinion that once the battle began to rage inside the borders of the Fatherland itself, German resistance would be stubborn. Eisenhower and the Russian commanders, intent upon minimising casualties in the final onslaught on Germany, and in an endeavour to bring about a speedy collapse of armed resistance, pressed for the use of maximum air power on both military and civilian targets in order to achieve a swift and decisive victory for the smallest number of Allied casualties. While it was agreed between the British, US and Russian Chiefs of Staff that massive aerial bombardment was a key to speedy victory, there were however conflicting views as to how such bombing could be best applied. General Carl Spaatz, commanding the US Strategic Air Forces in Europe, was in favour of first priority being given to the destruction of the Luftwaffe and, in particular, to the factories producing jet engines, in view of the recent appearance of the Messerschmitt 262, a jet-engined fighter of outstanding performance which he regarded as being a very serious threat to his day-bombers.

The Royal Navy, on the other hand, was concerned about the new Type XXI U-boats, which were faster under water than their predecessors and were equipped with the ingenious Schnorkel breathing device, which enabled them to stay below the surface for much longer periods than previously, and permitted them to charge their batteries whilst submerged.* The Navy wanted priority of attack to be accorded to the production facilities of these U-boats. In fact, the new threat to shipping posed by the Type XXIs never materialised, because of area bombing by Bomber Command and precision attacks by the US Eighth and Fifteenth Bomber Commands, all of which did serious damage to factories making vital components for these U-boats. The submarine menace was also lessened by Bomber Command's attacks on communication centres and canals, which disrupted supplies of prefabricated U-boat sections to the shipyards, and by the bombing of the shipyards themselves. Speer wrote in *Inside the Third Reich*, that: 'We would have been able to keep our promise of delivering forty boats a month by early 1945, however badly the war was going otherwise, if air raids had not destroyed a third of the submarines at the dockyards.' In addition, Bomber Command's extensive sea-mining operations in the Baltic, Kiel Canal and North Sea coastal areas of Germany prevented those U-boats which had been completed from becoming operational, except in limited numbers. An indirect consequence of the mining was

* U-boat batteries were charged by diesel generators which, before the Schnorkel device, could only be operated when the craft was on the surface.

expressed by the German admiral responsible for training crews, who complained that: 'Without trained crews there can be no U-boat offensive, but without a training area free of constantly laid and relaid airborne mines there can be no trained crews.'

Portal, however, did not agree with either Spaatz or the Royal Navy. He did not believe that priority in favour of attacks on the Luftwaffe or on U-boat targets was justified, unless it was thought that the war would continue until the end of 1945. He himself was of the opinion that victory could be achieved by May, provided that the newly launched Russian land offensive was successful, and he held the view that priority for attacks on oil and communications offered the best way of ensuring success for the Soviet armies, while at the same time offering the greatest assistance to the advancing British and American armies in the west. If oil and fuel supplies were denied to Germany's air and mechanised forces, and if military supplies could not be delivered to the different fronts, then, he argued, the collapse must be swift. He included, as attacks on communications, the bombing of towns lying in the path of the Russian, British and American advances.

It was now that Churchill entered the lists. On the night of 25 January, he discussed with Sir Archibald Sinclair, the Secretary of State for Air, the plans for the deployment of the Royal Air Force at this critical stage of the war. In particular, the Prime Minister wanted to know what plans existed for 'basting the Germans in their retreat from Breslau'. With the Crimean Conference at Yalta due to begin on 4 February, when Churchill and his Chiefs of Staff would meet Stalin, Roosevelt and their Chiefs of Staff, the Prime Minister wanted to know how he could demonstrate to the Russians the contribution that the British and US strategic air forces could make to the Soviet campaign in the east. On 26 January, the day after his meeting with Churchill, Sinclair consulted with Portal, who advised him that that oil should continue to have absolute priority, and that attacks in support of the Russian and other Allied advances should come next. Portal agreed, however, that in certain circumstances support of the Russian armies should have first priority, and he expressed the view that, after oil, 'We should use available effort in one big attack on Berlin and attacks on Dresden, Leipzig, Chemnitz, or any other cities where a severe blitz will not only cause confusion in the evacuation from the East but will also hamper the movement of troops from the West.' The four cities mentioned were focal points in the German system of communications behind the Eastern Front; the sowing of confusion which would interfere with the orderly movement of German troops in these areas would be invaluable to the Russians.

On the same day as he consulted with Portal, Sinclair answered Churchill's query of the previous night. In his minute to the Prime

Minister, he stated that plans for harrying the German retreat from Breslau was the prerogative of the Tactical Air Forces, rather than of Bomber Command and the US Strategic Bomber Forces. He went on to state that he felt strongly that 'the best use of our heavy bombers at the present time lies in maintaining the attack upon German oil plants whenever weather permits'. The benefits of such attacks, he said, would be felt equally by the Russians and by the British and American armies. There might be occasions, he added, if weather was unsuitable for attacks upon oil targets (which, being small, required precision bombing), when area attacks could be made on large cities in Eastern Germany such as Berlin, Dresden, Leipzig and Chemnitz, since these were not only administrative centres controlling military and civilian movements, but also main communication centres through which the bulk of military traffic had to move. Sinclair finished by saying that strategic bombing plans were now under examination. Churchill, however, was clearly not satisfied that sufficient urgency was being applied to the matter of supporting the Russians by bombing German towns lying in the path of their advances. In a most peremptory note to Sinclair, dated 26 January 1945, he wrote:

> I did not ask you last night about plans for harrying the German retreat from Breslau. On the contrary, I asked whether Berlin, and no doubt other large cities in East Germany, should not now be considered especially attractive targets. I am glad that this is 'under examination'. Pray report to me tomorrow what is going to be done.

Now the die was cast. On 28 January priorities were urgently reviewed by Portal, his Deputy Chief of the Air Staff, Air Marshal Sir Norman Bottomley, and Spaatz, particularly in respect of the Berlin-Dresden-Chemnitz-Leipzig plan. At this meeting it was agreed that Bottomley and Spaatz should immediately consult Eisenhower and his Deputy Supreme Commander, Tedder, about these priorities and should advise Portal, by signal to Malta, of their views. Portal was due to fly to Malta on the next morning for the preliminary meeting between Churchill, Roosevelt and the British and American Chiefs of Staff immediately prior to the conference with the Russians at Yalta.

On 1 February, following a meeting between Spaatz, Bottomley and Tedder at SHAEF in Brussels, the Vice-Chief of the Air Staff, Air Marshal Sir Douglas Evill, acting as CAS in Portal's absence, issued an Air Staff note on 'Strategic Bombing in Relation to the Present Russian Offensive'. This was discussed at a meeting of the Chiefs of Staff Committee on the same day, the representatives at this committee meeting being in fact, the Vice-Chiefs of Staff, since the Chiefs were all attending the Malta Conference. The note referred to the discussions between the Commanding General, US Strategic Air Forces in Europe, General Carl Spaatz, the Deputy Supreme Allied Commander, Air Chief Marshal Sir Arthur Tedder, and the Deputy Chief of the Air Staff, Air Marshal Sir Norman Bottomley, and the meeting agreed the new priorities for strategic bombing, for recommendation to the Chiefs of Staff in Malta.

On the following day, the Vice-Chiefs sent a signal, code-named 'Fleece 75', on the subject of strategic bombing. This signal listed the priorities as oil first, communications, with emphasis upon 'focal points of communication in the evacuation areas behind the Eastern Front, namely Berlin, Leipzig, Dresden and Chemnitz, or similar areas', second; tank factories third; jet fighter production fourth; and U-boat construction and assembly fifth.

At the meetings in Yalta, the US, British and Soviet Chiefs of Staff discussed the co-ordination of Allied offensive operations. The Russians had already reached the River Oder while the British and American armies were fast approaching the Rhine; it would not be long before the forces from the west and the east would find themselves rapidly approaching each other, and co-ordination was therefore essential, particularly in the matter of strategic bombing. At the plenary session General Antonov, Deputy Chief of Staff to the Red Army, submitted a note on the present Soviet offensive which included several suggestions as to how the Western Allies might contribute to its success – one way, he said, was to use strategic bombing to prevent the Germans from moving troops from the Western to the Eastern Front. Antonov asked for air attacks against communications, and suggested that, in particular, the Western Allied bombers should 'paralyse the Centres: Berlin and Leipzig', a plan very much in line with the thinking of Churchill and Portal. There arose, however, one difficulty: General Antonov also wanted to establish a bomb-line at this stage, which would pass through Stettin, Berlin, Dresden, the line of the River Elbe to Pardubitse, Brno, Vienna, Mariabor and Zagreb, east of which no bombing raids should be undertaken, although the towns through which the bomb-line passed should be allotted to the Western Allied air forces for attack. The proposal for such a bomb-line was made in order to preclude the danger of accidental bombing attacks upon advancing Russian troops. Portal was of the opinion that the suggested bomb-line was, at this date, too far to the west, and would prevent attacks by the British and US Strategic air forces on important oil targets, tank and self-propelled gun factories, and jet-engine production units which lay further to the east. General Kuter of the USAAF, who was attending the Yalta Conference in place of his Chief, General H.H. Arnold, who was ill at the time, supported Portal in his views, although in the event no agreement was reached on the matter.

The recommendations contained in 'Fleece 75' were adopted, however, and Spaatz and Harris were accordingly informed and issued with a revised directive.

Once more the bomber forces were to supply the main support for the Allied armies, in order to achieve victory as swiftly as possible and with the minimum losses of men and materials. They were to be the long-range artillery, as they had been in the invasion of Normandy, but now the targets were to be German towns and cities, and not French, Belgian and Dutch towns. Undoubtedly, the selection of these targets by the Joint Chiefs of Staff and the three Heads of Government was fully justified by the military situation at that time – the choice lay between the preservation of Allied or German lives.

On the night of 13/14 February 1945, the first of the raids on communication centres behind the Eastern Front was undertaken by RAF Bomber Command. The target was Dresden. The industrial area and marshalling yards in that city had already been assaulted by the US Eighth Bomber Command on 4 October 1944 with 30 bombers, and again on 16 January 1945 with 133 bombers. In the Bomber Command attack on 13/14 February, 786 heavies out of 804 despatched dropped 2,447.4 tons of bombs in a split raid, the first half of which was undertaken from above ten-tenths cloud. This cloud had cleared in time for the second half of the raid, and crews were therefore able to judge the first as successful and bomb where they could see extensive fires. The overall bomb-load consisted of 1,471.7 tons of HE and 1,175.7 tons of incendiary. Photographs taken on the 15th confirmed reports of success by crews, and the German and neutral press admitted that tremendous damage had been inflicted upon the town. How much of this damage was attributable to the RAF could not be determined because US Eighth Bomber Command attacked Dresden with 316 bombers on the morning of 14th February, and again on the 15th with 211 bombers. The final raid on Dresden, on 2 March, was also made by US Eighth Bomber Command with 406 aircraft.

RAF Bomber Command's raid on Dresden was immediately followed by a heavy attack on Chemnitz on the night of 14/15 February, when 663 heavy bombers out of 707 despatched dropped 2,108.6 tons, of which 788.8 were HE and 1,319.8 incendiary. On the night of 5/6 March Chemnitz was again the target for a major attack, when 672 Bomber Command aircraft out of 714 despatched dropped 1,978.7 tons of bombs, 1,105.5 tons of HE and 873.2 of incendiary. These raids resulted in extensive devastation. Leipzig did not receive attention until the day of 10 April and the night of the 10th/11th, when, amongst other transportation targets in the area of the Eastern Front, the marshalling yards of Leipzig/Engledorf, Leipzig/Mockau and Leipzig/Wahren were heavily attacked by Bomber Command. All through-lines at Engledorf and Wahren were cut, as were most lines at Mockau, and there was extensive destruction to wagon shops and other facilities, which included the complete devastation of the locomotive depot at Engledorf. In fact, the bombing of Dresden, Chemnitz and Leipzig by RAF and US Eighth Bomber Commands achieved exactly what had been demanded by the Joint Chiefs of Staff, Eisenhower and the Russians – devastation and utter confusion in these German communications and military administrative centres lying in front of the advancing Russian and Allied armies.

The direct support given to the Russians absorbed only a part of the effort applied by RAF Bomber Command and US Eighth Bomber Command. Their contribution to the success of the Allied land offensives led by Eisenhower was immense. From 1 January to 30 April 1945, RAF Bomber Command alone flew 54,742 sorties, dropping 181,403 tons of bombs on oil targets, communication centres in the Ruhr and Western Germany, and other targets in support of the Allied armies. In January the Command dropped 34,381 tons, in February 45,889 tons, in March 67,637 tons, and in April 33,496 tons. The 2,647.4 tons on Dresden, 4,087.3 tons on Chemnitz in two raids, and 1,058.1 tons on Leipzig, represented a relatively small percentage of the total tonnage dropped by Bomber Command in the months of January, February, March and April. Indeed, the brunt of the bombing was concentrated on supporting the battles of the Western Front, which indirectly offered support to the Russians as well since it denied the Germans any chance of reinforcing their Eastern Front.

By the second week in March, Bomber Command's priority had become the preparation of the way for the crossing of the Rhine. The German forces were by this time thinly spread in defence of the Rhine, but Generalfeldmarschall Walther Model, Commander of Army Group B (which consisted of the German Fifteenth Army and Fifth Panzer Army, twenty-one divisions in all), had his headquarters in the Ruhr and his divisions available to move as reinforcements to the major points of the Allied attacks across the Rhine, once these were revealed. It was Bomber Command's task, in conjunction with the US Eighth and Ninth Air Forces, to prevent Model from moving any of his divisions, a task which was to be achieved by massive bombing of communication centres in the Ruhr as well as many other targets outside that area, together with the bombing of military concentrations. The aim was to create physical chaos and the total disruption of communications. The Ruhr targets were allocated to Bomber Command, with German airfields, camps and military barracks being the charge of US Eighth Bomber Command. The colossal bombing of the Ruhr included raids such as that on Essen when, on the 11 March, 4,738.2 tons of bombs were dropped by 1,053 heavy bombers, and that on Dortmund on the 12th, when 1,079 heavies unloaded 4,889.3 tons of bombs.

Bomber Command made other attacks on vital targets which required a high degree of precision bombing. The task of tackling these targets fell to No. 617 Squadron from No. 5 Group, which had specialised in bombing small targets and which was equipped with the adapted Lancasters that could carry Barnes Wallis's 12,000-pound 'Tallboy' and 22,000-pound 'Grand Slam' bombs. One of the main means of wrecking Model's ability to reinforce points in the German defence of the Rhine was to destroy the railway viaducts at Bielefeld, Altenbeken, and Arnsberg, which carried the main traffic lines from the Ruhr to the rest of Germany. In addition, there were allocated for attack a number of major railway-bridge targets which, if destroyed, would paralyse German troop movements in the Rhine and Ruhr area, and isolate the Ruhr from North Sea ports such as Hamburg, Bremerhaven, Bremen and Cuxhaven. The Bielefeld and Altenbeken viaducts were attacked on 22 February by eighteen and sixteen aircraft respectively, dropping 12,000-pounders. The Altenbeken viaduct was severed at the north end for a length of 140-150 yards, but the results of the Bielefeld attack were in doubt. This viaduct was again attacked, however, on 14 March, when the 22,000-pound 'Grand Slam' bomb was used for the first time. Fourteen Lancasters made the assault, which was highly successful, the huge bomb shattering two spans of the twin viaduct, destroying a length of more than 100 yards. In addition, thirteen 12,000-pounders dropped by the other aircraft totally put out of action a road by-pass which the Germans had hastily completed to provide an alternative route to the viaduct. The Arnsberg railway viaduct was also bombed on the 14th by fifteen Lancasters. One 'Grand Slam' and fourteen 'Tallboys' were dropped, but results were inconclusive. This important viaduct, which carried the main-line traffic eastwards from the Ruhr, was attacked again on the 19th by nineteen Lancasters dropping six 'Grand Slam' and thirteen ' Tallboy' bombs. This time there was no doubt about the success of the raid. The viaduct was completely severed, more than 100 feet of it collapsing into the river below, with the embankment being cut over a distance of 115 feet at the base of the northern slope. Thus, before 23 March,* the day planned for 'Operation Plunder', the Allied crossings of the Rhine, the three main routes connecting the Ruhr with the rest of Germany had been rendered unusable.

---

* In fact, US First Army captured intact the Rhine bridge at Remagen on 7 March and poured into the bridge-head; then, on 22 March, Patton's US Third Army took the bridge at Oppenheim. Montgomery's set-piece amphibious and airborne crossing of the Rhine began on 23 March, and was completed successfully by the following day.

Other important railway targets attacked and severed before the Rhine crossings started were Arbergen Bridge on the 21st, Nienberg Railway Bridge on the 22nd, and Bremen Bridge and Bad Oeynhausen Railway Bridge on the 23rd; railway marshalling yards associated with the area of the battle were also heavily bombed.

Bomber Command's most immediate and direct support for the crossing of the Rhine was that rendered to Field-Marshal Montgomery's Twenty-First Army Group, which was poised to cross at Wesel. Thirty-two separate attacks were made during the week ending at dawn on Sunday, 25 March, and of these seventeen were in direct preparation and support of the Twenty-First Army Group's assaults north and south of Wesel, five against marshalling yards, five against bridges, and seven against enemy troop concentrations. Perhaps the best examples of the Command's tactical support for the ground forces were the attacks made on troop concentrations in Wesel, on 23 March by 77 heavies dropping 435.5 tons of HE, and, again, on the night of the 23rd/24th, immediately prior to the start of the ground assault, when 200 heavy bombers dropped 1,091.5 tons of HE and 7.3 tons of incendiaries. These raids drew from Montgomery a message of gratitude, addressed to Harris, as C-in-C, Bomber Command:

> My grateful appreciation for the quite magnificent cooperation you have given us in the Battle of the Rhine. The bombing of Wesel last night was a masterpiece and was a decisive factor in making possible our entry into the town before midnight.
> Montgomery

A similarly appreciative message came from 1 Commando Brigade which, with the 51st Highland Division, had led the attack on Wesel after crossing the Rhine. Referring to the bombing which preceded the crossing, the message read: 'A very fine attack. Wesel was taken with only 36 casualties.'

In the week that ended at dawn on Sunday 25 March, 4,327 sorties were flown by Bomber Command, dropping 16,974.6 tons of bombs. It was the last week of massive bombing, for by this time the war had, in effect, been won – only during the week ending at dawn on 15 April was anything like this tonnage again dropped. In that week, 13,274.4 tons of bombs were directed against targets deeper in Germany, to support the Western Allied armies in their swift advance across enemy territory to link up with the Russians on a line roughly from Kiel and Lübeck, through Magdeburg, Karlsbad, Pilsen, Linz and Salzburg, to Trieste.

As it turned out, however, the whole question of the bombing policy suddenly became, late in March, the subject of a critical attack by Churchill, who hitherto had been the greatest proponent of the destruction of Germany city by city, and who, as late as January 1945, had been pressing for plans to attack targets on the Eastern Front in support of the Russians. In a most unexpected minute to General Ismay,* dated 28 March and marked for the Chiefs of Staff Committee, the Prime Minister wrote:

> It seems to me that the moment has come when the question of bombing of German cities simply for the sake of increasing the terror, though under other pretexts, should be reviewed. Otherwise we shall come into control of an utterly ruined land. We shall not, for instance, be able to get housing materials out of Germany for our own needs because some temporary provision would have to be made for the Germans themselves. The destruction of Dresden remains a serious query against the conduct of Allied bombing. I am of the opinion that military objectives must henceforward be more strictly studied in our own interests rather than that of the enemy.
>
> The Foreign Secretary has spoken to me on this subject, and I feel the need for more precise concentration upon military objectives, such as oil and communications behind the immediate battle-zone, rather than acts of terror and wanton destruction, however impressive.

A copy of this minute was also marked for the attention of Portal, as Chief of the Air Staff.

Acting almost immediately, Portal, made a strong protest against Churchill's minute at the eightieth meeting of the Chiefs of Staff Committee, held on 29 March. Portal said that the Allied aim in bombing the enemy's large cities had always been to destroy the industries and transportation services in those cities, and not to terrorise the civilian population of Germany – whereas 'terror bombing' had been a definite policy of Germany towards Britain. Moreover, recent Allied strategic bombing had been concentrated on targets determined by the Russian commanders, by Eisenhower, and by other Allied commanders, in order to support the military advances on the Eastern and Western Fronts, Dresden and Leipzig being examples of requests from the Russians and from Eisenhower. Eisenhower, after isolating the Ruhr, was intent upon making his main thrust from the west along the axis Erfurt-Leipzig-Dresden, thereby joining up with the Russians and cutting the German forces in two, while making a secondary advance through Regensburg to Linz, also to join up with the Russians and to prevent, as he put it, 'the consolidation of German resistance in the redoubt in Southern Germany'.

* General Sir Hastings (later Lord) Ismay, Deputy Secretary (Military) to the War Cabinet, 1940-45, Additional Secretary (Military) to the War Cabinet, 1945-46, and Chief of Staff to the Minister of Defence, 1940-46. This latter post was held by Churchill, as well as that of Prime Minister, during his wartime period in office – Ismay was both a close friend of and an important adviser to the Prime Minister.

In this he was supported by General George Marshall, the US Army Chief of Staff. The outcome of Portal's protests was that at the eighty-third meeting of the Chiefs of Staff Committee, held on 30 March, Churchill withdrew his minute, substituting the following two days later:

General Ismay for C.O.S. Committee, C.A.S.

It seems to me that the moment has come when the question of the so called 'area bombing' of German cities should be reviewed from the point of view of our own interests. If we come into control of an entirely ruined land, there will be a great shortage of accommodation for ourselves and our Allies: and we shall be unable to get housing materials out of Germany for our own needs because some temporary provision would have to be made for the Germans themselves. We must see to it that our attacks do not do more harm to ourselves in the long run than they do to the enemy's immediate war effort. Pray let me have your views.

W.S.C.
1.4.45

In any case, by the beginning of April 1945 Portal had come to the view that it was now necessary to review the bombing policy, and to discuss it with the British and American Chiefs of Staff. To this end he submitted to the COS Committee on 4 April a 'Note by the Air Staff on Area Bombing', which surveyed the directives of the January 1943 Casablanca Conference, and the subsequent 'Pointblank' Directive of 10 June 1943. After recalling the reasons for attacking industrial areas, with emphasis upon towns involved in the production of aircraft and U-boats and, later, those involved in oil production and others that were centres of communication, the CAS stated:

In spite of recent advances in our ability to make precise attacks at night, the operational considerations which have in the past necessitated area attacks still exist. Nevertheless, it is recognised that at this advanced stage of the war no great or immediate additional advantage can be expected from the attack of the remaining industrial centres of Germany, because it is improbable that the full effects of further area attacks upon the enemy's war industries will have time to mature before hostilities cease. Moreover, the number of targets suitable for area bombing is now much reduced as a result of our past attacks and the rapid advance of the Allied Armies. For these reasons, and since allied superiority in military resources is already overwhelming, the effort of the Strategical Air Forces is being directed primarily to secure the most immediate effect upon the enemy's ability to resist the Allies' advance into Germany. This is being achieved by draining the enemy's oil resources to the lowest possible level, by disrupting communications vital to the enemy's resistance and by affording direct support to the armies as necessary.

In his penultimate paragraph, Portal wrote:

We appreciate the importance of refraining from the unnecessary destruction of towns and facilities which will be needed by our own troops or for Allied reconstruction purposes. If, however, we were to restrict our bomber forces to visual precision attack we should certainly reduce the contribution which they can make towards hastening the collapse of the enemy. It is considered that area attacks are still justified strategically, insofar as they are calculated to assist in the advance of the Allied Armies into Germany or in shortening the period of the war. Any incidental further destruction of German cities which is likely to be involved in the time remaining will certainly be small in comparison with that already accomplished.

Finally, he gave his conclusions:

(a) Area bombing designed solely with the object of destroying or disorganising industrial areas should be discontinued;
(b) There should be no alteration to the current bombing directive such as would exclude area bombing;
(c) Area attacks may prove necessary against those targets, the destruction of which is calculated best to assist the advance of the Allied Armies into Germany or to have the most immediate effect upon the enemy's ability to continue armed resistance;
(d) Any ultimate political or economic disadvantages of area bombing necessitated by these operations should be accepted.

The ease with which the Allies swept across the German-occupied territories and the German homeland itself from June 1944 until the collapse of German resistance, following Hitler's suicide on 30 April, in the first week of May 1945, was unquestionably due to the long and efficiently executed strategic bomber offensive made by RAF Bomber Command from February 1942 until the end of the war, and to the powerful strategic offensive added by US Eighth Bomber Command in 1944 and 1945. The truth is that Germany's armaments production had been so effectively and progressively devastated by Bomber Command in 1942 and 1943, and by Bomber Command and US Eighth Bomber Command throughout 1944 and the beginning of 1945, that she had been unable to maintain her military forces in adequate fighting condition to survive the war she had started. Her losses of weapons, aircraft, and naval and merchant shipping had come to exceed the minimum necessary replacement rates, and the defence measures forced upon her by the bombing had denuded even further her armies on all fronts. Her military mobility, too, had suffered drastically due to the disruption of her transportation communications and the loss of essential oils supplies, all brought about by bombing. From the beginning of the war on 3 September 1939, until 3 May 1945, when by RAF Bomber Command made its last raid on Germany, the Command despatched 389,809 sorties against enemy targets in Germany, German-occupied territory and Italy, for the loss of 8,655 aircraft, a loss rate of just over 2.2 per cent. Of these sorties 336,037 were despatched on bombing raids, dropping a total of 955,044 tons of bombs; 19,025 were despatched on sea-mining missions, laying 47,307 mines, a total weight of 33,237 tons of mines; while the remainder were despatched on radio counter-measure flights, fighter support, decoy flights, intruder activities against enemy aerodromes, meteorological flights, and on reconnaissance and special operations such as dropping and retrieving agents operating in Occupied Europe. By far the greatest proportion of this effort was undertaken between February 1942 and May 1945 under the command of Air Chief Marshal Sir Arthur Harris and his Deputy, Air Marshal Sir Robert Saundby. Of the total sorties, 331,001 were despatched at their direction, dropping 906,973 tons of bombs and laying 45,428 sea-mines. It is to be noted that of the total weight of bombs dropped, 865,715 tons were dropped in 1943, 1944 and the first four months of 1945. In addition to this prodigious figure, US Eighth Bomber Command added, in 1943, 1944 and 1945, another 621.260 tons.

Bomber Command's efforts were not without cost. Out of a total of 70,253 officers, non-commissioned officers and airmen of the Royal Air Force killed and missing on operations between 3 September 1939 and 14 August 1945, 47,268 were killed on Bomber Command operations between 3 September 1939 and May 1945, the date of the German surrender. In addition, 8,090 were killed whilst undertaking non-operational duties and 530 ground staff were killed on active service – a total for the Command of 55,888 personnel killed or missing. Over and above this number, 9,162 of all ranks were wounded in action or on active service. But although these casualties were grievous, they had not been suffered in vain – RAF Bomber Command's contribution to victory had proved decisive.

Casualties suffered by the US Eighth and Fifteenth Air Forces, from the beginning of their first operations in Europe in August 1942 until 8 May 1945, amounted to 61,791 all ranks, of which 24,288 were killed,

18,804 wounded, and 18,699 missing.*

The losses endured by the Allied armies from 6 June 1944 – D-Day – until the end of the war with Germany at the beginning of May 1945 make an interesting comparison. British casualties totalled 179,726, of which 38,670 were killed, 122,930 wounded, and 18,126 missing, while US casualties amounted to 488,062, of which 87,107 were killed, 361,756 wounded, and 39,199 missing. Total casualties, including French, Polish and others, were 731,461, of which 137,292 were killed. Without the bomber offensive that began in 1942, casualties to the land forces would certainly have exceeded these figures several times over; indeed, the invasion of Europe could not have taken place, and defeat of the Allies, or an ignominious negotiated peace, with Germany laying down the terms of the treaty, might well have been the end result.

For Germany, the bombing offensive was disastrous not only because of the devastation to industry, but also because it forced the Germans to divert more and more production to the needs of defence against the bombing, at the expense of the requirements for the Army's offensives on the Eastern Front, in North Africa, in the rest of the Mediterranean theatre of war, and, latterly, in North-West Europe. In 1943 and 1944 the bombing of the German homeland became so intense and effective that defence measures demanded a level of production – production which had been already severely disrupted by the bombing – so high that the needs of the Army on all its fronts had to be drastically curtailed, with the result that Germany had to abandon the offensive and was soon in full retreat on all fronts. With the invasion of Europe by the Allies in June 1944, yet another front was opened which Germany was incapable of defending adequately.

In March and November of 1972, the author spent many days with the late Albert Speer at his home in Heidelberg, examining German records for the production of military equipment from 1942 to 1945. A number of these records had not been available to the Allies at the end of the war, having been kept hidden by some of Speer's wartime staff until they were handed back to him after his release from Spandau Prison in October 1966.† Speer told the author: 'I consider it fair to say that the air attacks in 1943 cost us a lost 10 per cent of our armaments production.' The US Bombing Survey team, operating in Germany at the end of the war, gave the figure for 1943 as 9 per cent of armaments production lost. Speer went on to say, however, that the figure in 1944 was at least 20 per cent and, in a further observation to the author on the subject of gun production, he added:

* Figures for personnel listed as 'missing' include those who were made prisoner.
† In 1946, the Nürnberg War Crimes Tribunal sentenced Speer, among others, to a long term in prison for his part in the Nazi conduct of the war.

In 1943, the total production of all heavier guns for the Army, that is from 10.5-cm. field howitzers upwards, and for 7.5-cm. anti-tank guns and 8.8-cm. anti-tank and anti-aircraft guns upwards, came to 23,223; but it should have been 25,000, but for the bombing which lost us in that year about 2,000 guns. In 1944 it was worse. The actual production was 36,746 guns, whereas it should have been about 45,000 – at a loss rate of 20 per cent we lost some 9,000 guns. Therefore in 1943 and 1944 we lost approximately 11,200 guns due to the bombing. But really we lost more, for our production programmes were even higher in 1943 and 1944 and without your bombing they would have been achieved. Another thing, too, you must remember. I told you last time you were here in March* that the only guns effective against the heavily armoured Russian tanks were the 8.8-cm. onwards to the 12.8-cm. anti-tank guns, of which the 8.8-cm., with its precision sight, had proved to be a wonderful anti-tank gun. The production of these 8.8-cm. to 12.8-cm. guns from 1942 up to and including 1944 was 19,713 guns, but only 3,172 were allocated to the Army, despite their desperate need for them against the Russians and, later, against the British and American Armies as well, because the rest were required for anti-aircraft defence against your bombing of the Ruhr, Berlin, and other industrial towns and areas. In fact, we had to divert 75 per cent of the production of them to defence against the bombers.

Speer added that hundreds of thousands of trained soldiers were held back from the Russian Front to man these guns, and a figure of 900,000 men had been conservatively estimated by the German authorities at the time. Quite apart from these trained troops, he said that the number of personnel engaged in air-raid precautions, bomb-disposal duties and bomb-damage repair organisations in 1943 and 1944 amounted to between 1,000,000 and 1,500,000, most of whom would otherwise have been recruited into the Army and sent to the Eastern Front.

Studying the figures for the production of military equipment, it is easy to understand why Germany had to give priority to home defence, and why this policy had become a matter vital to the nation's survival. In 1944, for example, small-arms production from 1 January to 30 September was 3,297,000 weapons against losses on the battlefield, over the same period, of 4,457,000, the worst case being rifles, of which 1,960,000 were produced against 3,470,000 lost in battle. Another example of the state of affairs in 1944 resulting from the Allied bombing is revealed in the figures for actual, as against planned, production

* Mentioned earlier – see Chapter XXIV.

of tanks and aircraft in 1944.* Production of tanks for the year was 17,625, against a programme of 38,400. Production of day- and night-fighter aircraft was 25,822 against a programme of 57,600, and the production of all types of aircraft was 39,925 against a programme of 93,600. Karl Saur, a department head in Speer's Ministry of Armaments and War Production, commented on the situation to the Ministry's Fighter Staff on 8 April 1944. Referring to the fact that steel production was far from satisfactory, he said:

> We must be clear about the fact that in addition to our production programme [for steel], the tank production programme must be considerably broadened. Here we have a second task, namely to keep the enemy bombers out of the country until such time as we have built the necessary tanks to be able to win the war with tanks. The war cannot be won with aircraft, but aircraft are our immediate task, so that we can create the possibility of producing tanks. We shall end the war in the East with tanks. This would create the pre-conditions which yesterday caused the Führer to say: 'If this tank production programe is realised, which is now underpinned in terms of the whole range of models, and all of the initial planning, then this tank programme will decide the war.' However, a pre-condition for this is 100 per cent completion of the Air Force programme, so that we can keep the enemy bombers out of the country in order to be able to continue production.

But the combined Allied bomber offensive negated these plans, as can be seen from the figures quoted above.

The oil figures for 1944 extracted from Speer's records for both production and reserves reveal an incredible state of affairs. Imports from neutral and German-allied countries, such as Rumania and Hungary, had virtually ceased by October 1944, and by January 1945 home production of essential supplies was almost at a standstill. Aviation fuel reserves in 1944 dropped from 574,000 metric tons held in April, to 22,000 held in November, and, by December, to nil. Monthly production dropped from 175,000 metric tons in April to 26,000 in December, and 12,000 in January 1945. Military fuel reserves – gasoline and diesel for tanks, motor transport, and so forth – dropped from 760,000 metric tons held in April 1944 to nil by December, and the production fell from 238,000 tons in April to 124,000 tons in December, and nil by January 1945. Portal's emphasis on the bombing of oil targets as a priority proved in fact to be fully justified.

Wherever one looks amongst the production records for 1944, the

* Figures taken from a German document, 'Statistics of Armaments Production of the Technical Office', dated 15 February 1945.

story is the same, whether for motor trucks, railway waggons or infantry munitions. Production of the latter, for example, was planned at a rate of 800,000,000 rounds per month, but the highest monthly output achieved was only 484,000,000 rounds; light and heavy howitzer munitions were planned at a rate of 6,200,000 rounds, but the highest monthly rate reached was only 3,923,000 rounds. Moreover, the disruption of production extended beyond just armaments to the production of goods essential to living.

The inability of Germany's production to meet the needs of her armed services was not just a condition of 1944. It had started in 1942, gathering momentum in 1943, and reaching a state of disaster during 1944 and 1945; and it was primarily due to the bombing of the Ruhr, Berlin and central Germany by RAF Bomber Command in 1942 and 1943, and to the combined bombing by RAF and US Eighth Bomber Commands in 1944 and 1945.

Comments made by some of the German leaders after the war are illuminating.

Generalfeldmarschall Albert Kesselring, who succeeded von Rundstedt as Commander-in-Chief in the West, stated that: 'Allied air power was the greatest single reason for the German defeat.'

Generalmajor Kolb, formerly in charge of technical training at the German Air Ministry, said: 'From the middle of 1940 onward Germany was forced into major revision of its strategic plans of operation. The power of Allied day and night bombing forced Germany on the defensive from that time on.'

Generalfeldmarschall Hugo Sperrle, Commander-in-Chief of Luftflotte 3 until the fall of Paris in August 1944, said that: 'Allied bombing was the dominant factor in the success of the invasion [of Normandy]. I believe the initial landing could have been made without assistance from the air forces, but the breakthrough that followed would have been impossible without the massive scale of bombing, particularly of the German communications far in the rear. Allied air power was the chief factor in Germany's defeat.'

Dr Hjalmar Horace Greeley Schacht a former German Finance Minister, believed that: 'Germany lost the war the day it started. Your bombers destroyed German production, and Allied production made the defeat of Germany certain.'

And, before he committed suicide, Reichsmarschall Hermann Göring said that: 'The Allies owe the success of the invasion to the air forces. They prepared the invasion; they made it possible; they carried it through.'

War had taken to the air, and that war had been won in the air, denying the Nazis their victory.

EPILOGUE

By the end of April 1945, RAF Bomber Command's task of destroying the German military might had come to an end. In place of that destruction, the Command now embarked upon new tasks – flying mercy errands to the liberated nations of Western Europe, and ferrying home those now released from the German prisoner-of-war camps. This new role began in the week ending at dawn on Sunday, 6 May. In that first week of May, 2,618 sorties were flown, dropping on appointed areas 5,188 tons of urgently needed food supplies for civilians in Northern Holland. A further 204 aircraft brought home to Britain 4,033 ex-prisoners-of-war. Such operations continued throughout May and June, and by Sunday, 10 June, 3,592 sorties by Lancaster and Halifax aircraft had brought home 74,529 ex-prisoners-of-war, and had repatriated 1,876 Belgians to their homeland. By Sunday, 13 May, 3,341 sorties had dropped 6,673 tons of food on appointed areas in Holland. By 12 August, 138 tons of urgently required medical supplies for the Polish Red Cross had been flown to Varrelbusch in Poland. More mercy errands were also flown by the US Eighth and Fifteenth Air Forces.

While the initial phases of aid to liberated Europe began to replace the years of destruction, the war against Japan in the Pacific continued. Preparations were therefore in hand for a Royal Air Force bombing contingent, code-named 'Tiger Force', to proceed to the Far East. This force was to consist of twenty squadrons comprising 400 heavy bombers, half from Britain and the remainder from the dominions that border the Pacific. As soon as it became clear that the Japanese stronghold on Okinawa would soon fall to the Americans, General Marshall offered that island as a base from which the first ten squadrons of British bombers could operate against the mainland of Japan. The plan, however, was overtaken by the world's two most startling events.

On 4 July 1945 British consent had been given, in principle, to the use against the Japanese of the atomic bomb, a weapon which had been under development in the USA for a considerable time. On 17 July, Henry Stimson, the US Secretary of State for War, called on Churchill and laid before him a sheet of paper on which was written: 'Babies satisfactorily born.' The American explained: 'It means that the experiment in the Mexican desert has come off. The atomic bomb is a reality.' The experiment to which Stimson referred had taken place on the previous day at Alamagordo in New Mexico, when a trial bomb had been detonated at the top of a 100-foot pylon. In order to witness the test, the observing scientists had sheltered behind massive concrete shields more than ten miles distant from the pylon. When the device was detonated, there had been a tremendous blast, and a vast column of flame and smoke had mushroomed up into the fringe of the earth's atmosphere. Devastation within a circle of a radius of one mile from the pylon was absolute – even beyond that, it was indescribably awful.

To avoid further losses of Allied lives – principally American lives, since the United States was the most heavily committed of the Allies in the Pacific and stood to suffer extensive casualties, perhaps as many as a quarter of a million killed and even greater numbers wounded – it was decided that the atomic bomb should be used against the Japanese mainland in a bid to finish the war swiftly. First, however, Japan was given the opportunity to surrender immediately and unconditionally. The terms for this surrender, dated 26 July 1945,* were submitted to Japan on the same day, and were promptly rejected by the Japanese military rulers. On 27 July, and on the succeeding days up to 5 August, leaflets were dropped over eleven Japanese cities, warning them that they would be subjected to heavy bombardment unless Japan surrendered. Three million copies of the surrender terms were also dropped by American B-29 bombers, the Superfortresses.

On 6 August 1945, during a raid by US Twentieth Air Force B-29s, the first atomic bomb was dropped on Hiroshima, with horrific results. The entire town was wiped out – Hiroshima disintegrated into dust and ashes. Within seconds, 71,379 people were killed and tens of thousands more were seriously injured, many being maimed for life. The total number of casualties, killed and wounded, has been put at 230,000.

On 9 August, the second atomic bomb was dropped on Nagasaki with similar results, although, because of its geographical position, the death roll and numbers of other casualties were somewhat less.

* Coincidentally, this was also the date on which Churchill resigned as Prime Minister, following the massive Labour victory in the General Election of 5 July.

On 14 August, Japan surrendered unconditionally. The war in the Pacific was over.

There is little doubt that the atom bomb raids were the immediate cause of Japan's surrender. They were, however, essentially the final blow, one that was too great to withstand. The long series of battles in the Pacific and Burma had already weakened Japan, and the Allied blockade of her communications by sea and air power had slowly negated her ability to wage war effectively. Finally, when the Americans gained island bases in the Pacific, bringing them nearer and nearer to the Japanese mainland, the intensive air bombardment by the B-29s brought about Japan's defeat. Admiral Suzuki, the Japanese Prime Minister since 5 April, said of the bombing: 'It seemed to me unavoidable that in the long run Japan would be almost destroyed by air attack, so that merely on the basis of the B-29s alone I was convinced that Japan should sue for peace. On top of the B-29 raids came the atomic bomb ...' He was supported in his views by Prince Fumimaro Konoye, a former Prime Minister, who stated that: 'Fundamentally the thing that brought about the determination to make peace was the prolonged bombing by the B-29s.'

In this theatre, too, the war had also been won in the air.

SOURCES

Sources have, in general, been enumerated in the Author's Preface, together with acknowledgements to individuals who provided information or who enabled me to have access to official documents. I have listed below the most important documentary sources; others are included in the Bibliography, as the most important books upon which I have drawn.

Material on Marshal of the Royal Air Force Sir Arthur Harris, C-in-C Bomber Command, from February 1942 until 1945, is largely taken from interviews with him. Additionally, much information on Bomber Command and on Harris and his Deputy, Saundby, comes from my own knowledge, drawn from the time when I served on Harris's staff from February 1942 to May 1945. Correspondence between Harris and Churchill is from Churchill's files. Information on RDF (Radar) comes mainly from my own papers but is also to be found on Bomber Command files BC/S 26180/16/RDF, BC/S 26180/45/RADAR, and in Air Ministry S6 dated 26 April 1944, and S9592 dated 24 July 1944 (AIR 14). Details of bombing raids are extracted from the Bomber Command Weekly Digest.

Other sources on bombing results are taken from 'On the Spot Assessments of Bomb Damage in Germany from 2nd. June 1942 to 31st. December 1944', compiled by Büro Ha of the Swiss Intelligence Service, and from Albert Speer's private papers and production records.

Detailed sources:

CAB COS 513 (JP)	26 October 1936
CAB COS 553 (JP)	26 January 1937
CAB DO (42) 47	20 May 1942
CAB WP (42) 374	24 August 1942
CAB COS (42) 379 (0)	3 November 1942

CAB JIC (43) 458	12 November 1943
Air Ministry OZ 332	20 January 1944
Air Ministry OZ 831	14 February 1944
Air Ministry AX 621	17 February 1944
CAB JIC (44) 80	4 March 1944
PREM 669	7 May 1944
PREM 670	7 May 1944
PREM 537	11 May 1944
CAB JIC (44) 228 (0)	3 June 1944
CAB JIC (44) 241	13 June 1944
CCS 741/6 (FAN 477)	15 January 1945
SHAEF S77217	31 January 1945
CAB COS (45) 92 (0)	1 February 1945
Air Ministry FLEECE 75	2 February 1945
Air Ministry JASON 139	5 February 1945
Air Ministry FLEECE 178	5 February 1945
Air Ministry JASON 164	6 February 1945
CAB COS Argonaut Conference YALTA	6 February 1945
CAB COS (Argonaut) 7	9 February 1945
PREM D 83/5	28 March 1945
PREM D 89/5	1 April 1945
PREM – associated correspondence between DCAS and C-in-C Bomber Command on Prime Minister's file	
CAB COS (45) 233 (0)	2 April 1945
CAB COS (45) 238 (0)	4 April 1945
CAB COS (45) 263 (0)	16 April 1945

In addition, many minutes and letters on Churchill's files between the CAS (Portal) and the C-in-C Bomber Command (Harris) have been used as sources.

BIBLIOGRAPHY

DOCUMENTS

Cabinet Office Historical Branch: War Cabinet Minutes, Chiefs of Staff Minutes, Prime Minister's (Churchill's) files, 1939-45.

Public Record Office and Air Historical Branch, Ministry of Defence: Air Ministry files, 1918-1945, and RAF Bomber Command files, 1939-1945.

Bomber Command Weekly Digest prepared by Intelligence: No. 1 (for week ended 12.00 hours Saturday, 18 April 1942) to No. 174 (for week ended 23.59 hours Sunday, 19 August 1945).

United States of America Strategic Bombing Survey.

Büro Ha of the Swiss Intelligence Service: 'On the Spot Assessments of Bomb Damage in Germany from 2nd. June, 1942, to 31st. December, 1944'. Provided to the author by the late Hans Hausamann, formerly Head of the Büro Ha.

Salisbury Reference Library: *Keesing's Contemporary Archives – Weekly Diary of World Events 1931 to 1946*

—— : *The Times History of the War* (World War 1), Vols. VIII, X and XIII.

Hansard

BOOKS

Anon: *Der Jüdische Krieg*, Nibelungenverlag, Germany, 1944.

Avon, the Earl of: *The Memoirs of Sir Anthony Eden*, Vols I & II, London, Cassell, 1965.

de la Bere, Professor R.: *A History of Cranwell*, Aldershot, Gale & Polden, 1934.

Boyle, A.: *Trenchard – Man of Vision*, London, Collins, 1962.

Butler, David, & Sloman, Anne: *British Political Facts 1900-1979*, Macmillan Press, n.d.

Churchill, Sir Winston L.S.: *The Second World War*, Vols I-VI, London, Cassell, 1948-54.

Gilbert, Martin: *Winston S. Churchill 1922-1939* (Vol. V), London, Heinemann, 1976.

Dietrich, Dr O.: *Das Buch der Deutschen Gaue*, Germany, Gauverlag Bayerische Ostmark, 1938.

Goebbels, Dr J.: *Das Eherne Herz, Reden und Aufsätze aus den Jahren 1941-1942*, Germany, Zentralverlag der NSDAP, 1943. *See also* Lochner, L.P.

Heiber, Helmut: *Adolf Hitler*, Germany, Oswald Wolff, 1961.

Hitler, Adolf: *Mein Kampf* (tr. Ralph Manheim), London, Hutchinson, 1969.

Impact, Books 1-8, sponsored by the US Air Force Historical Foundation (Books 6 and 7 in particular), New York, Parton, 1980.

Irving, D.: *The Destruction of Dresden*, London, William Kimber, 1963.

Konsalik, H.G.: *Stalingrad*, Germany, Hestia Verlag, 1968.

Kurz, Hans R.: *Nachrichtenzentrum Schweiz*, Switzerland, Verlag Huber, 1972.

Laffin, J.: *Swifter Than Eagles – A Biography of MRAF Sir John Salmond*, Edinburgh, Blackwood, 1964.

Lewis, P.: *The British Bomber Since 1914*, London, Putnam, 1974.

Lochner, L.P. (tr. and ed.): *The Goebbels Diaries*, London, Hamish Hamilton, 1948.

Matt, Alphins: *Zwischen Allen Fronten*, Switzerland, Verlag Huber, 1969.

Reitlinger, G.: *The Final Solution*, London, Vallentine Mitchell, 1961.

Richards, D.: *Portal of Hungerford*, London, Heinemann, 1976.

——, & St George Saunders, H.: *The Royal Air Force, 1939-1945,* vols I-III, London, HMSO, 1953, 1954.

Saundby, Air Marshal Sir Robert: *Air Bombardment*, New York, Harper, 1961.

Saward, Group Captain D.: *The Bomber's Eye*, London, Cassell, 1959.

—— : *'Bomber' Harris: the Authorised Biography*, London, Cassell/Buchan & Enright, 1984.

—— : *Bernard Lovell: A Biography*, London, Robert Hale, 1984.

Schliephake, H.: *The Birth of the Luftwaffe*, Shepperton, Ian Allan, 1971.

Speer, Dr A.: *Inside the Third Reich*, London, Weidenfeld & Nicolson, 1970.

Webster, Sir Charles, & Frankland, N.: *The Strategic Air Offensive Against Germany*, Vols I-IV, London, HMSO, 1961.

Winkelnkemper, Dr T.: *Der Grossangriff auf Köln*, Germany, Zentralverlag der NSDAP, 1942.

Wood, D., & Dempster, D.: *The Narrow Margin*, London, Hutchinson, 1961.

Index

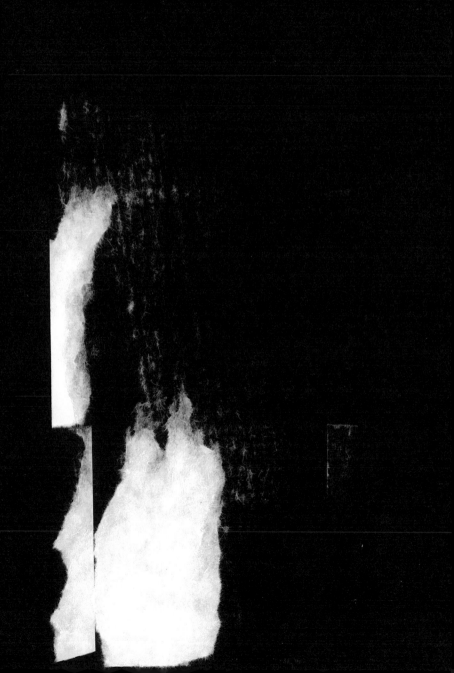